The MAILBOX®
The Idea Magazine For Teachers™

KINDERGARTEN

1995–1996
YEARBOOK

Jan Trautman
The Mailbox® Kindergarten Editor

The Education Center, Inc.
Greensboro, North Carolina

The Mailbox® 1995–1996 Kindergarten Yearbook

Editor In Chief: Margaret Michel
Editorial Manager: Julie Peck
Senior Editor: Jan Trautman
Early Childhood Editorial Director: Karen P. Shelton
Contributing Editors: Jayne Gammons, Ada Hanley Goren, Marie Iannetti, Mackie Rhodes
Copy Editors: Lynn Bemer Coble, Jennifer Rudisill, Gina Sutphin
Staff Artists: Jennifer T. Bennett, Cathy Spangler Bruce, Pam Crane, Teresa Davidson, Clevell Harris, Susan Hodnett, Sheila Krill, Rebecca Saunders, Barry Slate, Donna K. Teal
Contributing Artists: Marilynn G. Barr, Lucia Kemp Henry
Editorial Assistants: Elizabeth A. Findley, Wendy Svartz

ISBN 1-56234-136-7
ISSN 1088-5528

Copyright ©1996 by The Education Center, Inc.

All rights reserved except as here noted. No part of this publication may be reproduced or transmitted by any means, electronic or mechanical, without written permission from the publisher. Please direct written inquiries to the address below. Permission is granted to the original purchaser to reproduce pages for individual classroom use only and not for resale or distribution. Reproduction for an entire school or school system is prohibited.

The Education Center®, *The Mailbox*®, *Teacher's Helper*®, *The Mailbox*® Bookbag™, *Learning*™, and "the idea magazine for teachers,"™ and the mailbox/post/grass logo are trademarks of The Education Center, Inc., and may be the subject of one or more federal trademark registrations. All brand or product names are trademarks or registered trademarks of their respective companies.

Printed in the United States of America.

The Education Center, Inc.
P.O. Box 9753
Greensboro, NC 27429-0753

Look for *The Mailbox*® 1996-1997 Kindergarten Yearbook in the summer of 1997. The Education Center®, Inc., is the publisher of *The Mailbox*®, *Teacher's Helper*®, *The Mailbox*®Bookbag™, and *Learning*™ magazines, as well as other fine products and clubs. Look for these wherever quality teacher materials are sold, or call 1-800-334-0298.

Contents

Bulletin Boards 5

Arts & Crafts 21

Learning Centers 43

Children's Literature 63
    A Celebration Of Friendship: Books About Friendship 64
    Once Upon A Blue Moon: Books About The Moon And Night 70
    A Stitch In Time: Books About Blankets And Quilts 77
    Blowing In The Wind: Books About The Wind 84
    Eggs All Around: Books About Eggs 90
    Fish Tales: Books About Fish 96
    Getting Kids Into Books 103

Author Units 107
    Reading With Raffi 108
    Tales... By Tafuri 112
    Pfister's Pfabulous Pfriends 114
    Denise Fleming 116
    Nancy White Carlstrom 120
    Kevin's Kids 122

Math Units 125
    Math Masquerade 126
    Patterns, Patterns, Patterns 127
    Graphing Galore 130

Science Units 137
    "Sense-sational" Experiences With Taste and Smell 138
    "Sense-sational" Experiences With The Sense Of Touch 140
    "Sense-sational" Experiences With Hearing 142
    "Sense-sational" Experiences With The Sense of Sight 144
    The "Sense-sational" Sensory Fair 146

Multicultural ... 153
Journey To Germany ... 154
Jolly Olde England ... 156
Norway ... 158
Holiday Happenings: Celebrations of Hanukkah and Kwanzaa ... 162
Vive La France ... 164
India ... 166

Thematic Units ... 171
Welcome To School ... 172
A Family Affair ... 182
Ant Antics ... 184
No Bones About It! ... 191
If I Only Had A Scarecrow! ... 200
Paws, Claws, A Roar—And More! ... 208
At The Bakery ... 214
Positively Peanuts! ... 222
Pigs Aplenty! ... 224
On Top Of The World ... 233
Presenting Val's Pals In Rhyme Time ... 241
Animal Parents And Their Kids ... 248
The Strawberry Patch ... 256
We're Talkin' Turtles! ... 266
The Wild, Blue Yonder! ... 274

Kindergarten Café ... 281

Management Tips ... 301

Our Readers Write ... 305

Index ... 314

Bulletin Boards

Bulletin Boards

Marvelous Me!

Boost self-esteem with this picture-perfect display. For each student, decoratively cut around a brightly colored sheet of construction paper. To each sheet, attach a photo of a child and write "[Student's name] is marvelous because…." Have each child complete his sentence starter; then mount the completed projects on a board. Marvelous!

Joree King—Gr. K, Killarney Elementary, Orlando, FL

If it's to be... it starts with me!

These child-created "children" will convey a message of unity that will be admired by all. Provide each of your youngsters with a body shape cut from skin-toned construction paper. Have each child take a good look in a mirror, then decorate his shape using a variety of art supplies such as yarn, fabric, and wallpaper scraps. Mount the finished projects on a board with a title.

Beth Taylor Devlin, Dutch Lane Elementary School, Hicksville, NY

Reach Out And Be A Friend!

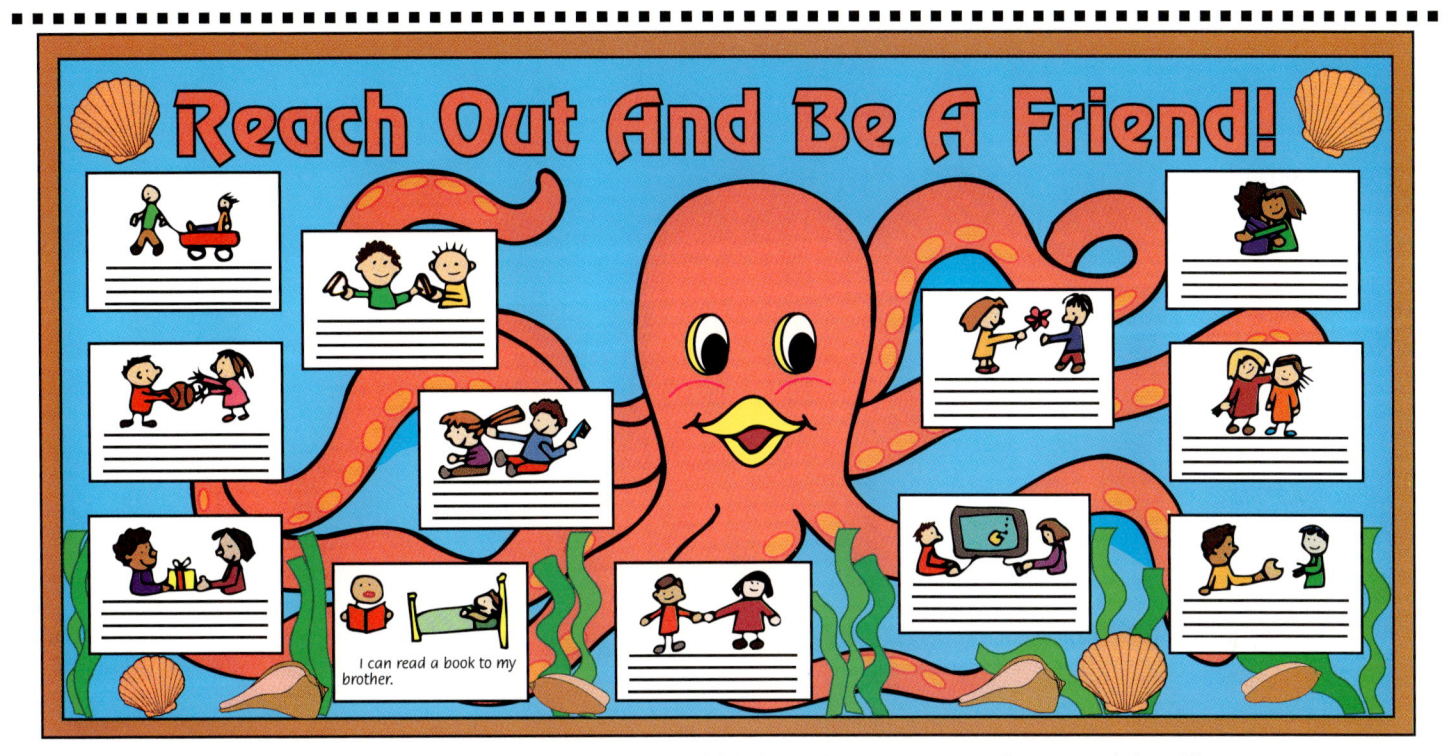

This extraordinary friendship display is just within reach! Ask each youngster to dictate and then illustrate one way to be a friend. Mount the illustrations on a bulletin-board background around a large octopus cutout. For an interesting 3-D effect, bend the arms of the octopus in various directions; then staple them to the board. Add tissue-paper seaweed to the bottom of the board, and hot glue real shells around the border. Fabulous!

Paula Mullahoo and Donna Lanchansky—Gr. K, Woodland School, Milford, MA

Welcome To Our School!

Something's fishy about this welcome-to-school display! On a wall or bulletin board, mount a humorous character enjoying the sand and surf. Write each student's name on a different fish cutout; then mount the cutouts on the board, so that together they form a larger fish shape. Write a catchy title on bubble-shaped cutouts. You won't have to fish for compliments with this display!

Tami Griffin—Gr. K, East Leesville Elementary, Leesville, LA

Bulletin Boards

In 1492, Columbus Sailed The Ocean Blue

Sail away with this unique Columbus Day display! On a wall or bulletin board, mount two sails, a flag, and one boat hull cut from bulletin-board paper. Have students color pictures of Columbus's ships on white art paper; then have each student paint over his illustration with blue watercolor paint. When dry, mount the pictures along the shapes of the sails. Anchors away for a great Columbus Day display!

Rena McCall and Mickey Highfill
Anne Watson Elementary, Bigelow, AR

Pokin' Around The Pumpkin Patch!

It's time to go pokin' around the pumpkin patch! Add a brown paper fence to a black background. To fill the patch with pumpkins, have each child stuff a paper lunch-size bag with newspaper, twist the top, and secure it with a rubber band. Have each child paint her bag to resemble a pumpkin. Pin the pumpkins to the board. Add a friendly scarecrow character to the board to guard the patch until the pumpkins are ripe for picking!

Nancy Hayes—Gr. K, Victor Haen School, Kaukauna, WI

Can You Guess Who?

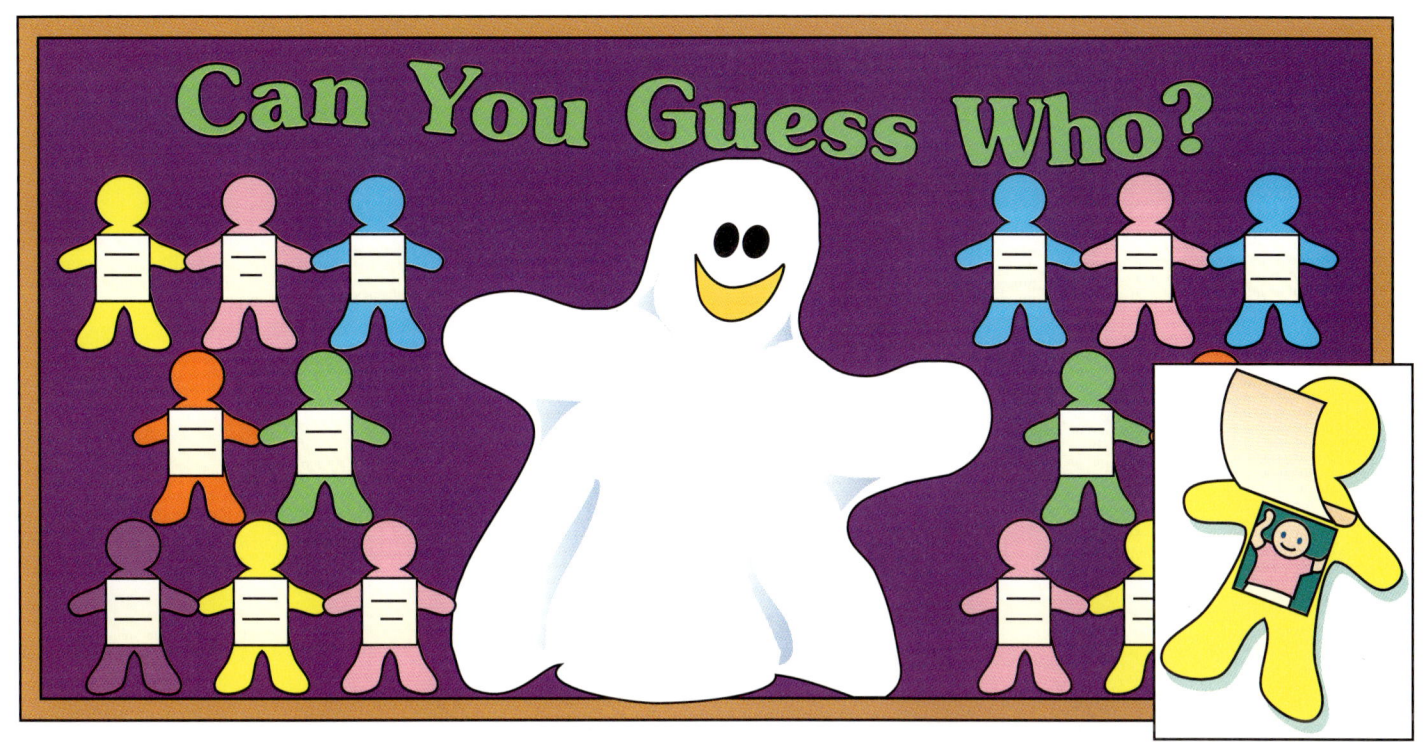

Here's a "spook-tacular" display for October. Loosely staple a large ghost cutout on a bulletin board, leaving a small section unstapled. Stuff the ghost with plastic grocery bags; then finish stapling it. Next mount a photo of each child (as an infant or a toddler) to a child-shaped cutout. Tape only the top edge of a sheet of paper labeled "Guess Who?" over each picture. Mount each child cutout around the ghost. Can *you* guess who?

Barbara Meyers—Gr. K, Fort Worth Country Day School, Fort Worth, TX

Thankful Hands

Get everyone's hands in on this great gobbler! Cut two paper grocery bags so that they open flat; then crumple the bags in water. When dry, mount the bags on the board and stuff with newspaper. Add head and leg cutouts to the turkey body. Have each child select a color of paint, then make handprints on a separate, large sheet of white art paper. After folding back the sides of the dried projects, staple them around the turkey's body to resemble feathers.

Beth Crawford and Barb Willis
John Celine School
Decorah, IA

Bulletin Boards

Countdown!

Let's count the days
'til Christmas
In an extraspecial way
And take a bell off Rudolph;
One bell every day.
Rudolph is our helper
And if we watch,
we'll see
When Christmas is upon us
With fun for you and me!

Rudolph is ready to help your youngsters count—backwards! Mount a reindeer cutout along with a copy of the poem (shown) onto a bulletin board. Use Sticky-Tac to attach the same number of large jingle bells onto the collar of the reindeer as there are days until the holiday. Surround Rudolph with your students' various holiday projects. Remove a bell each day and count down together. With this great display, you'll go down in history!

Debbie Korytoski—Gr. K, Pine Ridge Elementary, Ellerslie, GA

celebrate Hanukkah

Illuminate your room with a mural of your own school celebrating Hanukkah. Using construction paper and bulletin-board paper, create a display that resembles your school. Mount the school along with tree and bush cutouts (accented with tissue-paper leaves) and three-dimensional clouds. On white or yellow construction paper, use various art supplies to create Hanukkah scenes. Then mount the Hanukkah projects as windows of the school. Hanukkah is here!

Nancy Barad and Rona Cohen, Bet Yeladim Preschool, Columbia, MD

Snoozing, student-made bears are the subject of this wintry bulletin board. To create a hibernating hideout for bear art projects, mount a cave and tree cutout onto a blue background. Glue cotton batting over the cave and the branches of the tree. Mount wallpaper clouds and snowflake cutouts, along with a friendly sign, to add the finishing touches to this wintry scene.

Nancy Barad and Rona Cohen, Bet Yeladim Preschool, Columbia, MD

Using white chalk and assorted crayons, have each student draw a winter scene on a piece of light blue construction paper. Then have her dictate a corresponding story. Mount the projects on a dark blue background, along with snowflake cutouts and a title. Staple lengths of curled curling ribbon to the board. Then hang several snowflakes from the ceiling in front of the board. Let it snow! Let it snow! Let it snow!

Kathleen Sherbon—Gr. K, North County Christian School, Paso Robles, CA

Bulletin Boards..

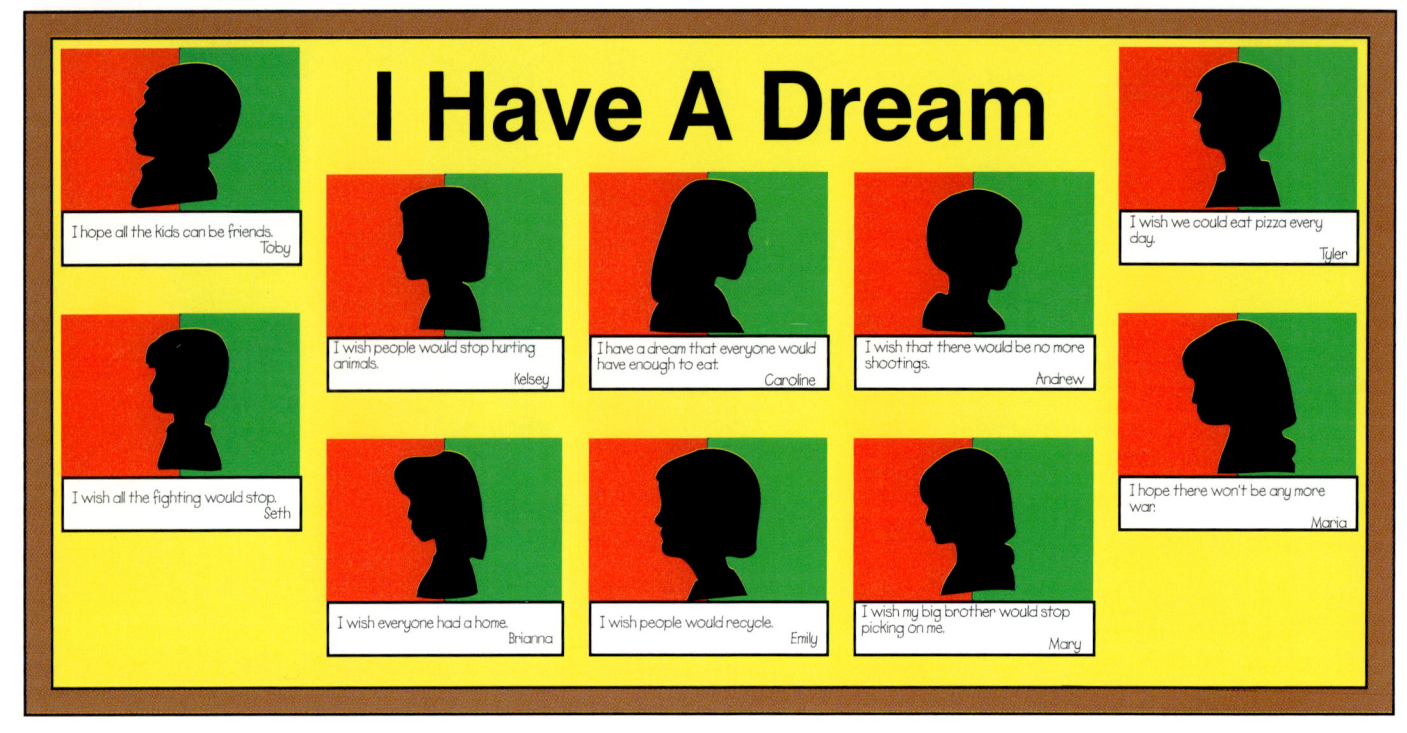

I Have A Dream

After discussing Martin Luther King, Jr., this bulletin board is a natural follow-up. Using an overhead projector, outline each child's profile on black construction paper and cut it out. For each child, tape a red and a green sheet of construction paper side by side; then mount his profile in the center. Give each child a 3" x 18" strip of paper on which to write (or dictate) his own dream for the world. Display each mounted profile with that child's written dream.

Adapted from an idea by Tracey Gest—Gr. K, Houston Elementary, Austin, TX

Kids put their hearts and hands into making this valentine display. Mount a large, white heart on a red background. Cut out a pink heart that is a little smaller than the white one. Have each child make a red handprint around the edge of the pink heart, then sign it when it dries. Use glitter glue to write a greeting. When that dries, mount the decorated heart on the board. Add sparkle by mounting a string of heart lights or a garland around the edge of the heart or the board.

Adapted from an idea by Barbara Meyers—Gr. K Fort Worth, TX

We're More Precious Than Gold!

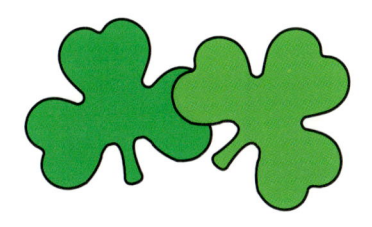

Highlight your precious little ones in this sparkling display. Enlarge and duplicate the leprechaun pattern on page 18. Color and cut out the pattern; then mount it near a large bulletin-board-paper pot. Have each child cut out a large, gold construction-paper coin, then glue his picture on it. After each child decorates his coin with glitter, mount each coin above the pot. Use glitter glue to write a seasonal message.

Beverly Brown—Grs. K–4
Ninety Six Elementary
Ninety Six, SC

Fly-Away Birds

Fly into the arrival of spring with these fine fellows. Have each child draw and cut out a bird shape from construction paper. Provide a variety of fabric scraps for students to cut and glue to their birds. When the glue is dry, have each child use markers to add details to his project. Have each child choose a spot on the board to mount his unique creation. Add a paper title cloud; then accent the board with cotton clouds and fringed construction-paper grass.

Kaye Sowell—Gr. K, Pelahatchie Elementary School, Brandon, MS

Bulletin Boards..

We're a Blooming Good Bunch!

In this case the more you add, the better it gets! Glue each child's photo inside a muffin liner. Mount the muffin-liner blooms along with construction-paper stems, leaves, and grass. Then encourage children to visit your art center and make spring things—such as butterflies, ladybugs, birds, rainbows, and clouds—to add to the board. Spring has definitely sprung!

Martha Ann Davis—Gr. K, Springfield Elementary, Greenwood, SC

Bountiful Spring!

Here's a showcase for a variety of spring art projects (see pages 94 and 34 for ideas). Cut out a large basket from butcher paper. Cut vertical slits in the basket. Weave twist ribbon (available at craft stores) through the slits. Add a twist-ribbon handle to the basket. Mount construction-paper grass along the bottom of the board and tissue-paper grass in the basket. Nestle art projects—there's a bunny pattern on page 19—amidst the grass.

Barbara Meyers, Fort Worth Country Day School, Fort Worth, TX

Mr. McGregor's Garden

peas
cucumbers
parsley
carrots
beans
onions
radishes
cabbages
potatoes

If you're studying rabbits, gardens, vegetables, or nutrition—this board's for you! Enlarge and duplicate the rabbit pattern on page 19. Color and cut out the rabbit; then mount it on a background. Encourage children to finger-paint pictures of garden foods. When the paint dries, instruct children to cut out their pictures. Mount each child's picture on the board and label it with cut-out letters.

Doris Hautala, Washington Elementary, Ely, MN

Honeybee Hotel

a e i
o   u

This board's designed for versatility! Mount beehives on a board. Label each hive with the skill(s) of your choice (such as vowels, as shown). Have children use art supplies to make bees. (There's a bee pattern on page 61.) Ask children to cut out pictures that have a beginning or middle vowel sound; then glue them to their bees. Store the bees in a bag. To use the board, have a child use pushpins to mount the bees on the appropriate hotel.

Adapted from an idea by Barbara Pasley, Energy Elementary, Energy, IL

Bulletin Boards..

June Is Busting Out All Over!

Give each child a small paper plate and several colorful "fillers" such as tissue-paper squares, buttons, aquarium gravel, yarn, and fabric scraps. Have each child paint a coat of glue over his plate, then cover the plate with the filler(s) of his choice. Instruct each child to cut out a construction-paper stem, leaves, and petals. When the center (the plate) is dry, have him glue the petals around the plate and mount the entire flower on the board.

America! America!

This board will inspire onlookers. Cut 4" x 18" strips of white paper—enough to make a border. Have children sponge-print red and blue stars on the strips. Staple the strips around a blue background. Next have children sponge-paint red, white, and blue heart shapes on the backs of light blue sentence strips. On another sheet of paper, have each child write and illustrate why he loves his country. Mount each page under the child's strip.

Wet Pets!

Brighten your classroom with a beautiful aquarium. Border the board with gray duct tape. Have children tear colorful construction-paper pieces and glue them on the board to resemble aquarium gravel. Add tissue-paper scenery and the water is ready for beautiful tropical fish. To make fish, have youngsters use fluorescent gloss tempera paint to paint fish shapes on waxed paper. When the fish dry, have children cut them out and add details with permanent markers.

Rose Semmel, Raritan Valley Community College Child Care, Somerville, NJ

We've Been Busy Bees!

With this board, children and their parents will be buzzing about their kindergarten accomplishments. For each child, duplicate the bee pattern (page 20) on construction paper. Have each child color his bee, then write his name on the flag. Then have each child write about and illustrate some of the things he has learned in kindergarten. Display each child's page on the board along with his bee page topper.

Adapted from an idea by Denise Westgard—Gr. K
Shiloh Christian School, Bismarck, ND

Leprechaun Pattern
Use with the bulletin board on page 13.

Pattern

Rabbit
Use with the top bulletin board on page 15.

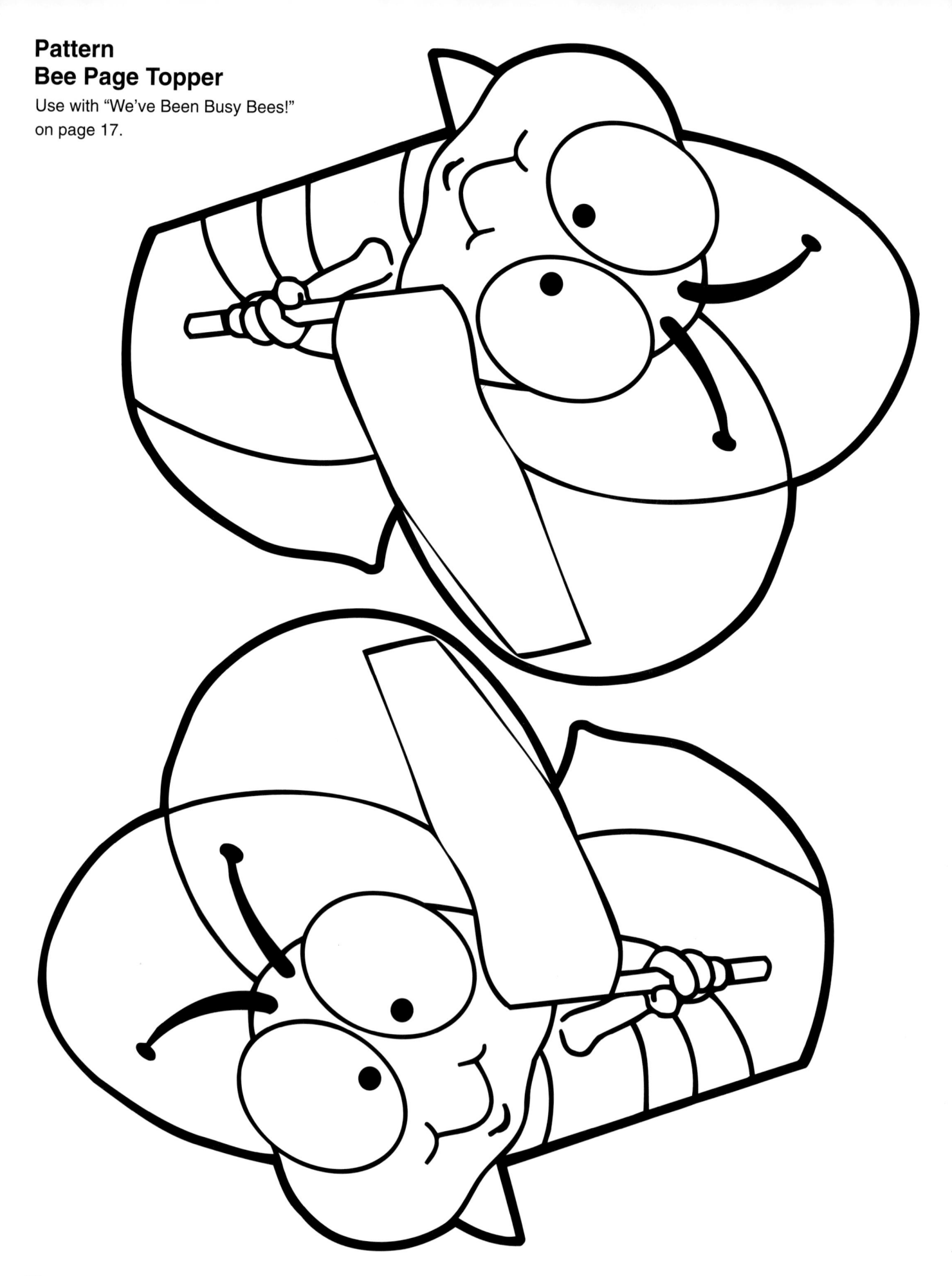

**Pattern
Bee Page Topper**
Use with "We've Been Busy Bees!"
on page 17.

©The Education Center, Inc. • THE MAILBOX® • Kindergarten • June/July 1996

Arts and Crafts

Arts & Crafts For Little Hands

Summer Sunflowers

Bring the last rays of summer sunshine into your classroom with these cheery sunflowers. To make a sunflower, paint the bottom of a paper bowl with yellow tempera paint. When the paint has dried, trace the rim of the bowl on yellow construction paper. Cut out the resulting circle. Squeeze a line of glue onto the rim of the bowl; then place the circle on top, covering the open portion of the bowl. Using scraps of yellow construction paper, cut out sunflower petals; then glue them around the circumference of the bowl. Glue sunflower seeds onto the center of the bowl. Attach a green stem and leaf cutouts, and your sunflower will be in full bloom. Brighten your learning environment by displaying the entire crop of sunflowers along a wall. Then watch your youngsters' sunny smiles as they enjoy a tasty treat of sunflower seeds.

Catherine E. Bray—Gr. K, Quadrille Academy, Indio, CA

A Tree For All Seasons

Branch out with these "tree-mendously" appealing art projects. Use these ideas to create beautiful trees throughout the year. Or, if you are doing a study of all the seasons, have each student create a tree to match his favorite time of the year. To make a tree trunk, cut a 4" x 10" rectangle from the panel of a brown paper bag. Starting at the top center, make a cut halfway down the length of the rectangle. Cut the scrap pieces of the bag into strips of varying lengths and widths. Working at a washable surface, pour a generous amount of glue onto both sides of the rectangle. Spread the glue over the entire piece, working the paper into a trunk with two branches. Press the trunk and branches onto a piece of construction paper. Repeat the gluing, shaping, and pressing process with the scraps to form additional branches. Let the project dry overnight. If desired, color the trunk and branches with brown or black crayons for added color and texture. Choose from the following suggestions to create sensational seasonal trees:

Fall Foliage: Press the wet trunk and branches onto dark-green construction paper. Glue small squares of yellow, red, and orange tissue paper onto the branches.

Winter Wonderland: Press the trunk and branches onto blue or gray construction paper. Leave the tree bare or dip a small piece of sponge into white paint. Press the sponge onto the branches.

Spring Blossoms: Press the trunk and branches onto green construction paper. Pour a small amount of red powder paint into a bag of popcorn; then shake the bag. Glue the popcorn to the tree for blossoms.

Summer Greenery: Press the trunk and branches onto yellow construction paper. Tear various shades of green construction paper into small pieces. Glue the scraps onto the branches.

Adapted from an idea by Mary E. Maurer, Children's Corner Daycare, Durant, OK

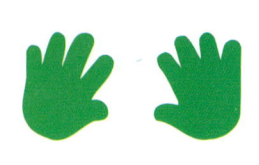

Critter Cages

Your youngsters will be wild about this zoo-animals project. To make a cage for a critter, accordian-fold a black piece of construction paper. Cut an *I* shape out of the paper as shown; then unfold. Using construction-paper scraps and other art materials, make a zoo animal for the cage; then glue the animal to a white piece of paper. Glue the top and bottom of the cage cutout to the background page. What a zoo!

Tammy Bruhn
Little Farm School
Ypsilanti, MI

Apple Wind Sock

Breeze into a new year by making an apple wind sock. To begin, glue red, yellow, and green apple cutouts onto a piece of fingerpaint paper. Add a number of similarly colored dot stickers. Cut crepe-paper streamers into varying lengths and attach them along the bottom edge of the paper. Bring the sides of the paper together and tape. On the top, punch four equally spaced holes; then attach string and suspend the wind sock from the ceiling or under a covered play area. This versatile craft can be adapted to suit any topic or holiday season.

Rose Semmel
Stanton Learning Center
Stanton, NJ

Stained-Glass Apples

The stained-glass effect of these apples is bright and beautiful. To begin, fold a piece of red, yellow, or green construction paper in half. Cut out a half-apple shape; then cut out the center of the apple as shown. Pour a generous amount of glue onto a sheet of waxed paper. Spread the glue over the paper using a paintbrush or fingers. Press red, yellow, and green tissue-paper squares over the glue, covering a space slightly larger than the apple cutout. Place the apple cutout onto the waxed paper and tissue squares, adding glue around the edge of the cutout as necessary. Dry overnight; then peel off the waxed paper. Trim the excess tissue paper from around the apple shape. Consider laminating the apples as a finishing touch. Display the apples on windows for a look that will brighten your classroom.

You've Been Framed

Here's a craft idea you can try when school pictures arrive. To get started on the project, glue a school picture to the center of a rectangle cut from plastic-grid craft canvas (available in a variety of colors at craft stores). Using a child's safety needle, weave brightly colored ribbons and cording through the canvas and around the picture. Attach a length of ribbon for hanging. What a perfect gift for National Grandparents Day!

Betty Silkunas
Oak Lane Day School
Blue Bell, PA

Happy Birthday To You!

Help children learn their birthdays while decorating these creative cakes. In advance, prepare cake-shaped templates. Trace a template on brightly colored tagboard; then cut on the resulting outline. Program the cake cutout with a name and birthday. Embellish the cake using a variety of art supplies such as yarn, colored glue, small decorating candies, and real candles. Consider using the completed projects to create a birthday graph or wall display.

Handy Magnets

Make handy magnet clips for holding student artwork. Begin by tracing a child's hand on tagboard; then cut out the shape. Label the cutout with the child's name or a cute phrase such as "Little Artist." Have each child decorate his hand cutout with an assortment of art supplies such as markers, glitter, and sequins. Onto the back of each decorated hand, glue a clothespin to which a magnet has been attached. When the glue is dry, the magnet clips can be sent home for each family's refrigerator art gallery. This craft is sure to be a hands-down favorite of parents.

Elizabeth Lyons—Gr. K
Tomahawk Elementary School
Lynchburg, VA

Arts & Crafts For Little Hands

Crafty Theme Tees

Encourage youngsters to show off your class's themes on these terrific T-shirts. Ask each child to bring an oversized, washed, solid-colored T-shirt from home. Have each child personalize his shirt using a fabric pen. To decorate his shirt after each unit or theme, have each child use fabric paint to make a small, theme-related picture on his shirt. Use a fabric pen to label each theme if desired. At the end of the year, this special shirt is bound to be a treasured keepsake.

Dawn Moore—Grs. K–1, Mt. View Elementary
Thorndike, ME

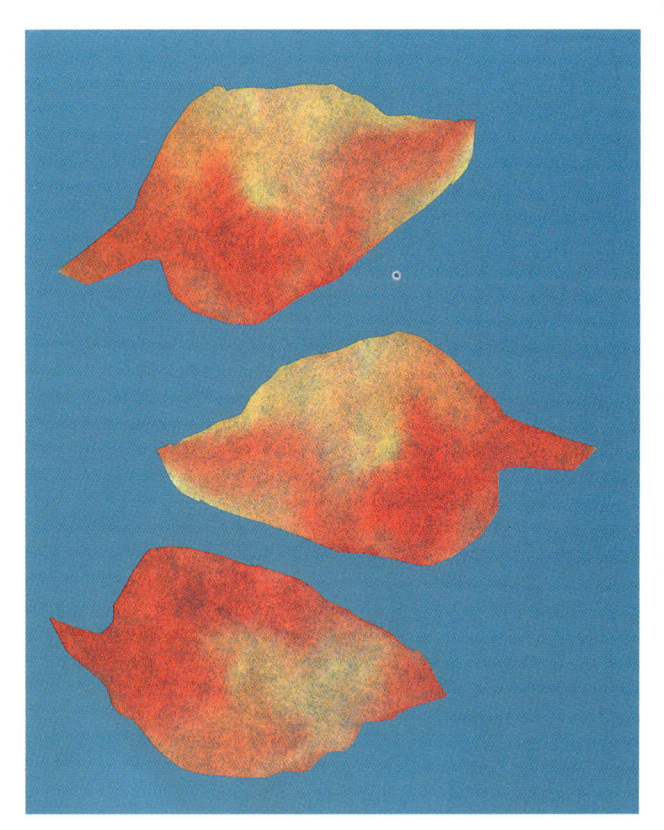

Colorful Foliage

Your little ones will love the colorful effect of these fall leaves. To make one, cut out a leaf shape from a coffee filter. Place a few drops of different-colored food coloring (such as orange, yellow, and red) and a few drops of water on a Styrofoam meat tray. Lay the leaf cutout on the meat tray, then set the leaf aside to dry. To vary this activity, fill each of several empty spray bottles with diluted food coloring; then mist a leaf cutout with different colors. Mount the leaves on a wall or bulletin board for a fun fall display.

Donna Henry, Portsmouth, VA

Jack-O'-Lanterns

These jack-o'-lanterns will add a festive touch to Halloween happenings. In advance, purchase a classroom supply of two-inch clay planting pots. To make a jack-o'-lantern, paint the clay pot orange. When the paint dries, turn the pot upside down; then use black Slick® paint to make a jack-o'-lantern face on it. Suspend each of the pots from a length of yarn and hang them from the ceiling. Jack-o'-lanterns everywhere!

Becky Gibson Watson, Camp Hill, AL

Indian Corn

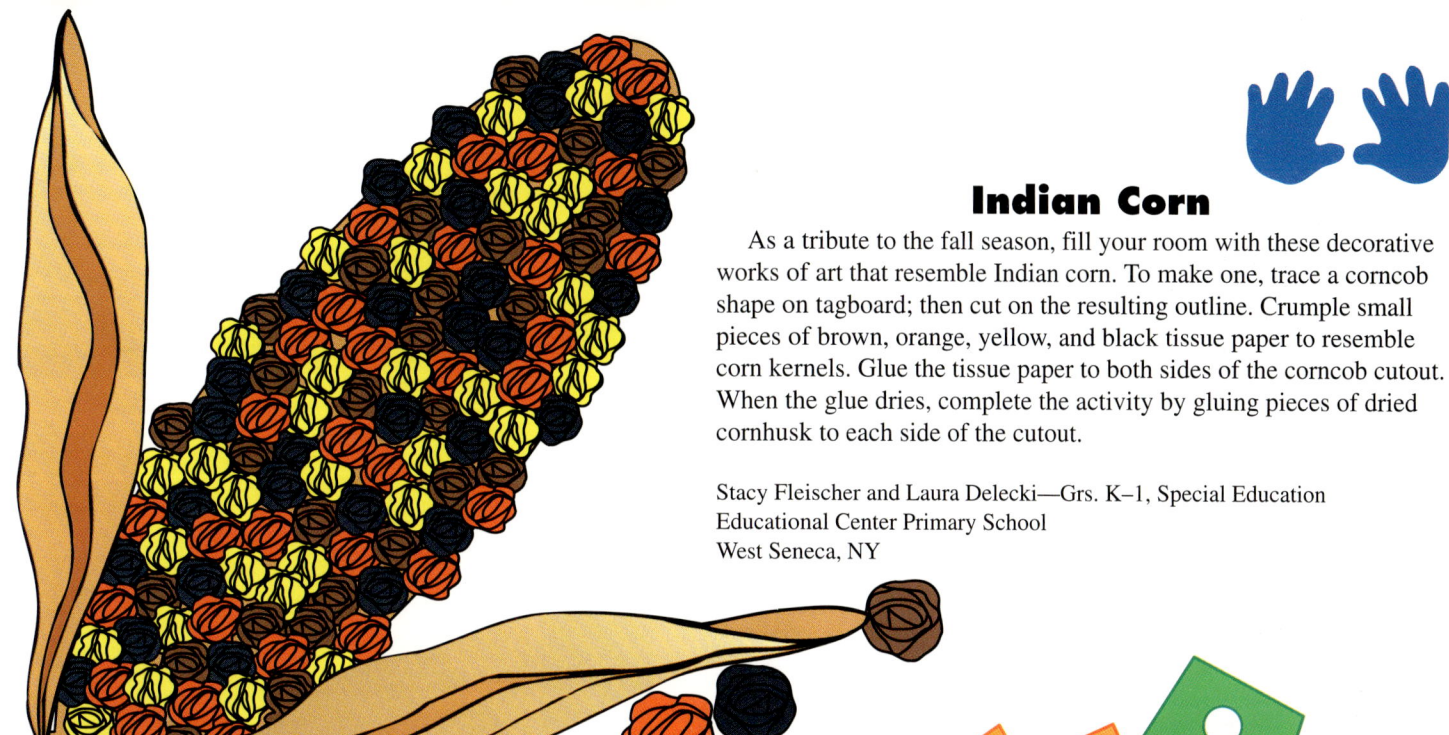

As a tribute to the fall season, fill your room with these decorative works of art that resemble Indian corn. To make one, trace a corncob shape on tagboard; then cut on the resulting outline. Crumple small pieces of brown, orange, yellow, and black tissue paper to resemble corn kernels. Glue the tissue paper to both sides of the corncob cutout. When the glue dries, complete the activity by gluing pieces of dried cornhusk to each side of the cutout.

Stacy Fleischer and Laura Delecki—Grs. K–1, Special Education
Educational Center Primary School
West Seneca, NY

Beaming Jack-O'-Lanterns

Illuminate your classroom with these glowing jack-o'-lanterns. To make one, cut or tear orange tissue paper into small pieces. Brush Mod Podge® on a plastic margarine lid; then layer the tissue paper atop the lid. Glue on construction-paper cutouts to make a jack-o'-lantern face. To the top of the lid, glue green tissue paper or curling ribbon; then brush on another layer of Mod Podge®. When dry, peel the tissue paper from the lid. Then punch a hole at the top of the jack-o'-lantern and tie a length of yarn through the hole. Hang these beaming jack-o'-lanterns on your classroom windows. How's that for haunting results?

Jane Kjosen, Underwood Elementary, Menomonee Falls, WI

Fall Leaf Prints

Adorn your classroom with this array of colorful fall foliage. In advance, collect a variety of fall leaves. To make a leaf print, paint the back of a leaf with brown, yellow, orange, red, or green paint. Place the leaf—paint side down—on a large sheet of construction paper. Lay a sheet of newspaper atop the leaf; then gently press and rub it. Remove the newspaper and leaf to reveal the print. Repeat this process several times, using different colors of paint.

Melissa L. Mapes—Pre-Kindergarten
Little People Land Preschool
St. Petersburg, FL

27

Fingerprint Turkeys

Now these fingerprint turkeys are something to gobble about! In advance, collect different brightly colored, nontoxic stamp pads. To make a turkey, press your thumb or finger onto a stamp pad, then onto a sheet of construction paper. Continue in this manner until the prints resemble the body of a turkey or a circular shape. Press another finger onto a different-colored stamp pad, then repeatedly onto the paper to resemble a row of turkey feathers. Continue in this manner, using a different color for each row of feathers. Then use a fine-tip marker to draw features on the fingerprints so that the picture resembles a turkey. Add to this great gobbler by gluing a copy of the poem (page 29) to the bottom of each paper.

Marsha A. Burks—Grs. K–1, Sheffield Elementary, Lynchburg, VA

All turkey birds are different,
From sea to shining sea.
And you'll never see another bird
Like this one to you from me.
Can you see what makes him different?
Do you need some helpful hints?
I made him from my very own
Thumb and fingerprints!
—Marsha A. Burks

Terrific Turkeys

Your little ones will have lots of fun when you set them loose on these grand gobblers. To make one, trace the turkey head (page 29) onto a folded sheet of construction paper. Also trace the tail on construction paper; then cut on the resulting outlines. Decorate the tail cutout with craft items such as glitter glue, Slick® paint, tissue paper, markers, crayons, feathers, or sequins and set it aside to dry. Glue wiggle eyes and a tissue-paper wattle on the turkey's head. Fold the tabs on the head cutout and glue it to the front of a paper cup. Glue the turkey's tail to the back of the cup. Fill the cup with the candy or nuts of your choice. Display the completed projects in your classroom; then have each child take his turkey home for the Thanksgiving holiday. Gobble, gobble!

Mary E. Maurer, Caddo, OK

Baking Dough

Your students will enjoy creating dough designs for jewelry, refrigerator magnets, or other decorations. They'll also love the fact that they can measure and mix the dough recipe on their own. Have each student mix and knead 4 tablespoons of flour, 1 tablespoon of salt, and 2 tablespoons of water. Have him roll the dough flat with a rolling pin, then use a cookie cutter or his hands to create his own dough designs. Bake the dough at 350° for 1 to 1 1/2 hours. Now that's a recipe for creativity!

Bonnie Pinkerton, Rockfield Elementary, Bowling Green, KY

Patterns

Use with "Terrific Turkeys" on page 28.

All turkey birds are different,
From sea to shining sea.
And you'll never see another bird
Like this one to you from me.
Can you see what makes him different?
Do you need some helpful hints?
I made him from my very own
Thumb and fingerprints!

—Marsha A. Burks

head

Place on fold.

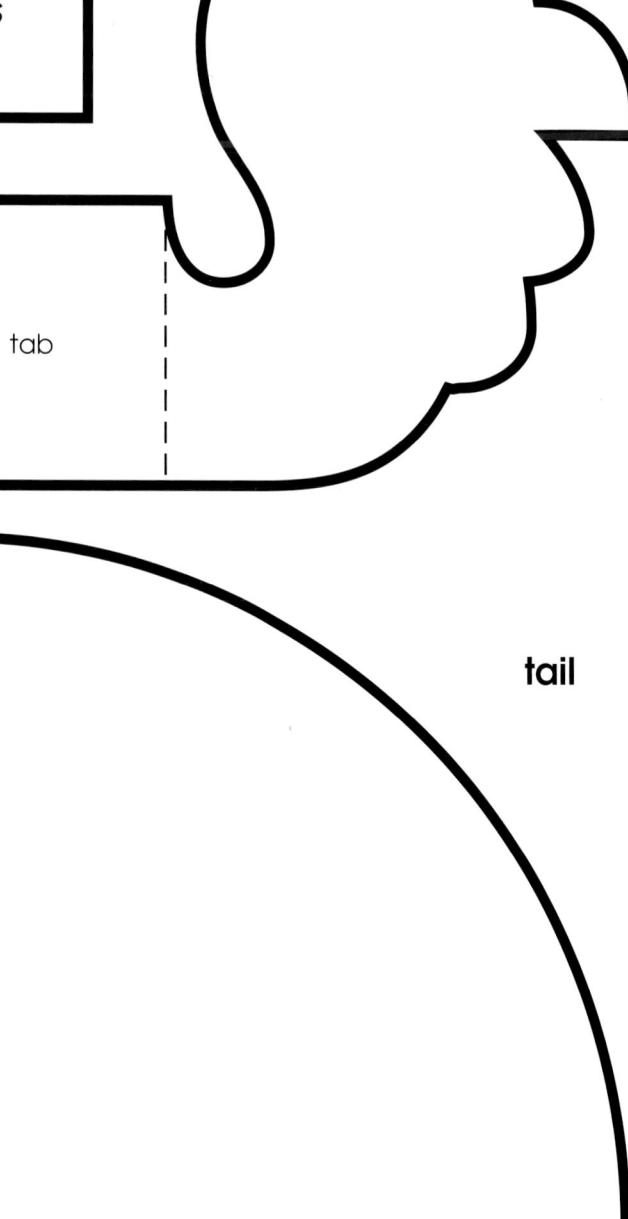

tab

tail

Arts & Crafts For Little Hands

Hung With Care...Everywhere!

Have your little ones make these eye-catching holiday stockings. To make a stocking ornament, fold a sheet of wallpaper in half. Trace a stocking pattern (or draw one) onto the wallpaper. Cut on the resulting outline through both paper thicknesses; then glue the two cutouts together. Embellish the stocking with pieces of ribbon, lace, sequins, and dried flowers. When the glue has dried, punch a hole near the top of the stocking; then suspend it from a tree using gold cord.

Linda Schwitzke
Headstart Preschool
Longview, WA

Trees With All The Trimmings

Oh Christmas Tree, oh Christmas Tree, how pretty you will be! To make one, draw a tree on green construction paper; then cut on the resulting outline. Use different-colored bingo markers, glitter glue, and Slick® fabric paint to decorate the tree. Then glue a star-shaped cutout to the top of the tree. Mount these terrific trees on a wall or bulletin board for a festive display.

Joyce Schmidt—Gr. K
North Pocono School District
Moscow, PA

Angel Ornaments

These cheerful cherubs will make a heavenly display in your classroom. To make one, draw an outline of an angel on tagboard; then cut on the resulting outline. Punch a hole in the top of the angel and tie on a gold-cord loop for hanging. Glue pearls, an assortment of small pasta shapes, and different-colored sequins onto the angel shape. Ooh! Aren't they heavenly?

Pat Gaddis—Pre-K
St. Timothy's Methodist Day School
Houston, TX

Wonderful Wreaths

Your little ones will enjoy making these festive holiday wreaths. To make a wreath, cut the center portion from a nine-inch paper plate. Glue holiday baking cups (turned inside out so that the design is showing) on the plate. When the glue is dry, glue a paper or ribbon bow to the wreath to complete the project. There you have it! A wonderful holiday wreath!

Martha Ann Davis—Gr. K
Springfield Elementary School
Greenwood, SC

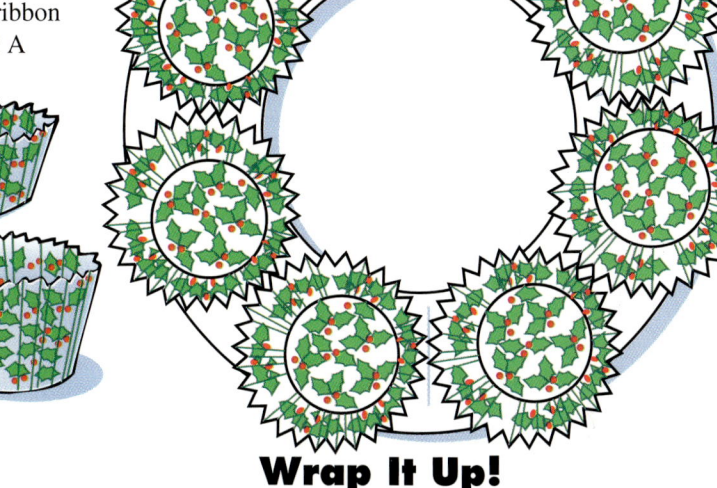

Wrap It Up!

Want to get your students wrapped up in a fun activity? If so, try this nifty art project. In advance cut sponges into various holiday shapes. Pour different colors of tempera paint into several pie tins. To make a sheet of wrapping paper, dip the holiday sponges into the tempera paint and repeatedly press them onto a sheet of newsprint, making the patterned design of your choice. After the paint dries, use the paper to gift wrap a special present.

Lori Hart
Sam Houston Elementary
Maryville, TN

"Hand-y" Holiday Prints

Whether it's reindeer or jolly old you-know-who—this idea will come in "hand-y." To make a Santa, assist each youngster in painting the palm of his hand with a selected skin tone of washable paint, and his fingers and thumb with white paint. Then have him press his hand onto a sheet of construction paper. When the paint dries, have him use Slick® fabric paint to add eyes, a nose, a mouth, a mustache, and a hat.

To make a reindeer, assist each child in painting his hand—but not his thumb—brown. Then have him press his hand onto a sheet of construction paper. Direct him to use his finger to spread the paint to "draw" antlers. When the paint dries, have him use Slick® fabric paint to make eyes and a nose on the reindeer's face. Mount these cheerful holiday works of art individually or attach them to a large sheet of bulletin-board paper to resemble a quilt.

Judy H. Dixon
Forest School
Owensboro, KY

A Wintry Snow Scene

Make your classroom a winter wonderland by displaying these cool works of art. In advance, spread Honeycomb® cereal on a sheet of newspaper; then use white tempera to paint the cereal. While the cereal is still wet, sprinkle the pieces with glitter and allow time for drying. To make a wintry snow scene, cut out and glue two or three white paper circles to a sheet of blue construction paper. Using markers or construction paper, transform the circles into a snow person by adding facial features and clothing. Then glue several pieces of the painted cereal onto the paper to resemble snowflakes. Use a white crayon to add any other snowy details. Brrr!

Robin Gorman—Gr. K
Potterville Elementary
Potterville, MI

Pinecone Trees

To make a tree, paint a pinecone green using tempera paint. Allow the paint to dry. Use an electric mixer to whip one part water and three parts of Ivory Snow®. Sprinkle salt and silver glitter in the mixture; then stir it. Using your fingers, dab the mixture onto the pinecone to resemble snow. Press a mound of white clay onto a small paper plate; then plant the pinecone in the clay. If desired, add small plastic animals to the clay to complete a wintry forest scene.

Rose Semmel
Stanton Learning Center
Stanton, NJ

"Scent-sational" Gingerbread Folk

Youngsters will run, run, as fast as they can to do this fun gingerbread-person art activity. To make one, copy the gingerbread person pattern (page 33) onto tagboard and cut it out. Then trace it onto the back of an 8" x 10" sheet of sandpaper. Using sharp, blunt-nosed scissors, cut out the sandpaper pattern. Rub a cinnamon stick across the rough side of the cutout. Then, using a mixture of white glue and white paint, decorate the gingerbread person. Attach a bow for the finishing touch. Mount these decorative gingerbread folk on a bulletin board to fill your room with the fragrance of cinnamon.

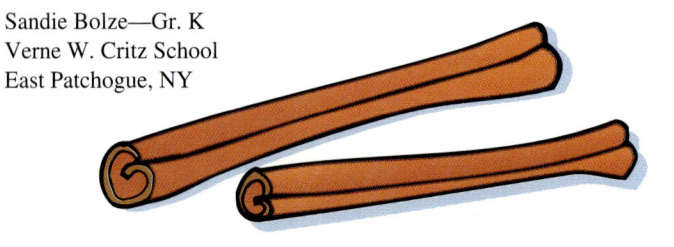

Sandie Bolze—Gr. K
Verne W. Critz School
East Patchogue, NY

Pattern
Use with " 'Scent-sational' Gingerbread Folk" on page 32.

Arts & Crafts
For Little Hands

Eyeglass Pin
Take a close look at this nifty art project. To make an eyeglass pin, cut out a magazine picture and glue it to the back of an eyeglass lens (check with your local eyewear store for old lenses). Trace the lens on a piece of felt and cut it out. Then glue the felt behind the magazine picture. Next hot-glue a pin back to the felt. Allow the glue to dry. This novel pin is perfect for gift giving!

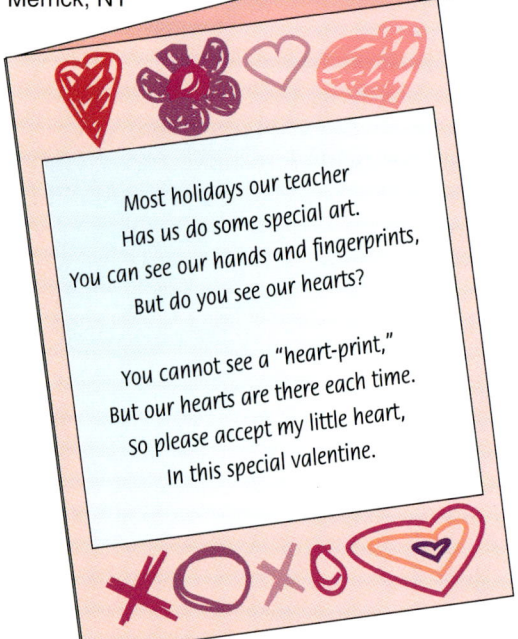

Ellen Arzt—Gr. K
Lakeside School
Merrick, NY

A Card With Heart
This sweet valentine card is sure to warm anybody's heart. To make a card, copy the poem shown onto white paper; then photocopy a classroom supply. To make a card, have each child glue a copy of the poem on a folded sheet of pink construction paper, then use crayons to make a decorative border. On a red sheet of construction paper, have each child trace both hands; then have him complete the drawing by rounding the bottom of both palms. Instruct each child to cut on the resulting outlines. Direct him to glue his school photo on the inside of the card. Then have him glue on just the palms of his hand cutouts (overlapping them as shown) to resemble a heart over his photo. What a heartwarming surprise!

Marsha A. Burks—Pre-K, Gr. K, and Special Education
Sheffield School
Lynchburg, VA

*Most holidays our teacher
Has us do some special art.
You can see our hands and fingerprints,
But do you see our hearts?*

*You cannot see a "heart-print,"
But our hearts are there each time.
So please accept my little heart,
In this special valentine.*

A Valentine's Day Card
This Valentine's Day card sure is a keeper! To make one, have each child draw a head-and-neck outline on skin-toned construction paper. Supply each child with a 2 1/2" x 18" strip of tagboard. Have each youngster trace both of his hands, then cut on the resulting outlines. Have him glue a hand cutout to each end of the tagboard strip, then glue the strip to the bottom of the head-and-neck cutout to resemble arms. Encourage each child to color and decorate the head pattern to resemble himself and color the arms as desired. Fold the arms towards the middle, overlapping them. Program each part of the card as shown.

Sharon Kudirko—Grs. K–2
Cooper School
Sheboygan, WI

Eggshell Rainbow

Looking for an interesting rainbow craft? If so, give this eggshell rainbow a try. In advance collect a supply of clean, dry, crushed eggshells. In each of several bowls, mix together two tablespoons of vinegar, a cup of hot water, and approximately ten drops of food coloring (using a different color for each bowl). Place some of the crushed eggshells in each bowl. Gently stir the eggshells until they absorb the desired amount of color. Spoon the eggshells onto paper towels and allow them to dry. To make a rainbow, use a paintbrush to spread glue in an arch shape onto a sheet of construction paper. Then sprinkle the eggshells onto the glue, using one color for each arch of the rainbow. Allow the glue to dry. To finish the project, glue cotton balls to each end of the rainbow to resemble clouds. Then brush an additional layer of diluted glue atop the eggshells. Now that's colorful!

Randalyn Larson
E. J. Memorial School
Jackson, MI

Lucky Horseshoe

You can never have too much luck on your side, and this art project ensures that you and your little ones aren't lacking! To make a lucky horseshoe, trace or draw a horseshoe on a sheet of black construction paper; then cut on the resulting outline. Also trace or draw three shamrocks; then cut them out. Decorate the shamrocks with sequins, glitter, stickers, and jewels. Position the horseshoe with the prongs up; then glue the shamrocks on the horseshoe cutout. (According to legend, horseshoes should be hung with the prongs up so the luck won't run out.) Display the horseshoes on your classroom door to wish good luck to all who enter!

Debra L. Erickson—Gr. K
Milan-Dummer Area Kindergarten
Milan, NH

Rainbow Wand

Making a rainbow wand is not only an artistic endeavor—it will also be lots of fun to use outdoors! To make a wand, cut a large paper plate in half; then cut off the rim of the plate. Color arches on the plate to resemble a rainbow. Next cut one-inch-wide lengths of various colors of crepe-paper streamers. Staple the streamers to one end of the plate. Take the rainbow wand outdoors and as you move about, let the colors flap in the wind!

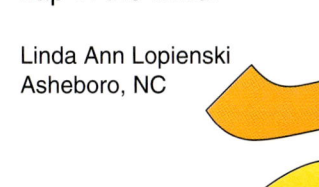

Linda Ann Lopienski
Asheboro, NC

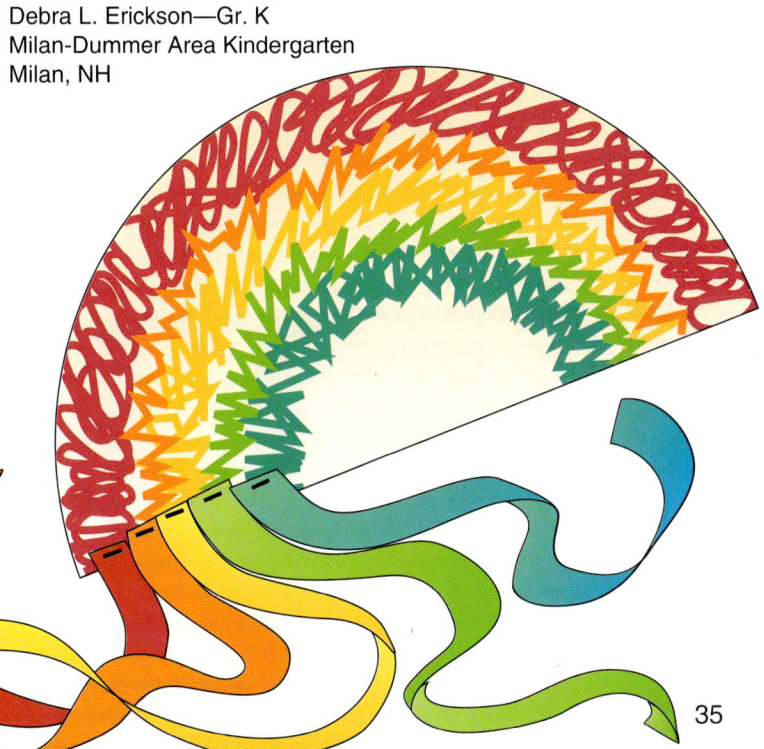

Fantastic Frames

Recycle old greeting cards to make these fantastic frames. To make a frame, cut off the front cover from an old greeting card. Then cut out the middle of the card, leaving a border that resembles a frame. (Cards that have border art work especially well.) Glue a child's artwork—one that is similar in size—to the back of the frame. Mount various framed masterpieces on a wall or bulletin board to make a classroom art gallery.

Tracey J. Quezada—Gr. K
Presentation Of Mary Academy
Hudson, NH

Buzzin' Bumblebees

Your little ones will be buzzin' to do this crafty activity. To make a bee, trace or draw a large bee shape on a double thickness of waxed paper; then cut on the resulting outline. Separate the bee cutouts. Sprinkle small amounts of yellow, black, and orange crayon shavings atop one bee cutout. Then place the other bee cutout atop the first one. Press a slightly warm iron on the bee; then lift the iron. (Do not slide the iron!) Repeat the process until all the crayon shavings have melted.

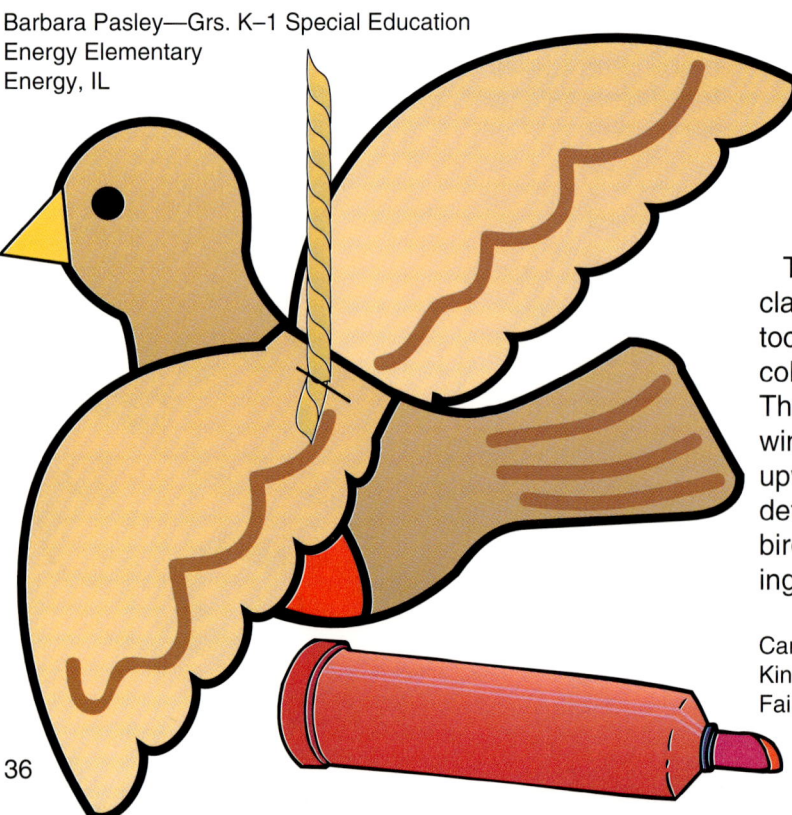

Barbara Pasley—Grs. K–1 Special Education
Energy Elementary
Energy, IL

Springtime Robin

These robin redbreasts are sure to give your classroom a touch of spring. To make a robin, photocopy the patterns on page 37 on the appropriate colors of construction paper. Cut out the patterns. Then glue the breast cutout on the bird. Staple the wings to the back of the bird; then fold the wings upward. Add a construction-paper beak and marker details. Then attach a length of string or yarn to the bird. Suspend these sweet "tweeties" from your ceiling for a fine-feathered display.

Carol Hargett
Kinderhaus III Early Learning Center
Fairborn, OH

Patterns
Use with "Springtime Robin" on page 36.

Finished Sample

body

wings

breast

©The Education Center, Inc. • THE MAILBOX® • Kindergarten • Feb/Mar 1996

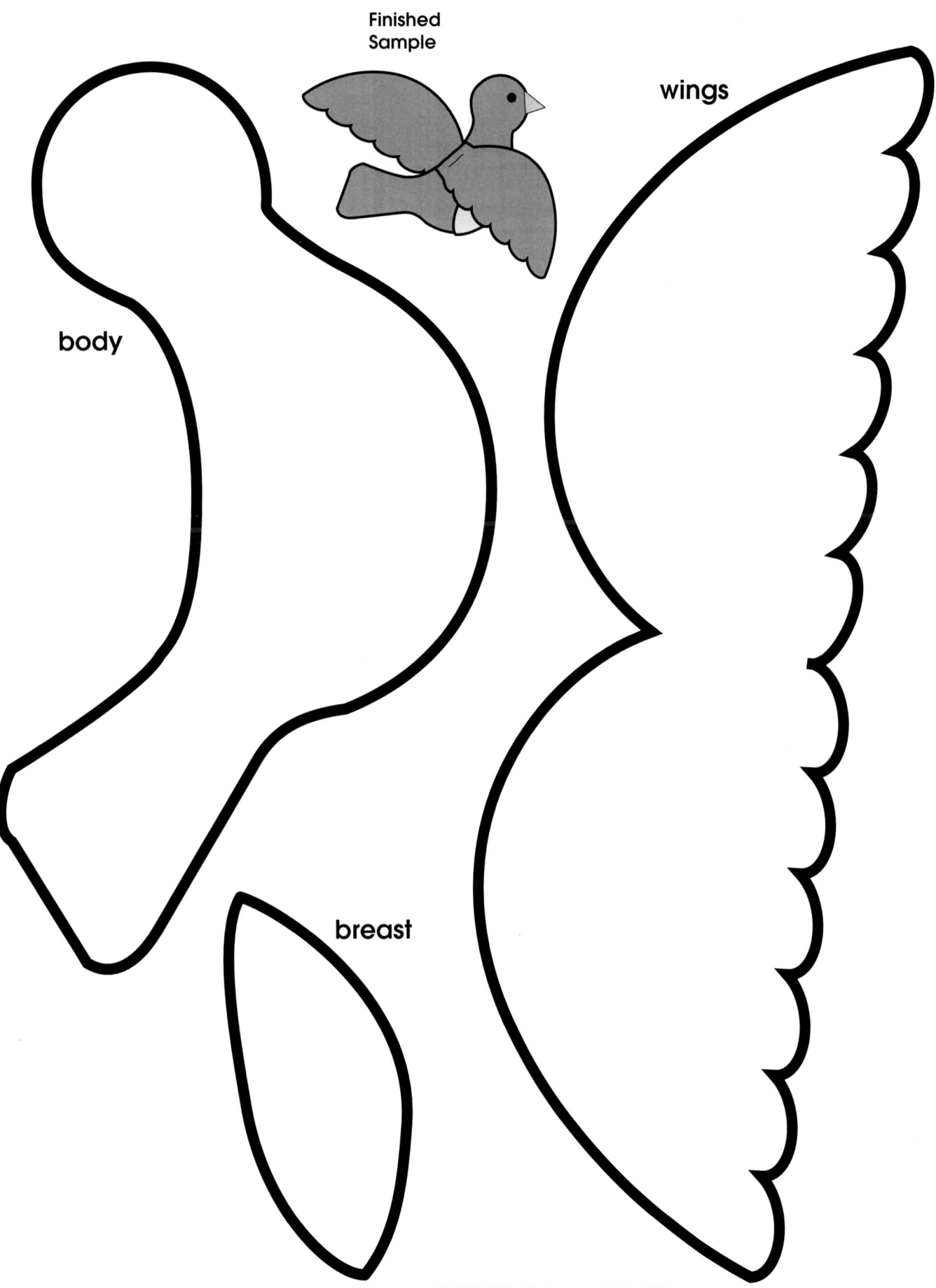

Arts & Crafts
For Little Hands

Fancy Eggs

These fancy eggs will be a festive addition to any bulletin-board basket (see page 14 for one idea). To make one egg, trace or draw an egg on construction paper; then cut it out. Cut a doily in half; then cut out the middle section from the doily. Glue the outer edge of the doily on the egg cutout; then trim the excess around the egg. Using different colors of tempera paint, sponge-paint the design of your choice on the egg. When the paint dries, the eggs are ready for displaying. "Egg-ceptional"!

Betsy Chaplick—Gr. K
Indianapolis, IN

A Sponge-Painted Bunny

A bit of sponge is what gives this fluffy-looking bunny its soft, furry look. To make one, use white chalk to trace or draw a rabbit shape onto a sheet of colored construction paper. Using a small sponge square and white tempera paint, sponge-paint inside the entire rabbit outline. Allow the paint to dry; then use markers to add facial features and other decorative details. What a cute bunny!

Barbara Meyers—Gr. K, Fort Worth Country Day School
Fort Worth, TX

Spring Basket

Fill this basket with decorative grass and eggs for a breath of springtime in your classroom. To make a basket, cut 2/3 off the top of a two-liter soda bottle. Discard the top portion of the bottle. Punch holes opposite each other near the rim of the bottle. Attach a long pipe cleaner from one hole to the other to form a handle. Then glue pastel-colored tissue-paper pieces on the bottle. When the glue dries, use puffy fabric paint to personalize the basket. When the paint dries, your basket is ready for filling!

Erlyne R. Osburn—Gr. K
Carousel School
Rancho Cordova, CA

Spring Has Sprung!

Welcome springtime with a spring picture that's really hands-on! In advance, copy the poem shown onto white paper; then duplicate a class supply on construction paper. To make this springtime scene, add art around the poem by pressing a fingertip on a stamp pad, then onto the construction paper. Continue in this manner—making designs to resemble birds, butterflies, insects, rabbits, flowers, and a sun. Then use a fine-tip marker to add details to your scene. Glue a fringed construction-paper strip at the bottom to resemble grass.

Marsha Burks—Grs. K–2
Sheffield Elementary
Lynchburg, VA

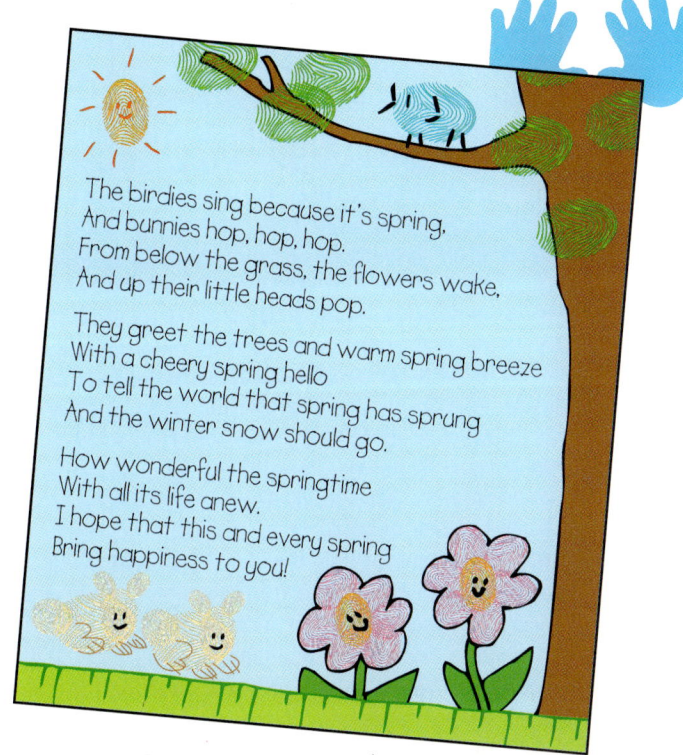

Snazzy Designs

Your budding artists' creative juices will surely flow with this unique project. In advance, color several small bowls of water with different colors of food coloring. Provide a dropper (such as an eyedropper) for each different color of water. To begin the project, use glue to make a design on a square of white tagboard. While the glue is wet, sprinkle salt atop it. Then gently tip the square to allow the excess salt to slide off. Next squeeze different colors of food coloring onto the salt—*one drop at a time.* (Youngsters will love watching the colors absorb into the salt!) Allow the glue to dry; then mount the design on a slightly larger square of colorful construction paper or tagboard. Mount the finished projects on a classroom wall or bulletin board for a snazzy springtime display.

Darlene Quinby
Calvary Episcopal School
Richmond, TX

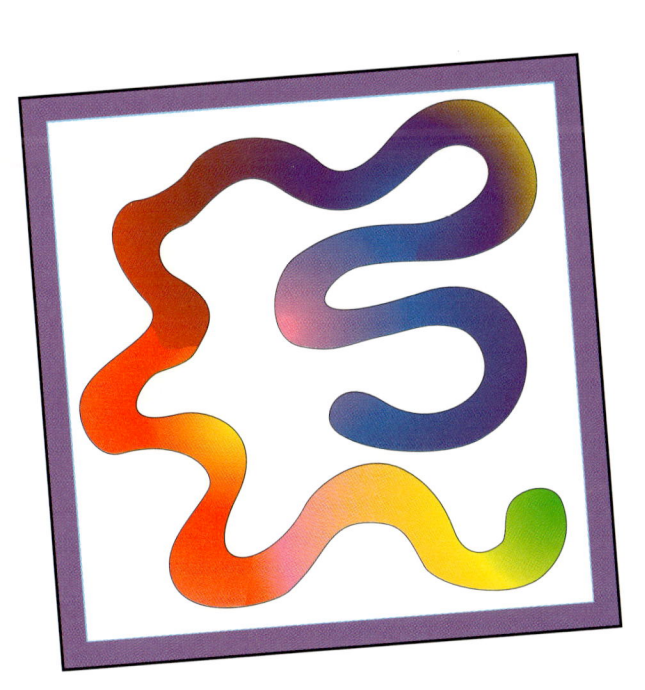

A Gift For Mom

What mom or grandmom wouldn't be thrilled to receive a beautiful vase of flowers from her little kindergartner? To make this vase, glue a length of ribbon around the cap from a large laundry-detergent bottle. Hot-glue a bow to the ribbon. Then insert floral foam into the lid so that it fits tightly. After arranging silk flowers in the foam, this gift is ready for an extraspecial delivery.

Faye Barker and Debbie Monk—Gr. K
Bethesda Elementary School
Durham, NC

Arts & Crafts
For Little Hands

Hot-Air Balloons
Watch the enthusiasm in your room take flight when your youngsters make these hot-air balloons. To make one, use markers and stickers to decorate a 5 1/2-ounce plastic cup. Fill the cup halfway with mixed plaster of paris. Then insert three drinking straws around the edge of the cup at one-third intervals. Next inflate a balloon and knot its end. Position the balloon between the three straws and tape the end of each straw to the balloon. Have each child use markers to decorate his balloon. Encourage little ones to take their balloons home to use as three-dimensional centerpieces!

Peggy Hundley Spitz
West Long Branch, NJ

Jellyfish
Here's a school of sea critters that your youngsters will be eager to make! To make a jellyfish, paint a half of a paper plate the color or colors of your choice, and allow it to dry. Use pinking shears to cut strips of tissue paper. Then glue the tissue-paper strips to the plate so that they hang down. To complete the project, use a marker to draw facial features on the jellyfish. Mount these colorful jellyfish on a wall or bulletin board for a special summer display.

Linda Anne Lopienski
Asheboro, NC

A Rock Lobster
This under-the-sea creature will really make a splash in your classroom. To make a rock lobster, cut off a row of three cardboard egg-carton cups. Paint the sections of the carton to resemble a lobster's body. When the paint dries, color and cut out a lobster tail and two claws. Glue the claw cutouts to one end of the lobster and the tail cutout to the other end. Then attach two pipe cleaners to resemble antennae. Glue two wiggle eyes to complete the lobster. Now this is a craft your little ones can put their claws on!

Ms. Guanipa—Gr. K
Covenant School
Arlington, MA

Dad's Day Apron

Dads will treasure these Father's Day presents for years to come. In advance, purchase a classroom supply of simple, white aprons (found at most craft stores). Provide each child with an apron. Have each child paint one of his hands with fabric paint, then press his hand onto the apron. Have him continue in this manner until he is happy with his design. When the paint dries, ask each child why he loves his dad or male friend or relative. Use a fabric pen to write his response on the apron. This nifty apron will brighten up Dad's day!

Daphne M. Orenshein—Gr. K
Yavneh Hebrew Academy
Los Angeles, CA

A Father's Day Magnet

No dad or caregiver will be able to resist this picture-perfect gift. In advance, photograph each of your students. To make one project, glue a photo to the center of a 6" x 6" square of sturdy cardboard. Have students glue colorful, scrunched-up, tissue-paper pieces on the cardboard to completely cover it. (You may want to do this in several sittings to ensure a thorough job.) When the glue dries, paint a coat of Mod Podge® over the picture frame. When that's completely dry, mount a piece of magnetic tape on the back. It's for you, Dad!

Seema Gersten
Harkham Hillel Hebrew Academy
Beverly Hills, CA

Coffee Bears

This project is not only fun to make, but it is also a really sensory experience. To make a coffee bear, trace a bear pattern (or draw one yourself) on a sheet of brown construction paper; then cut on the resulting outline. Draw facial features on the bear. Next spread glue on portions of the bear to represent its stomach, ears, and paws. Then sprinkle dried coffee grounds atop the glue. When the glue dries, shake off the excess coffee grounds. If you're in search of other sensory ideas, check out "Wonders Never Cease" on pages 138-151.

Sara Bockover—Gr. K
Keith Country Day School
Rockford, IL

Learning Centers

Spotlight on Centers

Apple Pickin'
Little ones will be delighted to do this "apple-tizing" number center. For each number you would like to include, photocopy the apple, stem, and leaf patterns (page 57) on construction paper. Program each apple with a numeral, each leaf with a number word, and each stem with dots. Laminate the patterns if desired. To use this center, a child matches the corresponding apples, stems, and leaves. Vary this center by providing a large supply of blank construction-paper apples so that each child can write the correct numeral on each apple.

Lynette McCaulley Pyne
Plainsboro, NJ

Soup Sort
Stir up some excitement when your students do this sorting center. Stock a center with a soup bowl filled with mixed dried beans, a ladle, and paper plates. To use this center, a child uses the ladle to scoop some beans onto a paper plate. To sort the beans, he categorizes them by size, color, texture, or shape; then he counts the beans in each group.

Althea A. Bleckley—Gr. K
South Rabun Elementary
Tiger, GA

Fish Watching
Encourage free exploration and discovery with this underwater science center. Place a fish-filled aquarium, several magnifying glasses, paper, and crayons in a center. To use this center, a child holds the magnifying glass at various distances in front of the aquarium and carefully examines the fish. He then illustrates what he observed and dictates a sentence about his picture. To vary the activity, supply the center with various craft items such as colored foil, construction paper, markers, and colored chalk for students to use to make fish similar to those in the tank. The high level of curiosity and interest at this center makes this activity a great catch!

Tina Costello—Developmental Kindergarten
Lincoln-Titus Elementary School
Crompond, NY

Spotlight on Centers

Spots On Spot
Here's a doggone fun math center to practice numeral recognition and counting. For each number that you would like to include in this center, photocopy the dog pattern (page 58). Program each dog's tag with a numeral. Then laminate them. Stock the center with a supply of black or brown buttons. To use this center, a child chooses a dog, reads the numeral, and then places the corresponding number of buttons on the dog cutout.

Laurie Mills—Gr. K
Stevenson Elementary
Stevenson, AL

Lace It Up!
Students will put their best feet forward when doing this center that practices fine-motor skills. Stock a center with shoes, boots, sneakers, and shoelaces of various colors and designs. To use this center, a child chooses a shoelace and uses it to lace a shoe, boot, or sneaker. If desired, encourage students to try their hands at tying the laces!

Betty Silkunas
Oak Lane Day School
Blue Bell, PA

Pancake Match
Youngsters will flip over this center that reinforces color/color word recognition. In advance, make 16 pancake cutouts; then pair them. Use markers to add a different color of syrup and a color word to each pair of pancakes. Place the pancake cutouts in a skillet. Then put the skillet and a spatula in a center. At this center, a child uses the spatula to remove each pancake; then he looks at the color of syrup and pairs it with the matching pancake.

Liz Mooney
Central Rayne Kindergarten
Rayne, LA

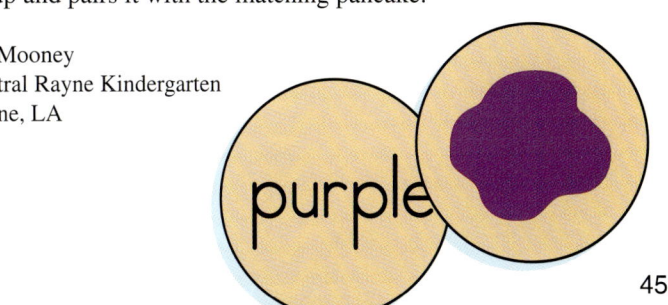

Spotlight on Centers

Taking A Close Look At Science

Create a science center in a jiffy using a shoe organizer with pockets. Place items such as seashells, rocks, tree bark, leaves, and pinecones in different resealable plastic bags. Insert each bag in a different pocket of the shoe organizer. Label each pocket with its contents. Place the filled shoe organizer and several magnifying glasses in a center. To use this center, a child chooses items of interest from a pocket and uses a magnifying glass to examine the items.

Patt Hall—Gr. K
Babson Park Elementary
Lake Wales, FL

Colored Kernels

This center is really popping with color recognition and counting skills. Using red, blue, yellow, and green markers, color a different-colored dot in the center of each of four different paper plates. Place the plates and a resealable bag of matching colored popcorn kernels in a center. To use this center, a child takes a handful of kernels from the bag and places the colored kernels on the corresponding paper plates. After sorting the colors, he counts the kernels on each plate to see which one has the most and which has the fewest kernels.

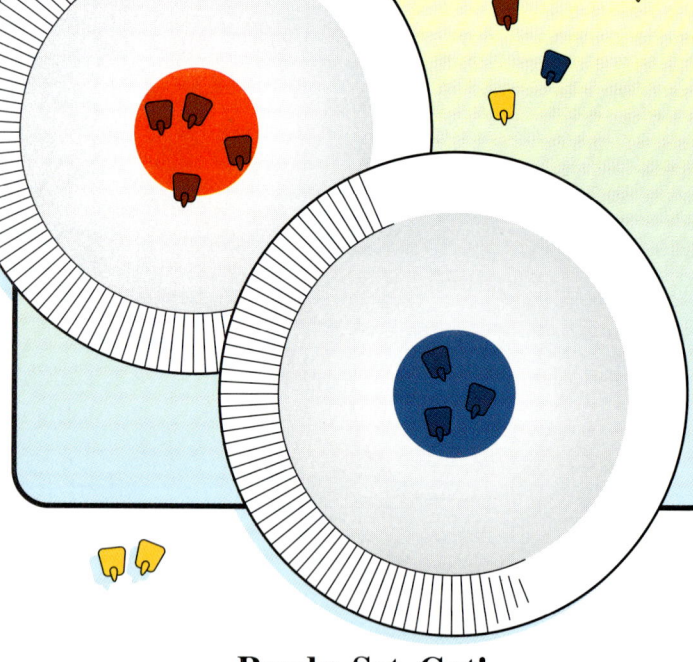

Gloria Barrow—Gr. K
Dundee Elementary
Dundee, FL

Ready, Set, Cut!

Save the ad section of newspapers for this center that provides lots of fine-motor practice. Place old newspapers, scissors, and a stapler in a center. To use this center, a child looks through the newspaper ads and cuts out the coupons of his choice. He then stacks the coupons and staples them together in a booklet. Allow youngsters to take their coupon books home for parents to use.

Ellen Bieleski—Gr. K
Elk Lake School
Dimock, PA

Spotlight on Centers

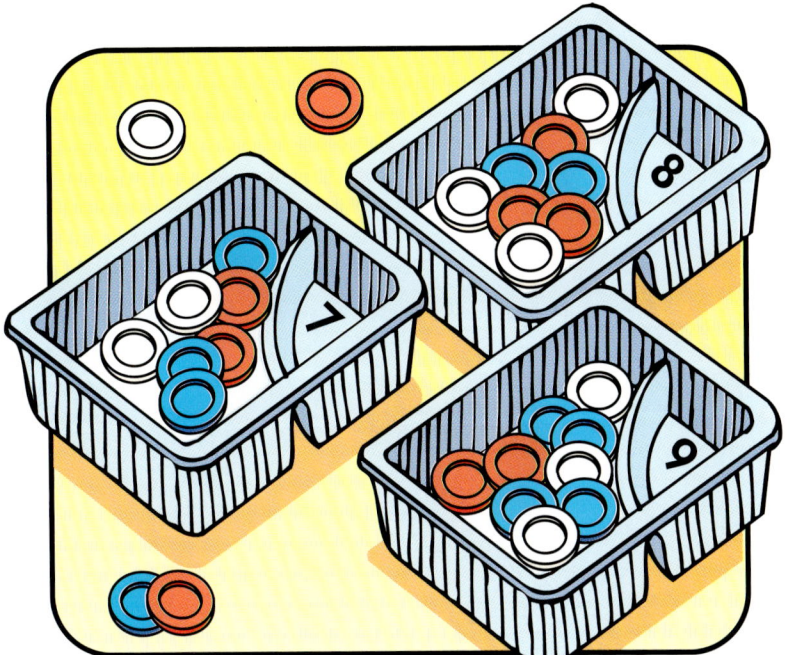

"Neato" Nacho Trays

Save nacho-and-cheese trays for this math center. Program the small divided area of each tray (where the cheese is placed) with a different numeral. Place several trays and a supply of small manipulatives such as marbles, poker chips, or buttons in a center. To use this center, a child chooses a tray, reads the numeral, and places the corresponding number of objects in the tray.

Betty L. Gomillion—Gr. K
South Leake Elementary
Walnut Grove, MS

Gourd Prints

This art center is a prime place for making gourd prints. In advance, cut various gourds in half. Pour tempera paints into shallow pans. Place the gourds, sheets of large construction paper, and the paints in a center. To use this center, a child dips a gourd into a color of paint, then presses it onto a sheet of construction paper. Have him continue in this manner, making the designs of his choice.

Katie Gaier—Gr. K
Parkview Elementary
Plymouth, WI

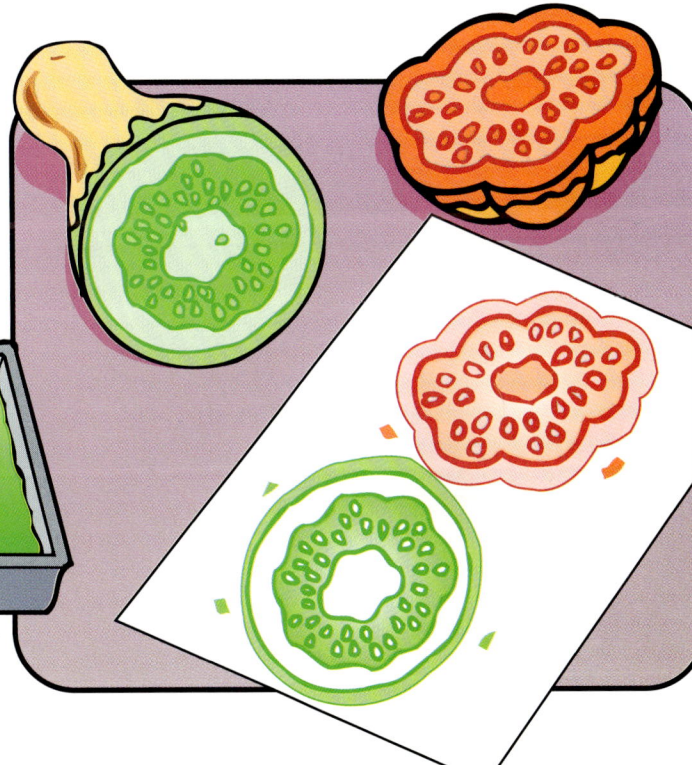

Chalkboard Letter-Recognition Center

Reinforce letter recognition with this magnetic activity that attracts attention. For each letter that you wish to study, cut out a pair of corresponding seasonal cutouts such as pumpkins and pumpkin leaves. Program the pumpkins with uppercase letters and the leaves with lowercase letters. Laminate the cutouts if desired. Attach a small piece of magnetic tape to the back of each cutout. Then, using colored chalk, draw a corresponding picture such as a pumpkin vine on a magnetic chalkboard. Mount the pumpkin leaves on the illustration. Place the pumpkins on a small table near the chalkboard. To use this center, a child chooses a pumpkin, reads the letter, and mounts it near the corresponding leaf.

Sally A. Camden
Cape Girardeau, MO

Spotlight on Centers

Nut Sorting

Your little ones will go nutty for this fun sorting center. In advance, collect a supply of Pringles® cans. Cover the outside of each can with wood-grain Con-Tact® covering to resemble a tree. Then cut a hole in the center of each can. Hot glue a different kind of nut to the top of each lid; then secure each lid on a can. Place the cans, a stuffed toy squirrel, and a basket filled with assorted nuts in a center. To do this activity, a child chooses a nut from the basket and places it inside the tree with the corresponding nut. Now that's nutty!

Kathy Hart
Mesa, AZ

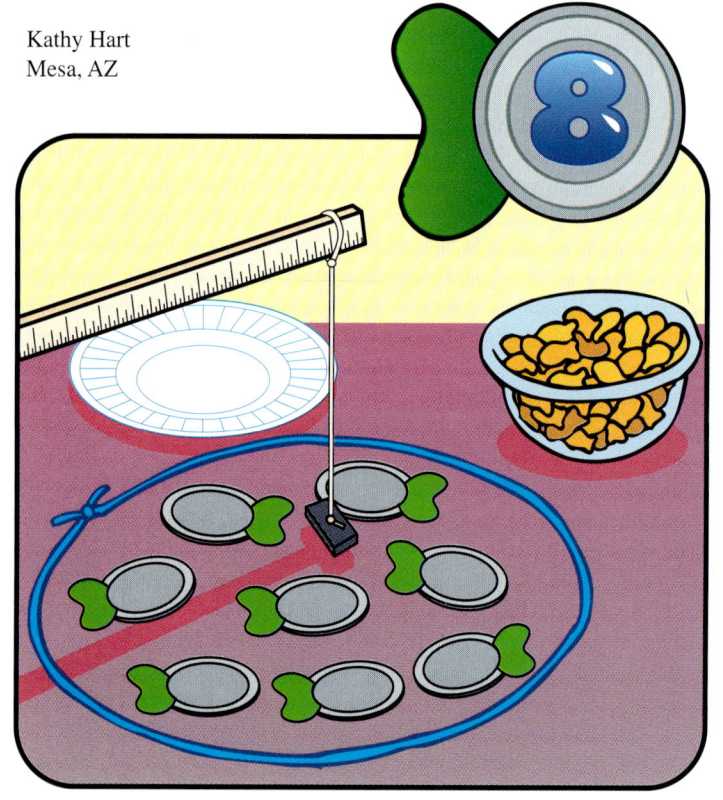

Fishing For Numbers

Here's a chance to provide youngsters with some number recognition skills that they can dive into. In advance, collect a supply of metal lids from frozen-juice cans. Using puffy paint or colored glue, program each lid with a different numeral. Glue a construction-paper fish tail to each lid so that it resembles a fish. When the paint and glue are dry, place the fish facedown on the floor. Arrange a length of blue yarn around the lids to represent a pond (or use a small wading pool). To make a fishing pole, tie a length of yarn to the end of a yardstick; then attach a piece of magnetic tape to the other end of the yarn. Place the fishing pole, a bowl of fish-shaped crackers, and a paper plate on a table near the pond. To use this center, a child uses the fishing pole to catch a fish, reads the numeral on the fish, and counts the corresponding number of fish-shaped crackers on the paper plate. (Provide a supply of unhandled crackers for snacking.)

Helen Andringa—Gr. K, Redeemer Christian School, Mesa, AZ

Clothespin Fun

Youngsters can practice name recognition, spelling, and alphabetical order all at one center. To make the center, glue wiggle eyes to a supply of spring-type clothespins. Using a marker, draw a nose and a mouth on each clothespin; then program an uppercase or lowercase letter on the other end of the clothespin. Place the clothespins in a basket. Next decorate a large, lidless cardboard box. Place the box, with the open side facing you, on a flat surface. Use a hole puncher to make a hole in each side of the box. Tie a length of clothesline or yarn through the holes. Place the box and the basket in a center. To use the center, a child clips the clothespins on the clothesline to spell his name or other words, or to put letters in alphabetical order.

Kimberly Turner
Booneville, KY

Spotlight on Centers

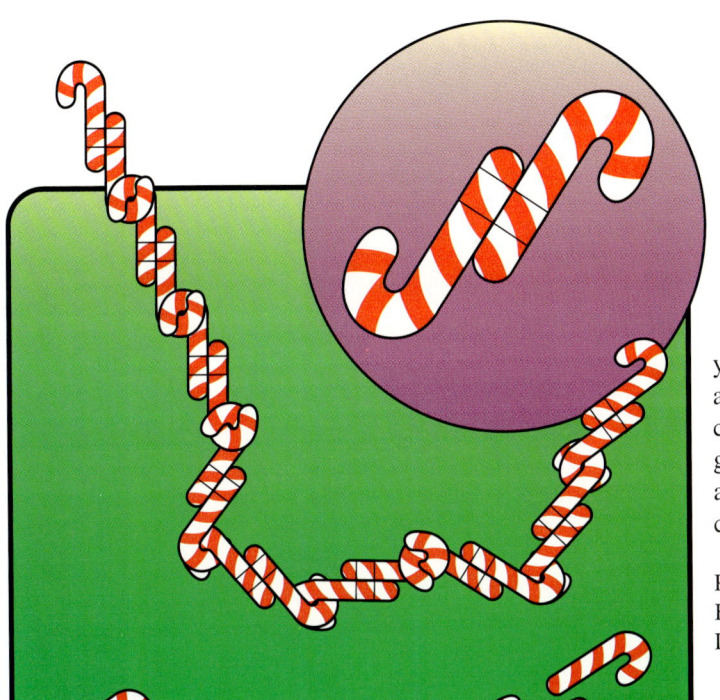

Candy Cane

With some candy canes and imagination, this center not only helps youngsters' fine-motor skills, but also provides lots of holiday fun. In advance, tape pairs of small candy canes together as shown. Place the candy canes in a center. To use this center, a student (or a small group of students) hooks together the candy canes to make a chain or a design. Reinforce math skills by asking students to estimate and count how many candy canes they have used. Ho, ho, ho!

Patt Hall—Gr. K
Babson Park Elementary
Lake Wales, FL

Cozy Quilts

Youngsters will snuggle up to this warm and cozy patterning center. To make the center, duplicate the quilt pattern on page 60. Cut out the quilt pattern and mount it on a sheet of tagboard; then laminate it if desired. From wallpaper cut out squares identical in size to those on the quilt. Place the wallpaper squares and the quilt in a center. To use this center, a child places the wallpaper squares on the quilt to make a patterned design of his choice. (To make a take-home project, stock the center with a copy of page 60 for each child. Then have each child glue the wallpaper squares to his page and color the rest of the picture.)

Carol Ulrich
Mt. Hood Christian Pre/K
Gresham, OR

It's A Wrap

Your little ones are sure to get wrapped up in fine-motor skills at this center. Stock a center with tape, bows, ribbons, scissors, note cards, pencils, various types of wrapping paper, and different-size blocks and boxes. To use this center, a child uses the paper and other materials to wrap and decorate the boxes and blocks. As a variation, a student may wish to place small items in the boxes before wrapping and giving them to another child in the center to open.

Lisa Brown
Kirbyville, TX

Spotlight on Centers

Write On!

Use a refrigerator box to make this unique writing center. To make the center, cut one side panel from a refrigerator box—or any large appliance box—so that it has a bottom panel and three sides. On the inside of the box, hang a small chalkboard and several pockets to hold various types of paper, stationery, and envelopes. Also mount appropriate seasonal/sight words on the panels. Then place a student desk on the bottom panel. Stock the desk with crayons, chalk, stencils, pencils, and markers. Then glue a copy of the writing center label (page 59) on the outside of the center. Encourage youngsters to decorate the outside of the box in their spare time. If desired, situate a typewriter nearby. To use this open-ended center, a child uses the materials provided to write stories or letters, draw pictures, or creatively write as he likes. The possibilities are endless!

Carol Willian—Gr. K
Strode Station Elementary
Winchester, KY

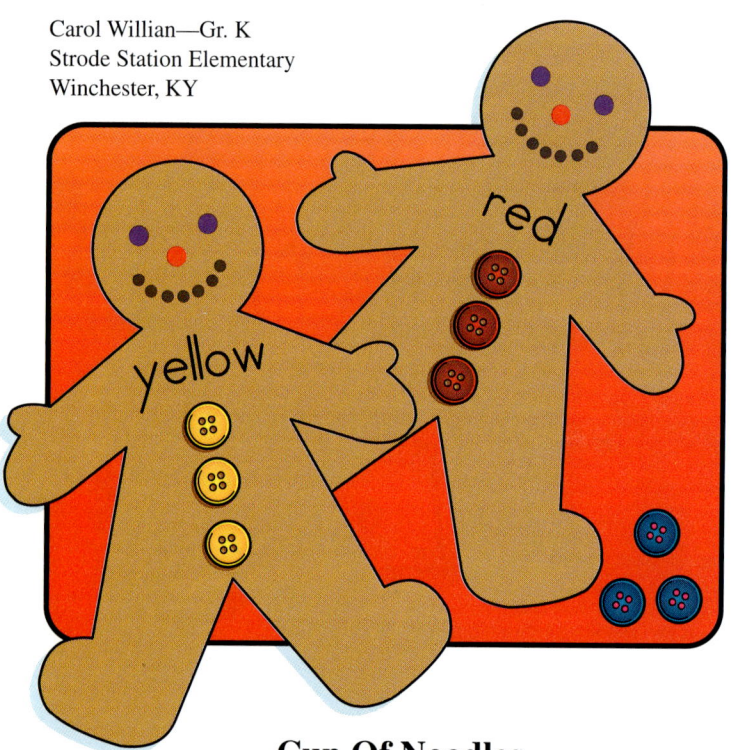

Run, Run, As Fast As You Can!

Here's a sweet way to practice color-word and color recognition. For each color that you would like to include in this center, cut a gingerbread-person shape from light brown construction paper. Use a marker to program each cutout with facial features and a different color word. Place the cutouts and matching colored buttons in a center. To use this center, a child chooses a gingerbread person, reads the color word, and places the matching colored buttons on the corresponding cutout. Can't catch me!

Liz Mooney—Gr. K
Central Rayne Kindergarten
Rayne, LA

Cup Of Noodles

This center sure has lots of "pasta-bilities." Stock your center with a bowl of different-colored assorted pasta (such as bow ties, elbows, and shells), paper cups, construction paper, and glue. To use this center, a child uses a paper cup to scoop some pasta from the bowl. After exploring his portion of pasta, he decides how he would like to sort—by color, shape, size, etc. Then he arranges and glues the pasta according to his desired categories on a sheet of construction paper. Now that's oodles of noodles!

Carol Mayo—Gr. K
Cypress Creek Elementary
Ruskin, FL

Spotlight on Centers

Cups Of Plenty!

Use empty plastic, snack-size pudding or fruit cups for this math center. In advance, collect ten pudding or fruit cups and program the outside of each cup with a different numeral from one to ten. Place the cups and counters (such as beads, buttons, or beans) in a center. To use this center, a child first puts the cups in numerical order, then fills each cup with the correct number of counters. As a variation, provide a supply of coins, label the cups accordingly, and have each child who visits the center place the coins in the corresponding cups.

Sue Langdon
Longwood Elementary
Shalimar, FL

A Message Center

Your little ones will be quick to visit this fun, hands-on center. Place a cookie sheet and a basket of magnetic letters and numbers in a center. To use this center, a child places the letters on the cookie sheet to spell or copy words, his name, or a message for the next child who visits the center. He may also place the numbers on the cookie sheet to create his phone number or put the numbers in numerical order.

Lynn Sanders
Hayes Elementary
Kennesaw, GA

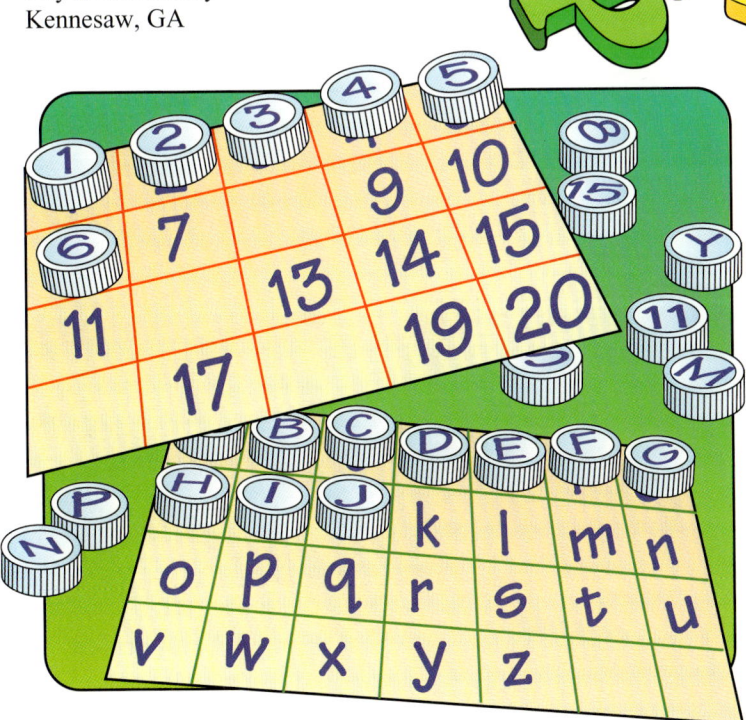

Letter And Number Boards

Visual discrimination, letter- and number recognition are all enhanced in this center. Draw a grid on several sheets of tagboard. Program each tagboard sheet with either numerals or letters; then laminate it. Also program a supply of plastic bottle caps with corresponding letters and numerals. Place the caps in a basket; then stock your center with the grids and the basket. To use the center, a child chooses a letter or numeral grid, then matches each bottle cap to the corresponding numeral or letter. Vary this activity by leaving some places on the grids blank. Then challenge each student to read the grid left to right and use the caps to fill in the blanks.

Barbara M. Marks
Kinderplace
Oshkosh, WI

Spotlight on Centers

Patterning With M&M's®
Little ones will have lots of fun in this sweet patterning center. Using different-colored bingo markers (in the colors found in a bag of M&M's®), program strips of construction paper with patterned designs. Place the programmed strips, blank construction-paper strips, bingo markers, and a cup of M&M's® in a center. To use this center, a child chooses a programmed strip and uses the candies to copy/continue the pattern on a blank construction-paper strip. Then the child may record his work by re-creating the pattern using the bingo markers. Provide a bowl of unhandled candies for youngsters to sample after a job well done!

Lisa Mascheri—Exceptional Education
Midway Elementary, Sanford, FL

Magnetic Colors
Students will be attracted to this magnetic color center. In advance, draw and cut out a variety of shapes and figures from different colors of construction paper. Also program construction-paper strips with the corresponding color words. Laminate the cutouts and the color-word strips; then attach a piece of magnetic tape to the back of each piece. Place the color cutouts, color words, and a magnetic board in a center. To use this center, a child arranges the color cutouts on the magnetic board. Then he reads each color word and matches it to the appropriate cutout.

Tara Stefanich—Gr. K
Merritt Elementary
Mt. Iron, MN

Water-Table Fun
Add some sparkle to your water table with this fun idea. Sprinkle different colors of glitter into the water. Then stock the table with various utensils such as measuring cups, funnels, sifters, ice-cream scoops, cups, and spoons. When a child visits this center, he may freely explore measuring, sifting, pouring, and volume with the utensils and the sparkling water. Splish, splash—what a blast!

Kristy Curless—Gr. K
Walnut Creek Day School
Columbia, MO

Spotlight on Centers

Egg Baskets
Your little ones will enjoy counting in this seasonal math center. In advance collect ten baskets. Program each basket with a different numeral from one to ten (or the numerals of your choice). Cut out and laminate 55 colorful construction-paper eggs. Place the baskets and the eggs in a center. To use the center, a child places the corresponding number of eggs in each basket. Extend the activity by having students then arrange the baskets in numerical order. For a variation, use plastic, colored eggs instead of construction-paper eggs.

Samita Arora
Rainbows United, Inc.
Wichita, KS

Lots Of Eggs!
Have your students give this "egg-cellent" center a try! For each number that you would like to include, use a permanent marker to program half of a plastic egg with the numeral. On the other half of each egg, attach the corresponding number of small stickers. Place the disassembled eggs in a basket; then put the basket and an empty egg carton in a center. To use the center, a child matches the corresponding egg halves, then arranges the assembled eggs in the egg carton.

Darlene Quinby
Calvary Episcopal School
Richmond, TX

Ice-Cube Tray Patterns
Little ones will be delighted to visit this cool patterning center. Stock your center with a bowl of different-colored pom-poms and several ice-cube trays. Encourage children to visit this center in pairs. Instruct each child in a pair to arrange pom-poms in one side of a different tray, making the color pattern of his choice. Then have the children in the pair switch trays and duplicate the pattern in their partner's tray.

Terri Whitaker—Gr. K
Barrington Place
Sugar Land, TX

Spotlight on Centers

Volcanic Math

This math center will provide an eruption of counting fun and fine-motor skills. For each number that you wish to include in your center, cut out a volcano shape from construction paper. Use a marker to program each cutout with a numeral or number word. Place the cutouts, a pair of tweezers, and a bowl of aquarium gravel (to represent volcanic rocks) in a center. To do this activity, a child uses the tweezers to place the correct number of rocks on each volcano.

Mary Philip—Gr. K
Relay Children's Center
Baltimore, MD

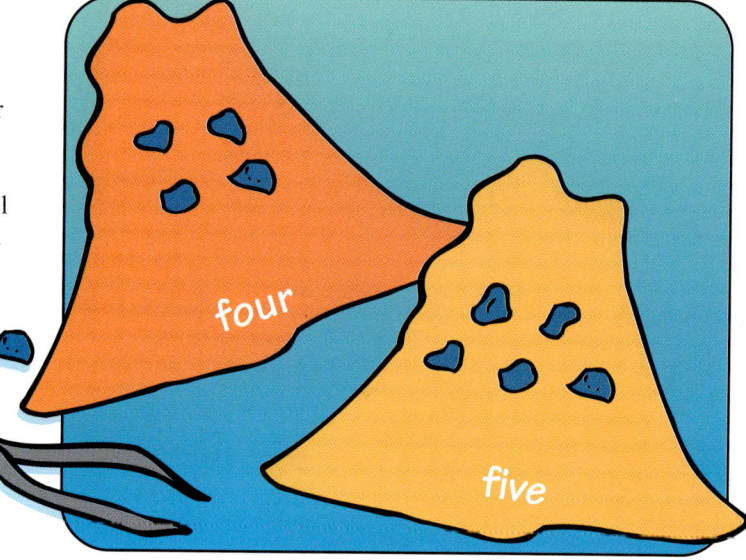

Seashell Matching

Since summer is approaching, this seashell center will be a nifty way for students to practice visual discrimination. In advance, collect pairs of different types of seashells. Place the seashells and a sand bucket in a center. To do this activity, a child sorts and matches the shells. As a variation, trace pairs of different types of seashell patterns on construction paper; then cut on the resulting outlines. Laminate the cutouts. Place the shell cutouts in a center and have students match the shell pairs.

Melissa Iverson
Academy Park Elementary
Bountiful, UT

The Reading Pool

With this suggestion you can transform your reading center into an oasis of learning. Position a small wading pool in your reading center; then toss in a few small, decorative pillows. Cut out a palm tree from bulletin-board paper and mount it on a wall near the center. Then cut out a few coconut shapes from construction paper and mount them on the tree. If desired, place a few artificial plants around the pool. Provide lots of sea-related literature for little ones to cozy up with in the reading pool. They'll be anxious to dive into a good book!

Jennifer Mitchell—Special Education
New Caney Elementary
New Caney, TX

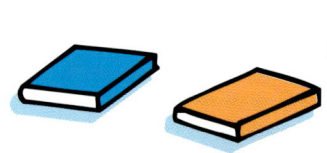

Spotlight on Centers

Writing Boxes

A-writing we will go with this fun-filled center! In advance, collect several plastic lunchboxes. Place items—such as pens, pencils, markers, crayons, stickers, stamps, stamp pads, glue sticks, a ruler, and a notepad—in each box. Place the writing boxes in a center. At this open-ended center, a child uses the materials provided to write stories or letters, draw pictures, or creatively write as he likes.

Jan Benson—Gr. K
Montevallo Elementary School
Montevallo, AL

Sensory Center

Create a center that will enrich the senses with this "sense-sational" idea. In advance collect several five-quart ice-cream buckets. In each bucket, store a different item, such as colored pasta, cornmeal, birdseed, milk-jug lids, rock salt, oatmeal, feathers, unpopped colored popcorn kernels, rice, and mixed dried beans. Place the buckets, measuring scoops, scales, bowls, an empty bucket, and measuring cups on the floor atop a tablecloth. To use this center, a child uses the kitchen tools to pour, estimate, measure, and weigh items from one of the buckets. Then he continues in the same manner, choosing another item. Cleanup will be a snap when you pour any spilled substances in the empty bucket for later use.

Susan Anker
White Bear Lake, MN

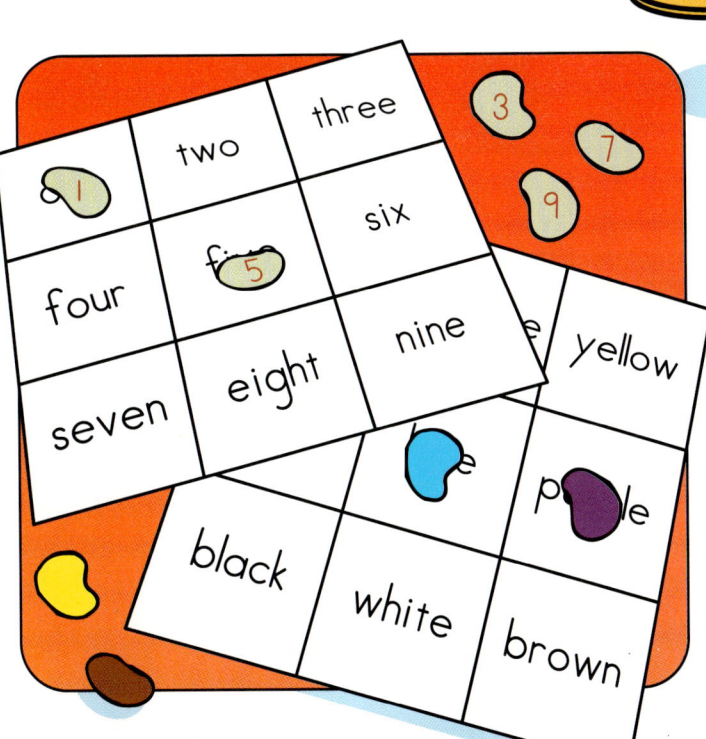

A New Twist On An Old Bean

This versatile center provides an opportunity to review the skill of your choice. Draw grids on several sheets of tagboard. Program each grid with the skill of your choice. (For example, you might program the grids with letters of the alphabet, shapes, numerals, or colors.) Laminate the sheets of tagboard. Then use a thin-lined permanent marker to program a supply of lima beans with the corresponding skill. Spray the lima beans with a coat of shellac. Store each set of lima beans in a basket; then put the grids and the baskets in a center. To use the center, a child chooses a grid and then matches each lima bean to the corresponding space in the grid.

Chris Jackson—Grs. K–1
Tench Tilghman Elementary School
Baltimore, MD

Spotlight on Centers

Look What's Buzzin'
Letter sounds will be the buzz at this phonics-related center. For each letter that you would like to include, photocopy the bee pattern and the honey-jar pattern (page 61) on construction paper. Color the bees with markers; then cut out the patterns. Program each bee with a letter. Then, for each letter, cut out a magazine picture with the same beginning sound. Glue each magazine picture to a honey jar and laminate the patterns if desired. Place the bees and the honey jars in a center. To use this center, a child matches each bee to the corresponding honey jar. (Program the backs of the honey jars for self-checking if desired.)

Melissa Iverson
Academy Park Elementary
Bountiful, UT

Flowerpot Blocks
Here's a springtime twist for a block center or reading center! In advance, use Slick® fabric paint to program one side of 26 (or more) plastic flowerpots with a different uppercase letter. Then program the back of each pot with a matching lowercase letter. To use this center, a child may arrange the pots in alphabetical order, stack them in alphabetical order, or use them to spell words.

Willette M. Munz
Little People Land
Pinellas Park, FL

Spots On Ladybugs
Need an idea to help youngsters practice simple addition? If so, this center hits the spot. Photocopy the ladybug pattern (page 62) several times. Place the ladybug patterns, a supply of black buttons (or paper dots), and several sets of numeral cards programmed from one to five in a center. To use this center, a child chooses a numeral card and places the corresponding number of buttons on one side of the ladybug. Then she chooses another card and places the corresponding number of buttons on the other side of the ladybug. She then counts the total number of buttons. If desired, provide paper and pencils, and encourage children to write out the number sentences as they work with the manipulatives.

Wendy Goodman—Grs. K–1
Charlotte, NC

Patterns

Use with "Apple Pickin' " on page 44.

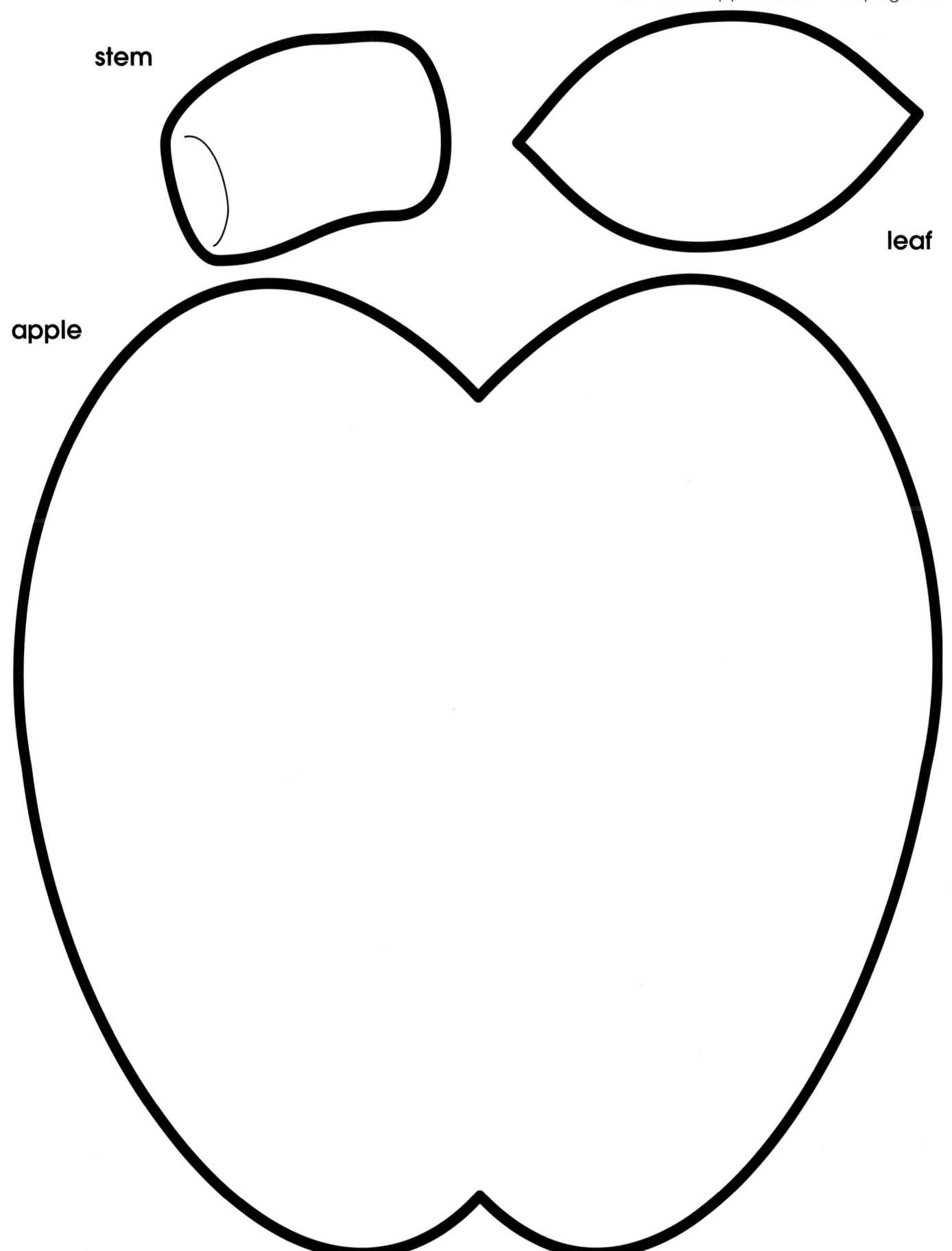

stem

leaf

apple

Pattern
Use with "Spots On Spot" on page 45.

dog

Center Label   Use with "Write On!" on page 50.

Writing Center

©The Education Center, Inc. • THE MAILBOX® • Kindergarten • Dec/Jan 1995–96

Note To The Teacher: Duplicate the label, color it, and cut around the bold lines. Glue the label onto a sheet of construction paper slightly larger than the label. Laminate the label if desired. Mount it on or near your writing center.

Pattern
Use with "Cozy Quilts" on page 49.

Pattern
Use with "Look What's Buzzin'" on page 56.

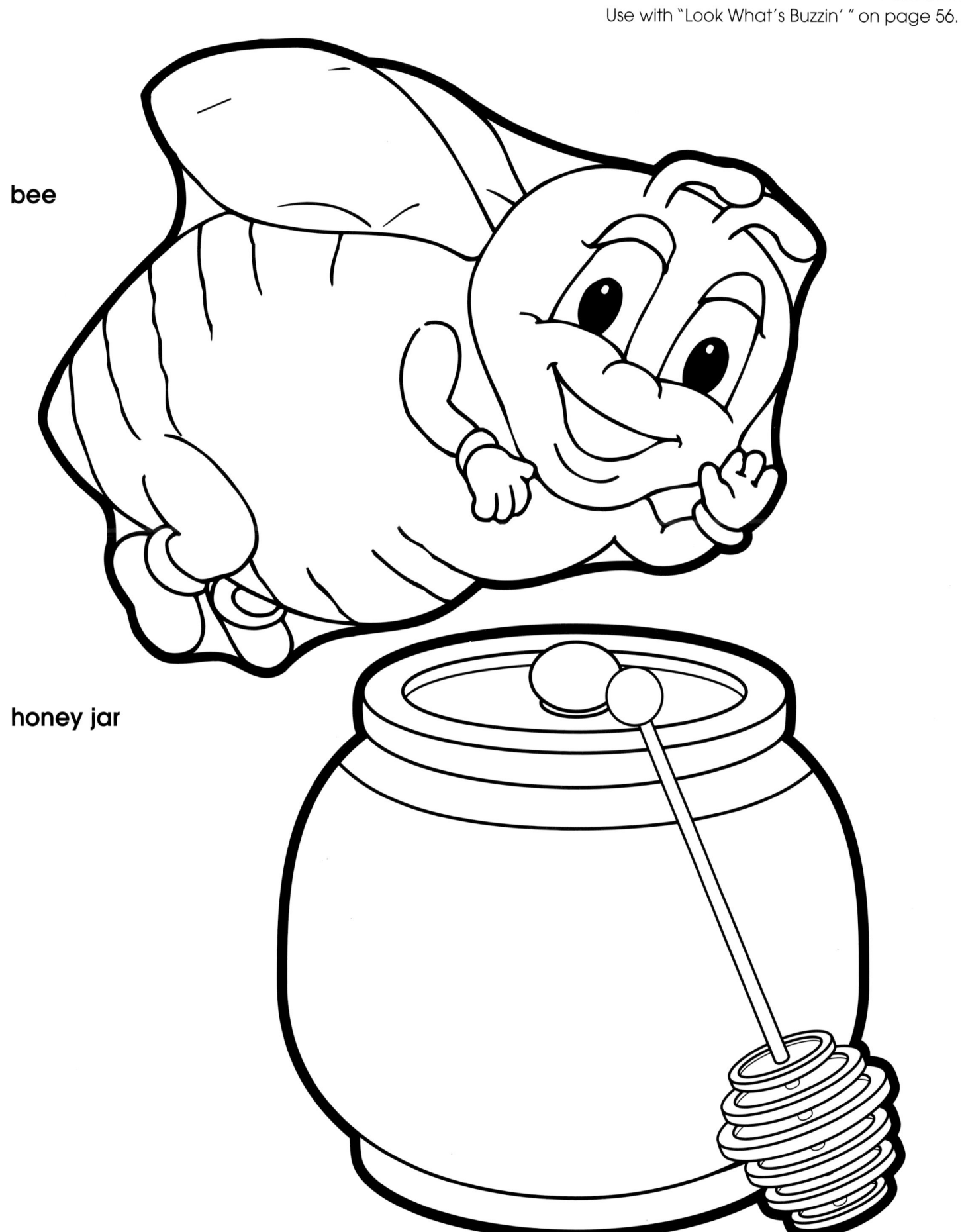

bee

honey jar

©The Education Center, Inc. • THE MAILBOX® • Kindergarten • April/May 1996

Ladybug Pattern
Use with "Spots On Ladybugs" on page 56.

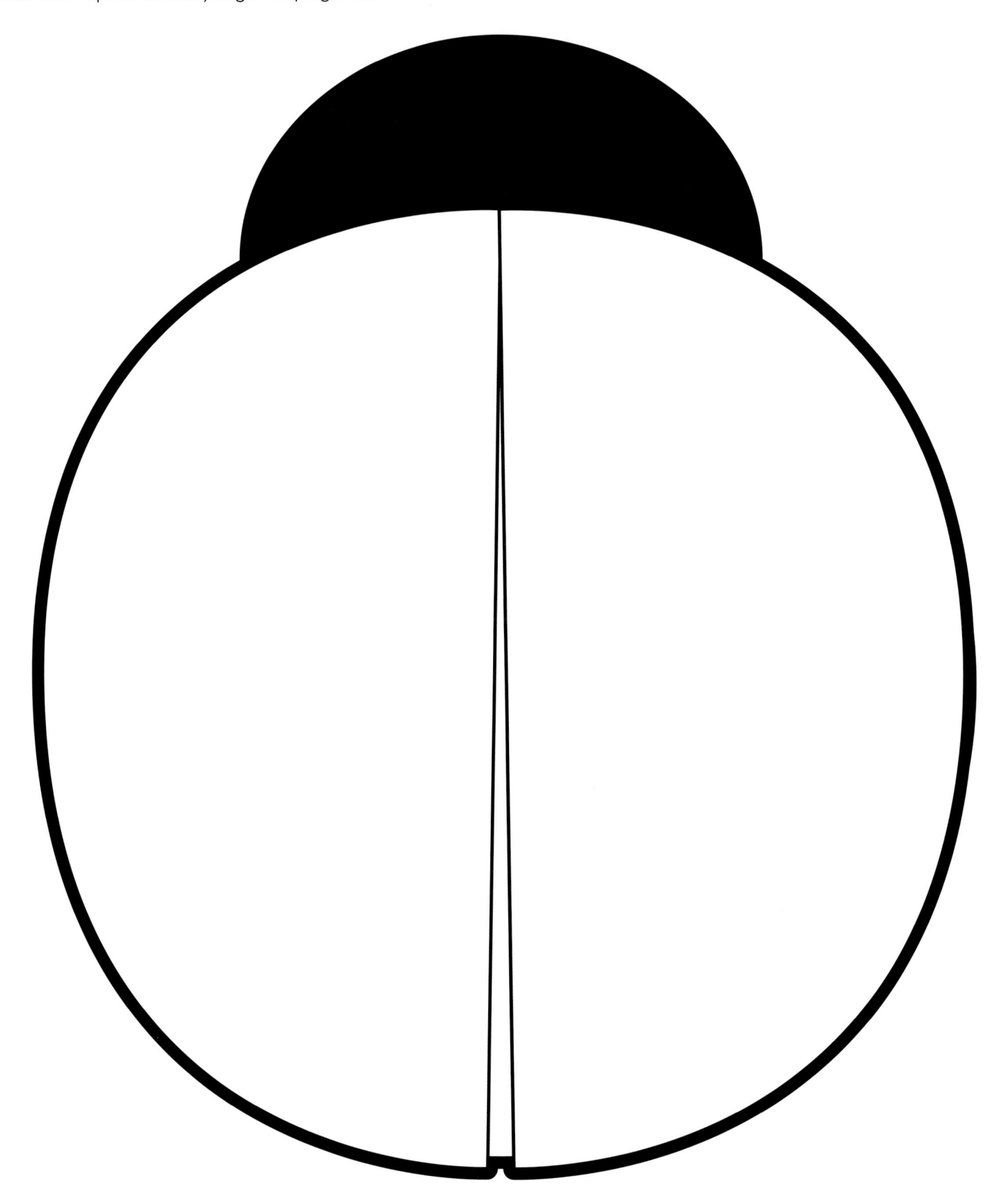

Children's Literature

A Celebration Of Friendship

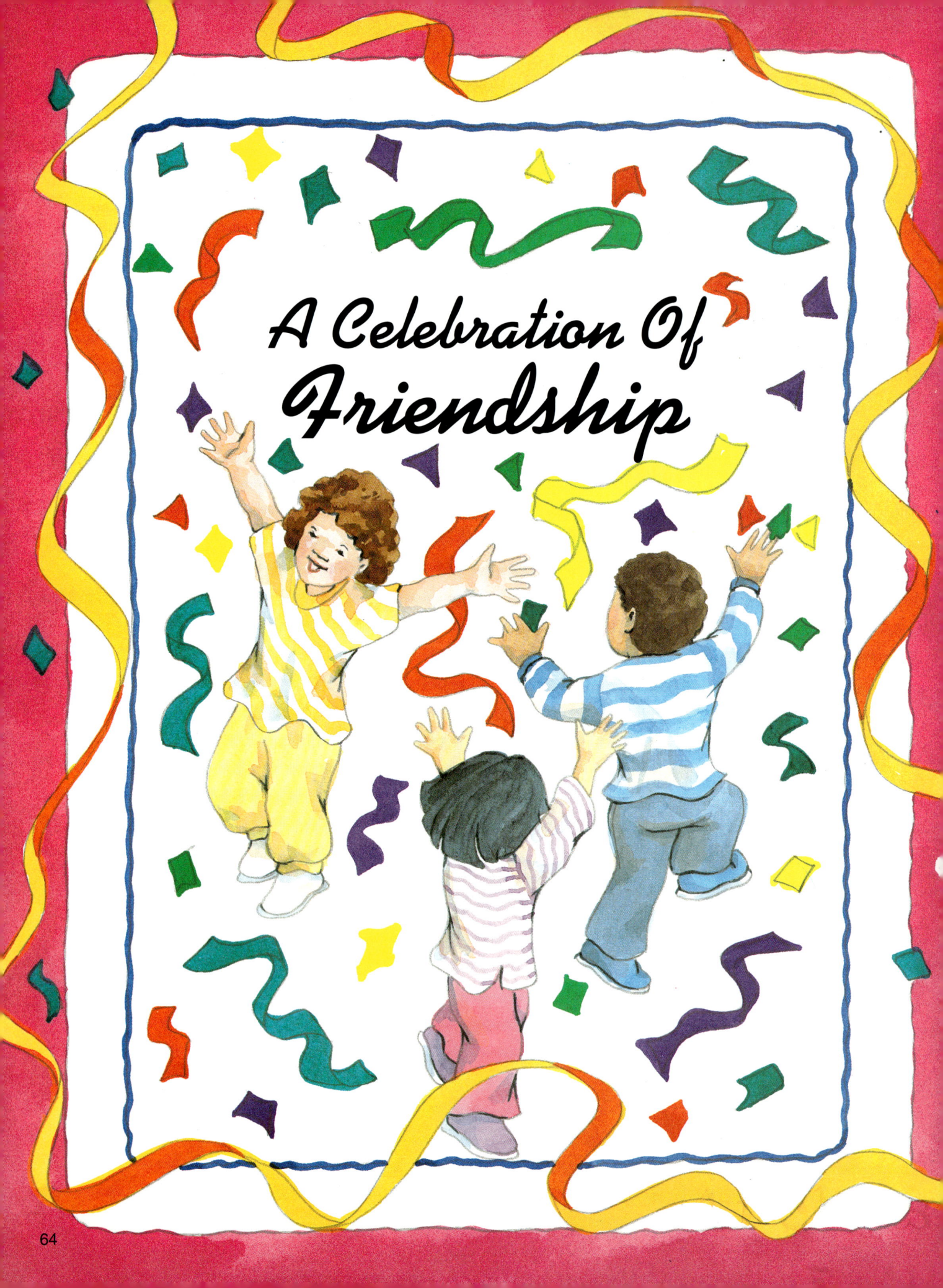

Friends
Written & Illustrated by Helme Heine
Published by Margaret K. McElderry Books

"Good friends always stick together." That's what Charlie Rooster, Johnny Mouse, and fat Percy, the pig, believe. Celebrate the joy of friendship with these carefree characters as you read this delightful book.

After sharing the book, discuss how the characters enjoyed each other's companionship as well as the tasks they accomplished together. Ask students to think about who their good friends are. Then have each child draw a picture of himself with his friends and write (or dictate) a sentence about his friends. If possible, take a picture of each child with his friends. Mount each developed picture, if taken, on the paper.

Diane E. Stark—Gr. K
Hawthorne Elementary
Kansas City, KS

Good friends *will* stick together with these circles of friendship. To make one, fold a square piece of paper in half diagonally to form a triangle. Fold the triangle in half again; then fold once more. To make sure you have folded the paper correctly, open the paper and look for eight sections. Refold the paper. Trace a child-shaped pattern (as shown) onto the folded paper. Keeping the paper folded, cut out the shape. Open the paper to find a circle of eight "friends" holding hands. Have each student decorate each child shape in his circle. Then ask him to write a friend's name on each shape or to dictate ideas about friendship to be written on each shape. Display the circles of friendship on a bulletin board titled "Good Friends Stick Together."

Jennifer Barton—Gr. K
Elizabeth Green School
Newington, CT

My Friends
Written & Illustrated by Taro Gomi
Published by Chronicle Books

A young girl recalls all that she has learned from her animal and people friends. Youngsters will enjoy the simple text and vibrant illustrations of Taro Gomi's charming book.

There is something to be learned from everything in the world around us. Help youngsters understand this idea by making a class book similar to the book *My Friends*. Brainstorm a list of animals; then talk about different actions or characteristics of each animal. For example, a fish swims and a lion roars. Ask each student to choose an animal to illustrate; then have him write (or dictate for you to write) a sentence about what he could learn from that animal. Bind the pages together with a cover. Title the book "Our Friends." Give each child an opportunity to take the book home for a night to share with his family.

Lisa Kranz—Gr. K
St. Ann School
Lansing, Il

Will I Have A Friend?
Written by Miriam Cohen
Illustrated by Lillian Hoban
Published by Macmillan Publishing Co., Inc.

Youngsters will identify with Jim's feelings as he spends his first day at school.

Use this reassuring story as a springboard for discussion about youngsters' feelings during the first days of school. Ask students to predict whether or not Jim will have a friend and if so, how Jim will meet his friend. After reading the book aloud, discuss the idea that everyone can be a friend to someone else in the class. On a chart, write several positive traits about each child that would make him a good friend. Then provide each child with a crown or an award ribbon cut from sturdy paper. Have each child personalize and decorate his item. Then write several positive words from the list on each child's crown or award.

Debbie Musser—Gr. K
Washington-Lee Elementary
Bristol, VA

The Rainbow Fish
Written & Illustrated by Marcus Pfister
Published by North-South Books

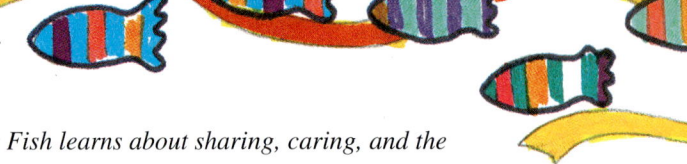

In this enchanting tale, the Rainbow Fish learns about sharing, caring, and the beauty that comes from within.

After reading the story aloud, discuss the importance of sharing in friendship. Then assist each child in making a Rainbow Fish book about sharing. To make a book, have each child cut two fish shapes (identical in size) from construction paper. Title one of the fish shapes "Sharing and Caring." Encourage the student to decorate this fish shape with paint, crayons, or markers. Using glitter and glue, have her make one shimmering scale on this fish. Place several sheets of paper (also cut in fish shapes) between the construction-paper fish, and bind them together to create a book. On each page, have the child illustrate and write (or dictate) ways that she can share and care.

Laurie Walegir—Gr. K
Twin Oaks Country Day School
Freeport, NY

Extend the beauty of this story by creating Rainbow Fish. Have each child paint rows of different colors on his own sheet of white art paper. After the paint dries, direct him to trace a fish pattern onto the paper and cut on the resulting outline. Onto the fish shape, glue a hole reinforcement for an eye and a small piece of tinfoil to represent the shimmering scale. Display the finished projects on a wall or bulletin board for a beautiful school of Rainbow Fish.

Barb Spero—Gr. K
Memorial School
Paramus, NJ

We Are Best Friends
Written & Illustrated by Aliki
Published by Greenwillow Books

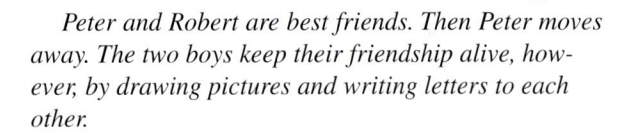

Peter and Robert are best friends. Then Peter moves away. The two boys keep their friendship alive, however, by drawing pictures and writing letters to each other.

Before reading the story aloud, show students the front cover and read the title. On a chart, create a list of things that good friends do together. Explain that in the story one of the boys moves away. Provide an opportunity for children who have moved, or have had a friend who moved, to share their stories. Ask students to predict whether or not the two boys will stay friends. Read *We Are Best Friends* aloud. As an extension to the story, provide an opportunity for youngsters in the class to write letters to each other. Begin by having students play together in pairs outside or in centers. Then announce that it is "time to move." Ask students to sit at separate tables from their partners. Have each child illustrate what he did with his partner. Then demonstrate how to write a letter by starting with the word "Dear" and ending with the writer's name. Have each student write (or dictate) a letter to his partner. Use the class mail center, if available, to mail the letters.

Do You Want To Be My Friend?
Written & Illustrated by Eric Carle
Published by Philomel Books

Travel along with a brave, little mouse as he seeks to find a friend. You'll discover a mystery and a few surprises along the way.

After sharing the story, make friendship necklaces. Provide each child with a length of string or ribbon that has been taped on one end. Write each child's name on the tape at the end of his string. Also give each child a supply of beads equal to the number of children in the class. (Wooden beads from a beaded carseat mat work nicely for this. For an added touch of fun, paint the beads green so that the necklaces will resemble the surprise character at the conclusion of the story.) Direct each child to go to each child in the class and ask the question, "Do you want to be my friend?" As each child answers, "Yes," he should give one of his beads to the child asking the question. As children receive beads, they can accept these tokens of friendship and thread them on their strings. After each child has completed his friendship necklace, allow each student to trade necklaces with someone with whom he would like to be better friends. To ensure fairness in this necklace exchange, consider drawing names or pairing children appropriately.

Adapted from an idea by Jody Weber and
Sheila Dozark—Gr. K
Boyer Valley Community School
Dunlap, IA

We Are All Alike...We Are All Different
Written & Illustrated by the Cheltenham Elementary School Kindergartners
Published by Scholastic Inc.

Use this book written by children, for children, to foster in youngsters the appreciation of similarities and differences among themselves.

As children learn to understand human diversity, they grow in self-esteem and acceptance of others. To help youngsters better understand diversity, try this activity. Pair students. Give each pair a piece of paper that has been folded in half. Unfold the page. Have each child take a good look at his partner, then draw his partner on one half of the page. Have the students write (or dictate for you to write) one way that they are alike and one way that they are different.

Extend the learning opportunities of this child-centered book with an art activity. Using skin-toned construction paper, cut out a body shape for each student. Also cut out a supply of large, red construction-paper hearts. Encourage each child to decorate his body shape using a variety of art supplies such as fabric, yarn, and markers. Have each child write his name on a heart cutout and glue the heart to the right hand of the decorated cutout. Attach the completed projects side by side along a wall or on a bulletin board. For a display that clearly communicates the message of friendship in a diverse world, cut out a globe design and attach it to a bulletin board. Then add the bodies and hearts around the globe design. Title the display "We are all alike. We are all different. We are all friends."

Beth Lemke
Coon Rapids, MN

Bein' With You This Way
Written by W. Nikola-Lisa
Illustrated by Michael Bryant
Published by Lee & Low Books, Inc.

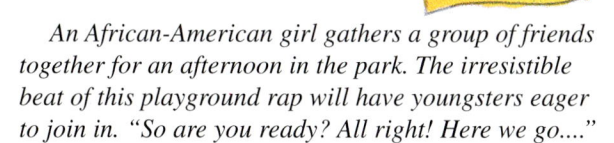

An African-American girl gathers a group of friends together for an afternoon in the park. The irresistible beat of this playground rap will have youngsters eager to join in. "So are you ready? All right! Here we go...."

This award-winning book is an excellent choice for introducing little ones to racial and physical differences. Read aloud *Bein' With You This Way*; then create a class version of the book. Write each page of the book's text on a separate sheet of construction paper. Title another sheet "Bein' With You This Way" to use as the cover. Then, on a warm, sunny day, take the class to the playground or on a field trip to a park. To capture the joy of "just bein' together," take candid photos of the children as they play. After the pictures have been developed, glue several of them around the text on each page in the class book. Laminate the covers and the pages of the book; then bind them together. Give each child an opportunity to take the book home to share with his family.

Jamaica's Find
Written by Juanita Havill
Illustrated by Anne Sibley O'Brien
Published by Houghton Mifflin Company

Jamaica finds a red hat and a cuddly toy dog at the park. She takes the hat to Lost and Found but can't resist keeping the dog. Later, when she returns the dog, she finds something even better. Youngsters will delight in the happy ending of this heartwarming story.

Read *Jamaica's Find* to the class; then have some fun with this secretive game of Lost and Found. Ask each child to bring a stuffed toy to school. Send a letter home to parents explaining the purpose of this activity and requesting that the toy be sent to school in a bag with the child's name attached. When it is time to play the game, collect everyone's bag; then redistribute the bags—giving each child a bag other than her own. Select a child to describe what her "lost" toy looked like. The children should look in the bags they are holding to see if the toy inside matches the description of the lost toy. The child with the matching toy can then announce that the lost toy has been "found." Continue play until each child has had a turn to describe her stuffed toy to the group.

The Doorbell Rang
Written & Illustrated by Pat Hutchins
Published by Greenwillow Books

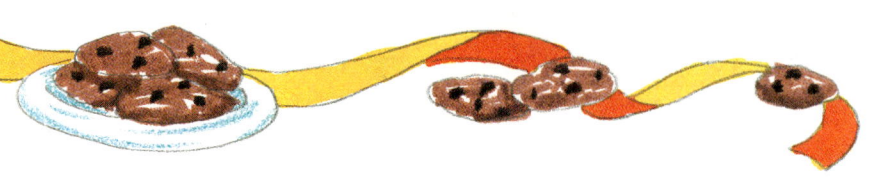

When this delightful story begins, there are a dozen cookies. Then the doorbell rings...and rings...and rings. The surprising conclusion of this story presents a lesson about the joy of sharing.

Before reading *The Doorbell Rang*, use this idea to help children solve the problem that will occur in the story. Show children a plate of 12 cookies. Ask two children, each holding a plate, to stand beside the cookies. As a class, decide how to divide the cookies fairly between the two children. Then ring a bell and invite two more children to stand with plates beside the first two children. Continue in this manner according to the book's text, until there are twelve children, each child with one cookie on his plate. Ring the bell once more. Again ask the class how the cookies could be shared; then have each standing child take a seat. At this point, read the story aloud. Ask students for their comments on the surprise ending; then provide them with an unexpected treat of chocolate chip cookies.

Extend the math opportunities of this story with a friendship counting activity. Ask each student to find a partner. Announce a series of directions for students to follow with their partner friends. For example, you might say, "Clap five times with your friend." (If you learn about a different number each week, use that number in your directions. Or choose a different number with each direction.) Consider having children find new partners after a series of directions. Youngsters will enjoy singing this song (sung to the tune of "Here We Go Round The Mulberry Bush") with their partners. Change the verse to match each different direction that you give.

Clap five times with your friend, with your friend, with your friend.
Clap five times with your friend; making friends is fun!

Sharon Johnson—Gr. K
Carver Kindergarten
Texarkana, AR

Jessica
Written & Illustrated by Kevin Henkes
Published by Scholastic Inc.

No one could see Jessica except Ruthie. "There is no Jessica," said Ruthie's parents. But there was.

Ruthie's imagination led to the discovery of her first friendship. After reading the story aloud, ask each student to think about what her imaginary friend would look like if she had one (and many probably do!). Brainstorm a list of things that could be done with an imaginary friend. Show youngsters the picture Ruthie painted of herself and Jessica at school. Discuss the reasons Ruthie painted the frowns on their faces and how she would paint the picture differently after she had met the real Jessica. Place the book in an art or painting center. Encourage each child who visits the center to paint a picture of herself and her imaginary friend. Have the student write her name and her imaginary friend's name on the paper.

Chrysanthemum
Written & Illustrated by Kevin Henkes 
Published by Greenwillow Books

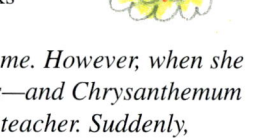

Chrysanthemum loves her name. However, when she goes to school, everyone giggles—and Chrysanthemum wilts. Then she meets her music teacher. Suddenly, Chrysanthemum blossoms.

The beginning of the year is the perfect time to read *Chrysanthemum*. After sharing the book, encourage discussion about each child's name. Ask children if they know why their parents chose their names. Count the number of letters in Chrysanthemum's name. Then help each child count the number of letters in his own first name. For each child, visually divide a sheet of paper into columns as shown (or use one-inch graph paper). Help each child write his name on the paper: one letter in each space. Group the names together based on the number of letters in each name. Then create a class graph. Reread the story later in the year and graph each child's last name in the same manner.

Barb Spero—Gr. K
Memorial School
Paramus, NJ

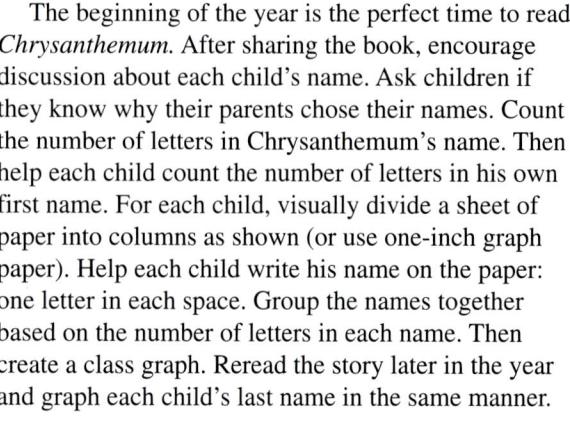

More Books About Friendship

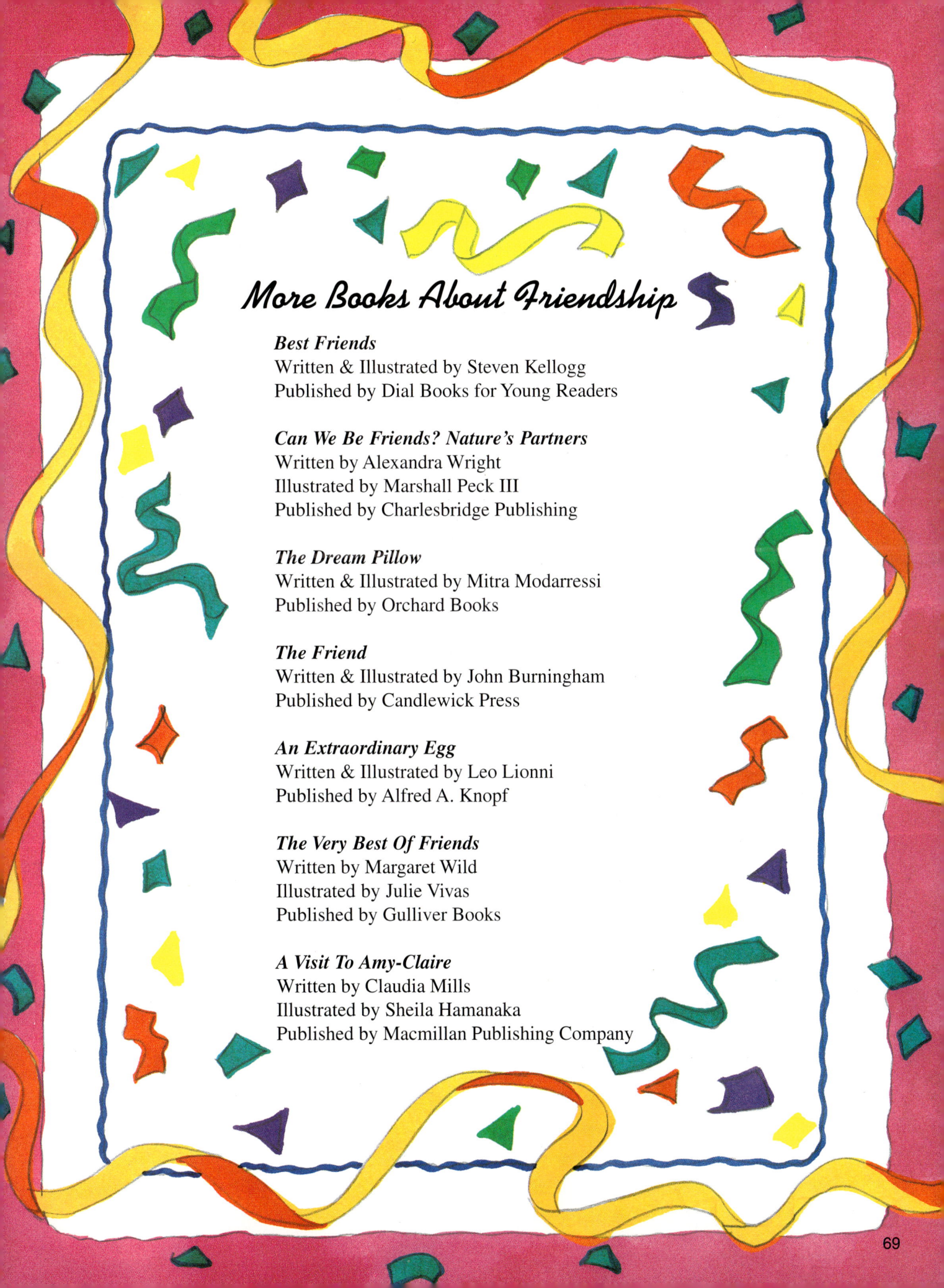

Best Friends
Written & Illustrated by Steven Kellogg
Published by Dial Books for Young Readers

Can We Be Friends? Nature's Partners
Written by Alexandra Wright
Illustrated by Marshall Peck III
Published by Charlesbridge Publishing

The Dream Pillow
Written & Illustrated by Mitra Modarressi
Published by Orchard Books

The Friend
Written & Illustrated by John Burningham
Published by Candlewick Press

An Extraordinary Egg
Written & Illustrated by Leo Lionni
Published by Alfred A. Knopf

The Very Best Of Friends
Written by Margaret Wild
Illustrated by Julie Vivas
Published by Gulliver Books

A Visit To Amy-Claire
Written by Claudia Mills
Illustrated by Sheila Hamanaka
Published by Macmillan Publishing Company

Once Upon A Blue Moon

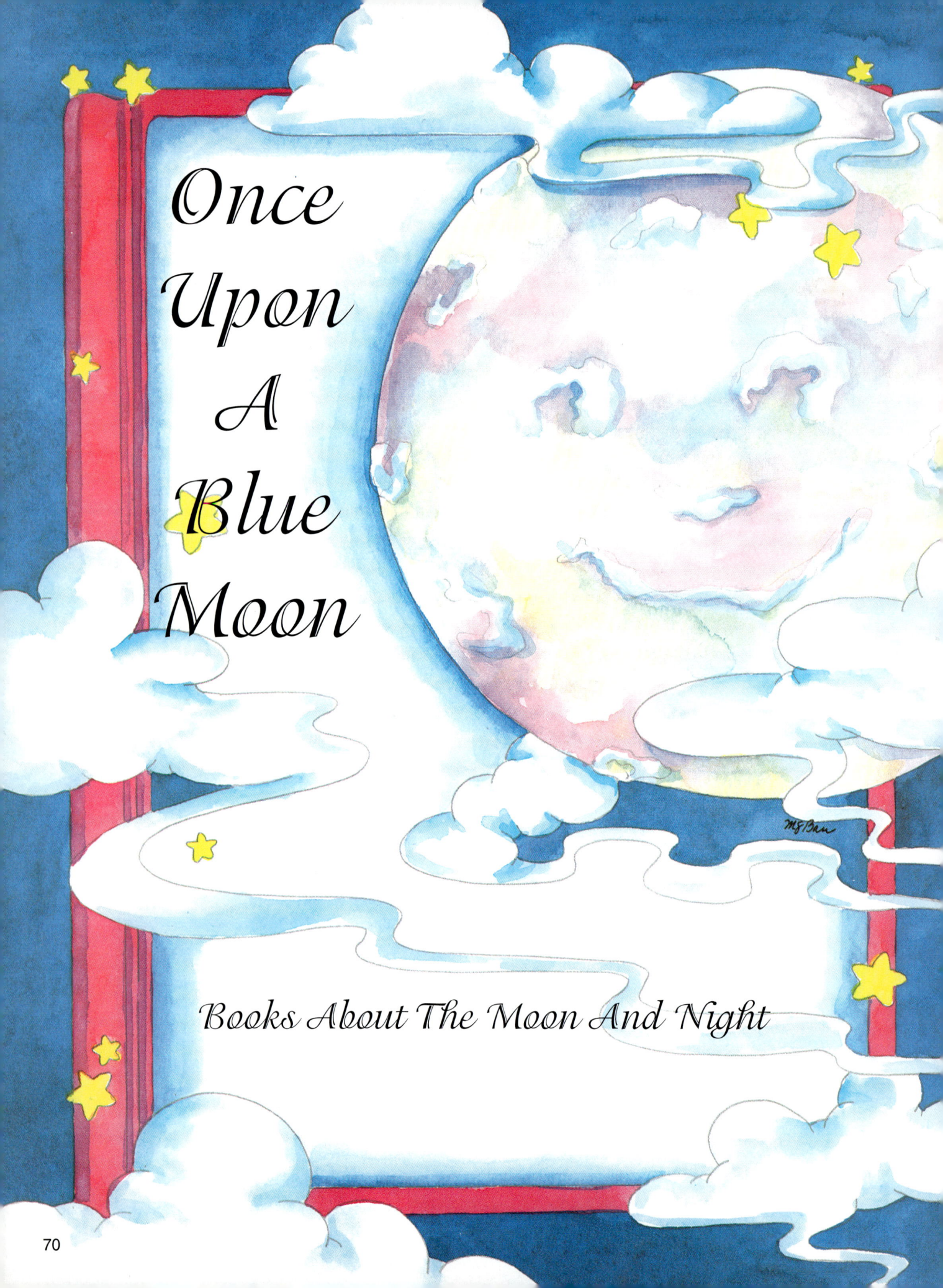

Books About The Moon And Night

Papa, Please Get The Moon For Me
Written & Illustrated by Eric Carle
Published by Scholastic Inc.

As a father sets out to get the moon for his little girl, the reader is fancifully drawn up and into the wondrous sky to experience the moon and its phases.

After sharing *Papa, Please Get The Moon For Me*, have students examine the clothing that Papa was wearing as he climbed the ladder. To help children separate fact from fiction, explain that there is no air, water, gravity, or sound on the moon. Its surface is covered with gray rocks, soil, and craters. Then display photographs of astronauts on the moon. Encourage students to look carefully at the astronauts' clothing. Then brainstorm a list of reasons why a space suit is necessary in space (such as for oxygen, warmth, and weight). Next have youngsters discuss how Papa traveled to the moon in the story. Then share photos of spacecraft that have actually traveled to the moon. Have students brainstorm what the spacecraft would have to be equipped to do to get the astronauts safely to the moon and home again.

Adapted from an idea by Randalyn Larson—Gr. K
Memorial School, Jackson, MI

I Want To Be An Astronaut
Written & Illustrated by Byron Barton
Published by Thomas Y. Crowell

Join the crew and blast off into an exciting space adventure. On this space mission you'll fly a shuttle, put on a space suit, and fix a satellite. 10–9–8…

I Want To Be An Astronaut is an excellent introductory book about being an astronaut. Have your youngsters complete this project which visually makes them a part of history. In advance, make a moon design by drizzling glue unevenly on a round tagboard circle. Sprinkle sand over the glue and let it dry. Then shake off the excess sand. To make a moon rubbing, have each child place a white piece of paper on top of the textured moon and use the side of a black crayon to rub the design onto the paper. Then have him cut out the moon. Provide each child with an astronaut pattern (page 76). If desired, have each child attach a small photo of his face to the astronaut. Glue a child-drawn American flag to a coffee-stirring stick. Attach the astronaut and flag to the moon for a historic moon landing.

Randalyn Larson—Gr. K

Goodnight Moon
Written by Margaret Wise Brown
Illustrated by Clement Hurd
Published by Harper & Row

In this classic story, a bunny—tucked in bed—says goodnight to his familiar surroundings. The gentle text and warm illustrations assure us that the bunny in the story—and possibly the reader—will find peaceful slumber.

For a naptime mood-setter, read *Goodnight Moon* to your class. Later create this bulletin board as a follow-up activity. Take a picture of each child in the class during naptime. Mount the photos on moon-shaped cutouts; then laminate them if desired. Display the photos on a board along with glittery stars and the title "Goodnight Class." For a finishing touch, have students decorate the borders with press-on star stickers.

Suzanne Costner—Preschool, Holy Trinity Preschool
Fayetteville, NC

Encourage your young authors to write and illustrate their own "Goodnight Moon" books. Provide each child with a long, rectangular length of white construction paper that has been accordion-folded in four sections. Direct each child to cut out a moon shape from construction paper and glue it to the front of the book. On each page, have him draw a picture of someone (or something) to whom he says, "Goodnight." Suggest that he alternate between full-color illustrations and black-and-white illustrations—similar to the style of Margaret Wise Brown. On each page, have him write the phrase "Goodnight, [person or object drawn]."

Alyson Wiecek—Gr. K, Levi Leonard Elementary School
Evansville, WI

Moon Rope: Un Lazo A La Luna
Written & Illustrated by Lois Ehlert
Published by Harcourt Brace Jovanovich, Publishers

A mole and a fox attempt to climb to the moon on a rope of braided grass. What happens in the story explains the lifestyle of the mole, and the face that some people claim to see in the moon.

Moon Rope is an adaptation of a Peruvian tale called "The Fox and the Mole." Lois Ehlert's art was inspired by the textiles and jewelry of the ancient Peruvian culture. It was believed that silver was a precious metal—the tears of the moon—and was used only to create objects of beauty. Provide materials for youngsters to make their own silverlike jewelry to resemble the fox in the moon. For each child, you will need one silvery piece of Friendly Plastic®, three rhinestones, and a safety pin. To make one fox-in-the-moon pin, heat a small pan of water on medium heat. Place the plastic in the pan and stir with a wooden spoon for about one minute or until the plastic is moldable. Remove the plastic from the water. Cut out a circle shape; then place the cutout in a bowl of cold water. After a few seconds, remove the circle and wipe dry. Using craft glue, mount the rhinestones to the plastic. When dry, hot-glue a safety pin to the back of the design. Students will be proud to wear these silvery fox pins, and to share the story that they represent.

Rabbit Mooncakes
Written & Illustrated by Hoong Yee Lee Krakauer
Published by Little, Brown and Company

Hoong Wei's family has gathered to celebrate the Harvest Moon Festival. Under the fullest and most glorious moon of the year, Hoong Wei learns that, with family, mistakes hardly matter at all.

After reading the story aloud, discuss the Chinese Harvest Moon Festival. This festival takes place at the time of the full moon nearest September 15. On this holiday, similar to Thanksgiving, families gather to feast, sing Chinese poem songs, eat mooncakes, and drink jasmine tea. Provide youngsters with an opportunity to celebrate the moon by eating rabbit mooncakes and drinking jasmine tea. Following the package directions, prepare the batter for a plain cake mix. Pour the batter in two 9" x 13" pans and bake. Using a cookie cutter shaped like a bunny, cut a rabbit-shaped cake for each youngster. Pour jasmine tea into small cups. Serve the treats and celebrate the moon!

How Night Came From The Sea: A Story From Brazil
Retold by Mary-Joan Gerson
Illustrated by Carla Golembe
Published by Little, Brown and Company

This Brazilian story tells of a sea goddess who brings night to the land where there has been only daylight. Boldly painted illustrations reveal the beauty and wonder that comes with the gift of night.

After reading the story aloud, have students create a list of animals that are active at night. Then encourage each child to paint, in vivid colors, an animal of his choice from the list. When dry, cut around the shape of each painting and place it in a large bag to resemble the bag of night in the story. Gather the children around the bag. As each picture is taken out of the bag, ask the artist to describe the night animal that he chose to paint. Then have him display the picture on a large sheet of blue bulletin-board paper. Display this mural along with the title "How Night Came From The Sea."

Why The Sun And The Moon Live In The Sky
Retold & Illustrated by Niki Daly
Published by Lothrop, Lee & Shepard Books

The sun, a traveler and seeker of beauty, and the moon, a being content to remain at home, invite the sea to visit. Will their home hold all the children of the sea?

This newly published version of a Nigerian creation myth is playfully illustrated and humorously told. As a class, compare and contrast this book with the Caldecott Honor book of the same title written by Elphinstone Dayrell and illustrated by Blair Lent (published by Scholastic Inc.). Then bring out the dramatic talents in your students by giving them the opportunity to act out the story of Why The Sun And The Moon Live In The Sky. Have students create masks depicting the sun, moon, ocean, and ocean animals in either the African style used in Lent's illustrations or the Renaissance style as shown in Daly's illustrations. After performing the story as a class, place the masks in a center for small groups of children to use independently.

Happy Birthday, Moon
Written & Illustrated by Frank Asch
Published by Prentice-Hall Books For Young Readers

A hat makes the perfect birthday gift for the moon—and a bear.

After sharing the story teach youngsters the poem (right). Then brainstorm a list of what the man in the moon might see as he looks down over the earth. Next make man-in-the-moon mobiles. Have each child cut out a large yellow circle and several stars. On white paper, have each child draw himself—as if he were the person in the moon—then cut out the drawing. Direct each child to glue his illustration to his moon. Attach the stars to the bottom of the moon with yarn. Ask each child to complete the sentence, "If I were the man in the moon, I would see...." Write the dictated response on a strip of paper and glue it to the moon mobile. Attach a length of string to the top of the moon and hang it for a celestial ceiling display.

Gay Taylor—Pre-K, West Point Elementary, West Point, GA

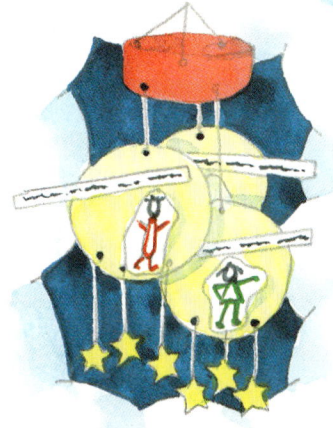

The man in the moon is shining bright,
For all to see on a dark, dark night.
From way up high, what will he see?
It might be you, or it might be me!

Lead students in a brainstorming session about what the moon might want for a birthday gift. Then provide each student with a piece of construction paper folded like a greeting card. Have each student decorate the front of the card with scraps of gift-wrapping paper and a miniature bow. Inside, have her draw a picture and write (or dictate) what she would give the moon as a birthday gift. Display these treasures near the title "Happy Birthday, Moon!"

Amy J. Rachlin, Jericho Early Childhood Center
Plainview, NY

After pointing out that Bear's gift to the moon was a *top hat,* ask students what type of hat they would like to see the moon wearing. Discuss several styles of hats; then show pictures or drawings of the moon's phases. Discuss which style of hat would best fit each phase of the moon. Launch creativity by providing students with an assortment of construction paper and various art supplies. Ask each child to choose a stage of the moon, then cut out a paper moon in that shape. After gluing the moon shape to a background sheet, have him design, cut out, and decorate a hat to glue on the moon. For a 3-D twist, give students Styrofoam-ball moons and a supply of construction paper. Encourage students to design hats for these moons to wear.

Sue Langdon, Longwood Elementary, Shalimar, FL

Conclude your *Happy Birthday, Moon* activities by having a birthday party for the moon. Ask children to make invitations for the party by drawing or gluing a moon shape on a folded sheet of construction paper. Assist the children in deciding whom to invite and in writing the appropriate information on the card. Before the party, decorate your room in a moon motif by displaying moon crafts, hanging sparkling paper stars, and draping glimmering streamers around. During the birthday party, serve moon juice (apple juice) and moon craters (chocolate chip cookies). Be sure to end the party by singing an enthusiastic round of "Happy Birthday" to the moon.

Ru Story-Huffman—Assistant Director
Pine Forest Regional Library, Richton, MS

Night In The Country
Written by Cynthia Rylant
Illustrated by Mary Szilagyi
Published by Bradbury Press

Listen to this melodious text and you'll hear the nighttime song of a frog, the "Pump!" of an apple falling, and the squeaks of a house that is trying to sleep. Listen—and you'll hear the sounds of night in the country.

After sharing and discussing this story, ask students to create a list of sounds that animals of the country—such as owls, frogs, and rabbits—might hear during the day. Using the list, assist your class in writing a new daytime version of the book. Have students illustrate the text; then title the classroom publication "Day In The Country." Place the bound book in the reading center along with the original nighttime version.

Jennifer Barton—Gr. K, Elizabeth Green School
Newington, CT

Good-Night, Owl!
Written & Illustrated by Pat Hutchins
Published by Aladdin Books

Owl tried to sleep while the other animals played. Then the moon came up....

Here's a follow-up art activity that will lead each youngster into a round of storytelling. After reading the story aloud, list the animals that lived in the tree with Owl. Next to each animal, write the sound that it made. Then have each student draw a tree on a piece of art paper. Next provide him with washable ink pads or tempera paint to make a thumbprint owl and sets of thumbprint animals in the branches of the tree. Using a fine-point marker, have him add details to the animals, along with their sound words. While looking at his finished picture, each child can tell his own cumulative version of Owl's sleepless day.

Kimberly Goddard—Gr. K, LaPorte Elementary, LaPorte, TX

The Moonglow Roll-O-Rama
Written & Illustrated by Dav Pilkey
Published by Orchard Books

The magic in the moonlight takes animals on an enchanted flight, wearing their roller skates, into the night.

Prior to sharing the book, ask children why they think many animals sleep during periods of the day. Then read the story aloud. After discussing the book, create "Moonglow Roll-O-Rama" mobiles. To make one, observe Pilkey's uses of color; then cut out a large posterboard circle. Cover the circle with a thin coat of glue; then sprinkle it with glitter. Draw or trace animal shapes onto black construction paper. Cut out the animals; then glue black, paper circles to their feet to resemble rollerskate wheels. Punch a hole in the top of each animal, and one hole for each animal in the bottom edge of the moon. Attach the cutouts to the moon with different lengths of fishing line. (This story is also a wonderful springboard for discussing friendship in diversity!)

Kimberly Madden—Gr. K, Falcon Elementary
Colorado Springs, CO

Goodnight, Goodnight
Written & Illustrated by Eve Rice
Published by Greenwillow Books

Goodnight creeps slowly over the town—but little kitten wants to play.

If possible, slightly dim the lights before reading the story aloud. After sharing the story, create a class "Goodnight, Goodnight" book. Encourage students to observe the illustrations of Eve Rice. Then provide each student with a black piece of construction paper, white and yellow chalk, and a yellow dot sticker or cutout. Ask her to create a "goodnight scene" using the supplies. Then have each child dictate a sentence about her scene for you to write on the bottom of the page. To prevent smudging, spray each picture with hairspray. Bind all of the pictures between construction-paper covers; then place the book in your reading center for further enjoyment.

Kimberly Goddard—Gr. K

More Books About The Moon And Night

Anansi The Spider: A Tale From The Ashanti
Adapted & Illustrated by Gerald McDermott
Published by Holt, Rinehart and Winston

The Moon Man
Written by Gerda Marie Scheidl
Translated & Adapted by J. Alison James
Illustrated by Józef Wilkon
Published by North-South Books

My Parents Think I'm Sleeping
Written by Jack Prelutsky
Illustrated by Yossi Abolafia
Published by Mulberry Books

Night On Neighborhood Street
Written by Eloise Greenfield
Illustrated by Jan Spivey Gilchrist
Published by Dial Books for Young Readers

No Moon, No Milk!
Written by Chris Babcock
Illustrated by Mark Teague
Published by Scholastic Inc.

Owl Moon
Written by Jane Yolen
Illustrated by John Schoenherr
Published by Scholastic Inc.

The Tale Of Rabbit And Coyote
Written by Tony Johnston
Illustrated by Tomie dePaola
Published by G. P. Putnam's Sons

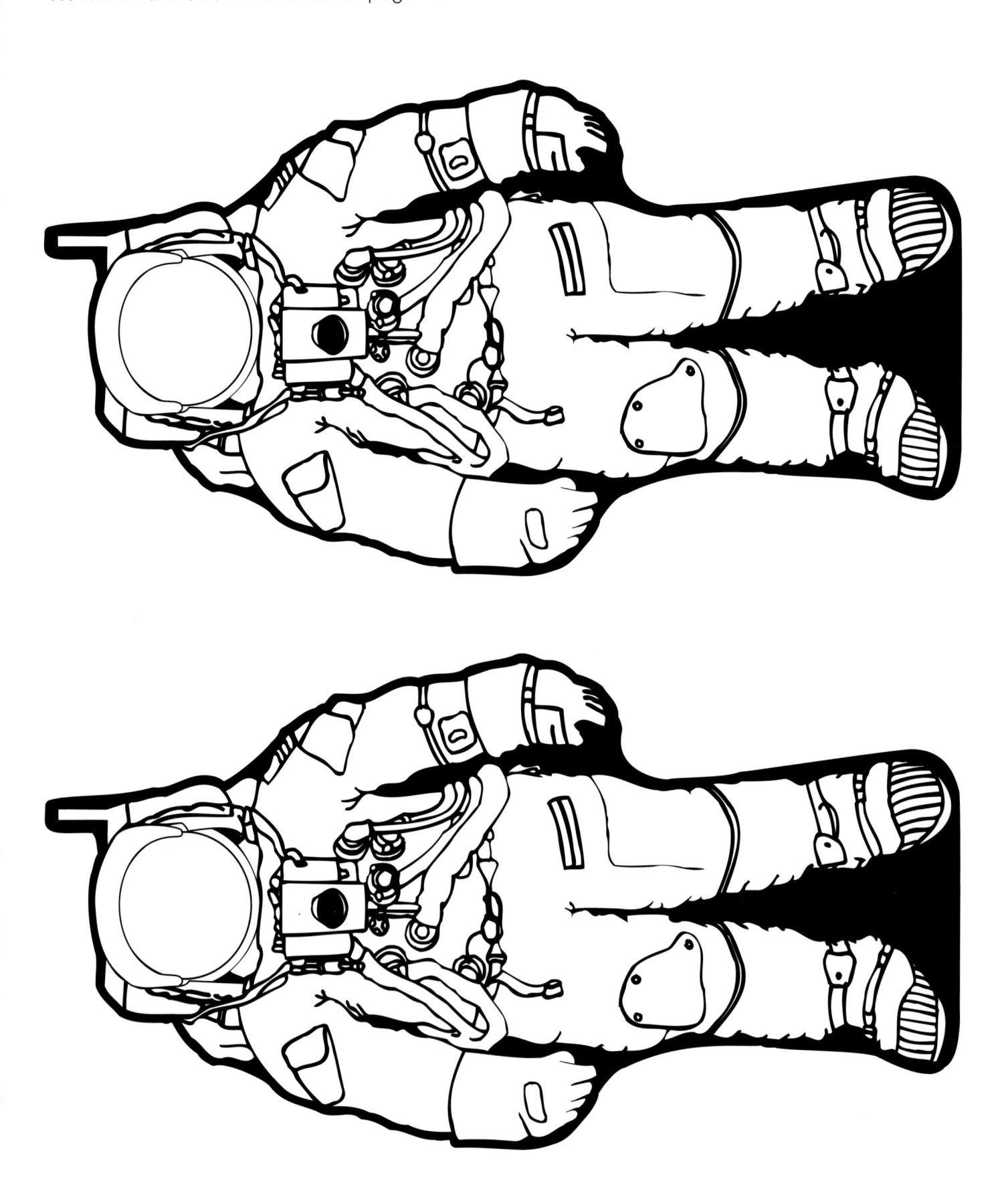

Patterns
Use with *I Want To Be An Astronaut* on page 71.

A Stitch In Time

A Cozy Collection Of Books About Blankets And Quilts

Eight Hands Round: A Patchwork Alphabet
Written by Ann Whitford Paul
Illustrated by Jeanette Winter
Published by HarperCollins Publishers

Woven into the patterns of patchwork quilts are the stories of the people who lived in early America. This beautifully illustrated book provides an introduction to these patterns and the people who created them.

Spread out a quilt and invite students to gather around as you share this story. Afterwards, give each child an eight-inch square of off-white paper. Have him manipulate pattern blocks on the square until he has created a design. Then have each child glue a precut, paper pattern-block shape (available at school supply stores) in the place of each pattern block. Ask each child to name his design and write/dictate the reason for that name. After sharing, make a quilt registry by placing each child's quilt block and writing in a photo album.

Rachel Kelley—Gr. K
Live Oak Elementary
Schertz, TX

Sweet Clara And The Freedom Quilt
Written by Deborah Hopkinson
Illustrated by James Ransome
Published by Alfred A. Knopf, Inc.

Sweet Clara learns to quilt to free herself from work in the fields. The quilt she creates leads herself, and many others, to an even greater freedom.

After sharing the story, have children examine the illustration of Clara's quilt. Look for Clara's sewn-on symbols such as the North Star, the pond, the boat, etc. On a chart, list landmarks in your community such as your school, main roads, and lakes. Have each child cut out a construction-paper house to represent his home. Also cut out additional landmarks that you discussed. Glue the cutouts to a large piece of bulletin-board paper. Add construction-paper, nine-patch quilt blocks to resemble Clara's freedom quilt.

Bobbie Lee Wagman
Milton, WI

Sam Johnson And The Blue Ribbon Quilt
Written & Illustrated by Lisa Campbell Ernst
Published by Lothrop, Lee & Shepard Books

Men in a quilting club? This surprising tale of turnabout relates that everyone can enjoy the art of quilting—and the art of cooperation!

In advance, survey children to see if they think that sewing is "women's work." Then share the book. Pause at the point of the surprise splash and have children brainstorm solutions to this dilemma. Finish reading the story. Then encourage children to cooperate by doing this quilt-pattern activity. To make quilt cards, obtain a quilt-pattern book from a library or craft store. Photocopy the pattern blocks. Color and cut out each block. Mount the blocks on tagboard; then write the name of the pattern on the back. Cut each card in half. Give a card-half to each child and have him find the person holding its match. When children find their matches, challenge them to speculate how their patterns got their names.

Rita Beiswenger
Crescent Avenue Weekday School
Fort Wayne, IN

Tar Beach
Written & Illustrated by Faith Ringgold
Published by Crown Publishers, Inc.

Flying will take you somewhere you'd like "to go that you can't get to any other way." For Cassie, and many others, flying is the way to freedom from whatever holds you down.

In advance, read the author information at the end of the book so you can paraphrase it for your class. After sharing the story and the author information, have children create their own story quilts. For each child, mark a 4-inch border around a large piece of art paper. Ask each child to paint a picture of a family memory on her paper. Write each child's story (as she dictates) along the top and bottom of her painting. Then have each child glue a border of 2-inch wallpaper squares around the edges of her paper. After sharing, display these works of art along with a copy of the book.

Rachel Kelley—Gr. K

The Quilt Story
Written by Tony Johnston
Illustrated by Tomie dePaola
Published by G. P. Putnam's Sons

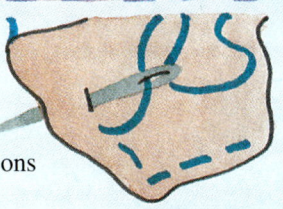

Quilts—like stories—become more meaningful when passed from one generation to the next. Travel through the years and across the miles with this quilt as it is sewn, loved, mended, and loved again.

After reading the story aloud, discuss the identity of the girl in the second half of the story. Encourage children to look for clues in the illustrations. Next discuss similarities in how the quilt helped both girls. For a story extension, create a class book titled "Our Quilt Stories." Ask each child to bring in a favorite quilt or blanket (see the request form on page 83). Take a picture of each child holding his blanket or quilt; then write as he dictates a story about his quilt. Mount the stories and pictures on construction paper and laminate if desired. Bind the pages together to create a book that youngsters will enjoy taking home to share with their families.

Kathryn Logan, Alaiedon Elementary School, Mason, MI

The Patchwork Quilt
Written by Valerie Flournoy
Illustrated by Jerry Pinkney
Published by Dial Books For Young Readers

A grandmother, mother, and daughter lovingly quilt a masterpiece made of family memories. Enrich a reading of the story by showing the "Reading Rainbow" episode that features The Patchwork Quilt. *LeVar Burton visits the Boston Children's Museum to watch children learning to create their own patchwork quilts.*

Follow up a reading of the story by discussing special family memories. Remind students that, like quilts, families are unique. Then create a bulletin board that will be a reminder of the variety of families represented in your class family. Ask each family to send in a family photo. Mount each photo on a piece of brightly colored construction paper. Arrange the photos in a design to resemble a quilt. Using a black marker, "join" the pieces together with lines that resemble stitches.

Mary Sutula
Orlando, FL

The Keeping Quilt
Written & Illustrated by Patricia Polacco
Published by Simon & Schuster, Inc.

After a family moves from Russia to America, they sew a quilt to help preserve the memories of the people they left behind. This is Patricia Polacco's story of the quilt that passed through four generations of her immigrant Jewish family.

In advance, prepare a gift sack for each child. To make one, cut a six-inch square of linen. Place an imitation gold coin, a silk flower, and a piece of rock salt in the center of the square. Bring the edges up to form a sack and tie it with a ribbon. Then share the story. Ask students to recall the uses of the quilt. Then discuss the tradition of giving a bride some gold, a flower, and some salt. Give each child a gift sack. As a class, compose a note to parents that explains the meanings of the sack's contents and encourages them to obtain a copy of the book to read together as a family. Duplicate the note for each child and attach it to his sack.

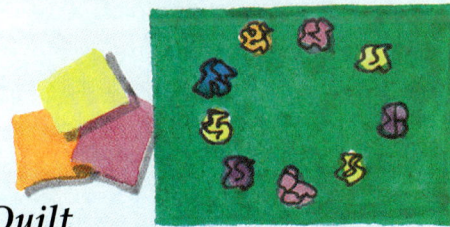

Luka's Quilt
Written & Illustrated by Georgia Guback
Published by Greenwillow Books

Luka's grandmother makes her a traditional Hawaiian quilt that turns out quite differently from what Luka expected. When Luka shows her disappointment, she and her grandmother stop feeling like best friends. How can they get their feelings and relationship patched up again?

After sharing *Luka's Quilt,* ask youngsters if they have ever received a gift that was not exactly what they expected. Did they, like Luka, show their disappointment? To solve their problem, Luka and her grandmother come to a colorful compromise that results in an optional floral quilt. Give youngsters an opportunity to make miniature floral quilts of their own. Provide each child with a piece of green construction paper and brightly colored tissue-paper squares. Direct each child to slightly crumple the squares, then glue them onto the paper to create a circle of tissue-paper flowers. Mount the projects on a larger piece of bulletin-board paper and display the finished project in your classroom.

Catherine V. Herber, Highland Preschool, Raleigh, NC

Owen
Written & Illustrated by Kevin Henkes
Published by Greenwillow Books

Owen has a favorite blanket that he loves with all of his heart. Now that it's time for Owen to start school, he must give Fuzzy up. Some snipping and sewing, however, lead to a happy solution for all.

Prior to sharing this Caldecott Honor Book, find out if your youngsters have favorite items such as blankets or special toys that they feel they could never part with. Then read *Owen* aloud. For a special time of sharing, have a Blanket Day in your classroom. Invite children to bring blankets to school (see the form on page 83); then try some blanket activities. Have each child show her blanket and tell where she got it or why it is special. Next make a floor graph with the blankets. Have the children take turns placing their folded blankets in categories such as "Quilts" or "Crocheted Blankets"; then discuss the results. Finally use the blankets for movement activities. For example, direct the children to put their blankets *over* them, *under* them, or *between* them.

Barbara Saul—Gr. K, Pine Hill School, Eureka, CA

Ten Little Rabbits
Written by Virginia Grossman
Illustrated by Sylvia Long
Published by Chronicle Books

A simple celebration of Native American traditions is tucked between the covers of this beautiful counting book.

After reading the book aloud, discuss the blankets shown throughout the book. Use the information at the back of the book to add to your discussion. Then, give youngsters an opportunity to make their own imitation Native American blankets. For each child, cut a rectangle from brown mailing paper or paper bags. Place the book, the papers, and markers in a center. Encourage each child to visit the center, look closely at the traditional Navajo blanket patterns shown in the book, and color his paper to resemble a blanket. To add a finishing touch, cut the ends to resemble fringe.

Jennifer Elsner—Gr. K
Child Development Center
Midland, TX

Geraldine's Blanket
Written & Illustrated by Holly Keller
Published by Greenwillow Books

Geraldine, like Owen, has a blanket that she takes wherever she goes. And Geraldine's parents, like Owen's, decide the time has come to put the blanket away. Snipping and sewing once again save the day.

Blanket-lovers young and old will love the triumphant ending of this story. Read aloud *Owen* and *Geraldine's Blanket.* As a class, compare and contrast the two stories. Then brainstorm a list of additional creative ways to keep a cherished blanket from certain doom. Have students draw pictures and write (or dictate) their creative methods for saving well-loved blankets. Bind the pages in a book titled "Save The Blankets!" Be sure to send the book of suggestions home (along with a copy of *Geraldine's Blanket*) for children to share with any parents who might be contemplating this dilemma themselves!

The Boy And The Quilt
Written by Shirley Kurtz
Illustrated by Cheryl Benner
Published by Good Books

This good-humored book is about a boy and his decision to make a quilt. After all, if his mother and sister can make quilts, so can he! The delightful illustrations will keep you in stitches. Included in the book are directions for making a patchwork quilt or comforter.

After hearing this story, youngsters will enjoy the predictable pattern of this poem and the accompanying flannelboard pieces. Reproduce five copies of the quilt pattern on page 83. Color the quilts. (Be sure to color one quilt red and blue.) Laminate and cut out the quilts; then back each one with flannel. Place the quilts on a flannelboard. As the class reads/recites each line, remove one quilt. For more fun, use real quilts or blankets. Ask five students to lie on the floor next to a stack of five folded quilts. As the class recites each line, take one quilt from the stack and cover one of the "sleeping" children. How cozy!

Five colorful quilts with patches galore;
One covered [child's name], and then there were four.

Four colorful quilts as pretty as can be;
One covered [child's name], and then there were three.

Three colorful quilts with patches red and blue;
One covered [child's name], and then there were two.

Two colorful quilts made just for fun;
One covered [child's name], and then there was one.

One colorful quilt left out in the sun;
It covered [child's name], and then there were none.

Kathryn Logan, Alaiedon Elementary School, Mason, MI

The Quilt
Written & Illustrated by Ann Jonas
Published by Greenwillow Books

A young girl tries to fall asleep under her new quilt. But the quilt looks like a town....

After sharing the story, try this cooperative art activity that reinforces patterning skills. Divide the class into groups of four or five students. Give each group a large sheet of construction paper, a supply of small wallpaper squares, and a skin-toned construction-paper circle for each child. Direct each group to arrange and glue the wallpaper squares on the paper to create a patterned patchwork quilt. Next have each child use art supplies to decorate his circle to resemble his face. Glue each child's decorated face shape to the back of his group's quilt, creating the appearance that each child is tucked beneath the covers. Good night!

Helaine Rooney—Gr. K
Georgian Forest Elementary
Silver Spring, MD

Coat Of Many Colors
Written by Dolly Parton
Illustrated by Judith Sutton
Published by HarperCollins Publishers

Dolly Parton's first best-selling song is based on her childhood in the mountains of Tennessee. Here, in book form, it is lovingly dedicated to "good mothers everywhere."

Read aloud *Coat Of Many Colors;* then listen to the song as sung by Dolly Parton. If *The Rag Coat* was read aloud, compare and contrast the two stories. Take a poll to find out which version students prefer. Ask them to explain their responses. If you have a class mascot that travels to children's homes at night, make a coat of many colors for him to wear when he goes visiting. Ask each child to bring a small scrap of material from home. To make the coat, sew the scraps together in patchwork style. Using a coat pattern designed for a stuffed toy, cut and sew a coat for the mascot to wear. On the mascot's next journey to each child's home, send along a copy of *Coat Of Many Colors* for the family to read together.

Kim Rainey—Gr. K, Bond Elementary
Assumption, IL

The Boy And The Cloth Of Dreams
Written by Jenny Koralek
Illustrated by James Mayhew
Published by Candlewick Press

A young boy is protected from nightmares by his cloth of dreams. When the quilt tears, nightmares escape through the holes. The boy must find courage within himself.

After reading the story aloud, discuss nightmares and how youngsters feel after waking up from a bad dream. Then have students make their own quilt of dreams. Iron a fusible material such as Trans-Web™ to the backs of different, brightly colored fabrics. Cut the fabrics into small, oddly shaped pieces and peel off the paper backing. Have each child look at the endpapers of the book, then give him a piece of dark blue fabric. (To prevent the fabric from fraying, cut it out with pinking shears.) Have each child arrange some cloth shapes on his blue fabric. Then iron the pieces to the fabric. Using gold glitter fabric paint, have the child paint around the edges of the shapes. Then have him paint stars on the shapes with white fabric paint. When dry, send the projects home with wishes for pleasant dreams.

The Rag Coat
Written & Illustrated by Lauren Mills
Published by Little, Brown and Company

Minna proudly wears her new coat to school and shares the stories sewn into its patchwork design. This uplifting story was inspired by tales from the Appalachian Mountains, a song by Dolly Parton, and the author's own childhood.

A reading of *The Rag Coat* is the perfect springboard to a discussion of values such as friendship, kindness, respect, and self-esteem. Follow up your class discussion with this art activity. Request that each child bring in a scrap of cloth. Then have her share a story about the cloth. Cut each child's scrap into smaller pieces; then combine all the pieces. Provide each child with a tagboard coat shape and encourage her to cover the shape with assorted fabric pieces. Have her glue the cloth on the coat; then trim around the edges. When the coats are complete, everyone will have a rag-coat like Minna's that is "full of stories."

Jamey Gillespie—Gr. K, Aloe Elementary, Victoria, TX

Cozy Up With These Additional Quilt-Making Ideas

Stock a paint center with ten-inch paper squares, sponges, and different colors of paints poured into pie pans. Encourage students to sponge-paint the papers. When dry, display the squares on a bulletin board to resemble a quilt.

Diane Frame—Pre-K, Fox Hollow Elementary
Port Richey, FL

Provide each child with a 5" x 6" piece of one-inch graph paper. Ask each child to color the squares on his paper using two different colors of crayons. Mount the completed papers together on a large piece of bulletin-board paper to create a class quilt.

Helen Zittel—Gr. K
Eden, NY

Provide each child with a large piece of construction paper and a supply of three-inch squares of wallpaper. Encourage the children to create patterns by gluing the squares to the paper. Display the miniature paper quilts.

Beth Pereira, Washington Academy
Belleville, NJ

More Books About Blankets And Quilts

The Quilt-Block History Of Pioneer Days With Projects Kids Can Make
Written by Mary Cobb
Illustrated by Jan Davey Ellis
Published by The Millbrook Press

The Josefina Story Quilt
Written by Eleanor Coerr
Illustrated by Bruce Degen
Published by Harper & Row, Publishers

Something From Nothing
Written & Illustrated by Phoebe Gilman
Published by Scholastic Inc.

The Patchwork Lady
Written by Mary K. Whittington
Illustrated by Jane Dyer
Published by Harcourt Brace Jovanovich

The Mountains Of Quilt
Written by Nancy Willard
Illustrated by Tomie dePaola
Published by Harcourt Brace Jovanovich

Pattern
Use with *The Boy And The Quilt* on page 80.

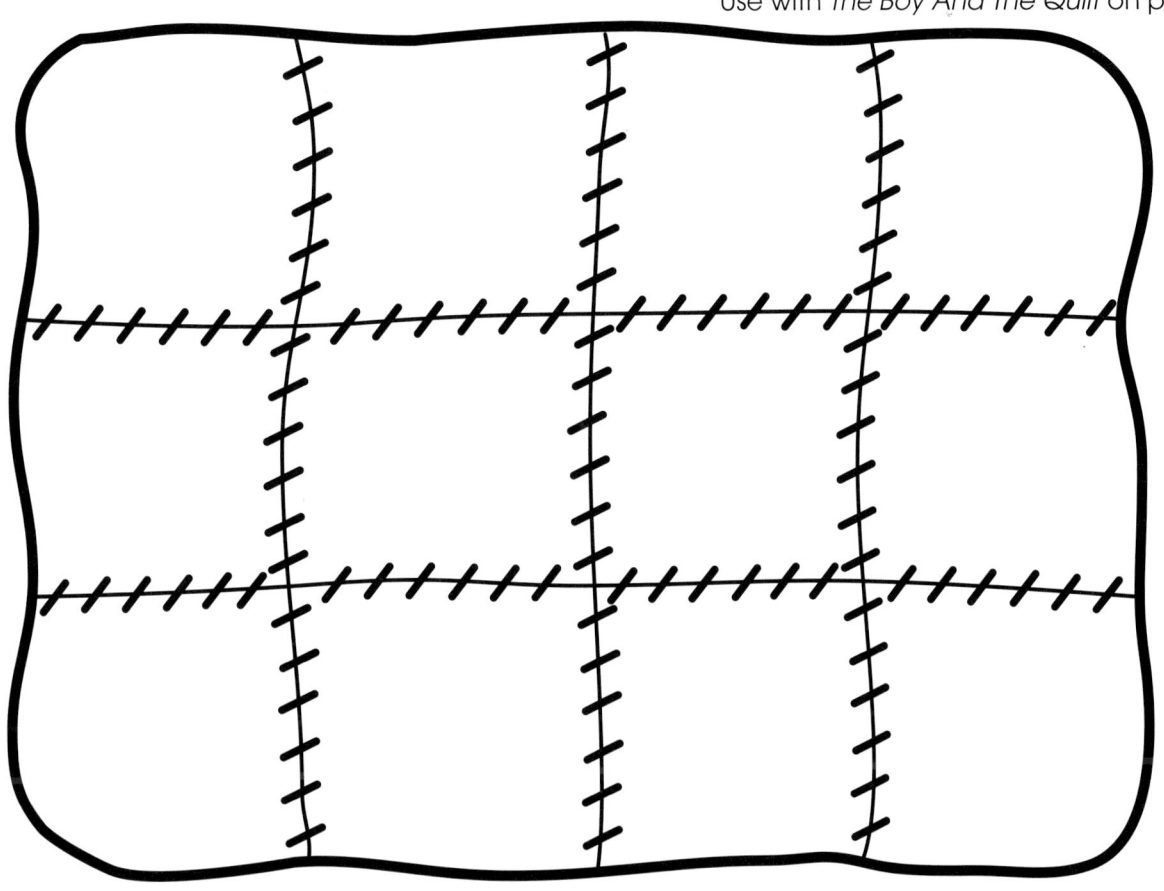

Use with *The Quilt Story* on page 79 and *Owen* on page 80.

Request Form

Dear Parent,

We are reading books about quilts and blankets. Please allow your child to bring a favorite quilt or blanket to school to share with the class. Send the quilt or blanket in a bag labeled with your child's name.

Thank you,

©The Education Center, Inc. • THE MAILBOX® • Kindergarten • Dec/Jan 1995–96

Blowing In The Wind

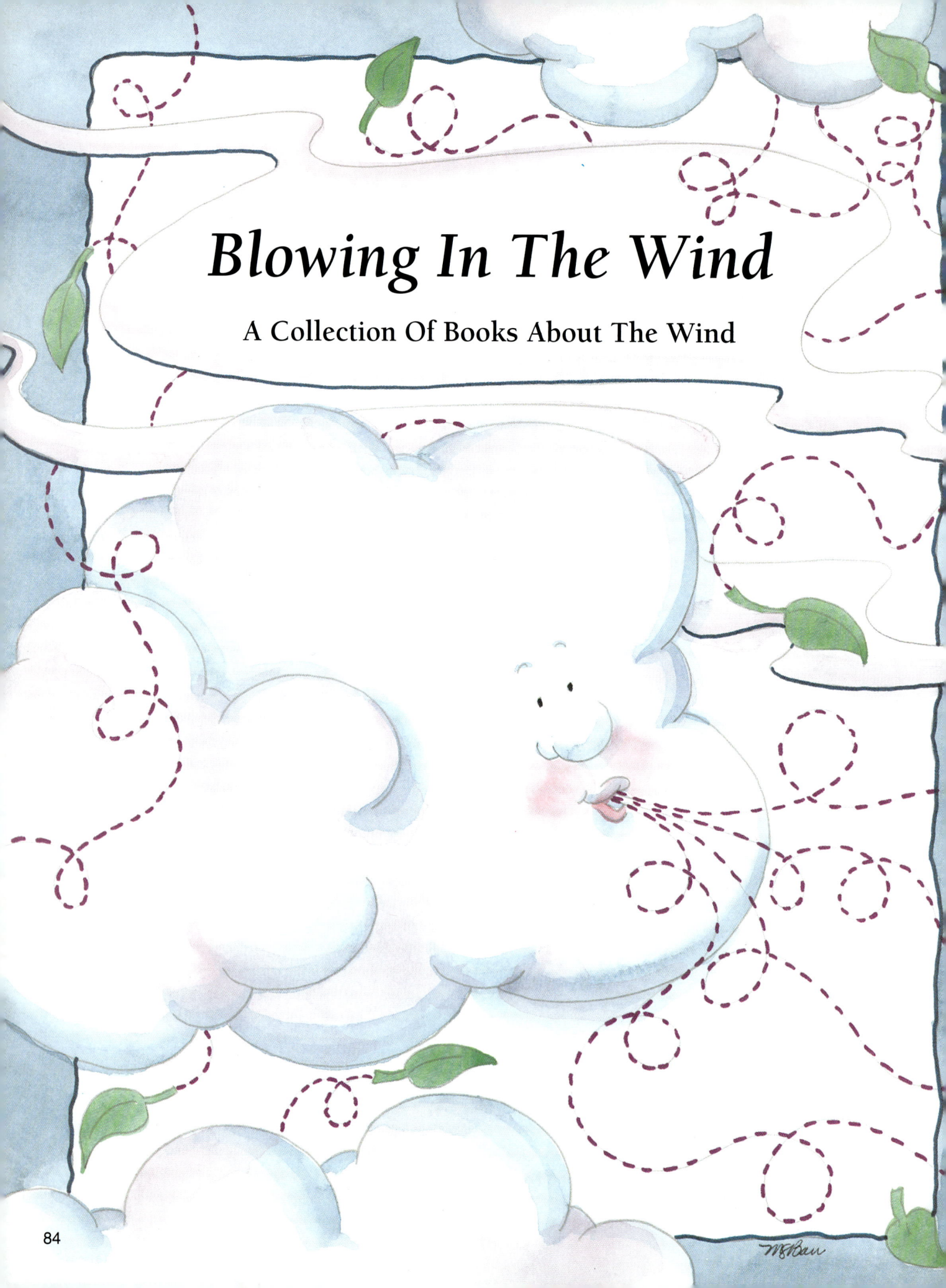

A Collection Of Books About The Wind

How Does The Wind Walk?
Written by Nancy White Carlstrom
Illustrated by Deborah Kogan Ray
Published by Macmillan Publishing Company

This beautifully illustrated book poetically describes how the wind moves through the four seasons of the year.

Explain to students that wind is moving air. Next discuss the idea that each child has air inside his body. To help students better understand these concepts, demonstrate the effects of moving air with these suggestions: Have each child blow into a cup of water with a straw. Have each child blow up a balloon and then release it. Encourage each child to blow on a pinwheel. Ask students to stand in front of a fan. Have children hold a set of wind chimes in front of a fan. Following each experiment, discuss with the class what they could see, hear, or feel as effects of the moving air.

Alison G. Hovda—Gr. K
St. Patrick's School
Fayetteville, NC

List the four seasons on a chart; then read aloud *How Does The Wind Walk?* Ask students to list evidence of the wind's movement during each different season. For a follow-up, try this creative-movement activity. Ask each child to find his own space in an open area; then provide each child with a scarf cut from sheer fabric. Play a musical selection and encourage children to move their scarves as if they were leaves in the wind. As the music ends, direct the children to let their scarf leaves flutter to the ground.

Jeanene Engelhardt—Gr. K
Workman Avenue School
West Covina, CA

How The Wind Plays
Written by Michael Lipson
Illustrated by Daniel Kirk
Published by Hyperion Books For Children

Oh, what a rascally character the wind can be! In this playful book, the wind is a mischievous child who is always at play.

After reading the book aloud, ask students to list the suggested ways that we can see the wind at play. Once youngsters are familiar with the song below (sung to the tune of "If You're Happy And You Know It"), encourage them to create new verses using their previously listed ideas.

Oh, the wind is blowing all the leaves around.
Oh, the wind is blowing all the leaves around.
It blows them all around; then they land back on the ground.
Oh, the wind is blowing all the leaves around.

Oh, the wind is flying all the kites so high.
Oh, the wind is flying all the kites so high.
The kites are flying high, so high up in the sky.
Oh, the wind is flying all the kites so high.

Brenda Hume—Gr. K
Sangaree Elementary School
Summerville, SC

Iva Dunnit And The Big Wind
Written by Carol Purdy
Illustrated by Steven Kellogg
Published by Dial Books For Young Readers

This tall tale captures the pioneer spirit of Iva Dunnit and her six children.

When the Big Wind blows into Cobb Hollow, Iva Dunnit and her six children must use their wits and their strength to save their house and their "livin'." Prior to sharing the book, collect pictures from scientific magazines of different types of storms involving wind—such as hurricanes and tornadoes. Then follow up a reading of this tall tale with a discussion of the effects of wind. As a class, brainstorm helpful effects of wind such as moving seeds, turning a windmill, and cooling people. Show students the collected pictures and brainstorm harmful effects of wind, such as destroying homes and causing erosion. Complete the lesson by having each child draw pictures of the helpful and harmful effects of wind.

Alison G. Hovda—Gr. K

The Wind Blew
Written & Illustrated by Pat Hutchins
Published by Macmillan Publishing Company

This blustery tale is so much fun you just might get carried away!

Before reading the book aloud, draw a picture of each item that the wind snatched up and tossed about in the story. Then read the story aloud. Ask students to recall the windblown items from the story. As each item is named, display the corresponding picture. Read the story again, asking students to sequence the pictures as you read. Place the pictures and the book in a center for students to enjoy independently.

Sherry Rosburg—Pre-Kindergarten
Redeemer Nursery School
Cincinnati, OH

Bring out the dramatic talents in your students by giving them opportunities to act out this hilarious story. In advance gather the props that will be needed such as an umbrella, an inflated balloon, a hat, etc. After reading the story aloud, encourage selected students to use the props to dramatize the story as you reread it. Don't forget to ask someone to be the wind!

Sue Lewis Lein—Four-Year-Olds, Kindergarten
St. Pius X Grade School
Wauwatosa, WI

After reading aloud *The Wind Blew,* create a class book based on this Pat Hutchins classic. Provide each student with a large piece of paper. Ask each child to illustrate an item that the wind might blow on a blustery day. Below his illustration, write each child's completion to the phrase "The wind blew…." Bind the pages between a titled cover to create a class book your children will want to read over and over again.

Diane Bonica and Kathy Devlin—Gr. K
Charles F. Tigard Elementary
Tigard, OR

This class mural will blow up a flurry of compliments. After reading the story, provide each student with various colors of construction paper, scissors, and glue. Ask each student to create an item of his choice that the wind might blow. Have each student mount his item on a large sheet of bulletin-board paper; then assist each child in labeling his item. Title the mural "What The Wind Blew," and display it on a wall or bulletin board.

Sharon Pitts—Gr. K
Grand Avenue Elementary School
Orlando, FL

The Tiny Seed
Written & Illustrated by Eric Carle
Published by Scholastic Inc.

Follow the adventures of a tiny seed as it is blown by the wind.

Read aloud and discuss *The Tiny Seed*. Demonstrate, by blowing through a straw, how the wind moved the seed. Then provide each student with a sunflower seed and a straw for his own experimentation. To add to the fun, encourage pairs of students to have seed races. Or extend the learning by providing other lightweight items for the students to blow with their straws.

Julie Hitt
Beaver Ridge Elementary
Norcross, GA

Gilberto And The Wind
Written & Illustrated by Marie Hall Ets
Published by The Viking Press

This classic story tells about Gilberto and his friend the wind. Together they sail a boat, spin a pinwheel, blow bubbles, and take a rest.

After reading aloud *Gilberto And The Wind*, point out that Marie Hall Ets used pencil and white chalk to illustrate her story. On a windy day, take students outside to observe the effects of the wind. Provide each child with a pencil and paper. Ask students to record their observations by drawing pictures. When you're back inside, provide students with white chalk to embellish their drawings. Encourage each child to discuss his drawing. Or have students write (or dictate) stories about their observations. Display the drawings and stories along with a copy of the book.

Alison G. Hovda—Gr. K
St. Patrick's School
Fayetteville, NC

Wind
Written by Ron Bacon
Illustrated by Phillippa Stichbury
Published by Scholastic Inc.

The simple rhyme of this book is an invitation to feel the wind and follow where it blows.

On a windy day, take the class outside and read *Wind* aloud. Reread the book, encouraging the children to move their hands and arms in a wavy manner, similar to the flowing print on each page. At a later time, read the book once more, encouraging the children to move their whole bodies to the rhythm of your words.

The Wind Garden
Written by Angela McAllister
Illustrated by Claire Fletcher
Published by Lothrop, Lee & Shepard Books

With the help of the wind, Ellie and Grandpa create a unique garden.

Extend this story by having children make pinwheels to plant in a class wind garden. To make a pinwheel, cut a 7" square of construction paper. Draw a circle in the center of the square; then color both sides of the square, not coloring in the circle. Cut a diagonal line from each corner of the square, stopping just before the circle in the center. Bring every other point toward the center of the paper, overlapping the points as they meet. Push a brad through the four overlapping points *only* and fasten it. (Do *not* push the brad through the circle.) Have each student stand his pinwheel in a long flower box that has been filled with sand or dirt. Place the completed wind garden near an open classroom window.

Julie Hitt

Mirandy And Brother Wind
Written by Patricia C. McKissack
Illustrated by Jerry Pinkney
Published by Alfred A. Knopf, Inc.

This Caldecott Honor book is so full of life it will blow you away! With the help of the wind, Mirandy and her partner win the Junior Cakewalk.

Celebrate this delightful story by having a Junior Cakewalk in your classroom. In advance have an adult volunteer prepare a cupcake for each child in the class. Arrange a classroom supply of chairs so that the chairs form a square and face outward. Play a selection of upbeat music and direct students to dance around the chairs. Remove one chair from the square; then stop the music. The child who is unable to find a seat selects the first cupcake. Continue the cakewalk until each child has a cupcake to enjoy.

Kate Taluga
Big Bend Community Coordinated Child Care
Tallahassee, FL

Wind Says Good Night
Written by Katy Rydell
Illustrated by David Jorgenson
Published by Houghton Mifflin Company

The animals and one restless child are awake. Then the weather changes and the wind says, "Good night."

Before reading *Wind Says Good Night,* use flannel to make each of the animal characters in the story. As you read this cumulative tale aloud, encourage listeners to join in. Then give each of the flannelboard pieces to a different listener. As you reread the story, ask each student to place his character on a flannelboard as it is mentioned. Later place the flannelboard pieces, the flannelboard, and the book in a center for students to enjoy independently.

Andrea M. Troisi
La Salle Middle School
Niagara Falls, NY

Blow Away Soon
Written by Betsy James
Illustrated by Anna Vojtech
Published by G. P. Putnam's Sons

When Nana shows Sophie how to build a blow-away-soon, Sophie learns that some things are to let go of and some things are to keep for a good long time.

After reading *Blow Away Soon,* discuss the items in the story that the wind blew away. Then display a collection of small objects such as leaves, seeds, pieces of paper, pebbles, and a spoon. Have the students sort the items that they predict the wind might blow away from those that will probably not blow away. (Provide labeled sorting mats if desired.) Next individually place each object in front of a small fan to see if it will blow away. Follow up the experiment with a discussion of the weight and shape of each object. If several large rocks are available, encourage students to build a blow-away-soon during a class outdoor time.

Cleo Velleman—Gr. K
Phoebe Hearst School
Metairie, LA

The Gates Of The Wind
Written by Kathryn Lasky
Illustrated by Janet Stevens
Published by Harcourt Brace & Company

Gamma Lee wants to make her home in the mountains at the Gates of the Wind. But will the wind let her?

After reading aloud *The Gates Of The Wind,* ask students if they would rather live in the valley or on the mountain at the gates of the wind. Prepare a bulletin board that depicts a mountain surrounded by a valley. Then take a picture of each student standing in front of a fan so that it appears that the student is being blown by the wind. Mount the photos of those students who said they would rather live on the mountain on the bulletin-board mountain. Mount the photos of those students who would rather live in the valley around the bulletin-board valley.

More Books About The Wind

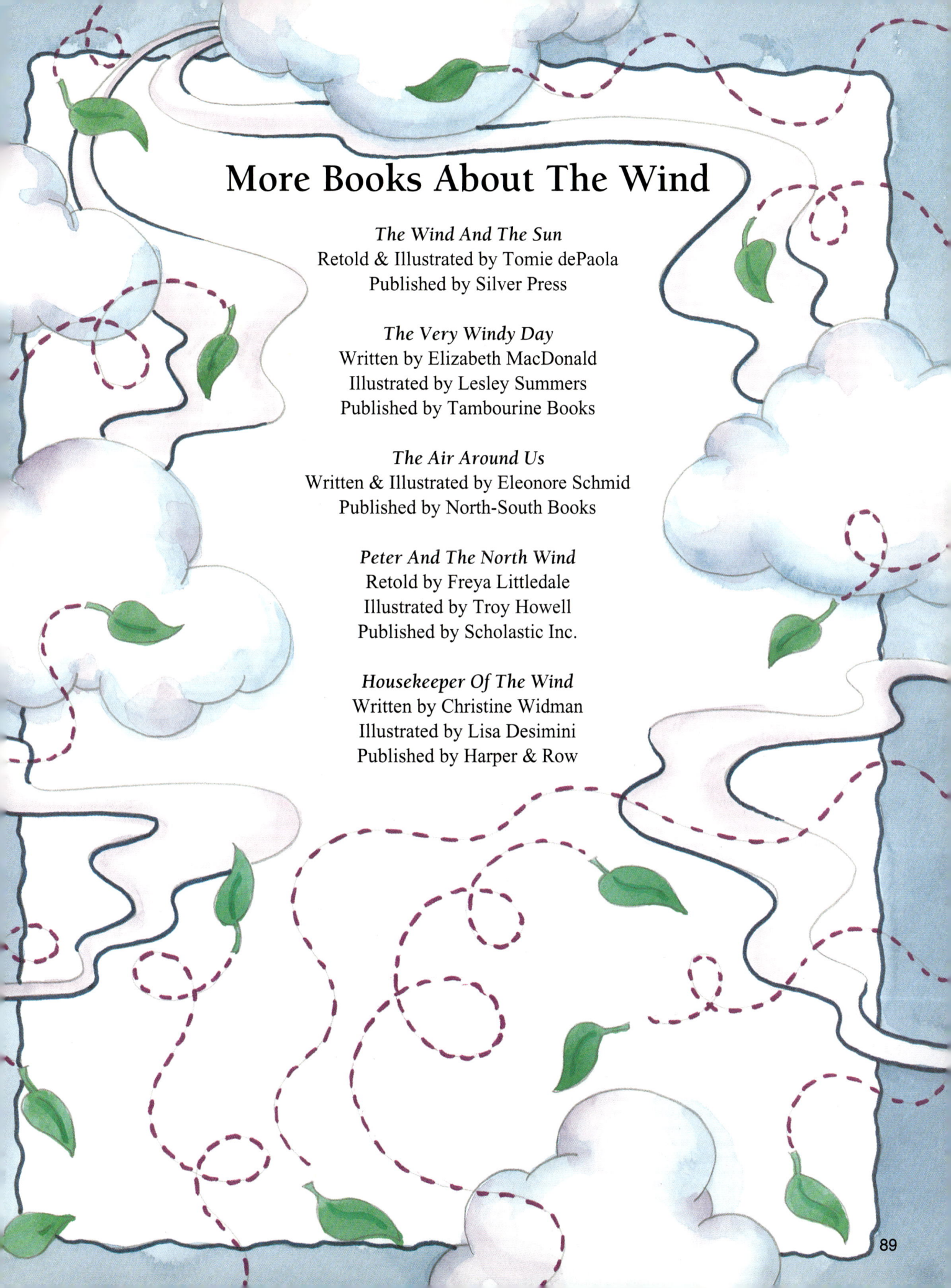

The Wind And The Sun
Retold & Illustrated by Tomie dePaola
Published by Silver Press

The Very Windy Day
Written by Elizabeth MacDonald
Illustrated by Lesley Summers
Published by Tambourine Books

The Air Around Us
Written & Illustrated by Eleonore Schmid
Published by North-South Books

Peter And The North Wind
Retold by Freya Littledale
Illustrated by Troy Howell
Published by Scholastic Inc.

Housekeeper Of The Wind
Written by Christine Widman
Illustrated by Lisa Desimini
Published by Harper & Row

Eggs All Around

Long before Horton hatched the egg, kids were curious about anything that taps its way out of a shell. After all, these miraculous and sometimes delicate ovals have the potential to turn out so many different ways: fried, scrambled, squawking, peeping, slithering—or even Sam-I-am green! Here's a collection of fiction and nonfiction books that are "eggs-actly" right for children who'd like to go peeping around eggshells.

Introduction and reviews contributed by Deborah Zink Roffino

Chickens Aren't The Only Ones
Written & Illustrated by Ruth Heller
Published by Grosset & Dunlap

Bold, bright illustrations complement the informative text in this "Reading Rainbow" selection. A touch of humor and rhyme leave youngsters with a wealth of information—and an impressive, new vocabulary word!

Before sharing this book, cut a construction-paper headband for each child. Label each headband with the word *oviparous*. Then read the book aloud. Afterwards write "oviparous" on the board. Practice pronouncing the word together. Then ask youngsters to recall what they learned from the book and suggest definitions. Next brainstorm a list of oviparous animals. Have each child use art supplies to create an animal from the list. Then attach each child's animal to a labeled headband. Encourage children to wear their headbands home and share what they've learned with their family members.

Dena Porter—Gr. K
Ozona Primary School
Ozona, TX

The Egg: A First Discovery Book
Created by Gallimard Jeunesse & Pascale de Bourgoing
Illustrated by René Mettler
Published by Scholastic Inc.

From the series with those coveted clear-overlay pages, here's a journey inside the shell to watch a chick develop. Also included are familiar birds, fish, and reptiles. Spiral-bound—this is the best of baby biology with text that is right on target.

After reading and discussing this book, have children look again at its last two pages. Conduct class surveys to find out how many children have tried each of the different types of eggs shown in the pictures. Then give each child a construction-paper egg. Encourage each child to write or dictate a favorite egg recipe. Ask each child to illustrate his recipe; then bind the recipes and illustrations together. Have each child share his recipe during a group reading time.

Linda Gordetsky—Grs. K–1
Banyan Creek Elementary
Delray Beach, FL

Egg: A Photographic Story Of Hatching
Written by Robert Burton
Photographed by Jane Burton & Kim Taylor
Published by Dorling Kindersley, Inc.

Maximum close-up photos reveal "eggs-quisite" details like the tiny pores in an ostrich egg that allow air to enter through the shell. Sequences of more than 20 animals hatching will feed kids' curiosities. Simply fascinating!

In advance, enlarge and photocopy several sets of pictures from this book. Use water-based markers to add color to the photocopied pictures. Cut out the pictures; then back each one with construction paper and laminate them. After sharing and discussing the book, place the sets of pictures and the book in a center. When a child visits the center, have him sequence a set of pictures to show the actual hatching process. Then encourage him to use the book to check his work.

Debbie Earley—Gr. K
Mountain View Elementary School
Kingsley, PA

A Nest Full Of Eggs
Written by Priscilla Belz Jenkins
Illustrated by Lizzy Rockwell
Published by HarperCollins

Before the mother robin can lay her pretty blue eggs, she must put together a nest. Simple science facts and realistic illustrations follow the baby birds' from their arrival until they spread their tiny wings and fly away.

Making these edible bird nests is a wonderful cooking extension to *A Nest Full Of Eggs*. After sharing the book, mix together the first three ingredients below. Then add the chow mein noodles and mix well. Have each child drop a spoonful of the mixture into a muffin liner, then use his greased fingers to mold the mixture into a nest. Then instruct each child to arrange several jelly-bean eggs in his nest. Oooh, beautiful to look at—and even better to eat!

1 7-oz. jar marshmallow creme
1/2 cup creamy peanut butter
4 tablespoons softened butter
1 8-oz. can chow mein noodles

Sharon Pasqua—Gr. K
Camino Grove School
Arcadia, CA

Nessa's Story
Written by Nancy Luenn
Illustrated by Neil Waldman
Published by Atheneum

On the lonely, frozen tundra, an Inuit girl happens upon a giant white egg and witnesses the hatching. The creature that emerges is a baby silaq—*a legendary animal that looks like a woolly mammoth.*

In advance, read the "Author's Note" at the back of the book. Then read the story aloud. Ask children to discuss what they think the silaq might be like. Then work on separating fact from fiction: Provide nonfiction egg-related books (pages 91 and 95) and two same-sized, construction-paper eggs for each child—one blank and one programmed as shown. Explain that nonfiction books are true; then encourage students to look through the books. On his blank egg, have each child draw a picture of an animal that really does hatch from an egg. Next have him copy the animal's name on the other egg, then cut on the dotted line. Use a brad to fasten the two egg pieces atop the illustrated egg cutout. Have each child share his finished project with the class. Are there any silaqs among them?

Randalyn Larson—Gr. K
Memorial School
Jackson, MI

An Extraordinary Egg
Written & Illustrated by Leo Lionni
Published by Alfred A. Knopf, Inc.

Leo Lionni has created a very simple—yet inviting—tale about three frogs who mistake an alligator egg for a chicken egg. Youngsters will get the joke that plays out in Lionni's trademark art style.

When you introduce this story to your children, create a little suspense by showing them only the title page—*not* the cover of the book. Ask each child to predict what is inside the egg; then read the story aloud. Afterwards discuss the predictions and the actual outcome. Then encourage each child to imagine what extraordinary thing Jessica will find next. Have each child write about and illustrate his idea on a sheet of construction paper. Bind all of the pages between two covers; then have each child share his page during a group reading time.

Cathy Collier—LDR
Southeastern Elementary
Chesapeake, VA

The Surprise Family
Written & Illustrated by Lynn Reiser
Published by Greenwillow Books

Eggshells are very temporary, but love is forever. This is a precious story about a little group who love each other—with their differences. Large type encourages early reading, and lively pictures propel the sweet story.

After sharing this story, discuss ways your class is kind of like a surprise family too. Each year you never know who will be in your classroom family! Encourage children to share their thoughts regarding what qualities make a good family member or friend. Then have small groups of children illustrate their ideas on poster-sized paper. During a group time, have the creators of each poster share their work with the rest of the class. Afterwards display the posters in your classroom to remind everybody of the message found in *The Surprise Family*.

Sonya Manson—Pre-K and Gr. K
Loma Linda, CA

Yes
Written & Illustrated by Josse Goffin
Published by Lothrop, Lee & Shepard Books

Enchanting pictures tell this wordless tale about a boy who tries to find the owner of an egg that he has discovered on a walk. Reviewing animals that lay eggs, this adventure with a twist requires that all thinking caps be pulled on tightly.

Before sharing this story with your class, bake a batch of surprise eggs. For each child, wrap a small, toy oviparous animal in canned biscuit dough. Bake these eggs (shaped dough) on greased cookie sheets at 350° until lightly browned. Then share the story with your youngsters. After discussing the tale, give each child an egg. Encourage each child to write/dictate a story about where he found his egg and to whom it might belong. Then have each child gently pull the egg apart to find the surprise inside. Have youngsters wrap up their stories using their surprise characters.

Mrs. Wren Aurelius—Gr. K
Krahn Elementary School
Spring, TX

Green Eggs And Ham
Written & Illustrated by Dr. Seuss
Published by Random House, Inc.

The magic of Seuss bursts through the pages of this book to captivate even the most reluctant of readers. This enormously popular Seuss selection is a must-see-and-read for any egg-related topic!

When you introduce your little ones to *Green Eggs And Ham,* be prepared to read it again, and again,…and again! Then extend the egg enthusiasm by setting up an egg-coloring center. Provide a hard-boiled egg for each child. Also provide prepared egg dyes in the primary colors: red, yellow, and blue. Encourage children to make predictions about and then experiment by dipping their eggs in combinations of colors. I do so like green eggs, and blue eggs, and orange eggs, and purple eggs,….

Kelly Crook—Gr. K
Blue Hill Elementary
Blue Hill, NE

Bently & Egg
Written & Illustrated by William Joyce
Published by HarperCollins Publishers

This springtime comedy chronicles the not-so-average incubation of a duck egg and its reluctant—but heroic—father figure.

After reading and discussing the ups and downs of poor Bently, design an obstacle course that includes some of the story-related events. For example, you might have each child carry a plastic egg on a spoon around a designated stuffed animal, then transfer the egg into a basket with a helium-filled balloon attached. Next have him carry the egg (in the basket) to a hat in which he carries the egg to the water table. At the water table, he places the egg in a toy boat and sails the boat to the other side—by blowing, fanning, or making waves. Finally he removes the egg, dries it off, and draws whatever he thinks might hatch from his egg—and names it, of course! Bind all of the pictures together; then have each child share his page with the class.

Theresa Lux—Pre-K
Pumpkin Patch
 Nursery School Centers Inc.
Guilderland, NY

Eggbert: The Slightly Cracked Egg
Written by Tom Ross
Illustrated by Rex Barron
Published by G. P. Putnam's Sons

Eggbert is an artist extraordinaire. His pictures are the talk of the fridge—until one dreadful day when it is discovered that Eggbert is slightly…(gasp!)…cracked. There begins Eggbert's journey to find a suitable place in the world for a slightly cracked egg.

This story is picture-perfect for portraying the idea that everybody is a little bit alike and a little bit different—and it is all perfectly natural! After reading and discussing this book with your children, ask each child to think of something that makes her just a little bit different or special. Then have each child illustrate and write/dictate about her idea. Bind all of the pages between two covers; then have each child share her page during a group time.

Tracey Rebock
Temple Emanuel
Cherry Hill, NJ

Hatch, Egg, Hatch!
Written by Shen Roddie
Illustrated by Frances Cony
Published by Little, Brown and Company

There may be lots of ways to cook an egg, but there's only one way to hatch it. Mother Hen learns patience in this touch-and-feel interactive book about a mother's love.

As you read this book aloud to your children, pause often to allow them to comment on Mother Hen's actions. Find out what advice they would offer Mother Hen. Then have each child make her own fluffy chick. Provide each child with a sheet of construction paper, white construction-paper scraps, two cotton balls, glue, a black marker, scissors, and chalk pastels. To make one chick, rub two cotton balls on a chalk pastel, gently pull the cotton balls apart to flatten them a bit, and glue them to the sheet of construction paper to resemble a chick. Use the chalk pastels and marker to add details. Next cut out two construction-paper egg halves; then glue them to the paper. Display the pictures along with the book and a title that reads "Our Eggs Have Hatched!"

Melissa Kile—Gr. K
Riner Elementary School
Riner, VA

The Easter Egg Farm
Written & Illustrated by Mary Jane Auch
Published by Holiday House, Inc.

Pauline is one unconventional chicken. Her eggs come out with the patterns of whatever stands in her field of vision. That makes for some fairly far-out Easter eggs and lots of fun on this brilliantly colored farm. Good lessons here on accepting diversity—and lots of inspiration for egg-decorating creativity! After sharing this book with your students, try any or all of the decorating techniques described below.

These eggs dry to a shiny enamel-like finish! To make one, cut out an egg shape from white poster board. In separate containers, mix condensed milk with different colors of food coloring. Using a separate paintbrush for each color, paint the egg with the mixtures. Tilt the egg in different directions, causing the colors to run together as desired. Then let the egg dry for about 48 hours to reveal a glossy shine.

Wendy Svenstrup
St. Mary's Preschool
Lafayette, IN

The home-school connection comes into play with this egg-decorating idea. Give each child a large, tagboard egg cutout. Have her take her egg home to decorate with her family members. Suggest that students and their families decorate with items such as pasta pieces, dried beans, fabric scraps, colored toothpicks, and sequins. Encourage each child to bring her decorated egg back to school to display in your classroom.

Nancy Blaschka
Comanche Primary
Comanche, TX

Use the crayon-resist art technique to decorate dozens of eggs for your springtime decor. Give each child a white construction-paper egg. Have him use heavy strokes of crayon to draw a design on the egg. Then use thinned tempera paint or watercolor paint to paint over the entire egg. The designs appear like magic!

Kelly A. Wong
Berlyn School
Ontario, CA

Finger-licking *is* allowed in this finger-painting project! Give each child one or more tagboard egg cutouts. Add food coloring to several different containers of light corn syrup. Then encourage children to finger-paint their eggs with the corn-syrup mixtures. Let the eggs dry for a day or two before displaying them on a board in a butcher-paper basket.

Janet A. Harris
Oquirrh Elementary
West Jordan, UT

More "Eggs-cellent" Reading

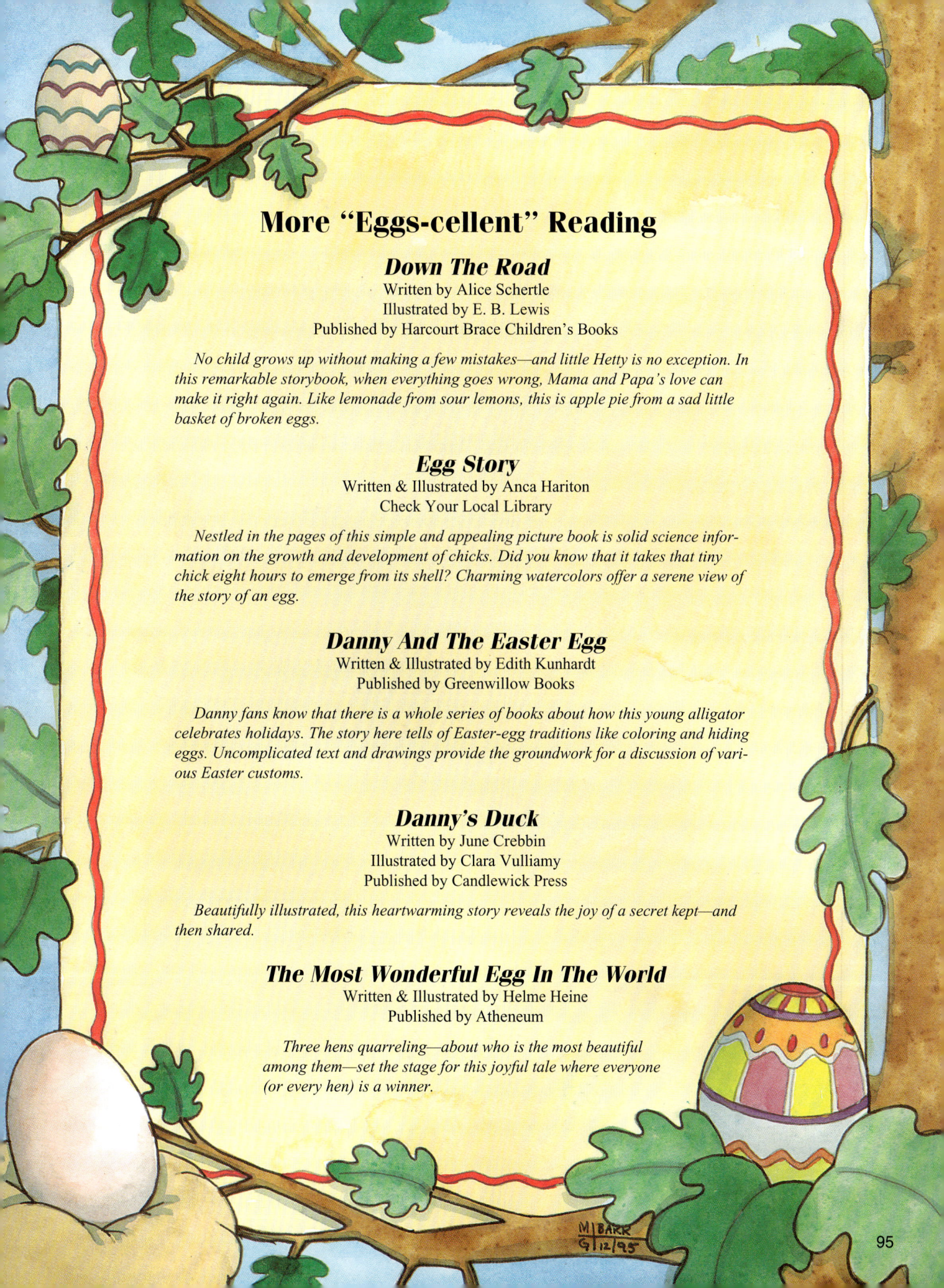

Down The Road
Written by Alice Schertle
Illustrated by E. B. Lewis
Published by Harcourt Brace Children's Books

No child grows up without making a few mistakes—and little Hetty is no exception. In this remarkable storybook, when everything goes wrong, Mama and Papa's love can make it right again. Like lemonade from sour lemons, this is apple pie from a sad little basket of broken eggs.

Egg Story
Written & Illustrated by Anca Hariton
Check Your Local Library

Nestled in the pages of this simple and appealing picture book is solid science information on the growth and development of chicks. Did you know that it takes that tiny chick eight hours to emerge from its shell? Charming watercolors offer a serene view of the story of an egg.

Danny And The Easter Egg
Written & Illustrated by Edith Kunhardt
Published by Greenwillow Books

Danny fans know that there is a whole series of books about how this young alligator celebrates holidays. The story here tells of Easter-egg traditions like coloring and hiding eggs. Uncomplicated text and drawings provide the groundwork for a discussion of various Easter customs.

Danny's Duck
Written by June Crebbin
Illustrated by Clara Vulliamy
Published by Candlewick Press

Beautifully illustrated, this heartwarming story reveals the joy of a secret kept—and then shared.

The Most Wonderful Egg In The World
Written & Illustrated by Helme Heine
Published by Atheneum

Three hens quarreling—about who is the most beautiful among them—set the stage for this joyful tale where everyone (or every hen) is a winner.

Fish Tales

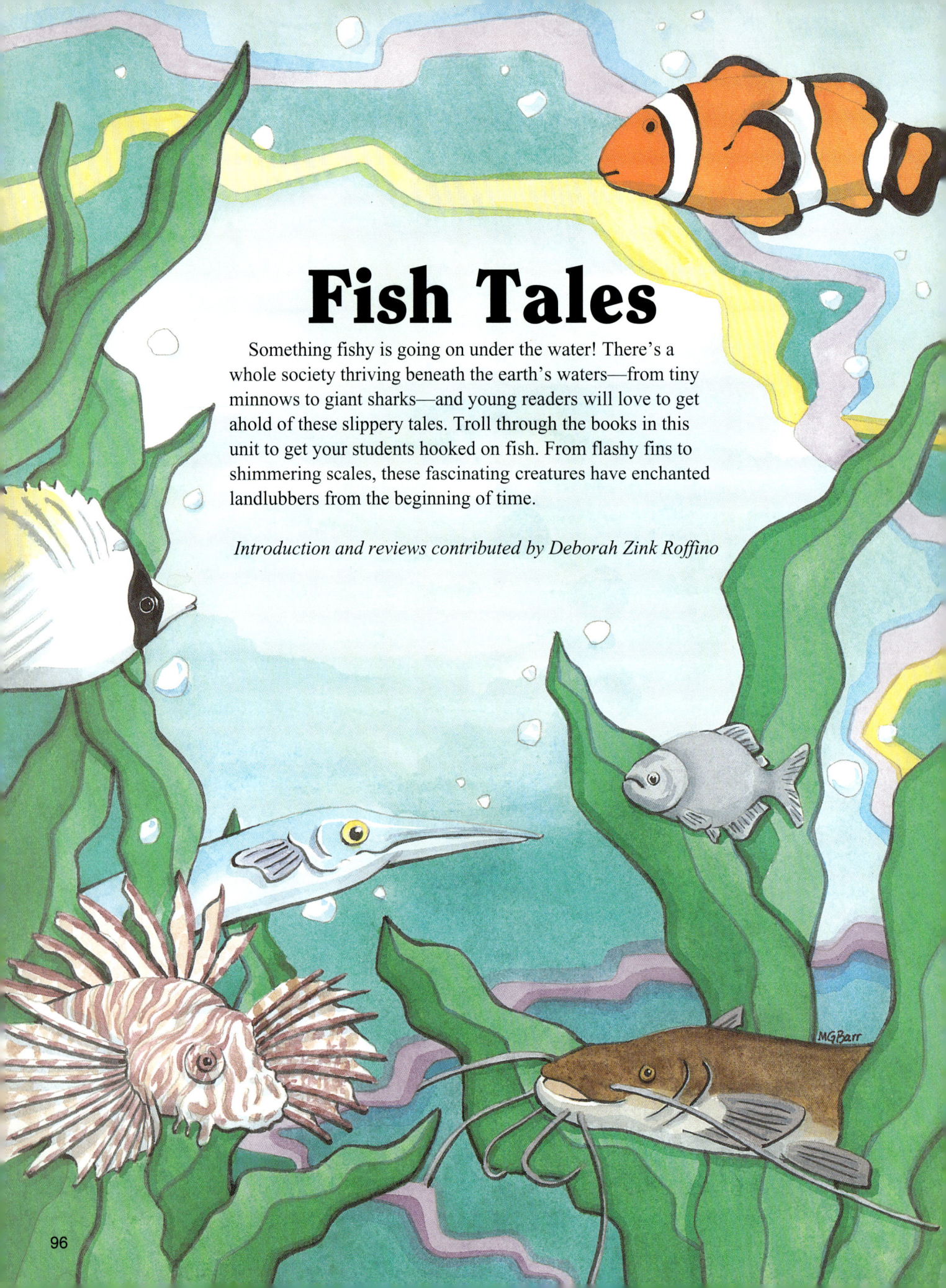

Something fishy is going on under the water! There's a whole society thriving beneath the earth's waters—from tiny minnows to giant sharks—and young readers will love to get ahold of these slippery tales. Troll through the books in this unit to get your students hooked on fish. From flashy fins to shimmering scales, these fascinating creatures have enchanted landlubbers from the beginning of time.

Introduction and reviews contributed by Deborah Zink Roffino

What's It Like To Be A Fish?
Written by Wendy Pfeffer
Illustrated by Holly Keller
Published by HarperCollins Publishers

From habits to habitats, here's a fine examination of the watery world of fish. There's a special emphasis on the fish that young children are most likely to encounter—the goldfish. The large text is complemented by bright, clear illustrations and the book closes with tips for setting up a goldfish bowl. After sharing this book with your youngsters, the following goldfish ideas are natural spin-offs to take your students swimming right across your curriculum.

Reel in those number skills with this fishy counting center. In advance, collect a supply of plastic fish (available at party-supply stores) and store them in a bowl. For each number that you'd like to include in your counting center, duplicate the fishbowl pattern (page 102) on construction paper. Add decorative details with markers; then laminate and cut out each bowl. Using a permanent marker, program each bowl with a different numeral or number word. Place the bowl of fish and the fishbowl cutouts in a center. To do this activity, a child arranges the fishbowls in numerical order. Then he places the correct number of fish on each fishbowl.

Denise K. Clay, Kehoe France School, New Orleans, LA

Use that handy goldfish gang to swim into patterning. Make workmats by laminating several sheets of blue construction paper or sentence strips. Provide a supply of toys or edible goldfish for manipulatives. Encourage each child to arrange the fish on a workmat to create the pattern of his choice. Then invite youngsters to read their patterns to each other.

Debbie Earley—Gr. K, Mountain View Elementary Kingsley, PA

This particular school of fish provides lots of nibbles as well as practice in sorting and graphing. In advance, gather at least three different types of edible goldfish (Pepperidge Farm® offers a wide variety). Give each child a random assortment of the goldfish and a simple bar graph. (If you'd like, you can program a copy of the fishbowl [page 102] with a bar graph; then reproduce it for each student.) Encourage each child to graph his goldfish. To extend this activity, have each child record his results on a large class graph. Then—as you nibble on the manipulatives—discuss what the graph reveals.

Chantelle M. Gist, Reid Elementary, Springfield, OH

Science concepts flow quite naturally out of all this fishy activity. Create an interactive science display by tracing the fish on page 13 of *What's It Like To Be A Fish?* Use water-based markers to add color to your picture; then back it with construction paper and cut it out. Next label nine strips of construction paper—four with the word "fin," and each of the remaining strips with "eye," "mouth," "gills," "scales," and "tail." Laminate all the pieces and prepare them for flannelboard or magnet-board use. Store all of the pieces in a resealable bag along with nine lengths of yarn (and some reusable adhesive if you're using a magnet board). To do this activity, a child places the fish on the board, then appropriately arranges the labels around the fish. If needed, she can use the yarn and adhesive to connect the labels to the appropriate fish parts. Encourage youngsters to check their work with the illustrations on pages 11 and 13 in the book.

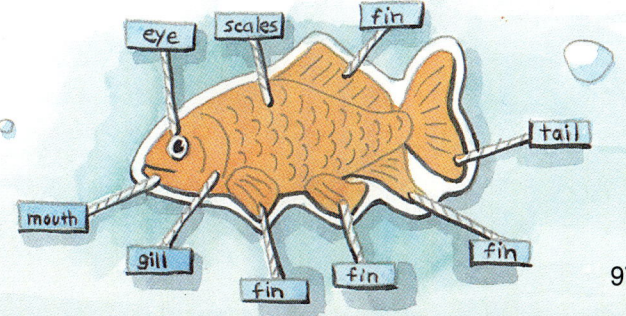

Sea Dragons And Rainbow Runners: Exploring Fish With Children
Written by Suzanne Samson, Illustrated by Preston Neel
Published by Roberts Rinehart Publishers

By its very title, this book invokes the imagination—and rightly so, for it is filled with a menagerie of oceanic whimsy. But if you look closely, you'll find that fact is carefully woven in with fiction. Which is fact and which is fiction? It's yours to tell!

After sharing this book, revisit each of the illustrations. Ask children to tell which parts of the illustrations they think are true and which parts they think are imaginary. Then take a look at the appendix at the back of the book, where you'll find information about each fish featured in the book. So how'd your class fare? Sometimes fact *is* stranger than fiction!

Crinkleroot's 25 Fish Every Child Should Know
Written & Illustrated by Jim Arnosky
Published by Simon & Schuster

In this book, various fish are presented by the very merry Mr. Crinkleroot. This simple directory is a good reference for anglers, teachers, artists, and curious kids.

This book presents an up-close-and-personal look at a variety of fish. Your little realists will dive into the detailed illustrations. And after a read-aloud, your emergent readers will love reading the large text and identifying each fish independently. In advance, purchase two identical sets of fish stickers (you should have at least two of each type of fish). Affix each sticker in one set to a large sheet of construction paper. Affix each sticker in the remaining set to another sheet of paper; then cut out each fish from that sheet. Laminate the whole fish mat and the fish cutouts. Store the small pieces in a Ziploc® bag and place them in a center along with the fish mat. After sharing the book, extend observation skills by encouraging children to visit this fish-related center. To do this activity, a child places the fish mat on a flat surface. He then matches each of the fish cutouts to the corresponding picture on the mat.

Denise K. Clay
Kehoe France School
New Orleans, LA

Fishy Facts
Written by Catherine Chermayeff & Nan Richardson
Illustrated by Ivan Chermayeff
Published by Harcourt Brace & Company

There's no floundering around here! Fish boldly appear in bright, sizzling colors to illustrate fabulous fish trivia on every page.

Fishy Facts presents a natural opportunity to introduce the concept of *facts* to your youngsters. After sharing the book, talk about the word *fact*. Guide children to summarize that a fact is a statement that is true. Then make your own class version of *Fishy Facts*. Give each child a large sheet of construction paper that is programmed at the top with "Did you know..." and at the bottom with "And that's a fact!" Encourage each child to illustrate a fact about fish that he has learned during your studies. Next have him write or dictate to complete the sentence starter on the page. Bind all the pages together to make a class book. Have each child share his page with the group. This class book is a great one to also share with your students' families—and that's a fact!

Hungry, Hungry Sharks
Written by Joanna Cole
Illustrated by Patricia Wynne
Published by Random House, Inc.

Sharks fascinate with their ferocity, and few kids can resist a good shark book. Here is a golden oldie that provides a simple discussion of different types of sharks and their behaviors.

After reading and discussing this book with your students, place it in your science center with additional shark books. Stock the center with art paper, crayons, and colored pencils. Encourage each child to closely examine the pictures of the type of shark that interests him the most. Then have him draw a picture of that shark and label it. If you have older students or adult volunteers available, encourage each student who shows a particular interest in sharks to ask a volunteer to help him find out more about his chosen shark. Youngsters will be thrilled to share their findings with the class. Afterward display the pictures along with the shark books.

A Swim Through The Sea
Written & Illustrated by Kristin Joy Pratt
Published by Dawn Publications (1-800-545-7475)

This exceptional alphabet book was named an Outstanding Science Trade Book in 1995. And to top that, it's authored and illustrated by a teenager! The pages—framed with ocean vocabulary—swirl with tropical watercolors. The large text is child-oriented, while the smaller text is packed with solid information for you or older readers.

Before sharing this book, divide a sheet of chart paper into two columns. Label one column "fish" and the other column "not fish." As you read the book aloud, ask youngsters to classify each animal featured. Some creatures may require additional discussion or a trip to an encyclopedia! Record your findings by having different students draw sketches in the appropriate columns or by copying the actual names of the creatures onto the chart.

After sharing this book from aesthetic and scientific angles, try this fanciful extension activity. Stock a center with a supply of letter stencils, construction paper, tissue paper, markers, and glue. As each child visits the center, encourage her to create a fish out of any letter of the alphabet. When each project is done, mount it above the appropriate letter on your classroom alphabet chart.

Adapted from an idea by
Diane Billman—Gr. K
Russell School
Smyrna, GA

Fish Eyes
Written & Illustrated by Lois Ehlert
Published by Harcourt Brace & Company

Holy mackerel! Neon colors add lots of splash to this appealing counting book. The fish eyes are actually peepholes to the next page—just right for peeking and poking around. Imaginative and fun, little ones are reeled in with these fanciful fish in a sea of navy blue.

The large, visible text makes this book a read-*along* as well as a read-aloud. After sharing this book, divide students into ten groups. Tell your students that you would like them to make a book that continues counting fish where the author left off. Assign a different number from 11–20 to each group, and supply each group with a sheet of blue construction paper. Ask each group to think of a describing word (adjective) for its group of fish. Write each group's number and dictation on its page. Then encourage students to use neon art supplies to create the corresponding amount and type of fish. Next direct each group to glue its fish to its blue paper. Sequence the pages; then bind them together between two covers. Encourage each group to share its page with the class.

Adapted from an idea by
Rachel Meseke Castro
Juneau Elementary
Juneau, WI

The Fish Skin
Written by Jamie Oliviero
Illustrated by Brent Morrisseau
Published by Hyperion Books For Children

From the Cree nation, this Native North American legend tells of a young boy who acquires the skin of a fish to save his people from drought. The surreal colors add to the fantasy, well-captured by a Native North American artist.

The theme of this story is harmony in nature, and the amazing fish is the star. As you begin to read the book aloud, pause after the first page of text. Find out if your youngsters think it was a good idea for the people to ask Cloud to stay away. Ask them to explain why or why not. Then finish reading the story aloud. Afterwards discuss what your students think the boy meant when he said that the people had learned that nature's cycle is good. Do your youngsters agree?

A Million Fish...More Or Less
Written by Patricia C. McKissack
Illustrated by Dena Schutzer
Published by Alfred A. Knopf, Inc.

The tales on the Bayou Clapateaux are tall alright! And young Hugh Thomas listens skeptically, wondering if there's a little truth-stretching going on. Then—after one eventful fishing trip—Hugh Thomas has a tall tale of his own to tell.

After reading and discussing this bayou tale, sing the story-related song below with your youngsters:

(sung to the tune of "Jimmy Crack Corn")

Caught a million fish,
What'll I do?
Caught a million fish,
What'll I do?
Caught a million fish,
What'll I do?
I'll bring them home to show to you!

Alligator ate some,
What'll I do?
Alligator ate some,
What'll I do?
Alligator ate some,
What'll I do?
I'll bring the rest to show to you!

(Repeat the second verse, inserting the phrases below.)

Raccoons ate some, what'll I do?....
Fish crows ate some, what'll I do?...
Hungry cat ate some, what'll I do?...

Three fish left, what'll I do?
Three fish left, what'll I do?
Three fish left, what'll I do?
I'll have to tell the tale to you!

Adapted from an idea by Rachel Meseke Castro
Juneau Elementary, Juneau, WI

The Sawfin Stickleback: A Very Fishy Story
Written by Catherine Friend
Illustrated by Dan Yaccarino
Published by Hyperion Books For Children

This whopper of a tale tells the story of the "TOTALLY HUMONGOUS Sawfin Stickleback." It is, indeed, a very fishy story and youngsters will get the joke that plays out in the bold, graphic art.

Being on the inside of the humor in this story will put your class in the mood for this variation of Pin The Tail On The Donkey. To prepare for the game, draw a fishing rod with a line and a hook on a sheet of poster board. Mount the poster on a wall at child height. After sharing the story, have each child use art supplies to create the fish of her choice. Laminate each fish. Give each child a piece of reusable adhesive to stick to the back of her fish. In turn, blindfold each child and have her try to attach her fish to the hook. Did *you* hook a whopper?

Denise K. Clay
Kehoe France School
New Orleans, LA

Swimmy
Written & Illustrated by Leo Lionni
Published by Pantheon Books

This Lionni classic is always a favorite. His insightful use of watercolors and collages submerge the reader in the underwater world of the unsuspecting, yet heroic, Swimmy.

After sharing this story, youngsters will be in the mood to create their own stylized Swimmy scenes. To make a bubbly background, you will need a shallow bowl, some bubble solution, blue food coloring, straws, and construction paper. Pour the bubble solution into the bowl. Add food coloring until the mixture is the desired shade of blue. Next use straws to blow bubbles until the bubbles begin to rise over the rim of the bowl. Then place a sheet of construction paper over the bowl. Repeat the process until the background is complete. When the paper is dry, glue on construction-paper and tissue-paper scenery. Then add red and/or black fingerprint fish to the scene. When the fish are dry, add details with fine-tipped markers. Display the scenes on a board titled "Swimmy Art."

Chantelle M. Gist
Reid Elementary
Springfield, OH

Diane Billman—Gr. K
Russell School
Smyrna, GA

More Books On The Line

Fiction

Rainbow Fish To The Rescue!
Written & Illustrated by Marcus Pfister
Published by North-South Books Inc.

"Only Joking!" Laughed The Lobster
Written & Illustrated by Colin West
Published by Candlewick Press

Big Al
Written by Andrew Clements
Illustrated by Yoshi
Published by Picture Book Studio

Nonfiction

Fearsome Fish
Written by Steve Parker
Illustrated by Ann Savage
Published by Raintree Steck-Vaughn Publishers

Weird And Wonderful Fish
Written & Illustrated by Colin S. Milkins
Published by Thomas Learning

**Pattern
Fishbowl**

Use with activities on page 97.

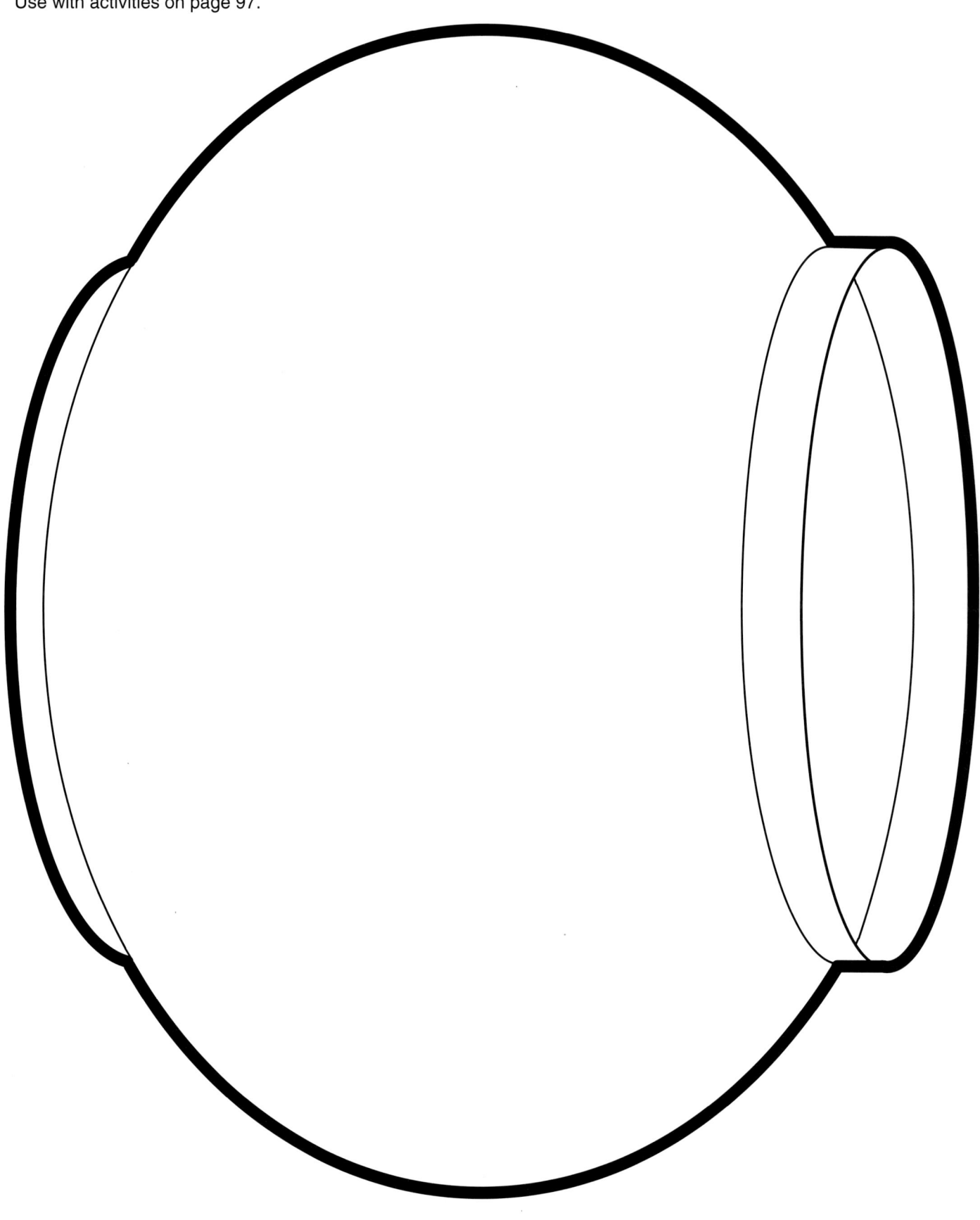

Getting Kids Into Books

Right On The Button
An assortment of classification activities will be right on the button after a reading of *The Button Box* by Margarette S. Reid (Dutton Children's Books). After sharing the book, discuss the variety of ways the boy in the story found to sort his grandmother's buttons. Then show students a tin or box of buttons that you have collected. (Garage sales or flea markets are a great source for buttons.) Divide the class into groups; then provide each group with a collection of buttons. Ask each group to work cooperatively to sort the buttons. Provide time for each group to share how they sorted their buttons. Later place the book and box of buttons in a center to be used for independent classification practice.

Denise Sinclair—Gr. K, Shiremanstown Elementary, Shiremanstown, PA

"Whooose" Owl Eyes?
This creative art project will be a wise extension to *Good-Night, Owl!* by Pat Hutchins (Aladdin Books). After reading the book aloud, instruct each student to draw, paint, or cut out an owl. Have him glue two connected rings from a plastic six-pack holder onto the owl to resemble eyes. To complete the project, add real feathers to the owl design. If desired, label the project with words identifying the various parts of the owl. Display the big-eyed owls on a bulletin board titled "Good Night, Owl!"

Kathy Curnow—Gr. K, Woolridge Elementary, Midlothian, VA

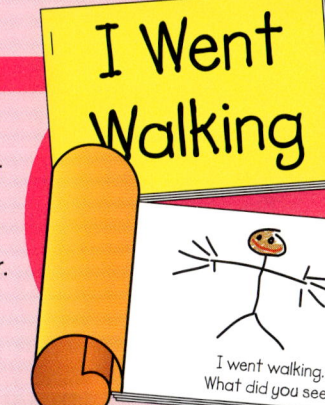

Let's Go Walking
Let's go walking. What will we see? When reading *I Went Walking* by Sue Williams (Gulliver Books), you'll see a young boy and his parade of whimsical animals. After enjoying the story and Julie Vivas's illustrations, give youngsters a chance to illustrate their own "I Went Walking" books. For each child, duplicate only the text of the book. Bind the pages together with a cover. Encourage each child to illustrate his book as desired. Then have him take the book home to share with his family.

Audrey Englehardt, South Roxana Elementary, South Roxana, IL

Tick, Tock: How Long Does It Take?
October is National Clock Month! Take the time to read aloud *Clocks And More Clocks* by Pat Hutchins (Young Readers Press, Inc.). Ask youngsters for their explanations as to why Mr. Higgins's clocks displayed different times. Then explore and record how long it takes your class to travel from the classroom to various parts of the school. Use a stopwatch to verify the length of time it takes the children to move from place to place. Then record the times on a chart as shown. At the end of the day or week, review the times and decide which destination was the closest and which was the farthest.

Lori J. Brown, LVBH Day Care Center, Palmyra, PA

Destination	Time
library	1 min. 47 secs.
cafeteria	56 secs.

Getting Kids Into Books

"I'll Huff And I'll Puff"

After sharing and comparing several versions of *The Three Little Pigs,* youngsters will be eager to retell the story with these projects. For each child, draw three house shapes on a sheet of tagboard. Provide each child with straw, toothpicks, and a small, rectangular piece of sponge and red paint. Also provide construction paper, glue, and scissors. Have each student apply the appropriate material on each house in the order they appear in the story. Then have each child draw and cut out a construction-paper wolf and three little pigs, and glue the cutouts to the picture. Encourage students to share their pictures with family members and retell the story.

Robin Souder—Gr. K, Kimball Wiles Elementary, Montevallo, AL

Inside A Mitten

The Mitten, adapted and illustrated by Jan Brett (G.P. Putnam's Sons), will inspire your little ones to participate in this circle activity. After sharing the story, have children sit in a circle on a rug. Review the animals in the order that they appear in the story. Then choose student volunteers to play the roles of the animals in the story. Place a large blanket in the center of the circle to represent the mitten and sing the song below as youngsters role-play climbing into the mitten.

(sung to the tune of "The Farmer In The Dell")

The mitten on the ground.
The mitten on the ground.
Heigh-ho! It's cold outside.
The mitten on the ground.

The [mole] snuggles in.
The [mole] snuggles in.
Heigh-ho! It's cold outside.
The [mole] snuggles in.

As the last student role-plays the mouse, have all of the students pretend to sneeze and fall out of the mitten.

Paula Laughtland, Edmonds, WA

Put Some Action Into The Alphabet

Get your little ones moving while they listen to *Action Alphabet* by Marty Neumeier and Byron Glaser (published by Greenwillow Books). Read the story aloud; then reread it and have your students do an action to represent the word on each page. On another day, read the book again, but before showing each page, have the students recall the word for that letter. Encourage students to brainstorm other action words that begin with that letter. Then create a class action-alphabet book. To make one, provide each child with a large sheet of construction paper. Assign each child a letter of the alphabet and have him illustrate an action word that has the same beginning sound. Bind the pages together along with a front cover entitled "Our Action Alphabet Book." Twist, bend, jump, or run. It all adds up to alphabet fun!

Suzanne Grade—Gr. K, Roe School, St. Louis, MO

Getting Kids Into Books

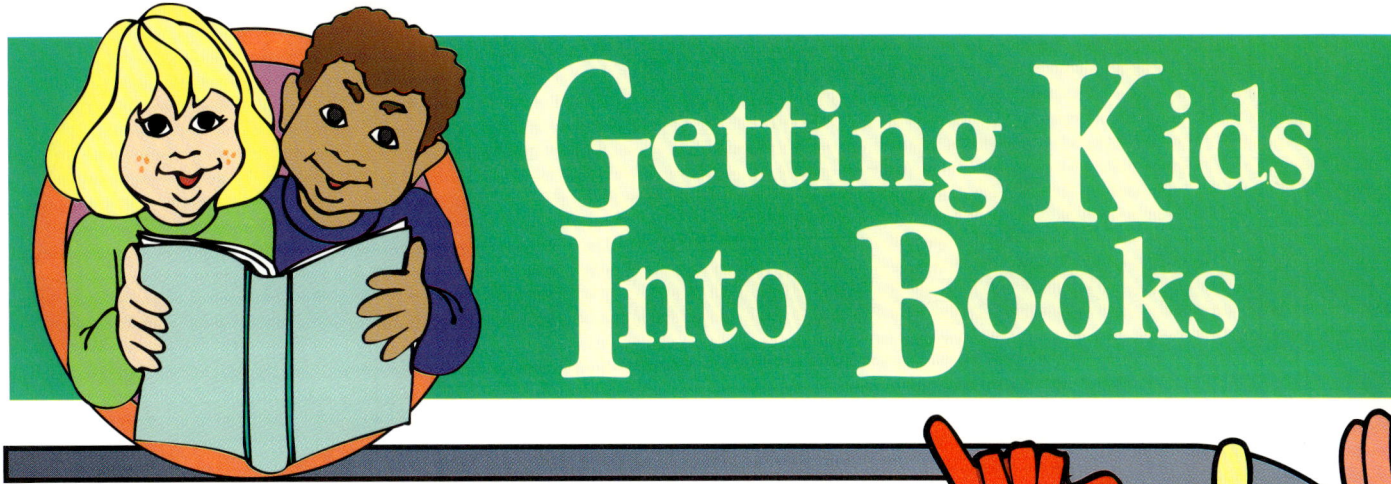

Sign-Language Flowers

This handsome display is a beautiful way to reinforce the manual alphabet. Share *The Handmade Alphabet* by Laura Rankin (Dial Books) with your class. As you display each elegant illustration, have students perform the corresponding hand sign. Then trace each child's right hand (with fingers just barely apart) onto different colors of construction paper until you have 24 hand shapes. Also trace two hands with fingers set wide apart. Cut out the hand shapes. Attach a green construction-paper stem to the base of each hand so that it resembles a flower. Then glue the stem to a construction-paper flowerpot. Label each pot with a different letter. Using the book's illustrations as a guide, fold the fingers of each hand-shaped flower so that it resembles the manual sign for the letter on the flowerpot. Glue the fingers in place when necessary. Mount the sign-language flowers in sequence along with the title "Do you know your ABCs?"

Barbara Pasley—Grs. K–1 Special Education, Energy School, Benton, IL

A Valentine Kiss

A reading of *Arthur's Valentine* by Marc Brown (Little, Brown, and Company) will inspire youngsters to make and give Valentine kisses! To make a kiss, give each child a six-inch strip of white paper, half of a 1 1/2-inch Styrofoam ball, and a six-inch square of aluminum foil. On his paper strip, have each child write "Love," and sign his name. Next have him place the flat side of the ball half on the foil. Then have him place one end of the strip under the ball. Making sure that the signed portion of the strip remains visible, help each child wrap the foil around the ball and mold it into a candy-kiss shape. Encourage each child to give his kiss to a parent or loved one. Close your eyes! Here comes a kiss!

Barb Spero—Gr. K, Memorial School, Paramus, NJ

Wait A Minute, Mr. Postman!

After reading and discussing *The Post Office Book* by Gail Gibbons (Thomas Y. Crowell), make a curb-style mailbox for your classroom mail center. Securely tape shut the flaps on a box. To make the box curved at one end, cut a piece of poster board the width of the box. Stand the box on end; then tape one end of the poster board to one side of what is now the top of the box. Arch the poster board over the top of the box and tape it to the other side. Next cover the whole structure with red, white, and blue paper. Label the box; then cut out a mail slot from the front and a mail-retrieval door from the back (as shown). If desired, cover the box with clear Con-Tact® covering. Place the mailbox in your mail center along with writing supplies and a copy of the book.

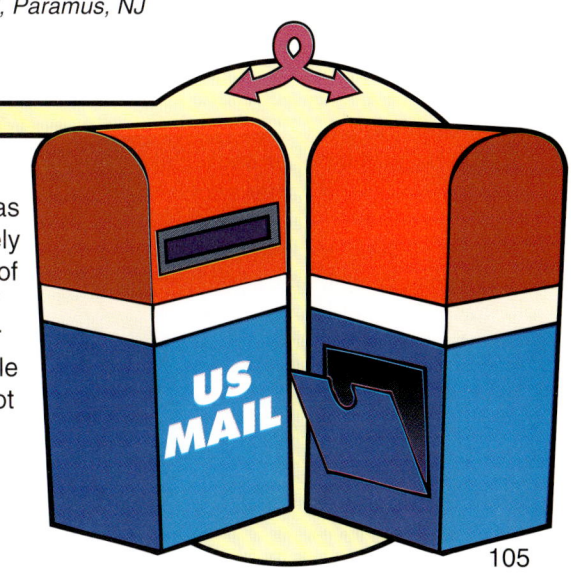

Karen Bryant, Rosa Taylor Elementary School, Macon, GA

Getting Kids Into Books

Who's Awake Tonight?

When night arrives, most of us turn out the lights and settle down for sleep after a busy day. Find out what certain animals do at night in *Animals At Night* by Sharon Peters (Troll Associates). After reading the story aloud, have your little ones create their own busy-night scenes with this simple lift-the-flap art project. To make one, cut out a brown tree trunk and a green treetop from construction paper. Glue the trunk to the bottom of a 9" x 12" sheet of black construction paper. Position the treetop above the trunk and glue only the top portion of it to the black paper. In doing so, the treetop will become a flap that can be lifted up. Glue a pair of wiggle eyes onto the front of the treetop. On the paper under the treetop, glue an animal sticker or drawing to correspond with an animal in the story. Embellish the sky with stars and a moon. Who's awake tonight? Lift the flap to see!

Laurie Mills—Gr. K, Stevenson Elementary, Stevenson, AL

From Seed To Carrot

Ruth Krauss's classic, *The Carrot Seed* (HarperCollins Children's Books), is the perfect story to give your little ones the scoop on both plant growth and patience. Before reading the story, paint a box brown—this will represent the ground. Inside the ground (box), place a package of carrot seeds, a hand trowel, a watering can, and a bag of ready-to-eat carrots. Read the story aloud. As you read about the related events in the story, remove and show each item from the ground. When you pull the carrots out at the end of the story, pass one to each child. While they're munching, discuss the story and the boy's feelings. It certainly takes a lot of patience to wait for those seeds to become carrots—and to eat those carrots!

Cheryl Gosling, The School House Preschool, Santa Cruz, CA

Counting Animals

Get your youngsters actively counting with these animal packets and *Who's Counting?* by Nancy Tafuri (Greenwillow Books). First cut animal shapes from felt for each set of animals in the story. Then place each set in a different resealable plastic bag. Put the plastic bags in a paper sack. Set up your flannelboard; then read the story aloud. Afterwards hold up the paper sack and sing this song.

(sung to the tune of "Frère Jacques")
I have something. I have something.
In my bag. In my bag.
Can you guess what's in it? Can you guess what's in it?
In my bag? In my bag?

Encourage children to guess the contents of the sack. After guessing, have each child reach into the sack and remove a plastic bag. Reread the story aloud. Have children place the animal cutouts from their bags on the flannelboard at the appropriate times in the story. Count each set of animals aloud with your students. Who's counting? We're all counting!

Nancy Clements, The Children's Center at 200 Park Avenue, New York, NY

Author Units

Reading With Raffi!

Using Raffi's Songs-To-Read In Your Classroom

Dear Teachers,

It's a delight for me to be able to speak to you through the pages of *The Mailbox®*, and to learn that, through my work, I am a regular visitor in your classrooms.

I have always believed that music can be a natural bridge between speaking and reading. I am honored that so many of you are using my songs and books to help bring your students to literacy, and are willing to take the time to share your ideas with other professionals.

My own work with children has brought me joy, satisfaction, and an ongoing feeling of wonder and delight. May your work reward you in all the same ways.

Thank you,

Raffi

Like Me And You
Illustrated by Lillian Hoban
Published by
Crown Books For Young Readers

This treasure of a book is a wonderful choice to use at the beginning of the year when students are just getting to know each other. Young readers will sing and say the names of children around the world as they are illustrated mailing letters to one another. After sharing the book with your children, discuss each of your students' names. When appropriate, talk about the culture from which each child's family originated. Invite parents from other cultures to visit your class to share information about their places of origin.

Down By The Bay
Illustrated by Nadine Bernard Westcott
Published by Crown Books For Young Readers

When he's in concert, Raffi sometimes jokes that the audience won't let him leave until he has sung this song with them! In this book, two friends use their imaginations and rhyme to create some of the silliest scenes you have ever laid eyes on! Share *Down By The Bay* with your children. After reading and discussing the book, teach the tune to your children and sing the book. Then announce that you are all going on an imaginary trip to the bay. Proceed by singing the song, inserting a different child's name and corresponding rhyming word each time. (If you can't think of real rhyming words—make them up!)

Jennifer Kreskai—Age 3-Gr. K, Kid's Land Inc.
South Bend, IN

"Have you ever seen Claire, playing with a bear..."

"Did you ever see Tony munching on baloney..."

Youngsters will be eager to create outlandish art projects to accompany their wild imaginings. Have each child choose a pair of rhyming words from *Down By The Bay* or a pair that he thought of on his own. Then provide a variety of art supplies and have each child illustrate his chosen rhyme. For example, a child could use a bingo marker to make polka dots on the tail of a whale cutout, or use fabric scraps to make a colorful bow tie for a construction-paper fly. Display the finished projects; then sing a verse of the song for each one.

Dawn Hurley, CUMC Child Care Center, Bethel Park, PA

After you've ventured "down by the bay, where the watermelons grow," a seed search makes a wonderful thematic extension into math. In advance, cut a large semicircle from poster board and color it to resemble a slice of watermelon. Program the cutout as shown. Then give each child a real watermelon wedge. Ask her to pick out all of the seeds and place them on a paper towel. After rinsing and drying the seeds, have each child count her seeds; then write her name on the graph to represent the number of seeds that she has. Encourage each child to help decorate the graph by gluing her seeds around the edges. When the graph is complete, discuss the results with your students.

Kim Gray, Warren Elementary School, Alvaton, KY

Baby Beluga
Illustrated by Ashley Wolff
Published by Crown Books For Young Readers

According to Raffi's experience, "Children love this song because it is a bright and tuneful love song for a baby whale. Hearing it and singing it is enough for them; they don't need to be told that it's trying to teach them anything." But a child who grows up with this song, says Raffi, is likely to become an adult who will—at the very least—be sensitive to reports about the fatal pollution of the water belugas live in. After sharing this book and song with your children, choose one (or both) of the following suggestions to make a whale-related art project.

Water-Spouting Beluga
Trace or draw a beluga on white construction paper; then cut it out. Glue the beluga onto a large sheet of blue construction paper. Use crayons to draw an ocean scene around the beluga. On another sheet of white paper, use watercolor paint to paint a long waterspout. Cut out the spout and glue it onto a craft stick or long pipe cleaner. Cut a slit near the top of the beluga's head. Slide the craft stick or pipe cleaner into the slit so that the waterspout appears to come from the beluga. As you read the story again, children can move the waterspout up and down.

Jennifer Barton—Gr. K, Elizabeth Green School, Newington, CT

Whale Watching
Display pictures of various types of whales. Encourage students to carefully study the pictures and discuss the differences among all of the whales. Then give each child (or small group of children) a long length of bulletin-board paper that has been folded in half vertically. Direct each child to draw the whale of his choice on the paper, adding crayon details as desired. Assist children in cutting out a double thickness of their whales. Staple around the outline of the cutouts, leaving an opening at the bottom. Have each child gently stuff his whale with newspaper or plastic grocery bags. Staple the whales on a ocean bulletin-board background. Mount a label near each individual whale.

Carol Steiner—Gr. K, Jackson Elementary School
Green Bay, WI

One Light, One Sun
Illustrated by Eugenie Fernandes
Published by Crown Books For Young Readers

This warm and wonderful ballad was written by Raffi to convey that all people, no matter how different, have very much in common. We have *one* light and *one* sun—enough for everyone! After sharing the book with your students, sing the song together. Encourage children to discuss the meaning of the story and song. Then have each child or small group of children use representations of items in the story to make a mobile. (Depending on the art techniques you choose to use, you might like to work on these mobiles in more than one sitting.) Here's one way to make a mobile: Cut a sun shape from construction paper. Glue on orange and yellow yarn to decorate the sun. Color or paint a construction-paper circle to resemble the world. Glue construction-paper shapes and scraps together to make a house. Cut out a construction-paper heart and decorate it with pink and red tissue paper and glitter. When the projects are dry, use yarn to hang them from a hanger. Display each mobile as a reminder of Raffi's song and the message that it carries.

Carmen Carpenter, Highland Preschool, Raleigh, NC

Five Little Ducks
Illustrated by Jose Aruego and Ariane Dewey
Published by Crown Books For Young Readers

In one version or another, this story has probably entered almost every kindergarten classroom. Your little ones are bound to love Raffi's version of the story with its delightful surprise ending. In advance, prepare five construction-paper duck cutouts. Make stick puppets by taping a craft stick to the back of each cutout. Then read the story aloud. After discussing the story, *sing* the story together. Then give each of the five duck puppets to different children. Have the children (ducks) stand side by side while the class sings the song. As each duck wanders off—according to the song's lyrics—have her squat down. When it's time for the wandering ducks to come back, direct each duck to take the hand of a classmate to come waddling back with her as her duckling. When the song is over, have the adult ducks give their puppets to the ducklings. Sing the song until everyone has had a turn to be a duck. But be forewarned—Raffi says that sometimes, it's hard to stop quacking once you start!

Terri Nix—Gr. K, Brauchle Elementary School,
San Antonio, TX

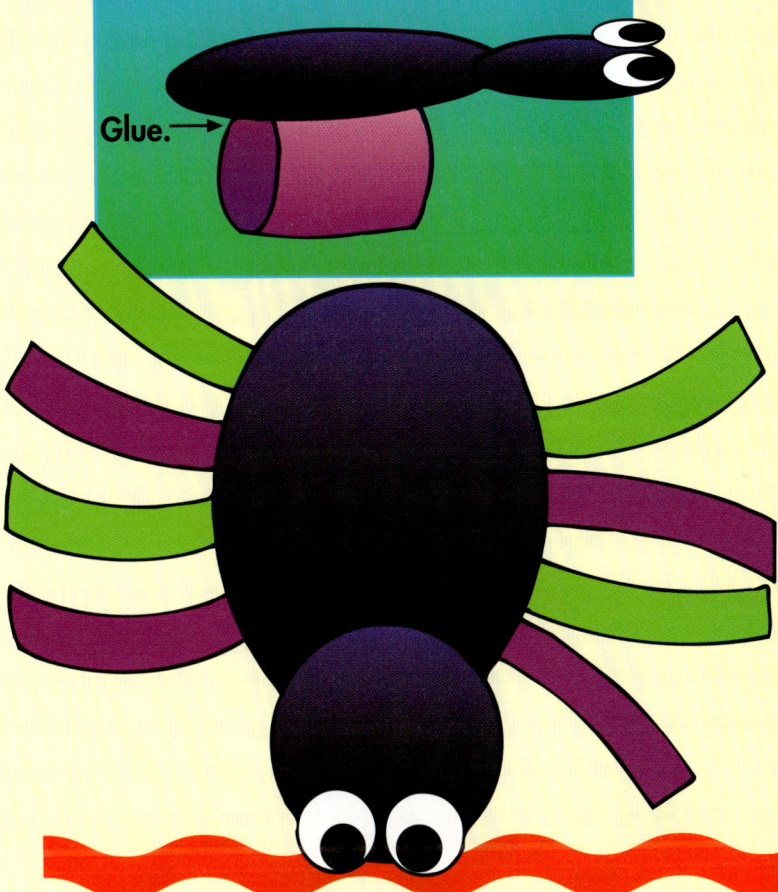

Spider On The Floor
Words and Music by Bill Russell
Illustrated by True Kelley
Published by Crown Books For Young Readers

Bill Russell taught Raffi this silly, spidery rhyming song that will entice even your most reluctant readers. After reading the book aloud, give each child a plastic spider ring or a small pom-pom. As you read the book aloud a second time, have each child move his spider on his own body according to the text.

Pamela Rose, St. Paul Lutheran Preschool, Bonduel, WI

Using Raffi's *Spider On The Wall* is one of the rare times that creepy crawlies will be welcome at storytime! Have each child make a spider from construction-paper pieces and wiggle eyes. Glue a construction-paper loop to the back of each spider to make a finger puppet. Ask each child to bring his finger puppet to storytime and manipulate his spider as you read the story aloud. Afterward ask each child to think of more body parts. Then call out a child's name. Using the format in the book, the child will say, "There's a spider on my [elbow], on my [elbow]." The other children move their spiders to the indicated body part. Then the child who chose that body part says, "But he jumps off!" Call out another child's name, continuing in the same manner until each child has had a turn to choose a body part.

Randalyn Larson—Gr. K, Memorial School,
Jackson, MI

Tales...By Tafuri

Using Nancy Tafuri's Books In Your Classroom

Being an only child until she was ten years old, Nancy Tafuri learned to enjoy her own company by coloring and painting for hours at a time! This love of art followed her into young adulthood when she entered the School of Visual Arts in New York City. "I adored shapes—" says the grown-up Nancy, "big, round, inviting shapes…which I felt would be perfect for the very young." And she was right! Children of all ages love her simple, uncluttered, yet emotionally affecting work. Nancy says that one of life's joys for her is "being able to take short lines of text or, in most cases, none at all and turn them into a package that can be held by small hands." So unwrap a package or two that was created with care—especially for your little ones—by Nancy Tafuri.

Have You Seen My Duckling?
Published by Greenwillow Books

Oh, no—a duckling is missing! Mother Duck and the rest of her brood swim around the pond frantically searching for the missing duckling. Page by page, clever viewers will soon realize that the little duckling really isn't lost at all—just adventuring. After sharing this book with your youngsters, create lots of opportunities for creative writing and sequencing events. Start by mounting a large construction-paper pond on a bulletin board. Then have each child use art materials to make a different character from the story—including the nest. (If you have more students than characters in the book, have some children embellish the pond scene with construction-paper details.) Then read the story again. As each character appears in the story, have a child pin the corresponding character to the board. Encourage children to improvise dialogue for each of the "speechless" characters in the story. Write the dialogue on paper speech bubbles; then mount the bubbles on the board. Add a title and you've got a wonderful display that youngsters can use to tell the story again and again!

Donna Adkins—Gr. K, Perritt Primary, Arkadelphia, AR

Early Morning In The Barn
Published by Greenwillow Books

When the sun comes up, the chicks are off to say "Good morning" to each of the barn's residents. The result? Well, try it in your classroom and see for yourself! As each new sound word is introduced in this book, assign the sound to a child or small group of children. Encourage each child to study her word and remember what it looks like. Then each time you point to that particular word, she can voice the part. Soon you'll have an original barnyard symphony in your classroom! Read the book again, switching parts as desired.

After sharing in a participatory reading of *Early Morning In The Barn* (see above), youngsters will be primed for this story-related reading activity. For each character in the book, cut out a tagboard card. Draw a picture of each animal in the book. Cut out each picture; then glue each picture to the left side of a different tagboard card. Write each animal's corresponding sound word on the right side of the card. Then make a puzzle cut between each picture and word. Store all of the pieces in a string-tie envelope. To do this activity, encourage children to use their reading skills to match each word to an animal picture.

Donna Adkins—Gr. K

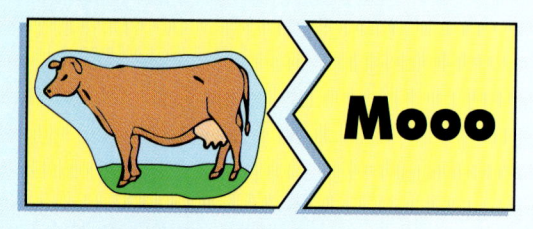

Dig a little further into the farm theme by encouraging students to create a classroom farm in your block area or sand table. Use toy animals, buildings, and people from your classroom collection. If you're short on any items, encourage children to create them using craft supplies. Keep a copy of the book close by so that youngsters can act out the story with their own farm.

Nancy Clements—Pre-K and K, The Children's Center, New York, NY

Who's Counting?
Published by Greenwillow Books

Who's counting? For starters, one curious little puppy! Youngsters can count along as this little puppy pads across the fields and through the barnyard to his final destination. After sharing this book with your students, have each child make a counting book of his own. First give each child ten sheets of paper. Instruct each child to write a different numeral and/or number word from one to ten on each page. Then have each child draw pictures to correspond with the number on each page. (Use rubber stamps for variety.) Bind each child's pages between construction-paper covers; then have him color and title the cover. Encourage each child to share his book during a group reading time.

Adapted from an idea by Samita Arora
Rainbows United, Inc., Wichita, KS

This counting book will be one of your students' favorite reading projects. Choose the numbers that you would like to study (for example, one–ten). For each number, position a child near a given number of objects (such as one hamster, two dress-up hats, etc); then snap a picture. Also take a picture of your entire class. For the last number, take a picture of that many children running; then take another picture of the same number of children playing. Program a sheet of construction paper for each number that you have included in your pictures. On the next-to-last page, write "[Ten] children…" On the last page, write "playing!" Glue the pictures to the corresponding pages and bind them all between two covers. Glue the class picture to the cover. You might even want to laminate this best-seller!

Mary Sutula, Orlando, FL

More Books By Nancy Tafuri
(Greenwillow Books)

All Year Long
The Barn Party
Do Not Disturb
Junglewalk
This Is The Farmer
Follow Me!

Books Illustrated By Nancy Tafuri
(Greenwillow Books)

Flap Your Wings And Try
Written by Charlotte Pomerantz

Asleep, Asleep
Written by Mirra Ginsburg

Across The Stream
Written by Mirra Ginsburg

Rabbit's Morning
Published by Greenwillow Books

When the sun was hot, Rabbit began his journey home. Nancy Tafuri invites the viewer to travel alongside Rabbit. Use this story as a springboard to discussing ordinal numbers and sequence of events. In advance, photocopy each of the animals in the book. (Be sure to include the mouse, hummingbird, opossum, swan, beaver, frog, porcupine, deer, pheasant, raccoon, skunk, and ladybug.) Mount each picture on construction paper. Next, leaving space between each word, write the ordinal number words (first–twelfth) across the board. Then share the story with your children. Afterwards ask children to recall which characters Rabbit saw first, second, third, etc. Mount the characters on the board under the appropriate ordinal number word. (Use the book as a research tool to recall the sequence of events.) Some of the order of events will be left up to class discretion!

Adapted from an idea by Sharon Roop—Gr. K
Slate Hill Elementary, Worthington, OH

Spots, Feathers, And Curly Tails
Published by Greenwillow Books

What causes youngsters' imaginations to kick into gear? Nancy Tafuri's *Spots, Feathers, And Curly Tails!* Before reading, show youngsters the cover of this book. Ask them to think about the title and the illustration to determine the setting of this book. When they have determined that it takes place on a farm, read the book aloud. Encourage youngsters to guess the answers to the text's questions before you turn the pages. Then choose another setting (such as the ocean or the zoo) and have each child think of an appropriate animal. Next give each child a large sheet of construction paper to fold in half. Instruct him to write a question about his animal on the folded side of the paper and illustrate it. Then have him open the paper and draw the entire animal on the inside. Have each child refold his paper and have the class try to guess his animal.

Pfister's Pfabulous Pfriends

Meet Marcus Pfister—author, illustrator, graphic designer, sculptor, painter, and photographer. In addition to his popular Penguin Pete and Hopper series, Pfister has authored two international best-sellers—*The Rainbow Fish* and *The Christmas Star*. It might interest you to know that several of his books are available in French, Spanish, and German. Pfister lives in Berne, Switzerland, with his wife and sons.

From *Penguin Pete and Little Tim* by Marcus Pfister, published by North-South Books, Inc., New York. Copyright ©1994 by Nord-Süd Verlag AG, Gossau Zürich, Switzerland.

Follow Penguin Pete!

The five books in Marcus Pfister's Penguin Pete series are delightful read-alouds for a winter or penguin unit. Introduce your students to the irresistible, big-eyed penguin by reading aloud *Penguin Pete.* Then travel with Pete on an adventurous fishing trip in *Penguin Pete's New Friends.* In *Penguin Pete And Pat,* Pete meets an adorable girl penguin with a blue beak. Pete finds adventure and a new friend in *Penguin Pete, Ahoy!,* but settles down to family life in *Penguin Pete And Little Tim.*

Penguin Facts

In addition to precious art and appealing stories, the books in the Penguin Pete series provide the perfect opportunity for youngsters to learn some fine-feathered facts about penguins. Visually divide a chart into two columns. Label one column "Penguin Facts" and the second column "Book Title." After reading each book aloud, ask students to list the facts about penguins that they deduced from the story. Write the dictated facts on the chart along with the title of the story that provided that information.

Penguin Facts	Book Title
Penguins lay eggs.	Penguin Pete and Pat
Penguins eat fish.	Penguin Pete's New Friends
Penguins swim well.	Penguin Pete, Ahoy!

Penguin Pete And Pat

When yellow-beaked Pete arrives home from his travels with Walter Whale, all of his friends—including a blue-beaked penguin named Pat—greet him. A romance, a wedding, and an egg soon follow. To their surprise, when little Tim is born, he has a green beak! After reading *Penguin Pete And Pat* aloud, give youngsters an opportunity to make unique penguins. To make one, cut a large, black construction-paper oval to represent the penguin's body. Then glue on two smaller ovals to resemble flippers. Next glue a white oval to the penguin's body and two small, white ovals to the top to resemble eyes. Color the eyes with a black marker. Finally add two orange triangles to resemble webbed feet. Blend two primary colors of your choice on a tagboard triangle beak to create a new color; then glue the beak to the penguin project.

Catherine V. Herber—PreK–3, Highland Preschool, Raleigh, NC

The Rainbow Fish

In this enchanting tale, the Rainbow Fish learns about sharing, caring, and the beauty that comes from within. A discussion of these values fits swimmingly with a reading of *The Rainbow Fish*. To extend the beauty of the story, choose from the following suggested activities:

Fancy Fish

These rainbow fish with their shimmering, silver scales will create a dazzling display. To make a rainbow fish, trace a fish onto a colored piece of construction paper; then cut it out. Paint the fish with several colors of tempera paint, swirling and mixing the colors for a unique effect. Sprinkle glitter over the wet paint and press on silver wrapping-paper scales. When dry, mount the fish onto a board along with several bulletin-board-paper waves.

Michelle Allen
Northwest Elementary, Ankeny, IA

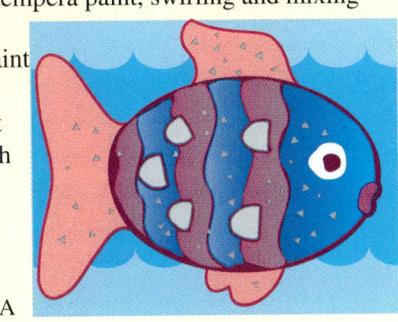

A Song About Sharing

After reading *The Rainbow Fish,* sing the first two verses of the song below. Then ask each child to imagine that he is the Rainbow Fish. Would he share his scales? Why or why not? Follow up the discussion by singing the song again, including the last verse if desired.

(sung to the tune of "The Muffin Man")
Have you heard of the Rainbow Fish,
The Rainbow Fish, the Rainbow Fish?
Have you heard of the Rainbow Fish?
He wouldn't share his scales.

If you were the Rainbow Fish,
The Rainbow Fish, the Rainbow Fish;
If you were the Rainbow Fish,
Would you share your scales?

If I were the Rainbow Fish,
The Rainbow Fish, the Rainbow Fish;
If I were the Rainbow Fish,
YES! I'd share my scales.

Adapted from an idea by Nell Nunn
Special Education
Ferson Creek School
St. Charles, IL

Special Scales

Wouldn't it be special if every child could have a sparkling, silver scale of her own? Before reading *The Rainbow Fish* aloud, safety-pin large sequins to a stuffed-toy fish or fish puppet. (A glittering bluefish puppet is available from Demco's Kids & Things™. Call 1-800-356-1200 and ask for item 171-4525 for the puppet or item 171-5583 for the book and puppet set.) Read the story aloud while animating the puppet; then pin one sequin scale to each child's shirt. These special scales will be a visual reminder to youngsters to share throughout the day.

Keitha-Lynn Stewart
Little Kids Day Care
Sissonville, WV

Creative Sharing

After viewing this cooperative art project, everyone will want to get their hands on *The Rainbow Fish*. Draw a large fish onto white poster board; then cut out the fish. Paint the fins and head of the fish to resemble Pfister's Rainbow Fish, leaving the center of the fish white. Using paint in various shades of blue, green, and purple, have each child press his handprints onto the center of the fish. Be sure to add a foil wrapping-paper scale. When the project is dry, consider displaying it in your school or community library.

Brenda Hume, Summerville, SC

More Pfister Fiction
Published by North-South Books

Hopper
Hopper Hunts For Spring
Hang On, Hopper!

Dazzle The Dinosaur
Chris & Croc
The Christmas Star

From *Penguin Pete and Little Tim* by Marcus Pfister, published by North-South Books, Inc., New York. Copyright ©1994 by Nord-Süd Verlag AG, Gossau Zürich, Switzerland.

Denise Fleming!
Using Denise Fleming's Books In Your Classroom

When you introduce children to a book by Denise Fleming, you're presenting a treat for the eyes *and* the ears. Denise Fleming's books take the reader on a joyous romp through color and concepts. Whether it's a nature lesson, a counting experience, or an introduction to wildlife and seasons, Denise Fleming has created an exhilarating collection of books that beckon to be read aloud.

Photograph by David Powers

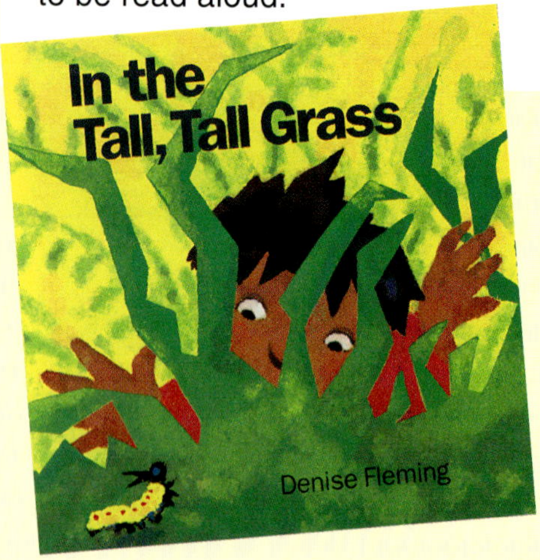

From *In the Tall, Tall Grass* by Denise Fleming; published by Henry Holt and Company, Inc. Copyright ©1991

In The Tall, Tall Grass
Published by Henry Holt And Company

With only a glance, Denise Fleming's bold, bright illustrations draw the reader into this outstanding nature tale. Crawl through the grass with a little caterpillar on a day's journey from sunlight to moonlight. There's a whole world to be discovered—in the tall, tall grass!

After sharing and discussing *In The Tall, Tall Grass,* youngsters will be primed to make these colorful, larger-than-life illustrations. Give each group of four or five students a large sheet of blue butcher paper (about 36" x 36"), a variety of colorful construction paper, and glue. Inspire youngsters to remember what kinds of things the caterpillar saw—or imagine what he *might* have seen—in the tall, tall grass. Then encourage each child in the group to tear and glue to create a minimural. Display each group's finished project along a wall with the title *"In The Tall, Tall Grass."*

Diane Bonica and Kathy Devlin—Gr. K
Charles F. Tigard School, Tigard, OR

Little hands will be immersed in the tall, tall grass with this story extension. In advance, cut a strip of tagboard that measures 2" x 6" for each child. Use a craft knife to cut two small finger holes at the bottom of each strip. Also fringe-cut enough green construction paper to tape to a table edge or bookcase to resemble grass. Then give each child one prepared tagboard strip, and provide a supply of construction paper, crayons, scissors, and glue. Encourage each child to use the art supplies to create a character from *In The Tall, Tall Grass.* Then have each child make a finger puppet by gluing his creature to his tagboard strip, leaving the holes open at the bottom of the strip. As you reread the book's text aloud, have children creep the appropriate characters through the tall, tall grass.

Andrea M. Troisi—Gr. K
La Salle Middle School
Niagara Falls, NY

Environmental studies, rhyming, and creativity all go into the making of this big book. As a class, brainstorm a list of environments around your school. Then "Fleming-ize" each of the listed environments. For example, you might write "In The Busy, Busy City" or "In The Big, Big Field." Then encourage each child to choose one of the environments and to write/dictate text and illustrate a creature(s) or object(s) that might be found in that particular environment. When each page is complete, have children sort their pictures into categories. Bind each category's pages between construction-paper covers; then have each child share her page with the class.

Sheri Dressler—Gr. K
Woodland School, Carpentersville, IL

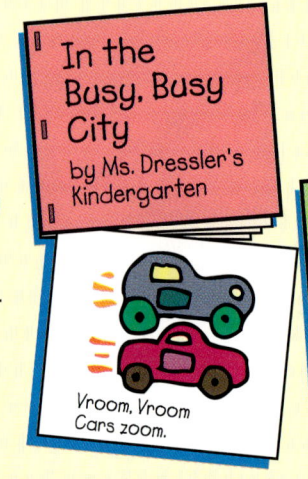

In the Busy, Busy City
by Ms. Dressler's Kindergarten

In the Big, Big Field
by Ms. Dressler's Kindergarten

Vroom, Vroom Cars zoom.

Barry Slate

In The Small, Small Pond
Published by Henry Holt And Company

From the tall, tall grass leaps a bright green frog, who lands right in the middle of springtime in the small, small pond! Denise Fleming's subtle introduction to the seasons gives readers a frog's-eye peek into the life and times in a small, small pond. Jump right in—you'll be glad you did!

Everyone will want to have a big, big part in creating this version of the small, small pond! To prepare for this ongoing class project, cover a bulletin board or wall with white paper. Roughly sketch an outlined cross section of the land, the pond, and the sky. Then have groups of children paint the land and the sky. When the background paint is dry, have children sponge-paint details on the land area. Also provide packing bubbles and blue paint to sponge-paint an interesting effect in the pond! Finish the preparations by mounting a title at the top of the display.

Stock your easel area with a supply of paper and colorful paints. As children visit the area, encourage them to paint any kind of creature that might be seen in the small, small pond. When each painting is dry, have the artist cut out her picture and select a place to staple or tape it to the scene. If desired, you can also create a 3-D effect by gently stuffing plastic grocery bags behind some of the creatures. You'll all be delighted to see the vast amounts of creativity in your small, small pond!

Diane Bonica and Kathy Devlin—Gr. K
Charles F. Tigard Elementary School, Tigard, OR

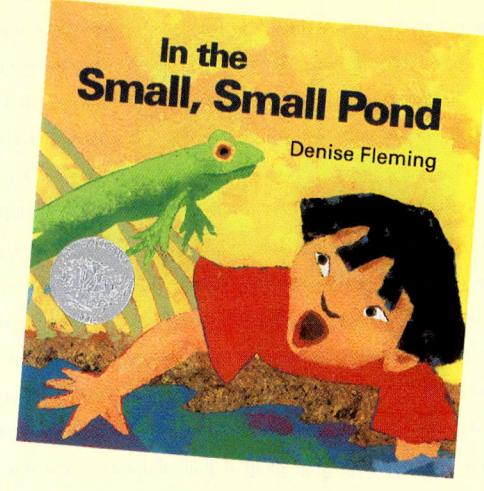

From *In the Small, Small Pond* by Denise Fleming; published by Henry Holt and Company, Inc. Copyright ©1993

After touring the pond with the little green frog in the book, youngsters will be enthusiastic to create a small, small pond in your classroom. Cover the bottom of your water table with clean sand; then add water. Provide a supply of foam meat trays, foam packing pieces, clean milk-carton panels, waterproof paints or paint markers, and scissors. Place all of these supplies near the water table. As children visit the area, encourage them to use the supplies to make animals and plant life that might be found in the small, small pond. Youngsters can use each others' creations to reenact the story or extend the story with plots of their own. Splash, splish; here comes a fish!

Carmen Carpenter—Pre-K
Highland Preschool
Raleigh, NC

Lunch
Published by Scholastic Inc.

This "lunch" is packed with a little, gray mouse who eats his way through an array of colorful fruits and vegetables—and a side order of rich vocabulary words! Just a few bites of this book can reinforce a variety of skills in your hungry learners.

From *Lunch* by Denise Fleming; published by Henry Holt and Company, Inc. Copyright ©1992

After reading and discussing the book with your children, give each child an opportunity to really *indulge* himself in the story! In advance color and/or cut out a picture to represent each of the foods in the book—a turnip, carrots, corn, peas, blueberries, grapes, apples, and watermelon. Mount each picture on a similarly shaped, construction-paper background; then laminate the pictures. Attach a loop of masking tape to the back of each picture. Then use face paint to paint a nose and whiskers on each child. Alternating between groups of eight children, give each child in the group a picture. As you read the text, have each child act out the part that corresponds with the picture he is holding. When each actor's respective part is over, have him press his picture onto his tummy. When the text reads "...he took a nap until...," direct each child to act the part. When you say, "...dinnertime!", have each child crawl off the stage, sniffing for dinner.

Patricia Moeser
University of Wisconsin-Madison
 Preschool Laboratory
Madison, WI

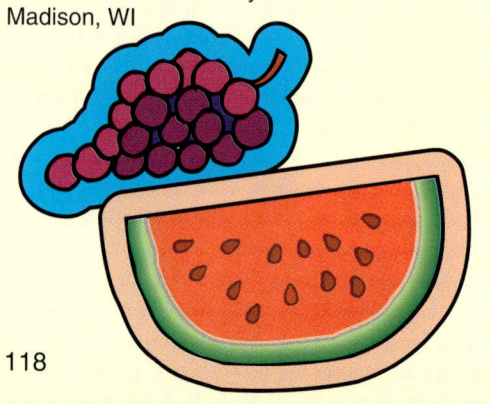

It's only natural that after lunch comes...dinner! So extend the story by writing a sequel entitled *Dinner*. Begin by recalling the types of foods that the mouse ate in *Lunch*. Guide children to determine that the mouse ate vegetables and fruits. Then encourage youngsters to brainstorm a list of foods that the mouse could eat for dinner. Assign each child (or small group of children) one of the foods listed; then encourage him to write/dictate text for and illustrate his page, being sure to include a mouse. Here's the tricky part: When each page is complete, decide on the order in which the mouse will eat the foods. Then challenge each child to color a spot on his mouse to represent the food(s) that the mouse has eaten before he gets to the child's particular food item. (Physically arranging children in sequence helps with this step.) Then bind the pages in order between illustrated construction-paper covers. Have each author/artist share his page during a group reading time.

Joyce Johnson—Gr. K
Bayshore Elementary
Bradenton, FL

With this activity, you'll be munching into math served on a bed of rich language development. Ask each child to bring in an uncut fruit or vegetable from home. On a table or countertop, graph the foods; then discuss the results. Also brainstorm additional ways of sorting the foods (such as by color, size, or shape); then do so. Afterward have each child draw and cut out a picture of the food item that he brought in. Glue each picture/group of pictures on a sheet of chart paper. Then wash and cut up each food item. As children sample each food, encourage them to call out words that describe each food. Write the words next to the respective picture on the chart paper. Follow up this tasting event by gluing a large mouse cutout to a sheet of poster board. In turn, have each child paint on a spot of color to represent his food item. Label the cutout similarly to the picture of the mouse on the last page of *Lunch*. Display the poster in your classroom.

Jennifer Strathdee
Palmer Elementary
Baldwinsville, NY

Barnyard Banter
Published by Henry Holt And Company, Inc.

This exuberant picture book is bursting with so much color, texture, and playful sound that even the most urban dwellers will feel as if they've been down on the farm for a spell. Denise Fleming has created a barnyard masterpiece!

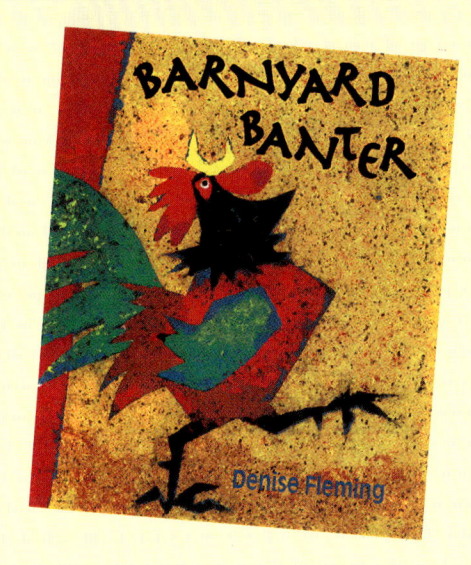

In *Barnyard Banter,* youngsters are introduced to sound words that might be just a little bit different than the sound words they have heard before. After sharing the book, reinforce this new vocabulary by singing the traditional "Old MacDonald" with the sound words from the book. Afterward isolate each of the sound words and discuss the rhyming pairs.

Carmen Carpenter—Pre-K
Highland Preschool, Raleigh, NC

Puzzles! Puzzles!

Your young puzzlers can honk, oink, and moo right along with the engaging *Barnyard Banter* Puzzle For Beginners. Then leap over to a seasonal tour with the big, shaped floor puzzle inspired by *In The Small, Small Pond.* Both of these lively puzzles are available from Briarpatch™ by calling 1-800-232-7427.

From *Barnyard Banter* by Denise Fleming; published by Henry Holt and Company, Inc. Copyright ©1994

Challenge your students to recall one character from the book that is on every page (except one), but never makes a sound. (Revisit the illustrations if necessary.) After children discover the yellow butterfly, encourage them to use position words to describe the butterfly's location on each page. For several consecutive mornings afterward, position a construction-paper butterfly in a different place in your room. When you gather for group time each day, ask who has located the butterfly and encourage children to use position words to guide you to the butterfly.

Jennifer Strathdee, Palmer Elementary, Baldwinsville, NY

This activity brings lots of barnyard noises, as well as emergent reading skills to your classroom. Cut out two tagboard cards for each talkative animal in the story. On one of each pair of cards, glue a cut-out picture of the animal. On the other card in each pair, write the corresponding sound word. (If you have an odd number of children in your class, make more than one card of any given sound to ensure that each child will have a card.) To begin, give each child a card. At your signal, have the children with sound cards make their sounds. Then encourage the children with picture cards to find their matches. When each card has been matched, mix up the cards and play another round. Ready, set,…let the barnyard banter begin!

Patty Welsh Cox—Gr. K
Austin Elementary School, Abilene, TX

Other Books By Denise Fleming

Count!
Published by Henry Holt And Company

Where Once There Was A Wood
Published by Henry Holt And Company

Nancy White Carlstrom

Nancy White Carlstrom has been a children's librarian, a schoolteacher, and the owner of her own bookstore! After the birth of her first child, she devoted her time to mothering and writing. Nancy White Carlstrom's popular *Jesse Bear, What Will You Wear?* had its origins in a song she sang while dressing her young son. When this story was accepted for publication, Carlstrom had already received 82 rejections on other stories! Thanks to her perseverance and dedication, Nancy White Carlstrom has since published numerous books to the delight of her devoted readers!

Who Gets The Sun Out Of Bed?
Illustrated by David McPhail
Published by Little, Brown and Company

"In the cold, dark winter, who gets the sun out of bed?" Not the spruce tree, nor the fire, nor the wind! So *who* gets the sun out of bed? Explore answers to this question with your youngsters prior to reading *Who Gets The Sun Out Of Bed?* Then, after reading the story aloud, have each child make this lazy sun project. Provide each child with a 12" x 18" sheet of construction paper and an eight-inch-square piece of fabric. To make a bed, have the student glue three edges of the fabric to the paper. Then have him glue pieces of tissue paper onto a construction-paper circle (sized to fit under the fabric square) to create a sun. To put the sun to bed, insert it under the open edge of the fabric. Remove the sun to get it out of bed. On his paper, encourage each child to write or dictate a statement telling who gets the sun out of bed. Display the pictures in your classroom windows.

Carmen Carpenter—Pre-K
Highland Preschool
Raleigh, NC

The Moon Came Too
Illustrated by Stella Ormai
Published by Macmillan Publishing Company

A little girl packs all of her treasures in preparation for a trip to her grandma's house. As she shares her favorite things with her grandma, the girl discovers that a very special treasure has come along too. After reading the story aloud, have students prepare this suitcase filled with some of their favorite things. For each child, cut the ends of a folded sheet of 12" x 18" construction paper to resemble handles on a suitcase. From catalogs and magazines, encourage the child to cut out pictures of some of his favorite things, such as toys, clothes, and nature items. Have him glue the pictures on his suitcase cutout to represent a packed bag. Then have the child cut a moon shape from white construction paper. On his moon, assist him as needed in writing "The moon came too." Attach one end of a length of yarn to the child's moon and the other end to his suitcase handle. Fold the suitcase in half, placing the moon inside. On the outside, have each child write his name. Encourage him to show his family the contents of his suitcase as he tells about the story.

Rise And Shine!
Illustrated by Dominic Catalano
Published by HarperCollins Publishers

Invite youngsters to bring to life this delightfully descriptive story about animal activity on a farm. After reading the story aloud, pair students and assign each pair a character from the story (for example, one pair may be roosters and another may be dogs). Then read the story again, this time encouraging each pair of students to listen for its assigned character. When the page with that pair's character is read, have the partners act out the movements and sounds described. For subsequent readings of the story, assign different characters to each pair.

Jesse Bear, What Will You Wear?

Illustrated by Bruce Degen
Published by Simon & Schuster

When asked what he will wear, Jesse Bear has an answer for every occasion. Not only does he wear his clothes; but he also wears his world and experiences. After reading this story, discuss the many things students wear. Include items—other than clothing—that may cover some or all of their bodies, even if only momentarily. For example, suggest that they wear glue during art, bubbles during a bubble-bath, and even a kiss for a very short time!

To extend the discussion, have each student describe the clothes he is wearing. Then provide him with a duplicated sheet of paper programmed with an outline of a bear and "_____ Bear, what will you wear? What will you wear to school? I'll wear my _____ to school." Have the child draw clothing on the bear to resemble his own. Then have him write his name and an article of his clothing on the lines. Place the completed pages between two construction-paper covers, staple them along the left edge, and title the class book "What Will You Wear?" Encourage student partners to read the book together.

Diane Billman—Gr. K
Russell School
Smyrna, GA

Better Not Get Wet, Jesse Bear

Illustrated by Bruce Degen
Published by Macmillan Publishing Company

Youngsters will become immersed in these splashy water stations after hearing this story. In advance, request that parents send swimsuits and towels to school with their children for a day of outdoor water play. On that day, prepare some of these water-activity stations with the suggested materials. Read the story aloud; then have children put on their swimsuits. Rotate small groups of students through each water station. Encourage them to tell about their activities and the materials as they play at each station. With all this water fun, youngsters will be drenched in delight!

- Dishwashing station: a water table, bubble solution, plastic dishes, and cleaning cloths
- Fishing station: a plastic aquarium, colored plastic or foam fish, and fishnets
- Plant-watering station: watering cans, plant sprayers, and real or plastic potted plants
- Birdbath station: a large, shallow dish and plastic or rubber birds
- Mud-puddle station: a tray of dirt, disposable plastic plates for holding the puddles, a pitcher of water, and rubber worms
- Swimming station: a plastic swimming pool, plastic boats, and a float

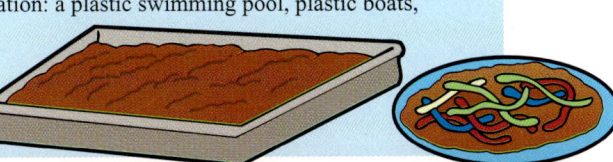

It's About Time, Jesse Bear: And Other Rhymes

Illustrated by Bruce Degen
Published by Macmillan Publishing Company

These Jesse Bear rhymes make perfect discussion-starters revolving around common childhood experiences. As each rhyme is read aloud, encourage students to tell about their own related experiences. If desired, ask them to dictate additional lines to the verse as you write their responses on chart paper. Then, for an extension activity to "Boxes Are Best," create a play center stocked with a few stuffed bears and a large variety of boxes in different shapes and sizes. In turn, have small groups of children play cooperatively in the center. Encourage them to build some of the items named in the rhyme as well as to make their own creations from the boxes.

More From The Carlstrom Collection

Blow Me A Kiss, Miss Lilly
Illustrated by Amy Schwartz
Published by Harper & Row, Publishers

Goodbye Geese
Illustrated by Ed Young
Published by Philomel Books

Northern Lullaby
Illustrated by Leo and Diane Dillon
Published by Philomel Books

(All Published by Macmillan Publishing Company)

How Do You Say It Today, Jesse Bear?
Illustrated by Bruce Degen

Happy Birthday, Jesse Bear!
Illustrated by Bruce Degen

Kiss Your Sister, Rose Marie!
Illustrated by Thor Wickstrom

Wild Wild Sunflower Child Anna
Illustrated by Jerry Pinkney

Kevin's Kids

Your youngsters will just love getting to know the "kids" created by Kevin Henkes. Through the eyes and hearts of characters such as tender Chrysanthemum and imaginative Jessica, Kevin Henkes shares the trials and triumphs of childhood. He approaches his characters with understanding rooted in his own personal and family experiences. With humor and sensitivity, Kevin Henkes generates empathy and affection for all kinds of kids. And—being a kid-at-heart himself—he communicates lessons that will last a lifetime.

Chrysanthemum
Published by Greenwillow Books

Chrysanthemum loved her absolutely perfect name. She loved to hear it, to see it, and to write it. That is—until the first day of school. That's when Chrysanthemum begins to think that her name is absolutely dreadful! It is only through the gentle understanding of a perceptive teacher that Chrysanthemum is able to—once again—blossom!

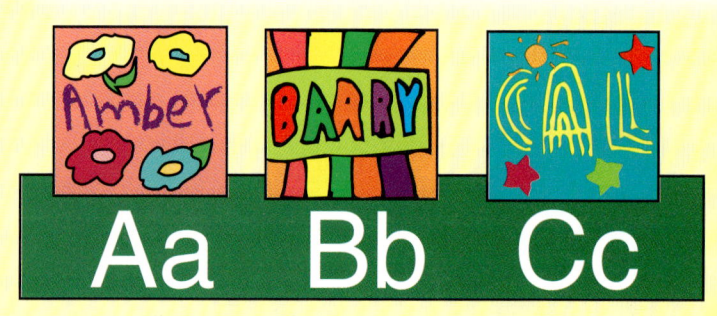

With this activity your youngsters can discover and appreciate the uniqueness of their own names. First write each child's name on a separate slip of paper and place it in a basket. Then read the story aloud. Next write "Chrysanthemum" at the top of a piece of chart paper. Count together the number of letters in that name. Then ask each student to predict whether his own name is longer, shorter, or the same length as Chrysanthemum's. Next pick a name from the basket and write that name on the chart. After the children identify the name, count the letters in it. Encourage youngsters to compare that name to "Chrysanthemum." Periodically continue to pick names and add them to the list so that each child's name is written on the chart. Finally have each child write his name on a sheet of construction paper. Encourage him to embellish his name with his own personal style of art. Display each child's name above the appropriate letter on your classroom alphabet chart. What an *absolutely perfect* display!

Laura Titsch
Public School 171
Long Island City, NY

After examining their own names, encourage youngsters to brainstorm a list of flower names. Write their suggestions on chart paper. Then have each child write his name on a sticky note and place it beside the flower name he would like to have as his own. Extend this activity by having each student create his own unique flower. In advance, cut a supply of colored tissue paper into assorted shapes and sizes. Pour liquid starch into a shallow tray. Cut a sheet of waxed paper for each student. Using a paintbrush, have each child spread the starch onto his waxed paper. Then have him arrange tissue-paper pieces on the starch to resemble a flower. Encourage each child to give his flower a name. When they've dried, frame the flowers with construction-paper strips. Display these one-of-a-kind flowers on your classroom windows for your one-of-a-kind little ones to enjoy.

Nan Hokanson
Sheboygan Falls, WI

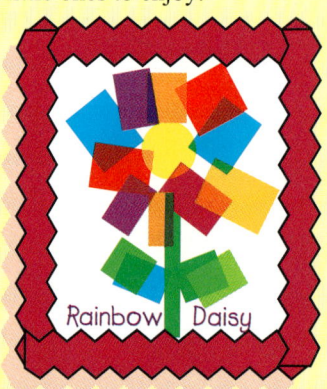

Bailey Goes Camping
Published by Greenwillow Books

Poor Bailey is too little to go camping—too little to join the fun that awaits his privileged older siblings. Then—to brooding Bailey's delight—Mama devises a plan that gives him the camping adventure of his life. After reading this story, have your very own class camping trip! Set up a small tent in the housekeeping area. Place nature items in the science center. Prepare a fishing game to put in another center. In the art area, provide materials to make a leaf-print project. During circle time, perform the rhyme and actions to "Going On A Bear Hunt," and tell silly ghost stories. And—for the finishing touch—have marshmallows for a snack!

Carmen Carpenter, Highland Preschool, Raleigh, NC

Owen
Published by Greenwillow Books

As the first day of school approaches, Owen is told that he cannot take his favorite blanket with him. But he just can't give up his not-so-fuzzy, yellow, go-everywhere, do-everything-with-him friend. After reading this story aloud, encourage youngsters to discuss how Owen feels about giving up his blanket. Find out if any of your students have had similar feelings. Then ask them to name some of their favorite things, and write their responses on chart paper. After discussing the items on the list, encourage each child to draw a picture of himself and his favorite thing. Have him write or dictate a statement about his picture. Display the pictures on a bulletin board titled "A Few Of Our Favorite Things."

Carmen Carpenter, Highland Preschool, Raleigh, NC

A Weekend With Wendell
Published by Greenwillow Books

This tale of a mischievous mouse and his antics during a sleepover weekend will be sure to spark talk and tales alike. After reading the story aloud, find out if your children have been on sleepovers. Encourage them to talk about their experiences. During the discussion, guide youngsters to suggest appropriate and inappropriate behavior for sleepovers. Then have your youngsters make sleepover pillows to serve as reminders for their next overnight stays. To start fold a sheet of 12" x 18" construction paper in half. Staple two sides together to resemble a pillowcase. Then assist each child in writing "When I sleep over, I will…," on her pillowcase. Next—on a sheet of 8 1/2" x 11" paper—encourage her to illustrate her completion to the sentence starter: this will be the pillow. When it's finished, slip the pillow into the pillowcase. Encourage each child to take her pillow home and place it in her suitcase. The next time she packs for a sleepover, she will find her pillow with useful reminders already packed.

Cathy Collier, Southeastern Elementary, Chesapeake, VA

Jessica
Published by Greenwillow Books

Jessica, Ruthie's imaginary friend, goes everywhere and does everything with Ruthie. When Ruthie goes to kindergarten, Jessica goes right along with her. Then Ruthie discovers a new friend in a most surprising way. Prepare ahead of time to make these hide-and-seek pictures as a follow-up activity to this book. First make a class supply of picture frames. To make one, fold a sheet of 9" x 12" construction paper in half once, then again. Then—starting at the long folded edge—cut 3/4 inch from each side so that the middle section of the paper can be removed. Unfold the paper and it will look like a double frame. To make the "glass" for the frame, cut a 9-inch length of 11 3/4-inch wide, colored plastic wrap. Fold the plastic wrap in half. Placing the folded side of the plastic wrap along one edge of the frame, glue it in place over the opening. Then glue along the edges of the other side of the frame and fold it over the wrap. Trim away any excess plastic wrap. With a permanent marker, write "My Best Friend" on the plastic wrap. Place the frame aside until the story has been read. As you read the book, ask your children to look carefully for Jessica on each page. Engage them in a discussion about imaginary and real friends. Then give each student half of a 9" x 12" sheet of white construction paper. Using a crayon the same color as the plastic wrap in the frame, encourage each child to draw a picture of his best friend—real or imaginary. When each picture is completed, place a frame over it. Staple along the top edge. Your youngsters will have great fun lifting the frames to reveal their best friends.

More Books By Kevin Henkes
Published by Greenwillow Books

Chester's Way

Grandpa & Bo

Julius, The Baby Of The World

Once Around The Block

Sheila Rae, The Brave

SHHHH

The Biggest Boy
(Illustrated by Nancy Tafuri)

Math Units

Math Masquerade!
Ideas To Develop Number Sense

Who: You and your students!
What: An exciting math masquerade filled with fun and learning opportunities.
When: Any time of the year.
Why: It's learning in disguise.
Where: Right in your own classroom.

Ring-A-Ling

If you're looking for a mathematical twist to cue your students to come to circle time, give this idea a ring. In advance, instruct students that when they hear you ring a bell, they are to listen carefully to the number of times it rings and then gather together at the circle-time area. When the students are seated, ask them how many times you rang the bell. This method not only gets your youngsters to circle time quickly, but also helps them practice counting skills.

Carol Willian—Gr. K
Strode Station Elementary
Winchester, KY

Photo Opportunities

Your youngsters are the stars in this classroom-made counting book. Choose a designated background such as playground equipment, a bulletin board, or an attractive outdoor setting. To make a counting book, photograph the designated area without children in the picture to represent the number zero. Then photograph one student in the same area to represent the number one. Continue in this manner until you have reached a desired number. Then mount each picture in numerical order on a separate sheet of construction paper. Label each page with the corresponding number word and numeral. Laminate the pages if desired. Bind the pages together and place the book in the math center for little ones to enjoy. For variety, coordinate the scenery with a particular theme. (You can also separate the pages and use them for sequencing activities.)

Mary S. Sutula
Orlando, FL

M&M's® Counting Book

"Pour out the candies. Get ready, get set. This counting book is the tastiest yet!" After reading aloud *The M&M's® Brand Chocolate Candies Counting Book* by Barbara Barbieri McGrath (Charlesbridge Publishing), try this sweet idea. Give each child a package of M&M's® and a white paper plate. Reread the book, and have each child use his candies to follow the directions on each page—even the directions about eating! Then instruct your little ones to set the candy wrapper aside for later.

For a fun follow-up, have each child make his own counting book. To make a book, provide each child with 12 sheets of paper. Have each youngster draw and color one candy on a sheet of paper; then write the numeral *one* (and the number word, if desired) under his drawing. Then have him draw and color two candies on another sheet; then write the numeral *two* under the drawing. Have each child continue in this manner until he has completed pages to the numeral *ten*. Instruct each student to stack the sheets in numerical order. Then place the sheets between the two additional sheets of paper and staple the pages together. Program the cover of each book with "My M&M's® Counting Book," and glue the empty candy wrapper to the cover.

Adapted from an idea by Samita Arora—Pre-K
Rainbows United, Inc.
Wichita, KS

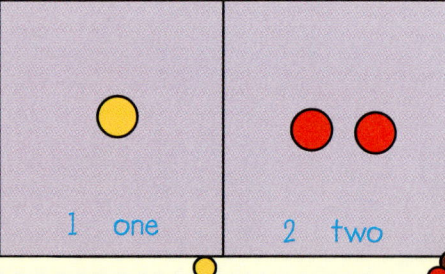

Patterns, Patterns, Patterns!

Help your little ones develop that all-important skill of patterning with the creative suggestions in this unit.

Pattern Talk

To begin this unit, point out simple patterns in the classroom, such as a pattern on a shirt or a repeated bulletin-board border pattern. Or model a repeated pattern using classroom supplies. Then brainstorm with your youngsters about different patterns that they know about. Write, as they dictate or point out, examples of different patterns. Guide the discussion so that youngsters can think about things in their everyday lives that repeat. For example, encourage students to think about patterns such as the days of the week, months of the year, and seasons.

Twinkling Lights

This festive idea will light up some holiday cheer in your classroom. Bring several strings of Christmas lights from home. Unscrew each bulb from the socket and mix the bulbs together. Seat youngsters in small groups on a rug. Provide each small group with a cord and bulbs. Have each group sort the bulbs by color; then use the bulbs to make a pattern. Ask each group to "read" their pattern to the other groups. Assist each group in replacing the bulbs in the sockets, making their color pattern. Then plug in each string of lights, turn off the classroom lights, and watch the color patterns light up your room. As an extension, ask students to bring in other holiday items such as gift wrap, stockings, candy, and plastic ornaments to use for patterning.

Lorrie Hartnett—Pre-K, Tom Green Elementary, Buda, TX

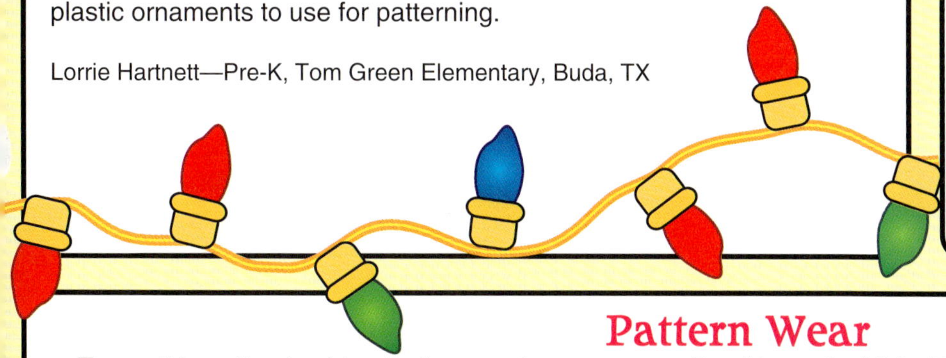

Fruit Kabobs

Here's a fun patterning idea that your little ones will really eat up! Supply each child with a plastic knife and assorted fruits such as orange, apple, and pear slices; grapes, and bananas. Have him cut up the fruit into chunks. Then provide each student with a wooden skewer and have him use the fruit chunks to create a fruit kabob, making a patterned design. After sharing their patterns with the class, allow your youngsters to eat their patterns!

Terri Whitaker—Gr. K, Barrington Place, Sugar Land, TX
Lynn Sanders—Gr. K, Hayes Elementary, Kennesaw, GA

Pattern Wear

Try on this patterning idea that youngsters can wear. Provide each child with a sentence strip and assorted construction-paper shape cutouts or assorted small objects such as buttons and pasta. Have each student glue the shape cutouts and/or objects to the sentence strip, making the pattern design of his choice. Fit each child's sentence strip around his waist to make a belt, or around his head to make a headband; then staple it. There you have it—pattern wear!

Terri Whitaker—Gr. K
Kelly A. Wong, Berlyn School, Ontario, CA

Moving Patterns

Get your little ones moving when doing this patterning activity. Start by showing your students two different actions. For example, you might touch your nose, then clap your hands; then repeat the actions. Have your students imitate you several times. Then add a third action. Have them repeat the group of actions several times; then add a fourth action to the pattern. Next ask for student volunteers to make up their own action patterns for the rest of the class to imitate. As a variation, do the actions to music.

E-I-E-I-O

You'll hear echoes of animal sounds with this center that resembles Old McDonald's farm. Write "Old McDonald's Farm" on a barn-shaped cutout; then glue the cutout to the top of a pencil box. Next use animal stamps or stickers to make animal-print patterns on construction-paper strips. Place the strips in the pencil box. To use this center, a child chooses a strip from the box, and from left to right makes the sound of each animal on the strip. Then he guesses the sound that would come next in the pattern.

Lisa Mascheri
Midway Elementary
Sanford, FL

moooo

Stegosaurus Patterning

Make no bones about it—this dinosaur center is a ton of fun. Cut out a large stegosaurus shape (without the spikes). From different-colored construction paper or wallpaper, cut out triangle-shaped spikes. To use this center, a child places the spikes in a pattern design on the dinosaur.

Charlene Pasker Carroll—Gr. K
Joseph Keels Elementary School
Columbia, SC

Musical Patterns

During circle time, have each student choose an instrument. Pair each child with another child who has a different instrument; then instruct each pair to invent their own musical pattern. Allow each pair to share their musical pattern with the rest of the class. As a variation, have your class sit in a circle with their instruments and use several instruments to make musical patterns.

Amy Allen and Lorraine Bennett
Cypress Creek Elementary
Ruskin, FL

Lining Up In Patterns

For a different method of lining up your youngsters, try this idea. Have your students get in line using a specific pattern. For example, you may have them get in line by using a boy, girl, boy, girl pattern. Or you may have youngsters get in line by distinctions in clothing such as color or type. Encourage your youngsters to think of different patterns each time you have them get in line.

Kelly A. Wong
Berlyn School
Ontario, CA

What Comes Next?

Encourage free exploration and discovery at this open-ended center. Stock a center with sentence strips and a supply of small items such as buttons, toothpicks, jug lids, paper clips, coins, and stickers. To use this center, a child arranges some of the items on a sentence strip to make the pattern design of his choice. Then encourage each youngster to share his pattern with a classmate and ask, "What comes next?"

Jug Lids

Students will flip their lids when using this nifty activity. In advance collect a large quantity of different-colored jug lids and the same colors of dot stickers. Arrange the dots on tagboard strips in different-colored patterns. Place the pattern strips and the lids in a center. To use the center, have a youngster choose a tagboard strip and use the lids to make the same pattern. Vary this activity by making pattern strips that require youngsters to "fill in the blanks" with the appropriate colors of lids.

Rachel Meseke Castro
Juneau Elementary School
Juneau, WI

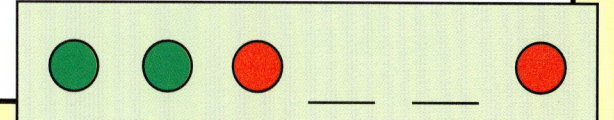

Circle-Time Fun

Have your little ones form a circle for this activity. Instruct each student in the circle to do a specific action to make a pattern. For example, you may instruct them to do a stand, stand, kneel pattern. Then have your youngsters verbalize the pattern they see. Repeat this activity several times, having them act out a different pattern each time. Then arrange half of your youngsters in a smaller circle. Have the group use their bodies to cooperatively make up their own pattern and have the rest of the class verbalize the pattern. Then give the other group an opportunity to do the same activity.

GRAPHING GALORE!

There's a whole lot of math—and more—packed into this assortment of teacher-recommended graphing ideas. Use these suggestions to reinforce skills such as collecting, organizing, displaying, and interpreting information.

REAL GRAPHS

PEANUT GRAPH

Your little ones will go nuts over this graphing activity. Place a large bowl of unshelled peanuts on a table. Ask each child to predict how many peanuts he can hold in one hand. Then, in turn, have each child take one handful of peanuts from the bowl. Have each youngster count his peanuts and compare the actual number to his prediction. Then instruct each student to align his peanuts in a designated spot. Have your youngsters examine the resulting graph and discuss which student(s) has the most, the least, or the same number of peanuts.

Adapted from an idea by Mary F. Philip—Gr. K
Relay Children's Center
Baltimore, MD

WHAT'S YOUR FAVORITE APPLE?

This "apple-tizing" tasting-and-graphing activity compares different types of apples and your youngsters' preferences. Provide a classroom supply of three different types of apples such as McIntosh, Granny Smith, and Golden Delicious. Label a large tabletop graph with each type of apple. Next slice pieces from each type of apple; then place the apple pieces in labeled bowls. Arrange the remaining apples behind the corresponding bowls. Then have each child taste each type of apple and decide which she likes best. Instruct her to choose an apple that represents her choice. Have each child place her chosen apple in the correct column on the graph. What's the most popular apple in *your* classroom?

Adapted from an idea by Alyson Wiecek—Gr. K
Levi Leonard Elementary School
Evansville, WI

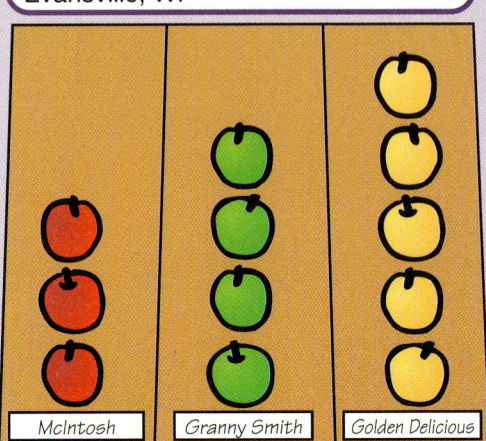

SNEAKIN' AROUND

Designate one day to be Sneaker Day. Instruct youngsters to wear sneakers on that specific day. Encourage each child to examine his sneakers to determine how they are held on his feet. Do they have Velcro® ties or shoelaces; or are they slip-ons? Label a large graph or a tiled floor with the different types of sneakers. Then have each child estimate how many shoes will be in each category. Next instruct each youngster to remove one of his sneakers and place it in the correct column on the graph. Discuss what the graph reveals. Did the results sneak up on you?

Adapted from an idea by Cindy Snyder—Gr. K
McGaughey Elementary
Mt. Zion, IL

SKITTLES®

Predicting, estimating, and comparing are just a few of the skills involved in this sweet graphing idea. For each small group of students, create a graph with a row for each of the colors found in a bag of Skittles® candy. Provide each group with a bag of Skittles®. Ask each child in the group to predict which color will appear most often. Have students pour the candies onto a paper plate and sort them according to color. Then have them place the candies on the graphs in the corresponding columns. Discuss what is revealed on each group's graph. And, of course, you'll have to have some unhandled candies for taste-testing!

YES OR NO?

Your youngsters and their opinions are the main ingredients in this spare-minute graphing activity. In advance, write the words "yes" and "no" at the top of a long, vertical strip of bulletin-board paper. For each child, glue footprint cutouts in both columns; then laminate the graph. When you have a spare minute or two, pose a yes-or-no question to your students such as "Do you like olives?" or "Did you eat cereal for breakfast?" After asking students the question, have them line up in the column of their choice. Chorally count each child in the two columns; then discuss the results. After your students become familiar with this activity, encourage them to generate their own yes-or-no questions.

Anita Ortiz—Gr. K
Red Sandstone Elementary
Vail, CO

SOUP'S ON!

Keep stirring up those graphing skills with this idea that's "Mmm, mmm, good!" Have each child bring a can of his favorite soup to school. Assist youngsters in sorting the different kinds of soup. Then label a large graph with the name of each soup and a picture cue. Have each student place his favorite soup in the appropriate place on the graph. Ask questions such as "Which column has the most cans?", "Which column has the least?", and "Are there any columns that have the same number?" As a follow-up activity, heat a few cans of the best-liked soups for your little ones to sample!

Kaye Sowell—Gr. K
Pelahatchie Elementary School
Pelahatchie, MS

PICTURE GRAPHS

LOOK WHAT'S POPPIN'!

This motivating graphing activity involves lots of tasting! First display several flavors of popcorn such as cheese, caramel, butter, and plain. Ask students to predict which flavor of popcorn will be liked best by the class. Next have each child taste a few pieces of each type of popcorn. Encourage him to choose a favorite flavor. Then give each child a white construction-paper popcorn cutout. Have him write his name on his popcorn, then color it to resemble his favorite flavor (for example, you could use orange to represent cheese, brown for caramel, yellow for butter, and white for plain). Label a graph with the different flavors of popcorn. Then have each child place his popcorn cutout in the appropriate row. Count the cutouts in each row. Then compare the results with youngsters' predictions.

Belinda Holland—Gr. K
Alamo Elementary
Fort Stockton, TX

WHAT'S FOR LUNCH?

"What would you like for lunch?" is the question asked of your students when doing this graphing activity. In advance photocopy each student's class photograph, or take a Polaroid® picture of each child. Attach the loop side of a piece of Velcro® to the back of each picture; then attach the hook side to a wall (or bulletin board) at students' eye level. Label the wall with the daily lunch choices and picture cues. (It works well to bind pictures of your rotating lunch choices on a metal ring. Then each day you can simply flip to the appropriate picture.) Then have each child place his picture in the column that represents his lunch choice. After determining which lunch is most popular on a specific day, ask other questions such as "What is David having for lunch today?"

Dana Gorman—Gr. K
North Mianus
Riverside, CT

HAPPY BIRTHDAY!

This teaching display doubles as a year-round room decoration. For each child, cut a large birthday-hat shape from colorful construction paper. Have each child personalize his hat and write his birthdate on it. Next encourage each child to decorate his hat as desired. Then program 12 tagboard strips with different months of the year. Mount the months on a wall; then assist each child in taping his hat above the appropriate month. When all of the hats are in place, ask your youngsters questions such as "In what month were the most people born?", "Who has a summer birthday?", and "Who has a winter birthday?" Leave the birthday chart on display all year. Happy birthday to you!

Amy Pritchett
Allen Day Elementary
High Point, NC

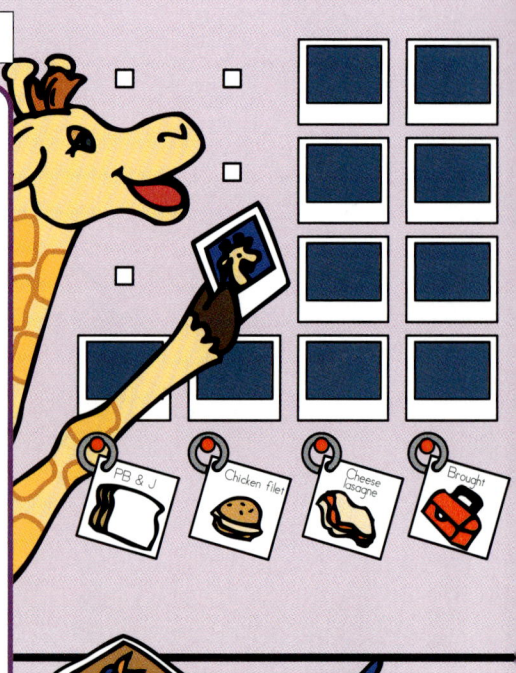

Spring	Summer	Fall	Winter

MY FAVORITE CENTER

Since youngsters typically have a few centers that they enjoy visiting more than others, why not put it to a vote? Write the name of each center on the chalkboard; then draw a picture cue next to each center's name. Give each student a white paper plate and crayons. On the plate, have each student copy the name of his favorite center and draw a picture of that center. Then collect the plates. While youngsters are not in the classroom, tape each plate above the corresponding label on the chalkboard. When youngsters return to your room, reveal the graph results. This graph will give you helpful information in determining which centers hold the most interest for your students.

Lois Maxam—Gr. K

TREES FOR ALL SEASONS

Winter, spring, summer, or fall—what's your favorite season of all? To do this activity, reproduce the tree pattern (page 135) for each child on construction paper. Ask each student to think about his favorite season and what a tree might look like during that season. Provide each child with craft items such as crayons, glue, tissue-paper pieces, paint, markers, and construction paper. Have each child cut out the tree pattern along the bold outline; then have him use the craft materials to create a tree to match his favorite season. Label a wall or bulletin board with the four seasons. After the pictures are dry, have each child mount his picture in the appropriate column. Discuss the graph results; then allow each student to share what his favorite season is and why.

Susan Brown—Gr. K
Southside Elementary
Tuscumbia, AL

ONCE UPON A TIME

This graphing activity will hold lots of mystery and intrigue. As you end a thematic unit, have your class vote on their favorite theme-related book. Display the books used during the unit on a table or chalkboard ledge for youngsters to examine. Ask youngsters to predict which story will be the class favorite. Then provide each child with a sheet of construction paper, and have him draw a picture that represents his favorite story (for example, if his favorite story during a bear unit was *Goldilocks And The Three Bears,* he might draw three bears). Have each child personalize his picture; then collect the pictures and secretly tabulate the pictures on a graph. At the end of the day, reveal the graph's results. Surprise!

Lois Maxam—Gr. K
Berry School
San Diego, CA

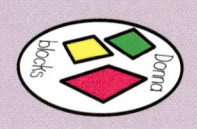

133

SYMBOLIC GRAPHS

SOURCES OF LIGHT

This bright idea integrates science and math. Send home a copy of the graph on page 136 with each child. Instruct each student to take the graph home to complete with a family member. Have each student graph the different sources of light in their home. Encourage each child to return his graph to share with the rest of the class. If you're really industrious, you could combine all of the information on the individual graphs to make a large class graph of light sources!

Kelly A. Wong
Berlyn School
Ontario, CA

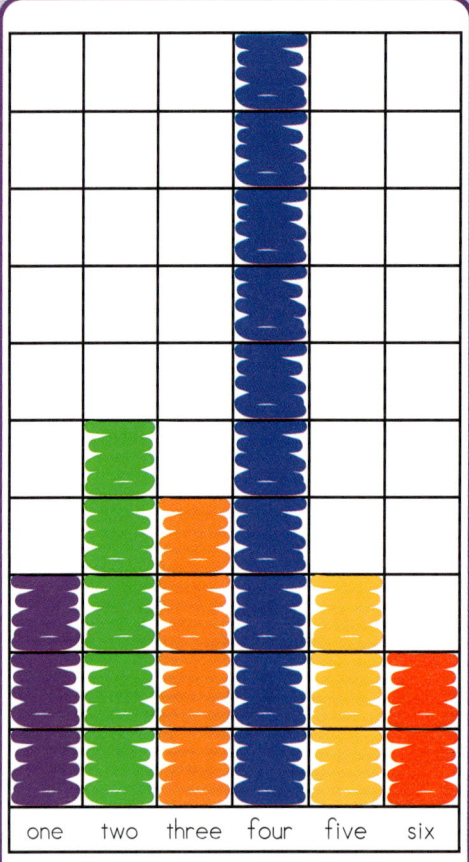

READY, SET, ROLL

Review counting and graphing with a roll of the die. Draw a grid on a sheet of white paper and label it with numerals from one to six. Photocopy a classroom supply of the graph. Place the graphs, crayons, a plastic cup, and a die in a center. To do this activity, a child places the die in the cup, shakes the cup, and rolls the die on the table. He then colors a square in the column above the numeral rolled on the die. For example, if he rolls a three, he colors a square in the "three" column. Have him continue in this manner until one column is completely filled. Ready, set, roll!

Wendy Svenstrup
St. Mary's Pre-school
Lafayette, IN

A TRAVELING BOOK OF GRAPHS

Make a book of class graphs for your little ones to take home and share with their family members. To make a book, draw a graph on a sheet of white paper. Photocopy a supply of the graphs to use each time you have a topic to graph. For example, you might graph students' favorite characters from books, vacation plans, etc. First label a copy of the graph with the choices. Students then mark their choices in a variety of ways. For example, on one graph you might have each student make a thumbprint in the appropriate place. On other graphs you might have children write their initials, glue their pictures, or attach stickers. When you have a collection of graphs, bind them together to make a book. Send the book home with one student each day to share with her family.

Sharon Pasqua—Gr. K
Camino Grove School
Arcadia, CA

Tree Pattern
Use with "Trees For All Seasons" on page 133.

©1996 The Education Center, Inc.

©The Education Center, Inc. • THE MAILBOX® • Kindergarten • April/May 1996

Name _____

SOURCES OF LIGHT GRAPH

9						
8						
7						
6						
5						
4						
3						
2						
1						
	windows	lightbulbs	lamps	flashlights	candles	other

Dear Parent,
   Help your child find all the sources of light you can at your house. Color how many of each kind you have on this graph. What kind of light does your family have the most of? What other kinds of light did you find? Which rooms had the most light? Which rooms had the least light? Please return the graph to school when completed.

                                                            Thank you,

©The Education Center, Inc. • THE MAILBOX® • Kindergarten • April/May 1996

Note To Teacher: Use with "Sources Of Light" on page 134.

Science Units

Wonders Never Cease

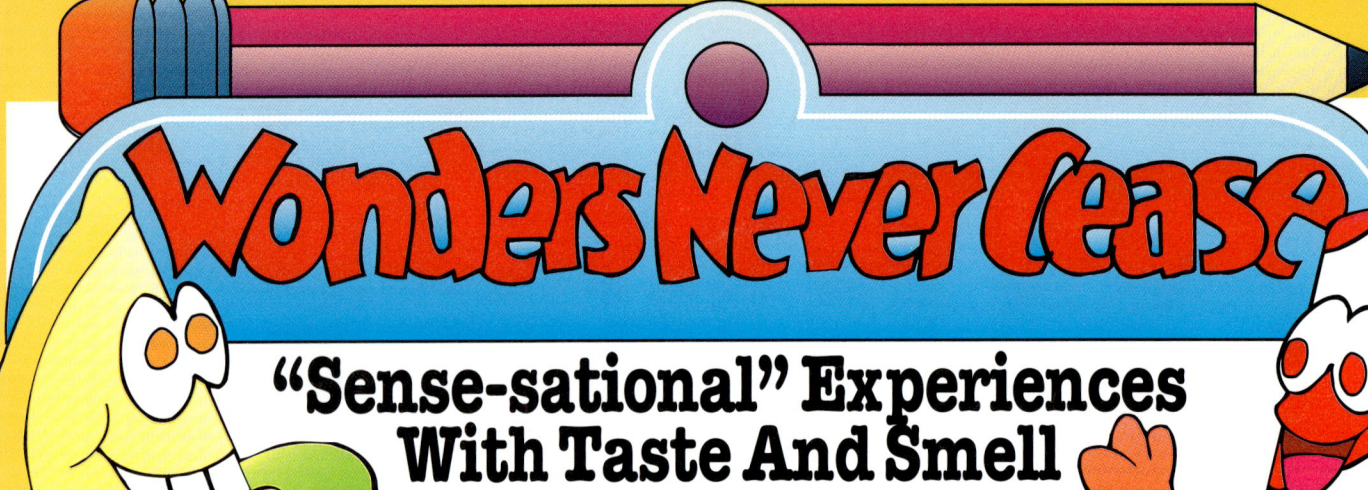

"Sense-sational" Experiences With Taste And Smell

Encourage your little ones to explore their senses of taste and smell with these activities that promote specific hands-on learning, and also provide limitless discovery opportunities.

by Marie Iannetti

What sense, aside from taste, do we need to taste food? Why? Write youngsters' responses on chart paper.

Experience 1
Potato Or Apple?

For each small group, you will need:
a raw apple (peeled and finely shredded on a plate)
a raw potato (peeled and finely shredded on a plate)
a nose clip
a blindfold
spoons
a pitcher of water
paper cups

Guided Discovery
Have each child take a turn being blindfolded and wearing a nose clip. Ask another child to place a small amount of the potato or apple on a spoon; then have the blindfolded child taste it. Next have him rinse his mouth with water and repeat the activity with the untasted food. Then repeat the activity **without** the use of the nose clip.

Science Circle Discussion Questions:
- Were you able to taste the foods when you wore the blindfold and the nose clip?
- How did each food taste?
- Were you able to taste the foods when you wore only the blindfold? Why?

What We Know
Our sense of taste is greatly affected by our sense of smell because our nasal passages lead to the tongue. Taste and smell are so closely linked that, when we taste food, it is really a combination of both senses. Some experts think that 80 percent of taste is due to smell. When we are unable to smell, it affects our ability to taste.

Variation
Have students repeat the activity using Coke® and 7-Up® in the taste test.

What do you do when you want to get a better smell of something? Why?
Write youngsters' responses on chart paper.

Experience 2
Only The Nose Knows!

For each small group, you will need:
several pieces of gauze
several baby-food jars (or small, lidded containers)
spray paint (optional)
scented items such as those listed below

Preparation:
Make smelly jars by collecting scented items such as peanut butter, onion, coffee, peppermint extract, orange peels, pickles, perfume, lemon juice, and cinnamon. Wrap a small portion of each item in a different piece of gauze and place it in a jar. Secure the lid on the jar. Cut out or draw pictures of each scented item; then color-code each jar and the back of the corresponding picture for self-checking. (Jars may be spray-painted to make them opaque, if desired.)

Guided Discovery
In turn, have each child open one jar at a time and smell its contents. Then have youngsters collaborate to match each jar to a corresponding picture. (Use the color-coding for self-checking.)

Science Circle Discussion Questions:
- Were you able to identify each jar's contents without seeing it? How?
- If you couldn't identify a smell right away, what did you do? Why?

What We Know
If you want to smell something in more detail, you sniff it. Sniffing brings more of the odor into the nose and closer to the organs of smell.

138

Extension Activities

Scented Pictures

Have your youngsters try this fragrant piece of artwork. To begin, mix 1/2 cup of cold water with a flavored gelatin mix. Use this mixture to paint a picture of the fruit that matches the flavor (or the design of your choice). When the painting is dry, use watercolor markers to add additional details. Display these masterpieces for a gallery that—for a while, anyway—smells as good as it looks.

Debby DePauw, Lincoln School, Rochelle, IL

Science Journals

Have your little ones make science journals to record their discoveries. Have each child color and personalize her journal cover. Place a supply of blank paper between the decorated cover and a construction-paper back cover; then staple the journal. When doing science-related activities, have students record and illustrate their observations in their journals.

Double The Scents

Create a page like the one shown to the right for each child. Fill in the blank with the word "Smell." Dip pairs of cotton balls in different extracts such as almond, vanilla, lemon, peppermint, and butterscotch. Place each cotton ball into a different film canister; then snap on the lid. Arrange the canisters in a center. To do this activity, a child removes the lid from each canister, smells its contents, and matches it with the corresponding canister. In each box, have each child draw an item that he smelled, then write/dictate a sentence under each picture.

Taste Table

Stock a table with various salty, sweet, sour, and bitter foods. Encourage your youngsters to taste each of the foods. Create a page like the one shown below for each child. Fill in the blank with the word "Taste." In each box, have each child draw a food that he tasted, then write/dictate a sentence under each picture.

Taste It!

Have a tasting party and serve unusual foods such as kiwifruits, dates, mangoes, avocados, artichokes, or other foods youngsters might not have tasted before.

Related Books

Taste by Mandy Suhr (Carolrhoda Books, Inc.)
Sense Suspense by Bruce McMillan (Scholastic Inc.)
Tasting by Henry Pluckrose (Franklin Watts Limited)
My Five Senses by Aliki (HarperCollins Publishers)

Wonders Never Cease

"Sense-sational" Experiences With The Sense Of Touch

Your little ones will explore the sense of touch with these tactile experiences.

Question:
Do you think hot and cold can affect our sense of touch? Why? Write youngsters' responses on chart paper.

Experience 1
Is It Hot Or Cold?

For each small group, you will need:
a cup of warm water
a cup of cold water
a cup of room-temperature water
ice cubes
one blue stick-on dot
one red stick-on dot

Preparation:
Place a blue dot on the cup of cold water and a red dot on the cup of warm water. Add one or two ice cubes to the cup of cold water.

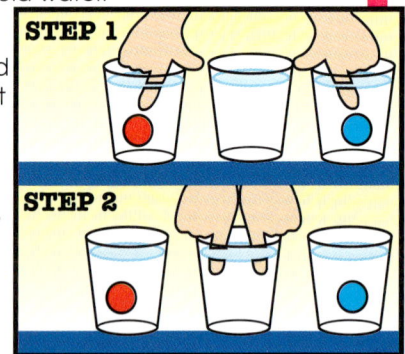

Guided Discovery:
In turn, have each child simultaneously dip his right index finger in the warm water and his left index finger in the cold water. Have him leave his fingers in the water for a minute or two. Then have him dip both fingers in the room-temperature water.

Science Circle Discussion Questions:
- How did your right finger feel when you dipped it into the room-temperature water?
- How did your left finger feel when you dipped it into the room-temperature water?
- Why do you think this happened?

What We Know:
The feeling in our fingertips is very sensitive because touch receptors are gathered very closely together on the tips of our fingers. Since the right finger was in the warm water for a time, it adjusted to the warm water, and when placed in the room-temperature water, it felt cold. Because the left finger was in the cold water for a time, it adjusted to the cold water, and when placed in the room-temperature water, it felt warm.

Question:
Can you match items just by using your sense of touch? How? Write youngsters' responses on chart paper.

Experience 2
Touch And Tell!

For each small group, you will need:
two cardboard boxes with lids
textured items such as those listed below

Preparation:
Collect two samples each of a variety of textured items such as cotton, velvet, sandpaper, burlap, foil, fur, and corduroy. Place one of each item in each of the boxes. Cut a hole in each box lid large enough for a child's hand to fit through; then place the lids on the boxes.

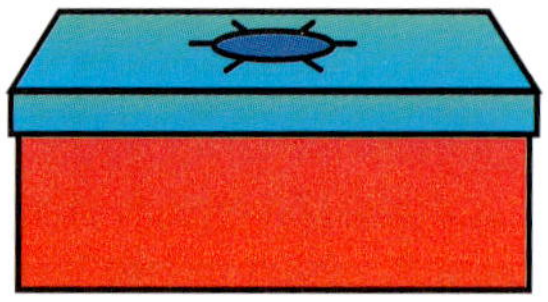

Guided Discovery:
In turn, have each child place one hand through the hole in one of the boxes and locate a texture, then pull it out of the box. Have him place his hand in the other box and locate the matching texture.

Science Circle Discovery Questions:
- Were you able to identify each texture without seeing it? How?
- How were the textures the same or different?

What We Know:
Since nerve endings in our fingertips are sensitive, they help us identify things by touching. They help us distinguish textures such as smooth, rough, silky, soft, or hard.

Extension Activities

A "Please Touch" Display

Have each child bring one to five items from home that have various textures. For example, he may bring ribbon, burlap, yarn, packing materials, cotton, or sandpaper. Attach the items to a large piece of poster board; then place it in a learning center for your youngsters to touch. Encourage students to use words such as smooth, rough, silky, bumpy, soft, and hard to describe the items. Vary the activity by having students classify the items by texture before attaching them to the poster board.

Center For Touching

Two senses are better than one, and you can prove it with this learning center. Cut out 10 or 12 tagboard cards. On each pair of cards, glue identical designs of yarn patterns. Display half of the cards, and stack the other half facedown. Place one card from the stack in a box, bag, or other container. To use this center, a student reaches inside the container without looking, feels the tactile pattern on the card, and indicates the matching card on display. Verify his guess by placing the card from the container beside the display version. Continue in this manner, placing another card in the container.

Texture Rubbings

Provide your students with various textured items such as coins, leaves, shoes with textured soles, textured wallpaper, and sandpaper letters and shapes. Have each student choose several different textured items. Then have him place a sheet of newsprint on the items and use the side of a crayon to repeatedly rub across the items. Display these terrific texture rubbings on a wall or bulletin board.

Related Books

Is It Rough? Is It Smooth? Is It Shiny?
Written & Illustrated by Tana Hoban
Published by Greenwillow Books

Sense Suspense: A Guessing Game For The Five Senses
Written & Photographed by Bruce McMillan
Published by Scholastic Inc.

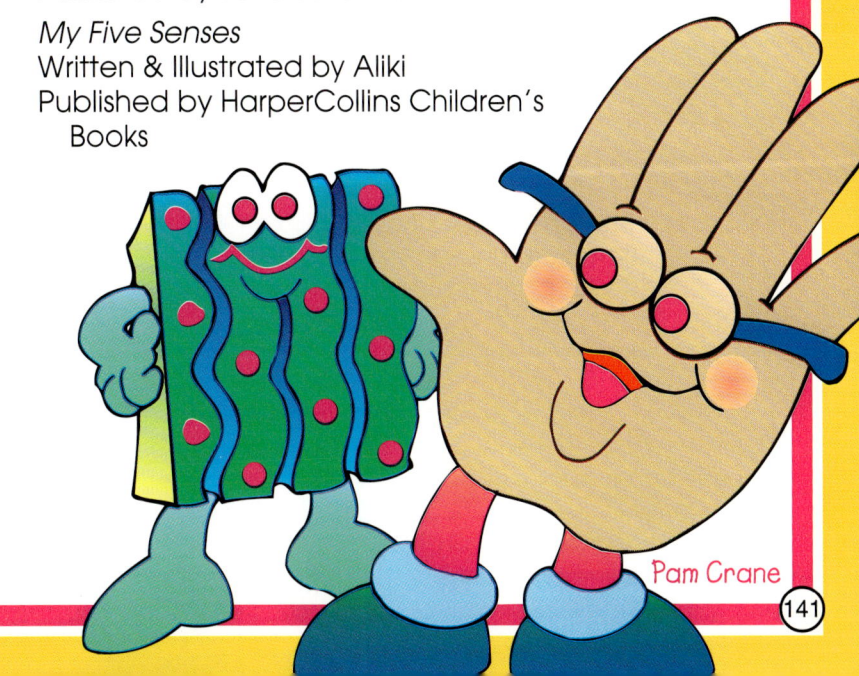

My Five Senses
Written & Illustrated by Aliki
Published by HarperCollins Children's Books

Pam Crane

Wonders Never Cease

"Sense-sational" Experiences With Hearing

Entice your little ones to explore their sense of hearing with these hands-on activities. Sound good?

by Marie Iannetti

How do you think a sound is made? Write youngsters' responses on chart paper.

Experience 1
Good Vibrations

Guided Discovery
Have each child lightly place his fingers on his throat. Instruct each student to make sounds such as whispering, humming, coughing, talking, singing, and growling. Then pair students, and have each child take a turn placing his fingers lightly on his partner's throat and repeating the activity. Discuss with your class that when they make sounds, their vocal cords move back and forth very fast. That back-and-forth movement is called a *vibration*.

Science Circle Discussion Questions:
- Did each sound produce the same vibrations?
- What were the differences in the vibrations?
- Was there a difference in vibrations when you touched your partner's throat? If so, what was the difference?

What We Know
Every sound is produced by vibrations. When we sing, talk, cough, whisper, hum, or growl, air is pushed from our lungs over our vocal cords. The air that flows over our vocal cords makes them vibrate or shake, and this produces sounds.

Can you see vibrations? Write youngsters' responses on chart paper.

Experience 2
Dancing Rice

For each small group, you will need:
a coffee can or plastic bowl
a rubber band
a sheet of plastic wrap—a little bigger than the top of the can or bowl
a spoon
a spoonful of uncooked rice
tape

Preparation:
Make a drum by stretching the plastic wrap over the top of the can/bowl and securing it tightly with the rubber band. Tape the edges of the plastic wrap to the can/bowl so that the wrap remains taut.

Guided Discovery
Have one child in each group sprinkle some rice on the top of the drum. Instruct another student to use the spoon to tap the top or side of the drum. Have your students carefully examine what happens. Then have another child repeat the activity, tapping slightly harder on the drum.

Science Circle Discussion Questions:
- What happened to the rice? Why?
- What happened when the drum was tapped harder?

What We Know
We can see the rice move and bounce on the drum because the plastic wrap is vibrating. Sometimes we can see vibrations or the effects of vibrations.

Extension Activities

What's That Sound?
Make an audiotape of different sounds such as a dog barking, a telephone ringing, a clock ticking, or dripping water. Draw or cut out a picture that corresponds with each sound; then mount each picture on a different sheet of construction paper. Mount the pictures on a wall at students' eye level. Have students listen as you play the sounds one at a time. Then have them match each sound to the corresponding picture. As a follow-up activity, brainstorm a list of sounds that students hear in the classroom, at home, and outside.

Ticktock
Set a loud-ticking alarm clock to ring in three minutes. Have your youngsters cover their eyes as you hide the clock in the classroom. Then ask students to use their sense of hearing to locate the clock. If they are unable to find the clock, the alarm will sound, alerting them to its specific location. Ticktock—where's the clock?

Shake, Shake, Shake!
Partially fill two empty film canisters with rice, two with paper clips, two with buttons, and two with pennies. Color-code the bottom of each canister for self-checking if desired. Place the eight canisters on a table. Have a small group of students take turns shaking the canisters and matching the pairs of canisters that sound alike.

Sound Detectors
Stock a center with pie pans, paper cups, empty cans, and boxes. Also provide several rubber bands of different thicknesses. Have your students place one or more rubber bands around the items and pluck the rubber band(s). Encourage youngsters to experiment with making high-pitched and low sounds.

Read All About It!
Set up a reading corner in your classroom with sound-related books such as the following:

Oh, What A Noisy Farm! by Harriet Ziefert (Tambourine Books)
Through Grandpa's Eyes by Patricia MacLachlan (HarperCollins Children's Books)
SHHHH! by Suzy Kline (Albert Whitman & Company)
Georgia Music by Helen V. Griffith (Greenwillow Books)
The Orchestra by Mark Rubin (Firefly Books, Ltd.)
The Noise Lullaby by Jacqueline K. Ogburn (Lothrop, Lee & Shepard Books)

Wonders Never Cease

"Sense-sational" Experiences With The Sense Of Sight

Have your little ones take a look at the sense of sight with these eye-opening experiences.

Question:
Do you suppose that two eyes see better than one? Why or why not? Write youngsters' responses on chart paper.

Experience 1
One Eye Or Two?

For each pair of students, you will need:
a tagboard square with holes punched around the border
a shoelace
a stopwatch or a watch with a second hand
an eye patch

Guided Discovery:
Have one child in a student pair wear the eye patch, then try to thread the shoelace through the holes. Instruct the other child in the pair to time her partner. After noting the time, have the child repeat the activity *with both eyes open.* Then have the students switch roles.

Science Circle Discussion Questions:
- Was there a difference between sewing the card with both eyes open and sewing it with one eye shut? If so, why?
- Was there a difference in the time? If so, why?

What We Know:
Seeing with two eyes is called *binocular vision.* Each eye sees things slightly differently than the other. When we look at an image with two eyes, our brains combine the information we receive from each eye. With two eyes, we learn a little bit more about that image than we would learn with just one eye.

Question:
What do you think happens to the pupil (the black part) of your eye when you are in a dimly lit room? How about in bright light? Write youngsters' responses on chart paper.

Experience 2
A Wide-Eyed Activity

Guided Discovery:
Have student pairs stand in a darkened area of your room. Instruct each child to examine his partner's pupils. Then have both children move outside on a sunny day or to a brightly lit area of your classroom. Once again, have each child examine his partner's pupils.

Science Circle Discussion Questions:
- What happened to your partner's pupils in the dark? In the light?
- Why do you think the size changed?

What We Know:
The pupil is an opening. The iris (the colored part of your eye) has muscles that control the size of your pupil. In bright light, the pupil gets smaller to protect your eye from too much light. In dim light, the pupil gets bigger so that we have enough light to see.

Extension Activities

No Peeking
Inspire your little ones to appreciate their sense of sight. Have each child sit in front of a large sheet of construction paper and crayons. Instruct each child to close her eyes and try to draw a picture. As children work, ask them questions to guide them in thinking about how the loss of sight is affecting their tasks. After several minutes, have your students open their eyes and look at their drawings. Discuss how your youngsters felt during and after this activity.

Guess Who?
During circle time, describe a specific student's appearance. For example, you might describe the color of someone's hair and eyes, the type of clothing he is wearing, and any other physical characteristics about him. Using their sense of sight, have the other students identify the student. Did you guess who?

Look Around!
Use this activity to walk into in*sight*ful awareness. Begin by giving each of your students (or small groups) a magnifying glass. Then set out on a walk around the campus. Encourage each child to use the magnifying glass to examine items along the way. When you return to your classroom, find out what students saw this time that they hadn't ever seen before. For a variation, repeat the activity using several pairs of binoculars.

Each Peach Pear Plum
Each Peach Pear Plum by Janet and Allan Ahlberg (Scholastic Inc.) is a treat for the eyes. First read the book aloud without showing the pictures. Then re-read it, asking youngsters to use their sense of sight to find the specified character on each page. Then discuss the difference between just hearing the story, and hearing and seeing the story. Extend this activity by playing a game of I Spy.

Pam Crane

Wonders Never Cease

The "Sense-sational" Sensory Fair

Come one, come all to the Sensory Fair! Invite youngsters and their parents to explore and review the senses with these hands-on activities. Your classroom will be a place for fun and discovery with a classroom Sensory Fair.

by Marie Iannetti

Setting Up And Getting Ready

Send a completed copy of the parent note (page 150) home with each child. To prepare your classroom for the Sensory Fair, decorate with items such as balloons, crepe paper, and banners. To the front door of the room, tape a sign that reads "The Sensory Fair." Set up an area in your room for each activity in this unit. Display a sign near each center identifying the sense or senses used in that activity. Mount step-by-step directions at each area. Discuss the directions with your class. On the day of the fair, have students escort their parents as they visit each area.

Sight

Seeing is believing with this activity. Place a supply of small blocks and blindfolds in a center. Have students and parents visiting this center alternate wearing the blindfolds. Using the blocks, have each person attempt to build a tower. Then have them remove their blindfolds and build a tower with the use of their eyesight. Have them discuss the differences in both versions.

Your little ones will be wide-eyed when they examine the real importance of the sense of sight. Cut several eyeglass-frame shapes from double thicknesses of construction paper. Glue waxed paper between each pair of construction-paper frames so that the waxed paper covers each of the lens areas. Have each child and parent visiting the center alternate wearing a pair of these glasses while attempting to do a task such as putting a puzzle together or tying a shoelace. Then have him remove his glasses and discuss the activity with the other member of his group.

Hearing

Before parents and students visit this area, have a volunteer hide several familiar rhythm instruments behind a draped table. Have the volunteer play one instrument at a time, without displaying it. Encourage parents and students to use their sense of hearing to identify each instrument.

Naming that sound will be the object of this "sound-sational" idea. Place a tape player in a corner of your room with a tape of recorded sounds such as a door slamming, a bell ringing, water trickling, a vacuum cleaner sweeping, a telephone ringing, or a balloon bursting. Display an answer sheet nearby for parents' use. To use this center, encourage students and parents to use their sense of hearing to identify each sound.

Taste

Set up a tasting table in your room. Fill each of several paper plates with a different type of food such as salted popcorn, salted crackers, unsweetened chocolate, lemon slices, sour pickles, cookies, and marshmallows. Provide a duplicated supply of the reproducible on page 151. Have the visitors in the center taste each food and describe how it tastes. Then instruct them to draw a picture of each of the foods in the corresponding box.

It's the battle of the soft drinks! Challenge your little ones and their caregivers to use their sense of taste to tell them apart. Label the bottoms of some paper cups with "cola" and some with "diet cola." Fill each cup halfway with the corresponding cola. Have the participants at this center take a sip of the cola, then a sip of the diet cola. Ask if they can tell which is which.

147

Pam Crane

Touch

This center is a touch-and-match activity. Fill brown paper bags with several pairs of objects such as paper clips, dice, marbles, crayons, buttons, and milk-jug lids. Place the bags on a table at a center. To use this center—without looking in the bags— the participants touch the objects in the bags. Using their sense of touch, they try to find matching objects. When they think they have found a match, they take the objects out to check. Placing each pair of objects on the table, they continue in this manner until all of the matching pairs have been identified.

Touch and tell is the name of the game at this center. Cut a hole—large enough for a hand to fit through—in the bottom of a box. Then gather a supply of items with interesting textures such as a banana, an orange, uncooked pasta, cooked spaghetti, a walnut, and a chilled canned soft drink. Place these items in an opaque bag. To do this activity, have the parent stand the box on end with the open end facing away from the child. Next have the parent (secretly) place one of the items in the box. Then instruct the child to insert his hand through the hole and feel the object. Encourage him to use his sense of touch to identify the object. Have the parent and child continue in this manner until all of the objects have been guessed.

Smell

In advance, collect a variety of scented items such as coffee grains, perfume, onion, lemon, soap, peanut butter, and cinnamon. Wrap a small portion of each item or a sample on a cotton ball in a piece of gauze, and place it in an opaque container with a lid. Label the bottom of each container with its contents. Place the containers in a center. To use this center, have an adult lift the lid from a container and hold the container under the child's nose. Without looking, have the child smell the contents of each container and guess what it is.

Have the participants in this center make a scented picture. Stock a center with dark-colored construction paper and a variety of different scented soaps. To use the center, the participants use the soap to draw the design of their choice on the construction paper. Mmm...can you smell it?

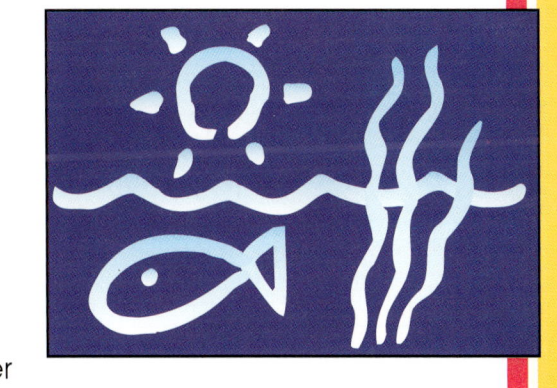

Invite parents and children to make a scented potpourri sachet at this center. Stock a center with a large bag of potpourri, net, rulers, scissors, gold wired ribbon, and rubber bands. To make a sachet, have parents assist each student in cutting a 14-inch circle of net. Have each child place a portion of potpourri in the center of the net. Have him gather the net around the potpourri and secure the top with a rubber band. Tie a length of gold wired ribbon around the rubber band; then tie a bow.

Parent Note
Use with "Setting Up And Getting Ready" on page 146.

Dear Parent,
   Our class has been learning about the five senses. You are invited to a Sensory Fair on _____ at _____.
                                                       (date)   (time)

We'd like you to participate with us in some fun sensory activities and see what we have learned!

Hope to see you there!

_____
(teacher)

©The Education Center, Inc. • THE MAILBOX® • Kindergarten • June/July 1996

Dear Parent,
   Our class has been learning about the five senses. You are invited to a Sensory Fair on _____ at _____.
                                                       (date)   (time)

We'd like you to participate with us in some fun sensory activities and see what we have learned!

Hope to see you there!

_____
(teacher)

©The Education Center, Inc. • THE MAILBOX® • Kindergarten • June/July 1996

Name _____

Sweet

Sour

Salty

Bitter

©The Education Center, Inc. • THE MAILBOX® • Kindergarten • June/July 1996

Note To The Teacher: Use with the first tasting activity on page 147

Multicultural Units

Journey To Germany

Entice youngsters with this child-sized peek into the fascinating country of Germany. As you study, you'll learn about the birthplace of many famous fairy tales, listen to some of Germany's famous composers, make a cuckoo clock and more. So come along—the journey has just begun!

by Elizabeth Trautman

Same And Different

As you and your young explorers investigate Germany, you'll find that there are many similarities between this European country and the United States. There are also a few very interesting differences. Keep track of your findings along the way by making a comparison chart to fill in as your students make appropriate discoveries. Write "Germany" at the top of a large sheet of chart paper. Visually divide the paper into two columns. Label one side "Same," and the other side "Different." Then encourage youngsters to browse through German magazines (available at local newsstands) and books about Germany such as *Enchantment Of The World: Germany* by Jim Hargrove (Childrens Press®). Guide children to verbalize the things that they notice and discuss whether they are similar to or different from your area of the country. Record students' observations on the chart. As you continue to study Germany, use this chart to record additional discoveries.

Germany

same	different
• clothes	• language
• buildings	• castles
• cars	• money
• people	
• sports	

Flying Proudly

Child-made German flags will add a regional flair to your Germany display and provide a meaningful opportunity to reinforce directional concepts. Give each child a white sheet of construction paper and paints, crayons, or colored pencils of black, red, and gold. Assist each child in visually dividing his paper into three equal, horizontal sections. Have each child color/paint the top section black, the middle section red, and the bottom section gold. In addition to displaying some of the finished flags in your Germany display area, mount a few of them onto your classroom windows and doors so passersby will know that you are studying Germany. Who knows what interesting tidbits someone else might be able to contribute to your studies!

Let's Speak German!

Since children are often intrigued by other languages, let them try out a few German words and phrases. Write the words on a large Germany-shaped cutout and post the cutout in your German display area. After introducing the words, encourage both children and adults to use them throughout your study of Germany. *Wunderbar!*

Guten Morgen—Good morning
Guten Tag—Good day
Bitte—Please
Danke—Thank you
Ja—Yes
Nein—No
Auf Wiedersehen—Good-bye
Kinder—children
Wunderbar—wonderful

one	eins
two	zwei
three	drei
four	vier
five	fünf
six	sechs
seven	sieben
eight	acht
nine	neun
ten	zehn

Schwarzwald
The Black Forest

Inspire youngsters to imagine the settings of some of the best-loved fairy tales as you or students tell stories such as *Snow White, Little Red Riding Hood,* and *Sleeping Beauty.* Encourage children to discuss what they think some of the scenes might have looked like. Then explain that although fairy tales are make-believe, many of the stories originated in a real place in Germany. Many of the stories were first told in the depths of the richly wooded *Schwarzwald*—German for "Black Forest." After this discussion, stock your art center with paper, shallow pans of paint, paintbrushes, and various sponge shapes. As each child visits the center, have her use the supplies to create a painting of what she thinks the Black Forest might look like. Enhance your Germany display area with the completed scenes and several fairy-tale books.

Cuckoo Clocks

Nestled along the streams and rivers of The Black Forest are little manufacturing towns. It is in those little towns that cuckoo clocks are made! Youngsters will pop up at the chance to make their own cuckoo clocks. To make one clock:

- Photocopy the patterns (page 168)) on construction paper. Use construction-paper cutouts, colored pencils, and crayons to decorate the clock, cuckoo, and weights (pinecone shapes) as desired; then cut them out.

- On a 3 1/2" construction-paper circle, write numerals to resemble a clock face. Glue the clock face onto the clock.

- Cut out two construction-paper clock hands and use a brad to attach them to the center of the clock face.

- Punch two holes in the bottom of the clock. Thread a length of string through the holes and tape each end of the string to a different weight.

- Make a support for the cuckoo by crisscrossing two 4" x 1/2" strips of paper as shown. Then glue one end of the support onto the clock and the other end onto the cuckoo.

After each child has made a cuckoo clock, read aloud *The Cuckoo-Clock Cuckoo* by Annegert Fuchshuber. As you read, have each child manipulate his clock to match the clock faces in the book. When each child's clock is "set," have children chorally "cuckoo" the appropriate number of times.

Worldwide Cuisine

Many world-famous foods and dishes originated in the German culture. Two such foods are hot dogs and sauerkraut! Sauerkraut was developed many years ago to keep cabbage from spoiling. Use the recipe below to make a mild-tasting sauerkraut; then have a hot dog and sauerkraut feast in your classroom!

Sauerkraut

Ingredients:
1 large head of cabbage
5 tsp. salt

Remove the outer leaves from the cabbage head. Cut out the core; then cut the cabbage into large chunks. Grate the cabbage. Put the cabbage into a large bowl and sprinkle it with the salt. Mix the cabbage and salt with your hands. Pack the cabbage *tightly* into glass baby-food jars. Set the lids *very loosely* on the jars. Place all of the jars in a baking pan to catch the juice drippings. After about seven to ten days, taste the sauerkraut. When the salty taste has diminished, it's ready to eat!

Music, Music, Music!

Music is a great tradition both in Germany's history and its present-day culture. Three of the most well-known German composers are Johann Sebastian Bach, Ludwig van Beethoven, and Robert Schumann. Introduce your students to these great masters by listening to pieces by each of the composers. *Hey, Ludwig!* is an especially lively collection of warm-hearted, energetic piano solos including works by Bach, Beethoven, and Schumann. It is available from Music For Little People at 1-800-727-2233.

155

Jolly Olde England

Introduce your young explorers to a land that has been called the birthplace of American culture. Use the following activities to see the sights, celebrate afternoon tea, sample children's literature, and more. Who knows? England might jolly well be your cup of tea!

ideas by Elizabeth Trautman

I Say, Old Chap!

Although English is the official language of England, there is a bit of difference between the English spoken in England and American English. Find out if your students know anyone who is originally from England. (Encourage children to think also of television and/or movie personalities such as Mary Poppins.) Then ask youngsters to tell you if they hear anything different in the way the English people speak. See if they can identify what the difference is. Then talk about the word *accent* and encourage youngsters to share when they discover someone else who has an English accent. (Some good examples include the narrator on "Pooh Corner" and the characters on "Jim Henson's Mother Goose Stories"—both on the Disney Channel—and Scar from *The Lion King*.) Perhaps your youngsters would like to work on crafting English accents of their own!

What A Sight!

Since you probably won't be taking your class on a field trip to England, try the next best thing to being there! Visit England's great capital city of London through Roxie Munroe's *The Inside-Outside Book Of London* (check your local library). With each turn of the page, your youngsters will travel from outside one of London's famous sights to a view from the inside of that sight. Acting as a travel guide, be sure to point out facts of interest (noted on the last page of the book) as you visit each of the sights. Ask children to describe and comment on what they see on each page. Find out if any of your students have seen similar sights in their lifetimes. Then compare the sights of London to the sights in your town/city. For example, how do the buses in your town compare to those seen on Regent Street?

Note: If *The Inside-Outside Book Of London* is not available, try using the pictures from *Living In London* by Anna Sproule or *London* by James E. Davis and Sharryl Davis Hawke.

What's The Word?

After being introduced to various English accents (see "I Say, Old Chap"), youngsters will be interested to learn some of the differences found in England's vocabulary. Write each pair of words from the list below on a piece of tagboard. Then draw or cut out a picture to represent each of the word pairs. Glue the picture to the tagboard. Share these picture cards with your students; then encourage them to use this new vocabulary during your study of England. Pip-pip! Cheerio!

England	United States
biscuits	cookies
bobby	police officer
bonnet	car hood
boot	car trunk
cheerio	good-bye
chips	french fries
crisps	potato chips
dustman	garbage collector
lift	elevator
lorry	truck
petrol	gasoline
sweets	candy
wireless	radio
on holiday	on vacation

London Bridge Is...What?

You heard right—London Bridge *was* falling down many, many years ago! After singing and playing the traditional "London Bridge," inform your students that London Bridge is one of 15 bridges that span the River Thames (pronounced *Temz*) in London. Over the years, London Bridge has been replaced and/or rebuilt several times. Encourage your youngsters to get a feel for bridge-building by creating a London-like scene in your block area. Using blue cloth or bulletin-board paper, create a winding river on the floor. In addition to blocks, stock the center with pieces of sturdy poster board, scissors, tape, craft sticks, and glue. Encourage youngsters to use the materials provided to make bridges across the river. If your youngsters get really ambitious, they might even like to construct some of the famous London sights (see "What A Sight!").

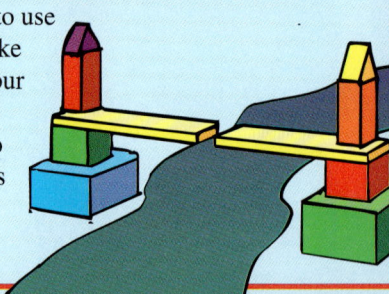

Get Out! Get Out!

One of England's special features is the royalty that has been a part of its history for centuries. Much of children's literature weaves the royal family into its storylines. One such story is Audrey and Don Wood's *King Bidgood's In The Bathtub* (Harcourt Brace Jovanovich, Publishers). Share this playful tale with your youngsters. After discussing the story, ask each child to imagine that he has been asked to help summon the king from his royal bathe. Have each child write about and illustrate how he would coax the king. Then bind all of the pages between covers entitled "Get Out! Get Out, Your Majesty!" Have each child share his page during a group reading time.

Setting Sail

If your study of England is taking place in November, seize the opportunity to discuss the Pilgrims and their journey to America. Using a world map, locate Plymouth on the southwest coast of England and what is now Plymouth in Massachusetts. Explain that the Pilgrims set sail in *The Mayflower* from Plymouth, England; then encourage youngsters to trace a possible route that the Pilgrims may have taken to reach the New World. Discuss the long journey and the hardships that the Pilgrims endured on their trip.

Follow up your discussion by making a bulletin board to remind students of this historical pilgrimage. Mount a construction-paper England and an America shape on a blue background. Duplicate the ship pattern (page 169) on construction paper for each child. Have each child cut out his ship, then create sails and masts from art supplies such as pipe cleaners, craft sticks, and construction paper. Then ask each child to write (or dictate) on a separate sheet of paper what he would hope to find in the New World. Attach his paper to the bottom of his ship; then mount them on a bulletin board entitled "Setting Sail."

If I sailed to a new country, I hope they would have soccer and the hot kind of gum.
Sammy

Teatime!

Teatime is a famous English tradition. People who have the time pause around 4 P.M. every day for a cup of tea and a snack. Find out what your students and their families are doing at this time of day. Discuss why this tradition may not be as popular in the United States. Then bring the English tradition right into your classroom! In advance, follow the recipe below and have each child participate in making a classroom batch of scones. Then choose an afternoon to celebrate an early-bird teatime. Serve tea and the class-made scones with jam. Mmmm… won't you join me for a cuppa?

Scones

1 1/2 cups flour
1/2 stick butter, softened
1/2 cup sugar
1/2 cup milk

Put flour and butter in a large bowl. Using a knife, cut the butter into small pieces. Then use your fingers to combine the mixture until it is crumbly. Add sugar and milk, and mix well with a spoon. Chill the dough for two hours or more. Then roll the dough into two-inch balls. Place the balls on a greased cookie sheet. Flatten the balls slightly with your hands or a large, greased spoon. Bake for 12 minutes at 450°.

Related Literature

The Big Concrete Lorry by Shirley Hughes
Published by Lothrop, Lee & Shepard Books

The King At The Door by Brock Cole
Published by Doubleday & Company, Inc.

London Bridge Is Falling Down! by Peter Spier
Published by Doubleday & Company, Inc.

Madeline In London by Ludwig Bemelmans
Published by Puffin Books

Norway

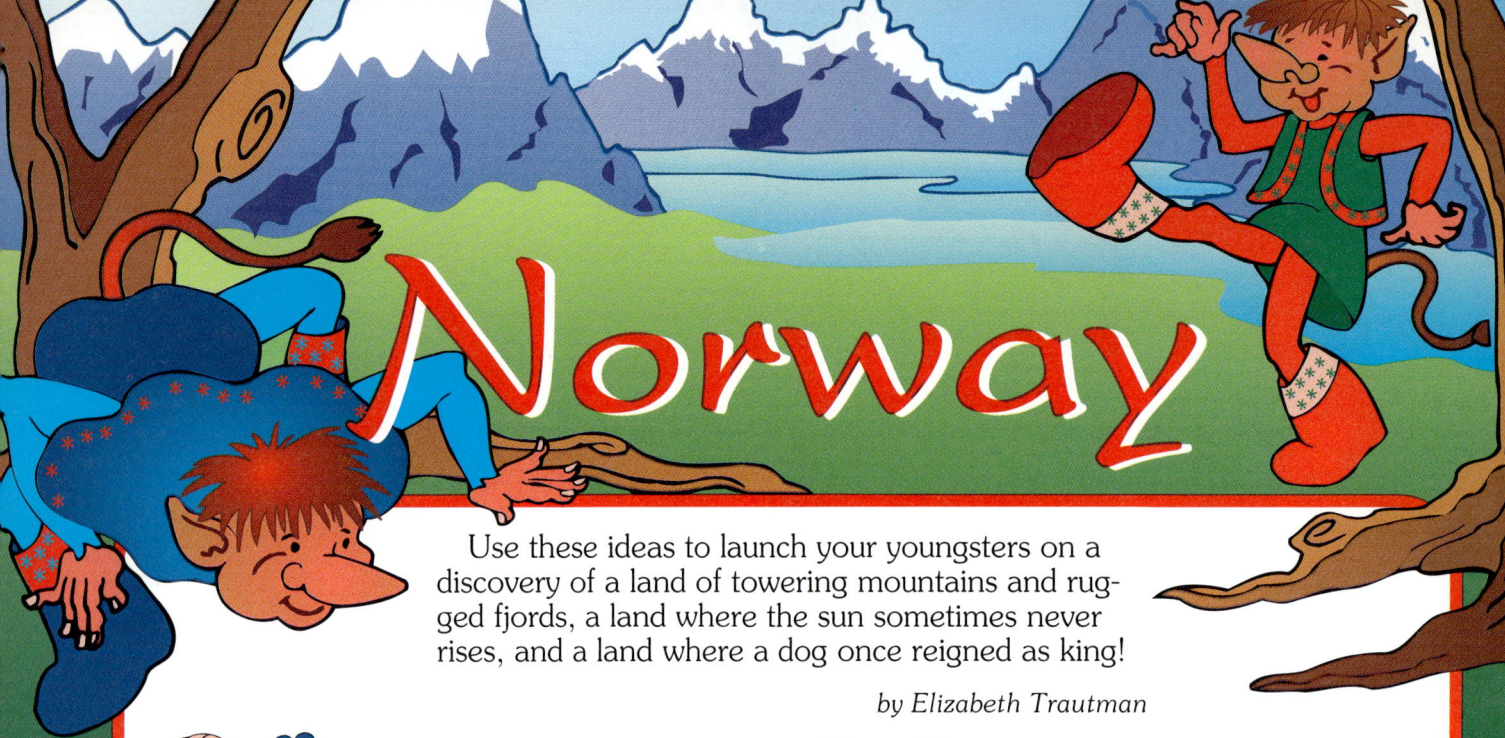

Use these ideas to launch your youngsters on a discovery of a land of towering mountains and rugged fjords, a land where the sun sometimes never rises, and a land where a dog once reigned as king!

by Elizabeth Trautman

Family Life

Invite your children to meet a typical Norwegian family by sharing *A Family In Norway* by Jetty St. John (Lerner Publications Company). Because the text is rather lengthy, preview the book ahead of time and prepare to paraphrase it for your youngsters. (There is a very helpful pronunciation guide on page 28.) As you share the book with your students, encourage them to discuss the ways in which Andrea's life is similar to/different from their lives. Use questions such as those below to guide your discussion. Then ask each child if he thinks it would be fun to visit Norway and have him explain his answer.

- From Andrea's house, she can see a fjord. What can you see from your house?
- In the summer, Andrea's family likes to eat meals on the patio, and often sees fishing boats or passenger boats passing by. Does your family eat outside in the summer? If so, where do you eat and what do you see?
- In Andrea's family, the children take turns doing the dishes after meals. Who does the dishes in your family?
- Andrea's brother Anders likes to go swimming in the fjord near his home. Where do you go swimming?
- Usually Mrs. Johansen and the children ride their bicycles to go shopping. How does your family travel around town?
- When Andrea's family goes on vacations, they like to hike in the mountains, ride horses, and ski. What do you like to do on your vacations?
- Dr. Johansen is a scientist. Who works in your family and what kinds of jobs do they do? (Did you notice how Dr. Johansen travels to work?)

What A Saga!

Norway's natural environment of majestic mountains, richly wooded forests, and wide-open spaces presents the perfect backdrop for wildly imaginative stories. Norwegian history contains many folktales of giants, trolls, fantastic beasts, and strong warriors. As the stories were told throughout the generations, many of the storytellers added a little more drama to heighten the fun of listening. The long stories or poems that described heroic activities of kings or mighty men were called *sagas*. Inspire your little ones to create a class-made saga. Begin by displaying reference-book pictures of Norway's landscape. Then encourage children to describe how they imagine trolls, giants, and fantastic beasts and people might look and act. Next, on a sheet of chart paper, write "Once upon a time, in the land of Norway, there lived...." Ask each child to dictate a sentence or two as you add it onto the saga. When your saga is complete, write the text (as you see fit) on separate sheets of construction paper; then have children illustrate the story. Bind the pages between illustrated covers and have each child (or group) share her page.

Troll Trouble

Explore the world of trolls and challenge your youngsters' creative problem-solving abilities by sharing *The Trouble With Trolls* by Jan Brett (Scholastic Inc.). As you can tell by reading the story, trolls were not known for their cleverness, and they often met their match in someone who outsmarted them. As you share this book with your students, pause at each problem in the story. Ask children to offer solutions to the problem at hand; then continue reading aloud. When you finish the story, look through the pictures in the book again. Pay close attention to the border art at the bottom of the pages. Encourage your students to create text for the story that takes place in those illustrations.

Can You Believe It?

Amaze students with this little-known fact about Norway. During the eleventh century—long, long ago!—the people of Norway chose a *dog* to be their king! The dog, King Suening-Saur, reigned for three years. Because he couldn't write, he signed all official documents with his paw print. Imagine that! Encourage youngsters to contemplate what other problems might arise if a dog were king. Then provide water-based stamp pads and have students sign some of their work with their "paw" prints. For an extension, stock an art center with various colors of stamp pads and paper. Have each child create a picture using only her fingerprints.

Flatbread Snacks

After-school snacks are an important part of any youngster's day—and the children of Norway are no different! Use the recipe that follows to make and sample a typical Norwegian snack. Flatbread is usually served with butter, jelly, or cheese. You might also like to try them with cinnamon and sugar or cream cheese.

Flatbread/Flatbrød

2 1/2 cups flour
1/4 cup vegetable oil
1 teaspoon baking soda
1/2 teaspoon salt
up to 1 cup buttermilk

Combine the first four ingredients in a large bowl and mix well. Add enough buttermilk to make a stiff dough. Knead the dough on a well-floured surface. Form a handful of dough into a ball; then press the ball into a flat circle. Using floured hands or a floured rolling pin, press/roll the dough into a very thin circle (approximately ten inches in diameter). Using cookie cutters, cut out shapes from the dough and place them on an ungreased cookie sheet. (Or simply score the dough circles and transfer them to the ungreased cookie sheet.) Bake at 350° for eight minutes or until the dough is lightly browned on the edges.

Whoa—Snow!

Here's a quick little Norway-related measuring activity that might astound some of your students. Cut three strips of bulletin-board paper, each one yard long. Then tell youngsters that in Norway, the snow in many areas is so deep that they have to close some of the roads for months. The snow is so deep, in fact, that it's measured in yards—not inches! Then, one at a time, tape the paper strips to a wall. Encourage children to compare the signified snow depth to themselves. Whoa—that's a lotta snow!

Literature Link

The Three Billy Goats Gruff
Written & Illustrated by Tim Arnold
Published by Margaret K. McElderry Books

The Man Who Kept House
Written by P. C. Asbjørnsen and J. E. Moe
Illustrated by Svend Otto S.
Published by Margaret K. McElderry Books

Welcome Back Sun
Written & Illustrated by Michael Emberley
Published by Little, Brown And Company

Jethro And Joel Were A Troll
Written & Illustrated by Bill Peet
Published by Houghton Mifflin Company

Star Light, Star Bright

Because Norway is located so far north, it has a very unusual rhythm of light and darkness. During the summer, the nights stay bright, with only a few hours of twilight. Imagine—you could walk your dog or read a book by natural light at midnight! However, just as the sun does not set during the summer, it also does not rise during the winter! Because of the long darkness, the colorful northern lights are greeted with great excitement. There is also a special interest in the intensity of the nighttime lights. The mixture of light from the moon and the stars, and the light reflected off the snow, creates an unusual effect. Have each child create a glowing winter scene to remind himself of the daylong nights in Norway. Using glow-in-the-dark paints and star stickers (available at craft stores), have each child create a picture of how he thinks the dark days of winter might look. Encourage youngsters to use additional art materials such as construction paper or chalk to create their pictures. Mount each finished project on a bulletin board entitled "The Winter Days Of Norway." Then turn off the lights to view each child's picture. (Use a flashlight to highlight each child's picture if desired.)

Christmas In Norway

It has been said that Christmas *(Jul)* is perhaps the favorite holiday in Norway. Early in November, holiday excitement builds and Norwegian children begin to count the days until Christmas! There is the same hustle and bustle in the big cities that is found in every other Christmas-celebrating city in the world. Decorated Christmas trees are displayed on public buildings everywhere, and Norway's natural forests add to the festive air. Why, they even have reindeer for inspiration!

There is an old saying in Norway—Christmas lasts until Easter because no one wants the festivities to end! If you're studying Norway during the winter months, experience a little bit of Christmas—Norwegian style!

Christmas Cooking

In Norway, it is customary for homes to have at least seven different kinds of cookies on hand, as well as Christmas bread. And traditionally all this baking is done by December 21! Catch your youngsters up in the enthusiasm of holiday baking by preparing this simplified recipe for Christmas bread. Mmmm, it's beginning to smell a lot like Christmas!

Christmas Bread/Julebrød

frozen white bread dough, defrosted
 (approx. 1 loaf per 5 children)
chopped nuts
raisins (softened by soaking in a
 small amount of warm water)
red and green candied cherries
 (chopped and shaken in flour)

With floured hands, divide the dough into portions—one for each child. Have each child press desired fruits and nuts into his dough. Next have each child flour his hands and a sheet of waxed paper, then knead his dough until the fruits and nuts are mixed in. Set the loaves on a greased cookie sheet and cover them with a slightly damp towel. Allow the dough to rise in a warm place until it doubles (about two hours). Instruct each child to punch down his loaf; then let the dough rise again (covered). Bake the loaves at 350° for 20 minutes or until the tops are golden brown. This Christmas bread can be eaten plain or topped with icing made from powdered sugar and milk, then sprinkled with nuts.

For The Birds

Norwegian Christmas hospitality even includes the birds! Traditionally a *julenek*—a sheaf of oats mounted on a pole—is set up in a yard. Your youngsters will be delighted to offer these modified juleneks to your neighborhood birds. To make one, spread peanut butter on one side of a rice cake. Carefully poke a pipe cleaner through the top of the rice cake—leaving a wide margin so the rice cake won't easily break—and form a loop. Gently press the coated rice cake in oats or birdseed. Hang each julenek from a tree branch and observe your guests!

Oh, Deer!

No doubt your youngsters will be drawn to the lovable reindeer in Jan Brett's *The Wild Christmas Reindeer* (G. P. Putnam's Sons). After sharing and discussing the story, tell youngsters that wild and herded reindeer can be found in Norway. Then have youngsters look carefully at the reindeer in the story. Encourage them to use terms such as *antlers* and *hooves* when they are describing the reindeer. Then have each child make a fanciful version of a reindeer from a crisp-rice cereal mixture. To make one, mix up a batch of crisp-rice marshmallow treats. With buttered hands, have each child mold a portion of the warm mixture into the shape of a reindeer head. Then have each child add pretzel pieces for antlers. Next direct each child to use chocolate chips for the eyes and nose. (If you'd like, substitute colorful gumdrops for the reindeer noses!)

Holiday

Candles, ribbons, and twinkling lights...
All are here on these holiday nights.
With mothers, fathers, sisters, brothers...
Some celebrate one way, and others, another.
But if you look closely, way down in your heart,
You might find that we're really not so far apart.
For it's families, and friends, and love, and thanksgiving
That bring us together in the joy of true giving.

Use the following ideas to develop awareness of and/or celebrate Hanukkah and Kwanzaa.

Happy, Happy Hanukkah!

Hanukkah Lights, Hanukkah Nights by Leslie Kimmelman (HarperCollins) offers a simple, yet energetic introduction to the beloved traditions and symbols of the eight joyous nights of Hanukkah. After sharing this book with your youngsters, ask each child to share related experiences from his family's holiday traditions. Find out if any of your students have relatives who come from far and wide, grandmothers who sip chicken soup, or cousins who play and sing together. (If desired, record the comments on chart paper.) Conclude your discussion by guiding your little ones in summarizing both the similarities and the diversities within your group.

Glittery Menorah

Brighten your classroom with these dazzling displays. To make a glittery menorah, paint nine craft sticks the color of your choice, and paint nine foam packing pieces to resemble flames. When the paint is dry, make a menorah base by gluing the craft sticks to a sheet of construction paper (as shown). Then cut off approximately two inches from eight of nine pipe cleaners. Arrange and glue the pipe cleaners on the paper so that the tallest pipe cleaner is in the middle. Glue a flame at the tip of each pipe cleaner. Add the finishing touch by squeezing glue around the flames. Sprinkle glitter on the glue; then let it dry. Shake off the excess glitter and display each child's finished project in your classroom.

Adapted from an idea by Bernice Regenstein
Bricktown, NJ

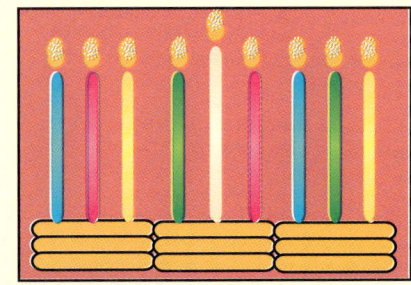

Spin, Dreidel, Spin

After reading some of the Hanukkah-related literature selections (see the literature list), your youngsters will be primed to get some hands-on experience with the game of dreidel. *Let's Play Dreidel!* is a book/cassette/dreidel set published by Kar-Ben Copies, Inc. (1-800-4-KARBEN). The cassette contains several upbeat dreidel-related songs. The book explains the way the game is played and the meanings of the symbols on the dreidel. Variations for the game are also presented. The set includes a dreidel so your youngsters can begin playing immediately. If you're thinking of playing dreidel with your little ones, this set might give you some ideas for lively alternatives.

The Literature Link

Toby Belfer Never Had A Christmas Tree
Written by Gloria Teles Pushker
Illustrated by Judith Hierstein
(Pelican Publishing Company)

Latkes And Applesauce: A Hanukkah Story
Written by Fran Manushkin
Illustrated by Robin Spowart
(Scholastic Inc.)

The Gift
Written by Aliana Brodmann
Illustrated by Anthony Carnabuci
(Simon & Schuster Books For Young Readers)

Light The Lights! A Story About Celebrating Hanukkah & Christmas
Written & Illustrated by Margaret Moorman
(Scholastic Inc.)

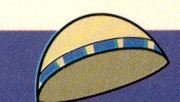

Happenings

Kwanzaa

Many African people throughout history have celebrated a "first fruits" harvest holiday. The elements included in most of these holidays were family and friends gathering together, giving thanks, remembering ancestors, evaluating their lives during the past year, and making plans for the coming year. There was usually singing, dancing, and feasting during this seven-day celebration.

In 1966 Dr. Maulana Karenga started a new African-American holiday that is intended to preserve African values and traditions. *Kwanzaa,* as the holiday is named, is celebrated for seven days beginning December 26 and ending January 1. Give your youngsters a greater understanding of Kwanzaa by reading aloud your choice of books from the literature list.

Kwanzaa Display

After sharing some of the Kwanzaa literature, have each of your youngsters choose from the following activities to contribute to the making of a stunning Kwanzaa display in your classroom. When each child has contributed at least one item to the display, encourage each child to share what he has made with the class and recall its significance.

The Colors Of Kwanzaa

The traditional colors of Kwanzaa are black, red, and green. Black represents the color of the people. Red stands for the struggles of the people. Green represents the rolling hills of Africa and is also the color of hope. Stock your art center with sheets of art paper; black, red, and green paints; and tissue paper. Encourage children to use the supplies to create original designs in the colors of Kwanzaa.

A Bountiful Harvest

During the Kwanzaa celebration, a basket filled with *mazao* (mah-ZAH-oo), or crops, serves as a symbol of the African harvest and thanksgiving. To set up a crop-making station in your classroom, provide a classroom supply of sculpting clay and small pieces of leather shoelaces or pipe cleaners. Encourage children to visit the station and sculpt crops such as apples, pears, grapes, bananas, and ears of corn. Pieces of leather shoelaces or pipe cleaners can be added for stems. (Use dull pencil points for texturizing if desired.) Allow the sculptures to dry for approximately one week. Then have each sculptor paint his crop with authentic colors. When the crops are dry, arrange them in a basket in your Kwanzaa display.

Preparing The Table

In Africa it is an old custom to make things by hand. Encourage children to work together to create a *mkeke* (m-KAY-kah), or placemat, for your Kwanzaa display. Fold a large sheet of black construction paper in half. Starting at the fold, cut parallel lines (equal distances apart) to within two inches of the ends of the paper. Unfold the paper and lay it on a flat surface. Using red and green lengths of yarn and construction paper—slightly longer in length than the width of the black paper—have students weave the yarn and paper in and out of the slits in the black paper. Children may weave in under-over patterns or create original pattern designs. When the weaving is finished, turn the project over and secure the ends of the yarn and paper strips with tape. Place the finished mkeke in your display area.

The Literature Link

Kwanzaa
Written by Deborah M. Newton Chocolate
Illustrated by Melodye Rosales
(Childrens Press®, Inc.)

Imani's Gift At Kwanzaa
Written by Denise Burden-Patmon
Illustrated by Floyd Cooper
(Picture Book Studio)

Kwanzaa
Written by A. P. Porter
Illustrated by Janice Lee Porter
(Carolrhoda Books, Inc.)

My First Kwanzaa Book
Written by Deborah M. Newton Chocolate
Illustrated by Cal Massey
(Scholastic Inc.)

VIVE LA FRANCE

Cross the Atlantic Ocean to explore a land that has been called "everyone's second home." You'll see a famous landmark, sample some cheeses, speak a little French, and more! So gather your youngsters together and...bon voyage!

ideas by Elizabeth Trautman

THE LAY OF THE LAND

Did you know that France is said to be shaped roughly like a hexagon? Before beginning this activity, cut out a large France shape from bulletin-board paper. (If desired, use an opaque projector to enlarge and trace the France shape in the illustration.) Then encourage your young geographers to carefully examine France on a variety of maps such as a world map, a globe, and encyclopedia maps. Challenge children to locate the six sides of France. After the six sides have been identified, guide children in using their beginning map skills to determine that three of the country's sides are bordered by water and three sides are mostly mountainous. As a class, decide on a map legend and have children paint the appropriate sides of the country accordingly. When the paint is dry, display the map on a bulletin board with other France-related projects.

FLY THE COLORS

These child-made flags will enable children to identify the flag of France, as well as reinforce left and right directionality. As you do this activity, display pictures of the flag of France for youngsters' reference. Using 8 1/2" x 11" sheets of white art paper, have children follow along as you demonstrate how to fold the paper into three equal sections. Then have each child open his paper and turn it over (to keep the edges flat). Direct each child to finger-paint the left section blue and the right section red, leaving the middle section white. When the flags are dry, add them to your France display. These colorful banners will signal to all who enter your classroom that you are studying France. And you never know what interesting tidbits a passerby might be able to contribute to your study—so fly those colors high!

PASS THE CHEESE, PLEASE

Throughout the years, France has become well-known for its fine cheeses. Although Brie, Camembert, and Roquefort are the most popular cheeses, there are over 400 types of cheeses produced in France. Imagine—you could eat a different cheese each day of the year, and then some! In honor of your study of France, organize a cheese taste-testing party. Prepare a chart similar to the one shown. Ask parent volunteers to send specific types of cheeses to school. Also have crackers handy to munch on between cheese types. When you're ready to test the cheeses, encourage children to use their senses of sight, touch, smell, and taste to evaluate each type of cheese. Then have each child record her opinion in the taste column. When the tasting is complete, use the chart to discuss favorites and least favorites.

UP, UP—AND AWAY!

Just a little bit of French history can lead to these colorful crafts. Tell your youngsters that the first people to fly in a hot-air balloon were the Montgolfier brothers from France. However, before these *people* took to balloon flight, they tried it out on a duck, a rooster, and a sheep! (The animals landed safely after an eight-minute flight.) Give each child a white sheet of art paper and a variety of colorful art supplies such as paints, markers, colored pencils, glitter glue, and fabric scraps. Encourage each child to use the supplies to create an original hot-air balloon. (Designing these balloons provides a great opportunity to reinforce patterning concepts!) After each child has cut out his balloon shape, have him color and cut out his choice of animals and/or people to glue to a construction-paper balloon basket. Then attach the balloon to the basket with lengths of yarn. Place the finished projects on exhibit in your France display.

PARLEZ-VOUS FRANÇAIS?

Since the French language is known for being one of the most charming languages to listen to, enhance your studies by having youngsters punctuate their everyday conversations with some of these common words and phrases.

Hello.	Bonjour.	\bō-zhūr\ or \bō(n)-zhūr\
Good-bye.	Au revoir.	\ō-rə-vwar\
Please.	S'il vous plaît.	\sēl-vū-plĕ\
Thank you.	Merci.	\mar-sē\
Excuse me.	Pardonnez-moi.	\pär-də-nā-mwä\
How are you?	Comment allez-vous?	\kəm-ən-tă-lā-vū\
I am fine.	Je vais bien.	\zhə-vĕ-byĕ\

THE SYMBOL OF PARIS

When visitors arrive in Paris, the Eiffel Tower—known as the symbol of Paris—is always at the top of their sightseeing list. Help your youngsters get a feel for this popular Parisian attraction by displaying several pictures of the Eiffel Tower from books such as *The Inside-Outside Book Of Paris* by Roxie Munro (Dutton Children's Books), *We Live In France* by James Tomlins, and encyclopedia pictures. Explain that the Eiffel Tower was built by a man named Alexandre Gustave Eiffel, who wanted to show how steel and iron could be used to build tall structures. Then display the pictures near your block center as inspiration for your budding engineers to build tall structures of their own. Encourage youngsters to try to build towers that will stand steadily as they get taller and taller. Post a class list near the center and invite children to record the number of blocks used in their structures. How high can you go?

Justin	22 blocks
Kori	18 blocks
Taylor	16 blocks
Katie	24 blocks
Steve	26 blocks

THE LITERATURE LINK

Mirette On The High Wire
Written & Illustrated by Emily Arnold McCully
Published by Scholastic Inc.

Minou
Written by Mindy Bingham
Illustrated by Itoko Maeno
Published by Advocacy Press

The Madeline Series
Written & Illustrated by Ludwig Bemelmans
Published by The Viking Press

The Cows Are Going To Paris
Written by David Kirby &
    Allen Woodman
Illustrated by Chris L. Demarest
Published by Boyds Mills Press, Inc.

Tulips
Written by Jay O'Callahan
Illustrated by Debrah Santini
Published by Picture Book Studio

India

It's hard to imagine that halfway around the world lies one of the earth's oldest and most colorful civilizations. Use the ideas in this unit to take a little peek into the faraway land of India.

ideas contributed by Elizabeth Trautman

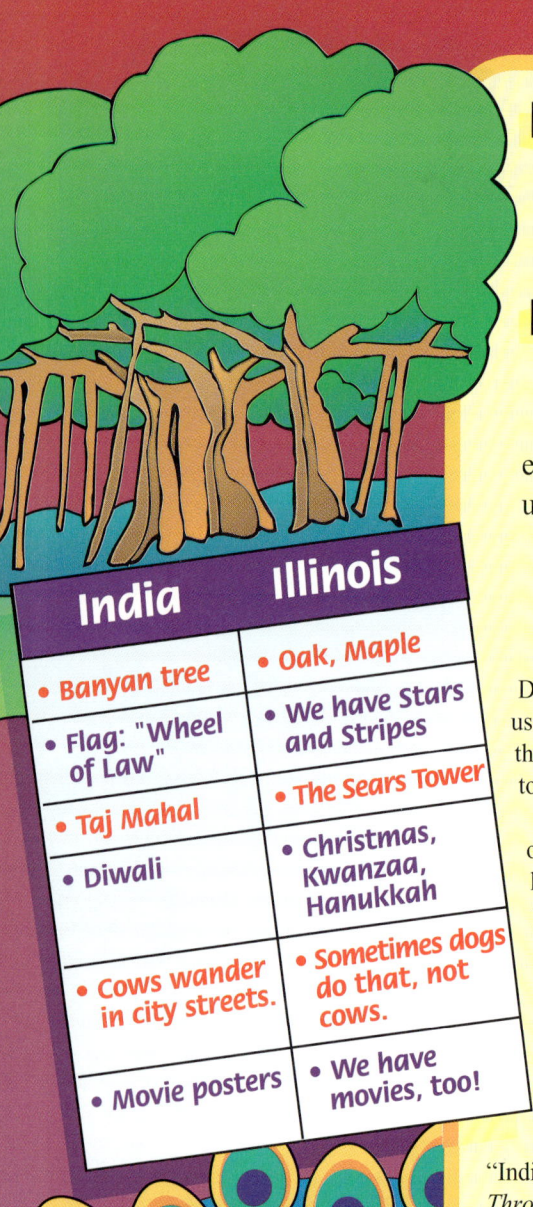

India	Illinois
• Banyan tree	• Oak, Maple
• Flag: "Wheel of Law"	• We have Stars and Stripes
• Taj Mahal	• The Sears Tower
• Diwali	• Christmas, Kwanzaa, Hanukkah
• Cows wander in city streets.	• Sometimes dogs do that, not cows.
• Movie posters	• We have movies, too!

A One...And A Two...And A Three!

Dipping into a little bit of the language of India is as easy as one, two, three when you use Jim Haskins's *Count Your Way Through India* (Carolrhoda Books, Inc.). Because the text is lengthy in some parts, preview the book ahead of time so you will be prepared to paraphrase for your youngsters when necessary.

Before you begin sharing the book, tell your youngsters that the official language of India is *Hindi*. As you read the first number in the book (in Hindi), encourage your little ones to repeat it after you; then discuss the page. When you go on to the next page, have youngsters repeat that number after you. Then—before you discuss that page, turn back a page and say the numbers in sequence (i.e. "ache, dough"). Continue through the book in this manner. Before you know it, you'll all be counting to ten in Hindi!

Same And Different

Encourage your children to make comparisons between what they are learning about India and your area of the country. Label the left side of a sheet of chart paper "India" and the right side "[your state]." Then revisit the illustrations in *Count Your Way Through India*. Encourage youngsters to name things that catch their attention in the illustrations or the text. Write their responses on the chart paper. When you've worked your way through the book, reread your list together. Then, as a class, determine which elements in the list have similar counterparts in your state and which do not. Discuss the results, guiding children to come to the conclusion that some things in India are very much the same and some things are *way different!*

The National Bird

With all the beautiful colors that are seen in India, it just seems to follow naturally that the peacock is the national bird of India. Encourage your children to create colorful peacocks to add to your India display. To make a peacock, cut out a construction-paper peacock body. Glue the cutout in the center near the bottom of a sheet of art paper. Use an oval-shaped sponge dipped in green paint to make prints around the peacock's body. When that paint dries, sponge-paint the center of each oval with a smaller oval-shaped sponge dipped in blue paint. When that paint is dry, sponge-paint the center of each design with an even smaller round sponge dipped in black paint. To complete this colorful bird, paint an eye on the peacock's face and add other details as desired.

Totally Tea

If you and your students were suddenly transported to the streets of India, you would find yourselves among numerous street stalls where people sell beverages. Since India is the world's largest producer of tea, a wide variety of teas is readily available there. One common type of tea is known as *masal chay* (spiced tea). Follow the recipe at left to prepare a sample of masal chay for each of your youngsters. After tasting the masal chay, poll your class for their reactions to the taste.

In a large pot, bring the water to a boil. Add the loose tea. Steep for ten minutes. Add the milk and heat to *near* boiling again. Stir in the sugar and spices. Before serving, reheat to warm, then pour the liquid through a fine strainer. Makes approximately 20 half-cup servings.

Masal Chay
5 c. water
6 tsp. loose tea
5 c. milk
1/3 c. sugar
1/2 tsp. cinnamon
1/2 tsp. cloves

Colorful Cloth

One of the first things a visitor in India will notice is the brilliant and beautiful colors and patterns of the fabrics. Many of these fabrics have been hand-painted using techniques that have been passed down from generation to generation. Design touches of India for your classroom by creating some colorful cloths of your own. Display pictures of Indian fabric from sources such as *India* by Anita Ganeri and Jonardon Ganeri (Raintree Steck-Vaughn Publishers) and *Enchantment Of The World: India* by Sylvia McNair (Childrens Press®). Provide shallow pans, each with several layers of paper towels. Soak the towel layers in each of the pans with a different bright color of washable kids' paint. Supply a variety of printing items such as cut sponges, green peppers, carved potatoes, or pasta pieces glued to the bottoms of film canisters. Give each child a piece of muslin and encourage him to use the supplies to create a colorful piece of Indian cloth. Display the dried cloths in your India display area.

Today Is Tomorrow

"Did you know that right now in India, children just like you are getting ready for bed?" After asking this question, find out if your students know why Indian children would be doing such a strange thing. Then read aloud *Somewhere In The World Right Now* by Stacey Schuett (Alfred A. Knopf, Inc.). After discussing the book, take a look at your world map or globe. Point out India and your state. Emphasize how far away India is. In fact, it is just about halfway around the world! Because it is so far away, India is in a different *time zone*. That means in India, the time is about 12 hours ahead of the United States.

To demonstrate the time difference, have half of your class move to an area of the room designated "India." Have the other half of the class stand in an area designated "[your state]." Give each group a large manipulative clock. Have each group set its clock for a given time such as 9:00. Then tell one group that, for them, it is 9:00 in the morning. Tell the other group that, for them, it is 9:00 at night. Ask each group what they might be doing at their given time.

Smell-A-Roma

Indian food is full of spices. So full, in fact, that some of the spicy Indian foods just might knock your socks off! Some of the main spices used in India are cumin, coriander, ginger, cinnamon, cloves, cardamom, chilies, fennel, and turmeric. Gather a collection of these spices and put them in separate numbered containers. Place the containers and a labeled chart at a center and declare a "Smell-A-Roma"! As participants visit the center, have them smell each of the spices. Ask each person to choose the spice that he likes best; then write his name across from the corresponding number in the chart. Is there a favorite Indian spice among your group?

1	Cloves	Katie, Ben, Eva, Tasha, Stevie, Emily, Jose, Tim, Kim
2	Coriander	Todd, Eddie, Fred
3	Fennel	Karen, Laura
	Ginger	Linda, Terry, Jackson, Don, Margo, Danny
	urmeric	Larry, Sherry, Moe

167

Patterns
Use with "Cuckoo Clocks" on page 155.

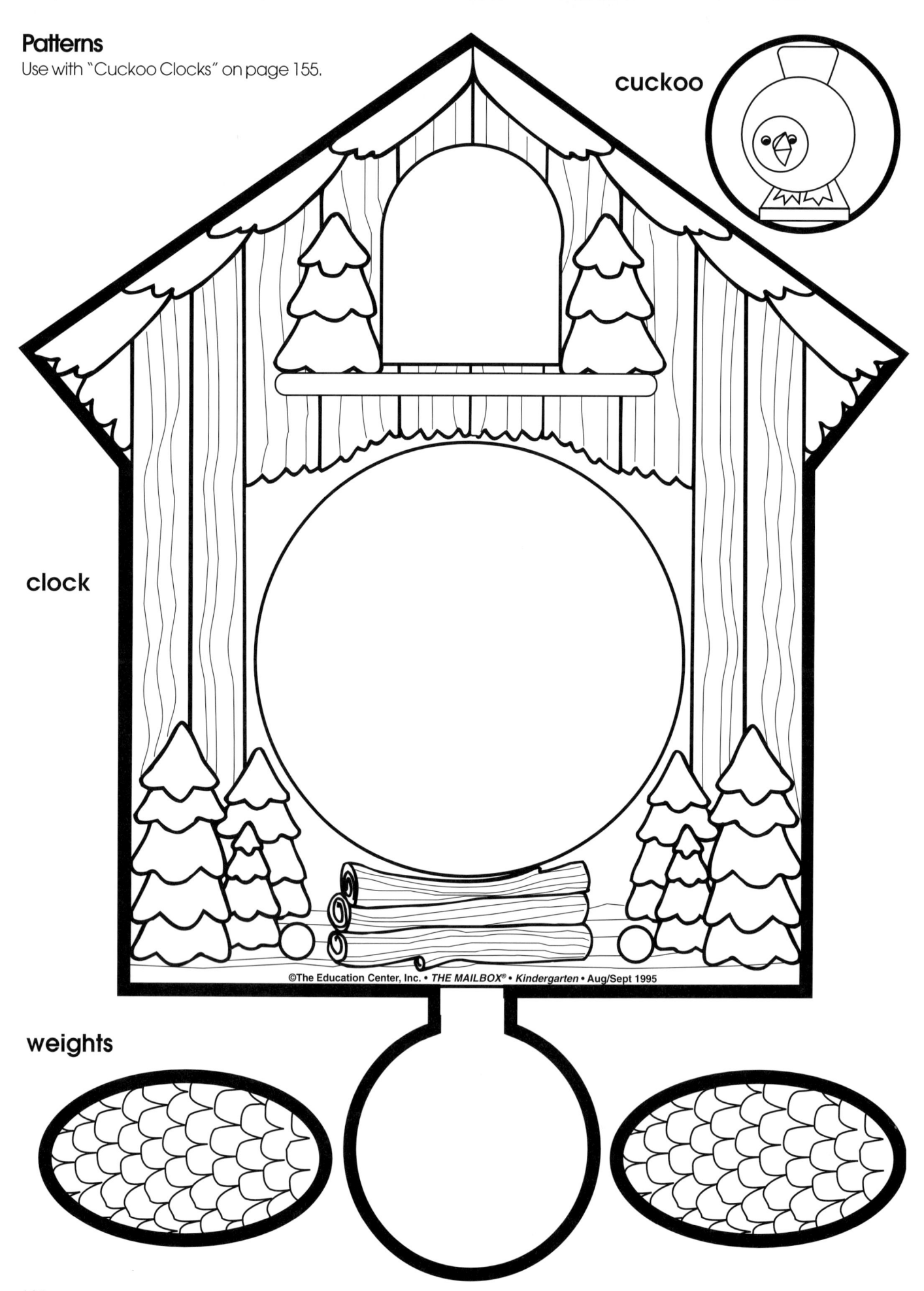

cuckoo

clock

weights

168

ship

Pattern
Use with "Setting Sail" on page 157.

Thematic Units

Welcome To School

It's always exciting for teachers and students when the first days of a new school year roll around. Use this collection of bus-themed ideas to meet and greet your little ones with warmth and security. In practically no time at all, you'll find that everyone is ready to climb on board and head off towards a totally terrific school year!

by Lucia Kemp Henry

Can't Wait To See You!

Calm those first-day jitters and create a sense of positive anticipation by letting your new class know that you are thinking about them. A week or two before school begins, send a welcome-to-school pack to each child. To make one pack, write a note similar to the one shown. Then photocopy the note and the nametag and class token (page 176) on colorful construction paper. Personalize the class token and the nametag; then laminate and cut them out. Place the nametag, token, and notecard in a manila envelope along with a photograph of yourself. (If desired, make an additional copy of the name tag label and use it as a mailing label on the envelope.) This little contact will do big things to create a sense of welcome and warmth for your new arrivals.

Ms. Lucy Proia
21A Guyer Street
High Point, NC 24856

Luke Bolka
14

Dear Luke,
I am very excited about our first day of school. I'm looking forward to having you in my classroom. We will have lots of fun and we'll learn many new things this year.
Please wear your school bus nametag when you come to school on the first day. Bring your class token too. I have some special activities planned!
See you soon!
Ms. Proia

Class Token
Luke
for first-day fun!

Luke

First-Day Decor

This happy, yellow school bus can be the friendly reminder that lets your little ones know just where they belong. Use an opaque projector to enlarge the school-bus pattern (page 177) on bright yellow bulletin-board paper. Add construction-paper details to the bus if desired. Then write your name on the bus and tape it to your classroom door. On the first day of school, stand near the decorated door to greet your students. If you made the nametags and tokens described in "Can't Wait To See You!", ask each child for his class token and check to be sure that he is wearing his nametag. (Have a few extra nametags and tokens available for children who forget to bring their own.) Bringing the class token and nametag from home will give each child a sense of responsibility and belonging. And seeing that school-bus door will assure each child that he's at just the right stop!

Ms. Proia's Class

Bus Business

Prepare for a pretend bus trip by sharing Raffi's *Wheels On The Bus* (Crown Publishers, Inc.). After reading the book aloud, prepare for a dramatic singing version of the text! Arrange children's chairs bus-style—in two long, parallel rows. Display the personalized class tokens (from "Can't Wait To See You!") on a nearby table. As you call each child, have her find the token with her name on it, hand it to you, and find a seat on the bus. Sitting in the pretend bus creates just the right atmosphere for singing "The Wheels On The Bus." Teach this song to your little ones, complete with all the actions and sound effects. Encourage youngsters to add original verses with their own actions and sound effects—and sing away!

Tour Bus

Use this bus-related activity to introduce students to your school personnel, acclimate them to their new surroundings, and practice walking in line. After sitting in the pretend bus (see "Bus Business" on page 172), have youngsters move away from the chairs and stand in line bus-style—in two long, parallel rows. Then explain that you are going to be in a pretend *moving* bus. And as you (the bus driver) move, all of the children should follow you without getting out of line. (If desired, have side-by-side partners hold hands.) After a little practice, guide the bus through your school, making stops to meet and greet school personnel and learn about other locations in your school. Take Polaroid™ pictures of significant people and places you see along the way. When you return to your classroom, mount the pictures on a sheet of chart paper. Discuss each of the pictures and add child-dictated labels near each picture. Display the chart at students' eye level so they can refer to it throughout the first weeks of school.

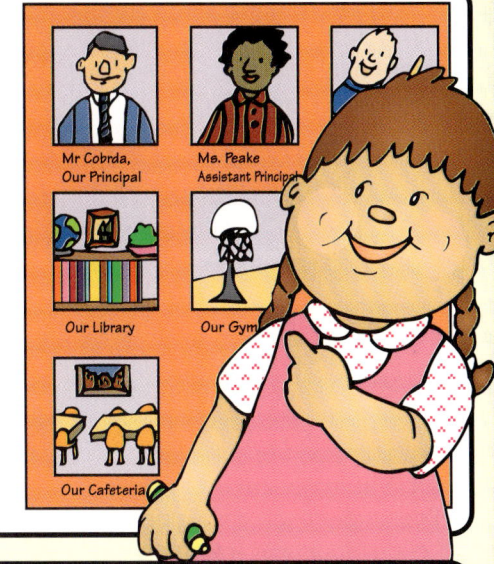

School-Bus Booklet

This foldout booklet is filled with a busload of child-centered, autobiographical activities. For each child, duplicate the booklet patterns (pages 178-181) on white construction paper. Have each child complete the booklet as follows:

Cover
Have each child write his name on the cover and color the page as desired.

Page 1
Have each child glue or draw a picture of himself in the center of the ribbon. Next have him trace his hand in the box or use paint to make a handprint. Then have each child write his name and age in the spaces provided.

Page 2
Read aloud the sentence starter at the bottom of the page. Have each child illustrate a completion to the sentence. Record each child's dictation at the bottom of the page.

Page 3
Have each child illustrate some of his classmates in the space provided. Then have him draw a picture of you in the box at the right.

Cut out all of the pages along the bold outlines. Glue the pages together where indicated (end-to-end). Fold the pages accordion-style so that the cover is on the top. Display each child's unfolded booklet on a bulletin board or wall.

Bus Totes

Since it seems to be especially difficult for little ones to keep track of items that need to travel from school to home or vice versa, help each child make a bus tote for that very purpose. For each child, duplicate the bus pattern (page 177) on construction paper. Have each child draw a picture of himself in the passenger window and color the page as he likes. Then write each child's name on his bus and cut it out. Glue each bus cutout to the front of a string-tie envelope. Laminate each envelope with the flap open. Using a craft knife, carefully slit the laminating film along the envelope opening. Use these sturdy totes to transport student work, newsletters, and other forms of teacher-parent communication from school to home *and* back again when necessary!

Welcome Aboard

Load this bus with each child's self-portrait, and you'll have an attractive room display that each child will feel proud to have had a hand in creating. In addition, you'll all get to know one another a little bit along the way. Provide an assortment of skin-toned construction paper and other art supplies such as crayons, yarn, fabric scraps, scissors, and glue. Have each child choose a color of paper and cut out a large circle to represent his head. Then have each child glue his head cutout onto a white sheet of construction paper and use the art supplies to create a self-portrait. Next cut out a large, yellow school-bus shape from bulletin-board paper. Mount the bus cutout and a title on a bulletin board. When each child's self-portrait is complete, assist him in selecting a place on the bus to staple his picture to resemble a child looking out of the bus's window.

When the display is finished, gather the children around the board and hold all of the class tokens (see "Can't Wait To See You!" on page 172) in your hand. One at a time, show a class token. When a child sees his name, have him point out his portrait on the bus display and tell his classmates a little bit about himself. When he is done sharing, have the class respond by saying, "Welcome aboard, [student's name]!"

Welcome Aboard!!
Mrs. Mayhew's Class

My name is Danielle and I am 5 and a half...

A Smooth Ride For Mrs. Ryan's Class

1. Keep your hands and feet to yourself.
2. Follow directions.
3. Be kind.
4. Ask for help when you need it.

A Smooth Ride

As you begin your first few days together as a class, facilitate a discussion encouraging children to think of ways that would enable everyone in the class to work and play well together. As a group, decide what you would like your class rules to be. Emphasize that when everyone follows the rules, things in your classroom are likely to be much more fun for everyone—a *smooth* ride! Write the rules on a sheet of chart paper. Then enlarge and duplicate the school bus on the nametag pattern (page 176). Write a title on the bus such as the one shown; then cut it out. Attach the bus cutout to the top of your list of rules and post the chart in a prominent place in your classroom.

Traveling To School

Talking about how students get to school will help you continue to get to know one another—and introduce graphing and other math skills at the same time. In advance, photocopy the nametag label (page 176) and the car and walk patterns (page 176) on construction paper. Color the patterns; then cut them out. Draw four columns on a sheet of chart paper. Glue the cutouts to the chart paper to serve as visual cues for the columns. Label the columns as shown. (Leave the fourth column open for another option. If all of your students ride in a bus or car, or walk, label the fourth column with an unlikely option such as "flying" and you'll have an opportunity to discuss the number zero.) Then have each child write his name or tape his class token (see "Can't Wait To See You!" on page 172) in the column that represents how he gets to school. When the graph is complete, discuss what it reveals by asking questions such as "How many children ride the bus?", "How many children walk to school?", and "Which number is greater?" While you're at it, this is a great springboard for a discussion on transportation!

We're So Glad You're In Our Classroom!

Use this little song as you bring closure to the end of your first school day. Singing it together will help students remember each other's names, and help each child feel welcome and special. Photocopy a classroom quantity of an award pattern on construction paper. Personalize and sign an award for each child. Then seat your youngsters in a circle. Sing the song below, replacing the boldfaced words with your school's name and several of your students' names each time you repeat it until you have mentioned each child in your classroom. As you sing each child's name, give her personalized award to her. Then sing the last verse, inserting the appropriate day of the week.

(sung to the tune of "The More We Get Together")

We're so glad you're in our classroom, our classroom, our classroom.
We're so glad you're in our classroom at **Washington School.**
We're glad to have **David,** and **Amy,** and **Jessica.**
We're so glad you're in our classroom at **Washington School.**

We'll see you all on **Tuesday,** on **Tuesday,** on **Tuesday.**
We'll see you all on **Tuesday,** at **Washington School.**

Books About School And Such

The Day The Teacher Went Bananas
Written by James Howe
Illustrated by Lillian Hoban
Published by E. P. Dutton

My Teacher Sleeps In School
Written by Leatie Weiss
Illustrated by Ellen Weiss
Published by Viking Kestrel

Jessica
Written & Illustrated by Kevin Henkes
Published by Scholastic Inc.

Time For School, Nathan!
Written & Illustrated by Lulu Delacre
Published by Scholastic Inc.

School Bus
Written & Illustrated by Donald Crews
Published by Greenwillow Books

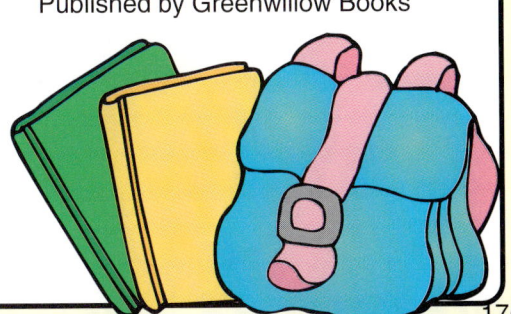

Patterns

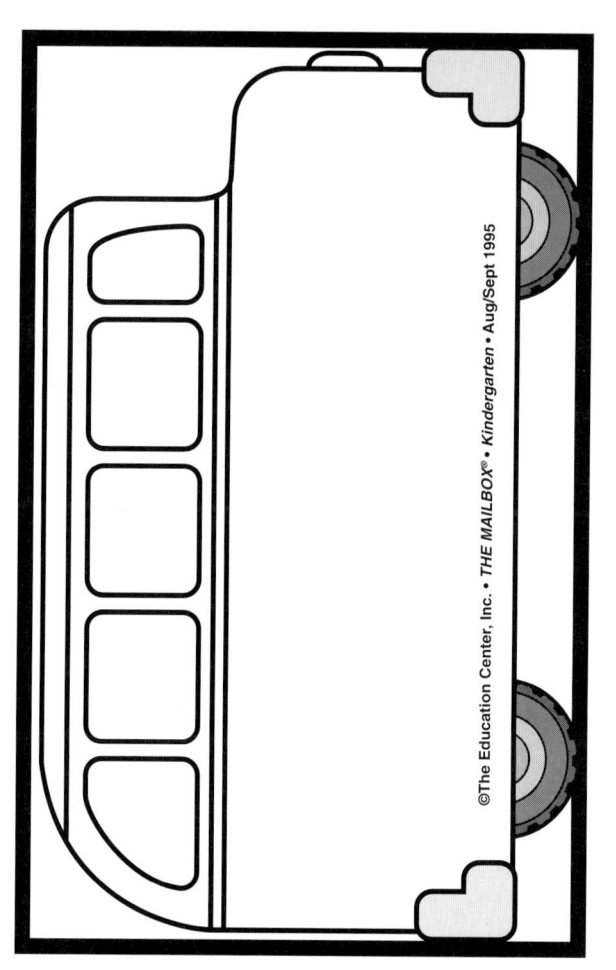

class token
Use with "Can't Wait To See You!", "First-Day Decor," and "Bus Business" (page 172); "Welcome Aboard" (page 174); and "Traveling To School" (page 175.)

nametag
Use with "Can't Wait To See You!" and "First-Day Decor" (page 172), "A Smooth Ride" (page 174), and "Traveling To School" (page 175).

Class Token for first-day fun!

Patterns
Use with "Traveling To School" on page 175.

car

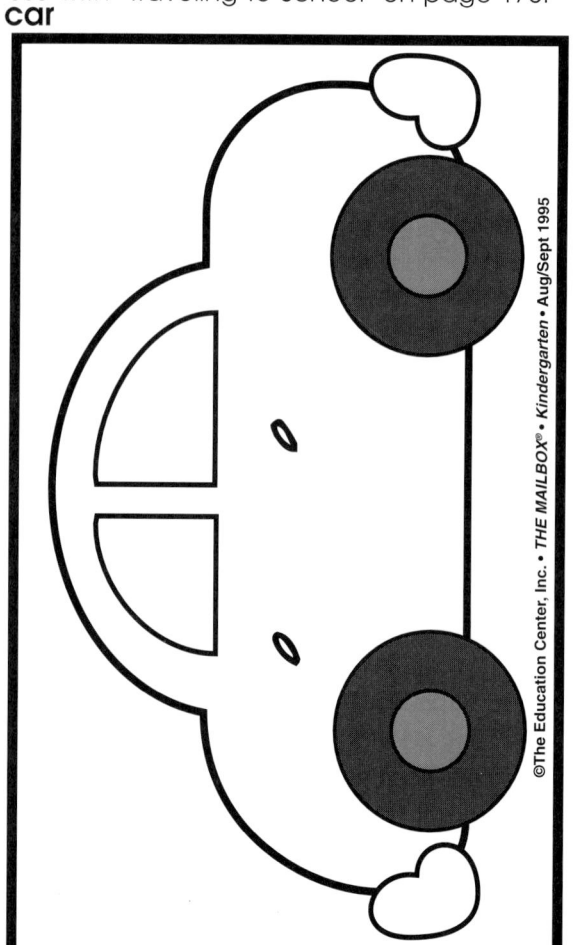

walk

**Pattern
school bus**
Use with "First-Day Decor" on page
172 and "Bus Totes" on page 173.

Booklet cover

Use with "School-Bus Booklet" on page 173.

My School Book

by _____

Glue page 1 here.

I am _____ years old.

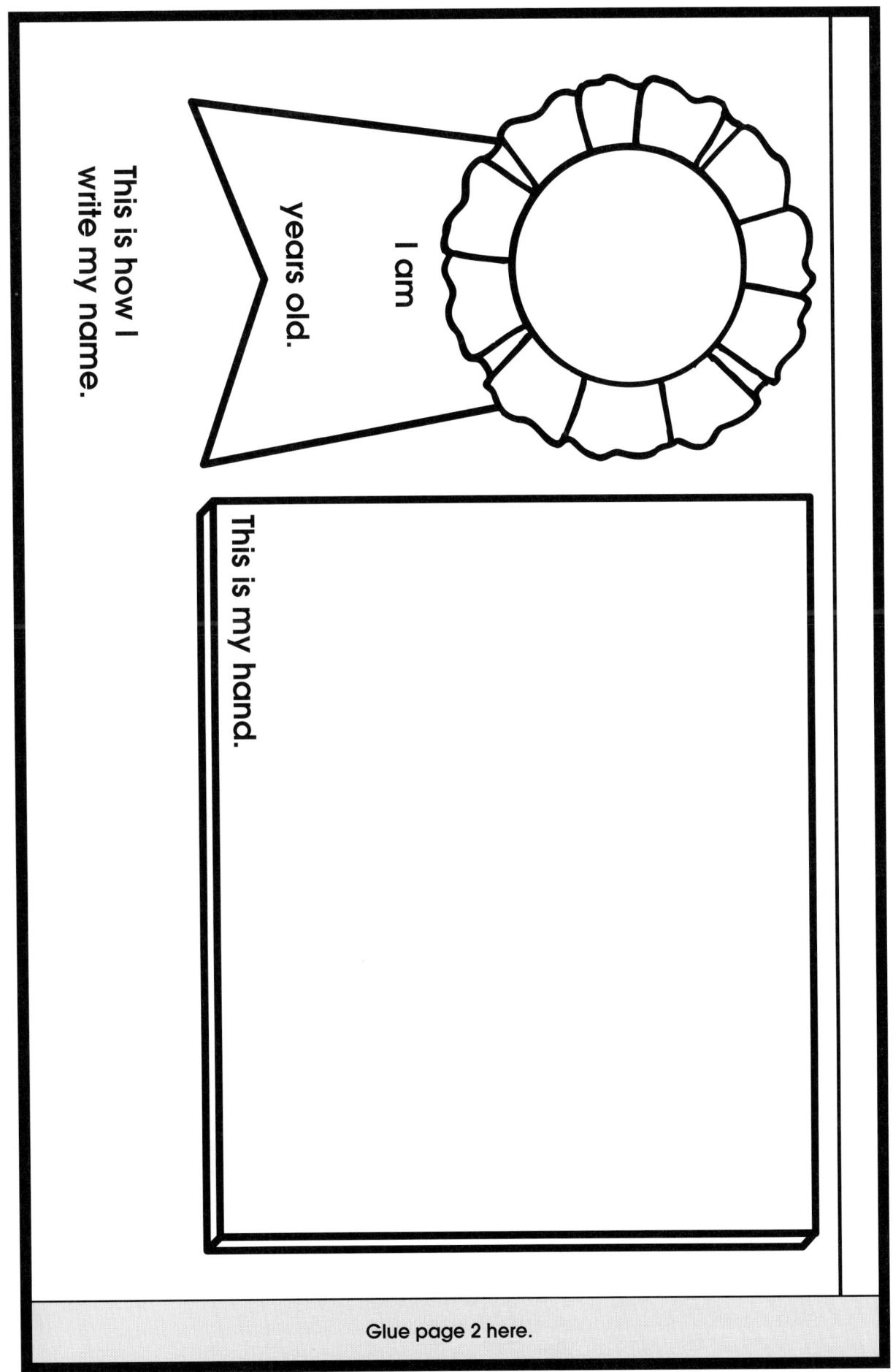

This is how I write my name.

This is my hand.

Glue page 2 here.

Booklet page 1
Use with "School-Bus Booklet" on page 173.

I want to learn about...

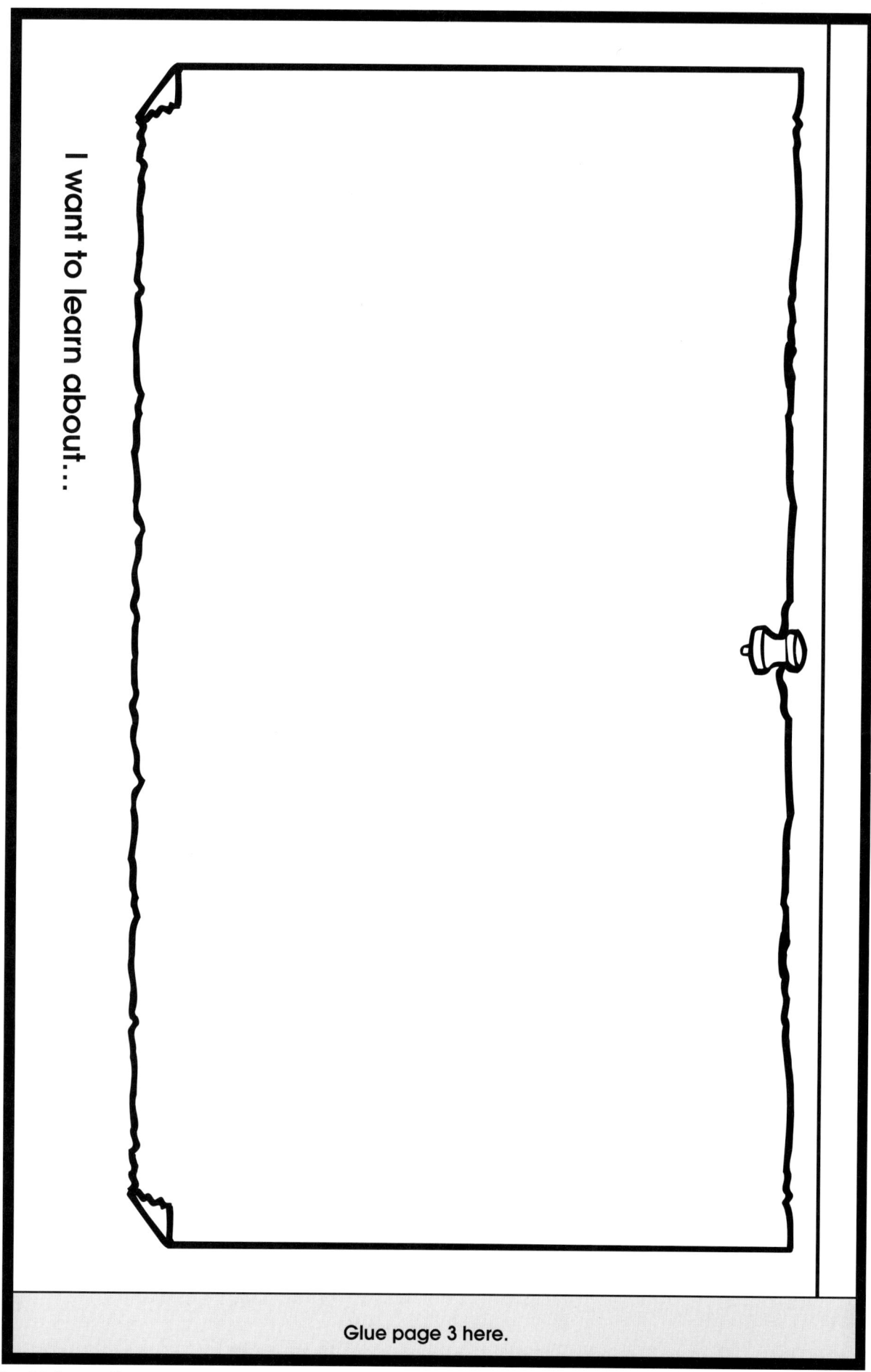

Glue page 3 here.

Booklet page 2
Use with "School-Bus Booklet" on page 173.

Here are some of my friends at school.

This is my teacher.

Booklet page 3
Use with "School-Bus Booklet" on page 173.

A Family Affair

Today's families come in all shapes and sizes. Though families of the 1990s may appear to look different from those of the past, the purposes of families remain the same. Families teach, protect, nurture, love, and provide for their children. Use the following activities to explore your students' individual families.

ideas contributed by Lucia Kemp Henry

What Is A Family?
Just what is a family anyway? Pose that question to your students and write their responses on chart paper. Then read aloud "What Is A Family?" from Mary Ann Hoberman's *Fathers, Mothers, Sisters, Brothers: A Collection Of Family Poems* (Scholastic Inc.). After discussing the poem, ask youngsters if they would like to add anything to their original definitions, and write their responses on the chart paper. Guide youngsters in summarizing the list to come up with a student-generated definition of *family*.

Family Portraits
The best thing about these family portraits is that youngsters don't have to dress up, comb their hair, or keep their clothes clean for a single minute. The beauty of it all truly comes from the crayon of the beholder! Prepare a bulletin board by mounting a construction-paper picture frame around the border. Then have each child think about who (and what) makes up his family. Give each child a large sheet of construction paper and crayons, paints, or other art materials. Have each child create a portrait of his family; then encourage him to write (or dictate) about his family. Provide time for each child to share his family portrait and creative writing during a group time. Encourage children to recognize the similarities and the unique traits among the families represented. Then mount each picture on the bulletin board.

Graphing Families
These graphs will help youngsters recognize the similarities and differences among their families. Make a graph for each family concept that you'd like to study. For example, you could make a graph for the number of people in a family, the number of children in a family, or the number of pets in a family. Photocopy each child's school photo several times. Have each child represent herself on each graph by mounting her photo in the appropriate column. As you summarize the graphs, be sure to give value to all of the families represented.

Family Traditions

While five- and six-year-olds may not be aware of their specific family traditions, this activity will help each child become aware of and appreciate her family traditions and the traditions of other families. Stimulate a discussion on family traditions by asking questions such as "What does your family do on weekends?", "How does your family celebrate birthdays?", and "What is your family's favorite food?" Help each child identify her family's tradition; then have her illustrate and write about their tradition. Post the finished projects on a bulletin board entitled "Tradition, Tradition!"

Family Show-And-Tell

Family show-and-tell provides a wonderful opportunity for each family to get to know you and your class and vice versa. Send a note home to each parent explaining family show-and-tell and asking each family to sign up for a particular day (see the illustration). Encourage families to come to school with as many family members as they can. If you have families that are from other cultures, be sure to have them share about those cultures with your children.

Dear Parent,
We are studying families in school and we'd love to meet yours! Please sign up for one of the dates below and bring as many family members as you can. Be prepared to share with us something that is special to your family. You could share photographs, a favorite family recipe, a song, a game, a pet,.... Be creative—we just want to get to know your family!
Thank you!
Ms. Henry

Sizing It Up

Explore each child's wishes regarding the size of family he thinks he would like to have. Record each child's wish. Then read aloud *Louanne Pig In The Perfect Family* by Nancy Carlson (Carolrhoda Books, Inc.). In this story, Louanne has a family of three—but she thinks that George's family of ten is the perfect size for a family. Children will laugh as well as think when Louanne gets a chance to experience the grass on the other side of the backyard fence!

After sharing the story, encourage children to discuss the advantages and disadvantages of having a large or small family. Then ask each child if he would like to change his family-size wish that you recorded earlier.

Our Classroom Family

Discuss with your youngsters the ways in which your class is like a family. Using the topic sentences below as discussion starters, encourage each child to share how each sentence applies to his family as well as your classroom family.

- We have lots of different people.
- We work and play together.
- We help each other.
- We care about each other's feelings.
- We disagree and compromise.

After your discussion, create a visual display of classroom unity. Draw a simple, outline person on a sheet of paper. Reproduce the pattern on construction paper for each child. Then ask each child to color his person to resemble himself. Cut out the people patterns; then mount them in a circle around the title "Our Classroom Family."

Family-Related Books

One Hundred Is A Family
Written by Pam Muñoz Ryan
Illustrated by Benrei Huang
Published by Hyperion Books For Children

Geraldine's Baby Brother
Written & Illustrated by Holly Keller
Published by Greenwillow Books

Octopus Hug
Written by Laurence Pringle
Illustrated by Kate Salley Palmer
Published by Boyds Mills Press

My Mom Travels A Lot
Written by Caroline Feller Bauer
Illustrated by Nancy Winslow Parker
Published by Frederick Warne

Her Majesty, Aunt Essie
Written & Illustrated by Amy Schwartz
Published by Bradbury Press

Horace
Written & Illustrated by Holly Keller
Published by Mulberry Books

Ant Antics

Go buggy with this unit on ants! By digging into the facts about ants, youngsters will learn social concepts such as cooperation, sharing, and living together in communities. Integrate your current math and language skills into these activities, and "ant-ticipate" lots of learning fun!

by Jayne Gammons

Question And Answer Anthills

Before you begin these ant activities, cut three large anthill shapes from brown bulletin-board paper. Title one anthill "What We Know About Ants"; the second, "What We Want To Know About Ants"; and the third, "What We Learned About Ants." Post the anthill shapes on a chalkboard or bulletin board. Using picture and reference books, show students pictures of ants. Encourage children to share facts they already know about ants. As they share, record the comments on the first anthill. Next ask students what they would like to know about ants. Record the questions on the second anthill. At the conclusion of the unit, ask students to recall what they have learned. Write the facts on the third anthill. Getting antsy? Get started!

Everybody Needs A Job

Ants are known as social insects because they live and work together in groups called *colonies*. Every ant in a colony has its own job to do, and all of the ants must work together to keep the colony alive. Make this social-studies concept, known as *division of labor,* relevant to your kindergartners. As a class, create a list of jobs current to the needs in your classroom. Have each youngster choose a job; then send her out to complete her assigned task. What busy little ants!

Extend this activity to your study of communities and community services by brainstorming a list of jobs people do in a town or city. Discuss why each of these jobs is important to the well-being of the community.

Barry Slate

We All Live Together

Most types of ants live together in a nest called an *anthill*. An anthill is made of dirt and leaves, and can have many miles of tunnels and hundreds of rooms inside. Discuss with your students the idea that the way ants live and work together in an anthill is similar to the way people live and work together in a city. Then have students create an anthill display. In advance, draw an anthill (with one room for each child) on a bulletin board. Have students press sponges dipped into brown paint onto the anthill shape. Next have students cut out construction-paper leaves, grass, and flowers. Mount the cutouts onto the bulletin board above the painted anthill. Name the anthill after your town. Have each child choose a room of the anthill. Then have him create the same number of thumbprint ants as there are people in his family. Label the ant families in your anthill town. Follow up this art project by reading aloud *Ant Cities* by Arthur Dorros (check your local library).

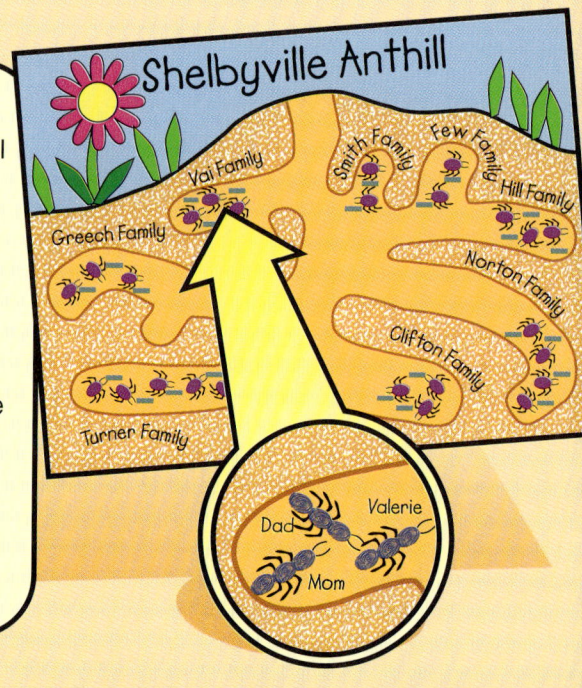

Picnic March

Get your picnic pals up and moving with this ant chant. While chanting the first verse, clap as you say each number word. While chanting the second verse, stomp as you say each number word.

One ant, **two** ants, **three** ants, **four**.
Our picnic is their grocery store.
Five ants, **six** ants, **seven** ants, **eight**.
They are crawling on my plate!

Eight ants, **seven** ants,
Stomp around.
Six ants, **five** ants,
On the ground.
Four ants, **three** ants,
On the run!
Two ants, **one** ant.
No more fun.

Let's Have A Picnic

Picnics mean warm weather, tasty food—and ants! When students go on a picnic at this center, an army of counting ants will follow close behind. To make the center, program a set of white paper plates with different numerals from one to ten. To make the plates look delicious, glue pictures of food cut from magazines onto each plate. Store the plates in a picnic basket. Using the pattern on page 189, duplicate a supply of 55 ants on brown construction paper. Laminate and cut out the ants. Spread a picnic tablecloth over a table or on the floor in a center. Place the basket of plates and the ant cutouts on the tablecloth. To use this center, a youngster selects a plate from the basket and reads the numeral on the plate. After counting out the corresponding number of ants, he then makes a trail of ants marching toward the plate.

Follow My Trail

When an ant finds food, he gets excited and wants to share the good news with his fellow ants! On the way back to the nest, he leaves a special trail by pressing his body on the ground. The other ants smell the trail and rush to the food. The more trails, the stronger the smell. After the food is gone, the ants return to their nest and the smell goes away. Play an ant-trail game to help youngsters understand the amazing way ants communicate in order to share food. To play, take your class to an open area such as a gym or playground. Gather students at one end of the area; then designate that space as the "nest." Spread a picnic cloth at the other end of the area; then designate that space as the "food." Have youngsters pretend to be ants; then give three perfume-spritzed cotton balls to each ant in your class. To begin the game, select one child to leave the nest and walk to the food. Instruct her to return to the nest, stopping three times to leave a cotton ball trail behind her. Upon returning to the nest, have her pick a partner. Instruct both ants to go back to the food. This time, the second ant returns to the nest, leaving a trail, and picks a partner. Continue in this manner until all of the ants are at the food. At this point, announce "Nest!" All ants should scurry back to the nest, picking up three cotton balls as they go.

On The Move

Dig into math with these manipulative math ants and workmats. For each child, photocopy the ant patterns (page 190) on red or brown construction paper and the anthill workmat (page 189) on tan construction paper. Laminate the ant designs and workmats; then cut them out.

Use the ants and workmats during a group math session to reinforce your current math curriculum needs. Provide each child in the group with a workmat and an equal number of ants. Instruct students to use the manipulatives to show a set of ants: equal to a number you announce, equal to a partner's set, with one more/less than a number you announce, or to match a story you tell ("Two ants were in a nest. One ant went to look for food."). After using the ants and workmats in a group, place the materials in a center for children to use during free time.

Leaf Nests

Though all ants live in groups, not all ants live in anthills. *Tailor* ants in Africa live in nests they make from leaves. These ants sew leaves together with their mouths, using silk thread made by the young ants. Have youngsters make leaf nests out of paper and yarn. To make a leaf nest, cut two identical leaf shapes from green construction paper. Holding the two leaves together, punch holes along the edges of the leaves. Sew the leaves together with a length of white yarn, leaving a section of the leaf nest open to create a pocket. Duplicate several sets of ants (page 190) on green construction paper. Cut the ants out; then give each student an equal amount to put in his leaf nest. Have each child take his nest of ants home, along with a letter encouraging parents to use the ants with the student to reinforce your current math skill.

Marching Ants

Army ants do not build nests. Instead, they move from place to place together in a long line, like marching soldiers. Teach youngsters the traditional tune "The Ants Go Marching." Keep a steady beat by tapping your hands on your knees while singing the song. Don't be surprised if students feel inspired to get up and march around! Then make walking in line fun by pretending to be army ants. Try marching two by two, three by three and so on until youngsters are in lines of ten. March on!

Once students are familiar with this tune, read aloud *Amazing Anthony Ant* by Lorna & Graham Philpot (Random House, Inc.). Youngsters will be amazed by Anthony Ant as they sing the song, follow the maze, and lift the flaps of this delightful book.

Big And Small

In *Two Bad Ants* by Chris Van Allsburg (Houghton Mifflin), two ants experience a dangerous adventure that convinces them to go back to the safety of their colony. Students will be held in suspense as you slowly read this book aloud. Encourage youngsters to examine the detailed illustrations, which are drawn from the ants' perspective. Challenge them to discover what the crystals, lake, and other dangers really are.

Your little ones will feel big when they realize that, to an ant, they are very large indeed. Stretch students' thinking by asking them to estimate the number of ants that could sit on a child's hand. Write the estimates on a large hand-shaped cutout. Then assist each child in tracing his own hand onto construction paper and cutting out the shape. Have each child fill his hand cutout with painted ants. To paint an ant, dip a cotton swab in black paint. For each ant, make three connected dots on the cutout. When the paint dries, add six legs and antennae with a black pen or marker. Conclude the activity by having each child count the number of ants on his hand cutout; then write the number on the back of the cutout.

I've Got Ants In My Pants! Dance

Are your students getting antsy? Quick! Have them stand in a circle. Select one child to have a pretend ant in his pants. Or give him a plastic ant to put in his pocket. Play lively music as the youngster wiggles, jiggles, and probably giggles. Have the other children clap their hands or stomp their feet to the rhythm of the music as they watch. After an appropriate length of time, give a signal for the ant to jump from the pants of the first child to the pants of another child in the circle. This child can then perform his own creative version of the "I've Got Ants In My Pants!" dance. The antics continue as the ant jumps from child to child around the circle.

Class Big Books/Student Small Books

Choose from the "ant-thology" of ideas below to create a variety of class- and student-made books. To make a class big book, duplicate a supply of the large ant pattern (page 189) on brown or red construction paper. Cut out each ant; then glue it onto a 12" x 18" piece of white construction paper. Using the ideas below, choose the type of book you would like to make; then program the ants accordingly. Assign each programmed page to a child or group of children to illustrate. Bind the book with a cover; then share the book during a group reading time.

To make an individual book for each child, duplicate and staple together a set of construction-paper booklet pages (page 190). Have each student write (or dictate for you to write) a title and her name, then decorate the front page to create a cover. On each of the following pages, have her program the ant designs and illustrate the pages. Students may wish to make their own versions of the class book or original books using the ideas suggested below.

Ant Antonyms—Program each ant with a pair of antonyms.

A Is For Ant—Program each ant with a word that begins with the letter *A*.

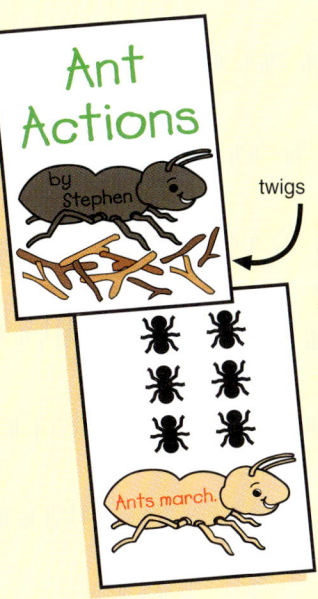

Ant Actions—Program each ant with a simple sentence describing ant actions.

The Ants Go Marching—Program each ant with a numeral or number word.

Let's Be "Observ-ant"

Venture outside with your class on any warm day and you are sure to find an anthill nearby. Or place a piece of bread on a windowsill or class patio to lure ants close enough for observation. Record class observations on a chart. When youngsters are studying ants, inform them that they are acting as *myrmecologists*—scientists who study ants.

To investigate ant life further, create a simple ant farm to put in a science center. Begin by filling a large jar with sifted dirt. Collect ants in a smaller jar. Be careful—some ants can bite or sting! Transfer the ants to the large jar. Put a tiny piece of bread and a small, damp sponge piece into the jar to provide the ants with food and water. Punch several small holes in the lid before placing it on the jar. Tape a piece of black construction paper around the jar so that the ants will live in the dark as they do underground. Then remove the paper when observing the ants. Place the ant farm in a science center along with crayons, pencils, and a booklet titled "Our Ant Farm." Encourage students to draw and write about their ant-farm observations in the booklet.

A Delicious Treat

As a treat for your hardworking youngsters, serve edible ants buried in individual anthills! Simply place several ants (chocolate-covered raisins) in a cup and cover them with crushed cookie crumbs. Or serve Ants On A Log—the traditional insect favorite made from celery sticks, peanut butter, and raisins. Tasty!

Get Busy Reading!

The Ant And The Elephant
Written & Illustrated by Bill Peet
Published by Houghton Mifflin

Antics! An Alphabetical Anthology
Written & Illustrated by Cathi Hepworth
Published by G. P. Putnam's Sons

The Ants Go Marching
(This book is out of print. Check your local library.)
Written by Berniece Freschet
Illustrated by Stefan Martin
Published by Charles Scribner's Sons

"I Can't" Said The Ant: A Second Book Of Nonsense
Written & Illustrated by Polly Cameron
Published by Coward, McCann & Geoghegan, Inc.

Step By Step
Written by Diane Wolkstein
Illustrated by Jos. A. Smith
Published by Morrow Junior Books

Anthill Workmat

Use with "On The Move" on page 186.

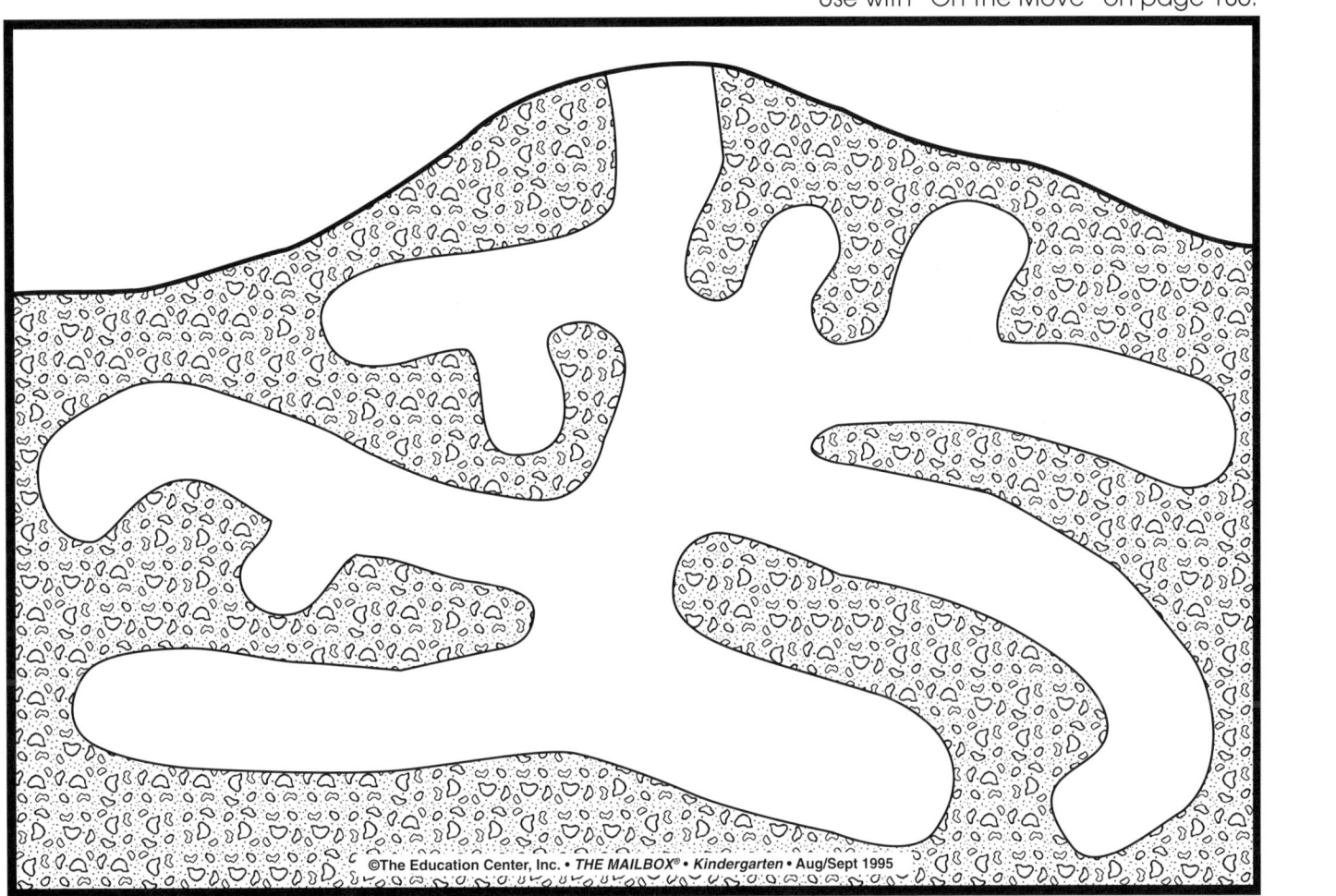

©The Education Center, Inc. • THE MAILBOX® • Kindergarten • Aug/Sept 1995

Ant Pattern

Use with "Let's Have A Picnic" on page 185 and "Class Big Books" on page 187.

©The Education Center, Inc. • THE MAILBOX® • Kindergarten • Aug/Sept 1995

189

Patterns
Ant Manipulatives
Use with "On The Move" and "Leaf Nests" on page 186.

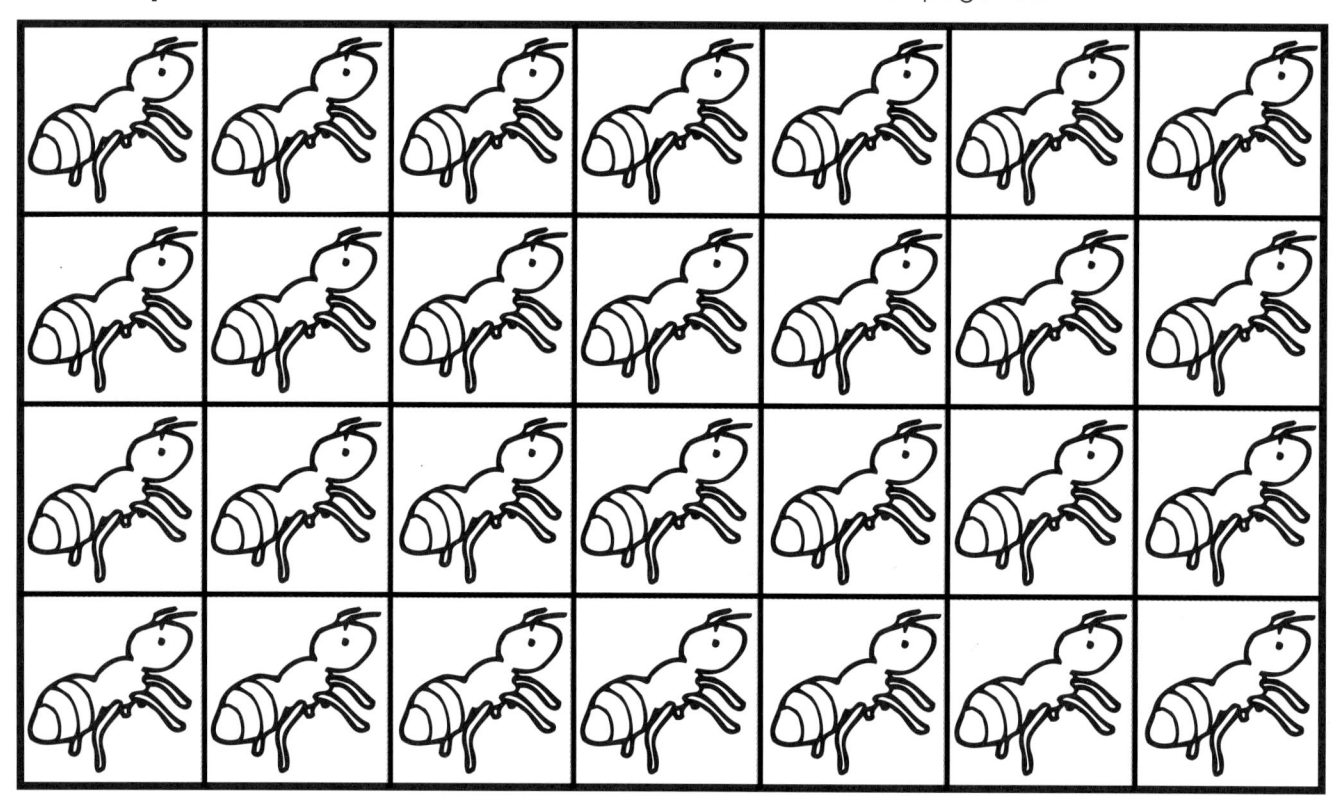

©The Education Center, Inc. • THE MAILBOX® • Kindergarten • Aug/Sept 1995

Booklet Pattern
Use with "Student Small Books" on page 187.

©The Education Center, Inc. • THE MAILBOX® • Kindergarten • Aug/Sept 1995

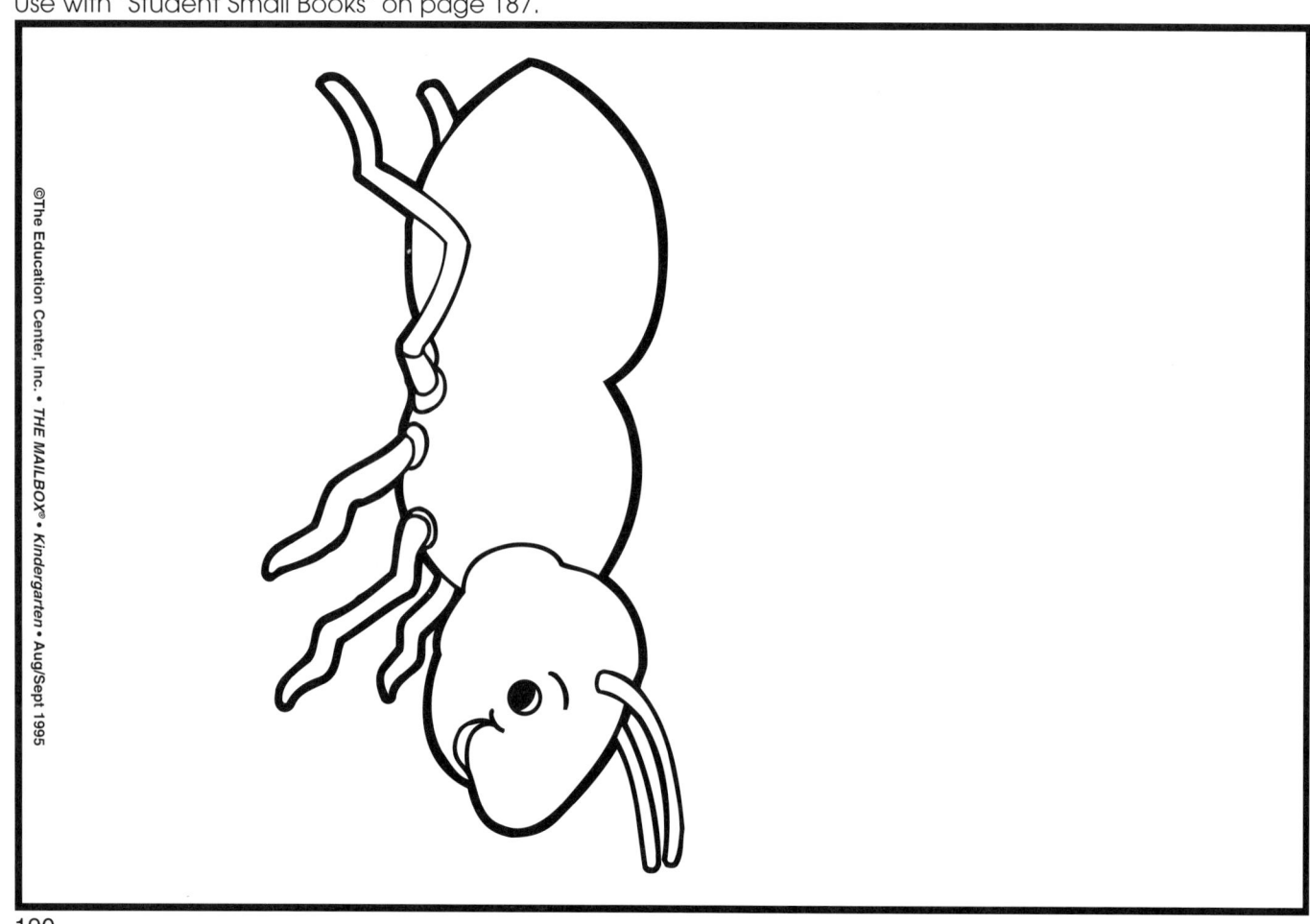

No Bones About It!

Take the scariness out of skeletons with this science-oriented unit all about bones.

by Lucia Kemp Henry

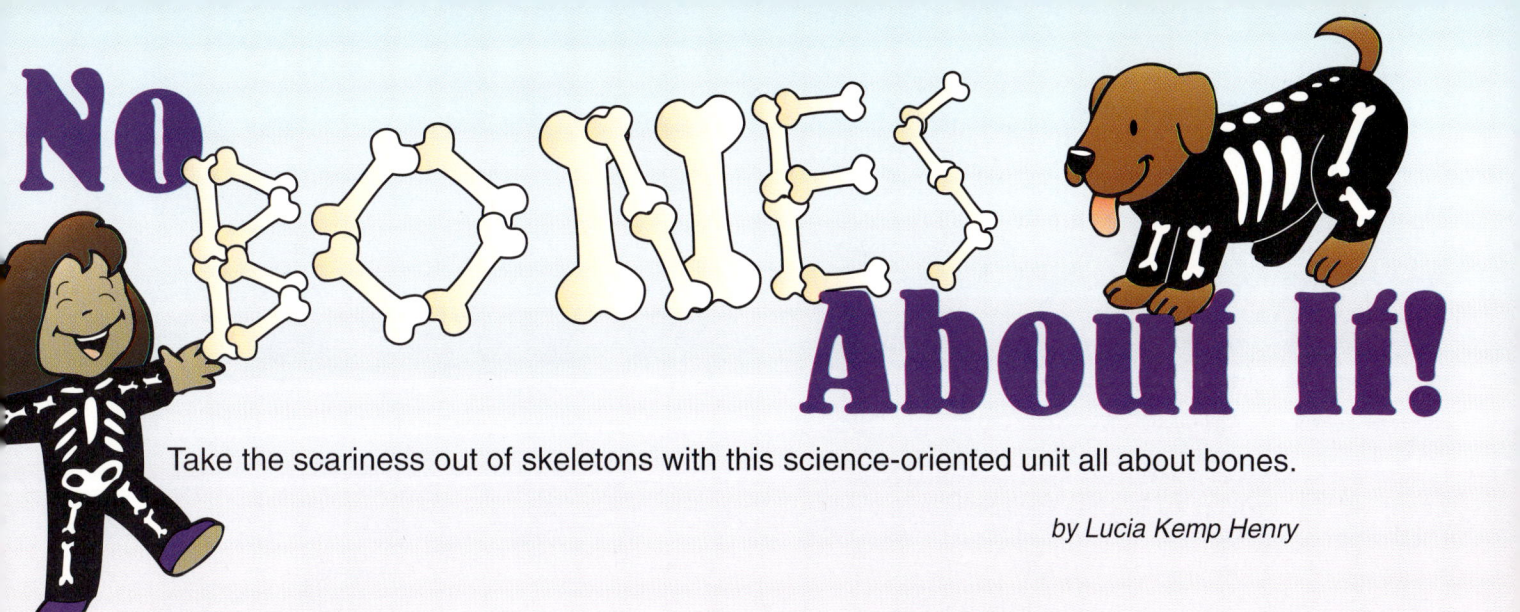

The Bone Basics

Bone up on the basics with these basic bone facts.

- Bones give our bodies shape.
- Bones give our bodies support.
- Bones protect us.
- Bones help us move.
- Bones grow.
- Bones are strong.
- Bones can break and mend.

X-Ray Play

Ask your local hospital X-ray lab to donate or loan old X-ray films which show the basic bones of the human body such as the skull, ribs, hand, arm, leg, foot, and spine. As you show youngsters each X-ray, have them silently guess which body part it represents. Ask each child to show her guess by pointing to that part of her own body. Display a word card alongside the X-ray; then ask the students to read the word on the card. If you are able to keep the films, consider putting them in a center along with the word cards. Students who visit the center can match each X-ray to its corresponding word card.

My Bones

This fun action poem will ensure that no one can be caught being a lazybones!

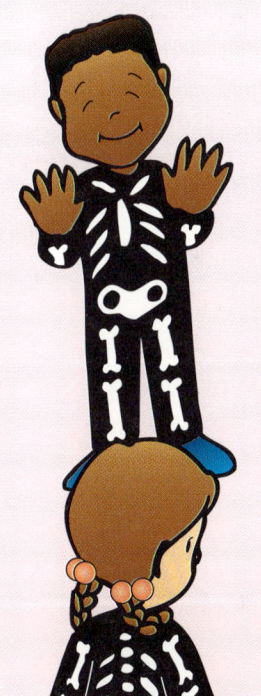

My bones are inside me.	*Point to chest.*
My bones are strong.	*Flex biceps.*
My bones help my body move all day long.	*Move around in place.*
Bones in my fingers.	*Wiggle fingers.*
Bones in my toes.	*Wiggle toes.*
Every bone is a bone that grows.	*Stoop down, then "grow" to tiptoes.*
Bones in my foot.	*Point to foot.*
Bones in my hand.	*Wave hand.*
My bones help me jump and hop and stand.	*Jump, hop, then stand tall.*
Bones in my back.	*Point to spine.*
Bones in my chest.	*Point to chest.*
Good, strong bones are the very best.	*Pose like a bodybuilder.*
Bones in my legs.	*Point to legs.*
Bones in my arms.	*Point to arms.*
Bones keep my heart and lungs from harm.	*Wrap arms around chest in a hug.*
Bones in my neck.	*Point to neck.*
Bones in my head.	*Point to head.*
My bones even work when I'm in bed!	*Pretend to sleep.*
My bones help me work.	*Pretend to work.*
My bones help me play.	*Pretend to play.*
My bones are inside me hidden away!	*Stand, arms and legs outstretched.*

—by Lucia Kemp Henry

Mr. Funny Bones Big Book

Discuss with youngsters how the bones in our bodies, along with our muscles, help us move in many different ways. Title a chart "Our bones help us...." Ask youngsters to brainstorm a list of movement words such as *hop, slide,* and *gallop.* Record the words on the chart. Then, as a class, make this silly big book using the skeleton patterns on page 194. Reduce the patterns slightly so that both pieces will fit on one page with space to spare. Duplicate a classroom supply of the patterns onto white construction paper. Have each child cut out the patterns. Ask him to arrange and glue the patterns on a large piece of black construction paper. Then have him use chalk to draw arm, hand, leg, and foot bones to show the movement of his choice. Program each child's page with the sentence "Mr. Funny Bones can [movement word]." Bind the pages between construction-paper covers. Encourage each child to share his page during a group reading time.

The Knee Bone's Connected To The Leg Bone...

This child-size skeleton puzzle will help youngsters learn the correct configuration of a human skeleton. Students will also learn to match bones to their corresponding body parts. To make a puzzle, ask a child to lie on a large sheet of bulletin-board paper. Trace around the child; then cut on the resulting outline. Enlarge the skeleton patterns on pages 194 and 195 so that they are proportionate to the body shape (about 150%). Laminate the patterns; then cut on the solid outlines. Place the body shape and the skeleton patterns in a center. Students who visit the center can place the skeleton pieces on the body shape in the correct position. If desired, assist each child in making his own skeleton puzzle.

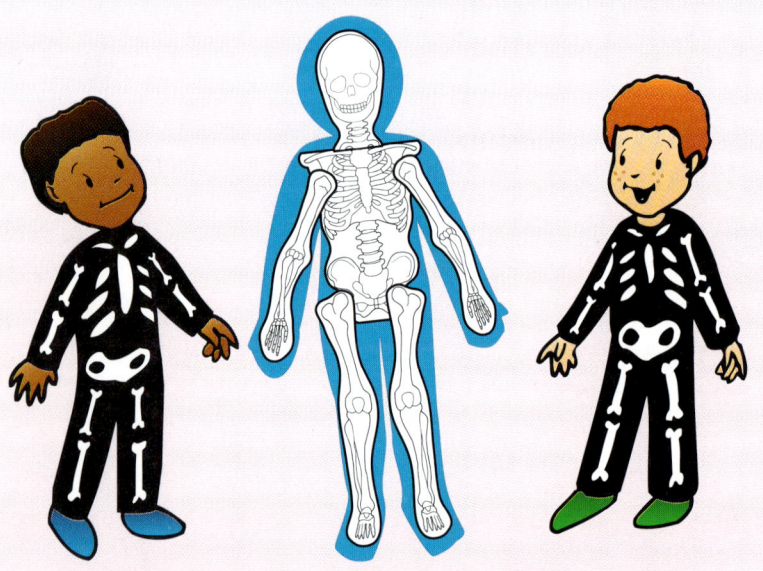

Animals Have Skeletons, Too!

Here's an exciting way to introduce youngsters to the concept that, just like people, many common animals have skeletons. Read aloud *The Glow-In-The-Dark Book Of Animal Skeletons* by Regina Kahney (Random House). Hold each page of the book under a light for a few seconds; then turn off the lights. Youngsters will be thrilled to see that the skeletons glow in the dark!

As a follow-up to reading this book, have youngsters make animal skeletons booklets. Reproduce the booklet pages (pages 196–198) in classroom quantities. Using a paper cutter, cut along the bold outlines; then provide each child with a set of pages. Ask her to stack the pages in numerical order with the title page on top and the end page on the bottom. Have each youngster follow along as you read each page. Discuss the illustrations for each animal, pointing out that each animal's body shape resembles its skeleton shape. Direct each child to color her pages. Consider providing youngsters with glow-in-the-dark crayons to color the illustration of each animal's skeleton. Staple the pages together. Encourage children to read their books at home with their families.

All About Bones

Make no bones about it! Students are sure to enjoy these skeleton center suggestions.

- Duplicate the skeleton patterns on pages 194 and 195. Cut out and assemble the skeleton; then display it in a writing center. Label the skeleton or display a set of cards labeled with words learned during the unit. Stock the center with white paper, scissors, glue, pencils, and colored construction paper. A student who visits this center can draw and cut out bone shapes, glue them onto a sheet of colored paper, and label his project.

- Use the animal skeletons booklet (pages 196-198) to create a simple matching game. Duplicate one set of the booklet pages. Using correction fluid, mask the page number on each illustrated booklet page. Reproduce the modified pages; then cut the pages apart to make cards. Glue each set of matching cards to the same color of construction paper. Laminate them for durability; then cut the cards apart. To use the cards, a child can match each skeleton illustration with the appropriate animal picture.

- Place a collection of books about bones and skeletons in a reading center. If possible, include a model of a human skeleton in the center. *The Bones & Skeleton Book* by Stephen Cumbaa (Somerville House Books Limited) can be purchased (at children's specialty shops) in a kit which includes a put-together skeleton model.

An Inside Look

With these exciting animal puppets, students will be able to see each animal's skeleton through the body illustration. Enlarge each animal body and skeleton pattern from the animal skeletons booklet (page 192). Be sure to leave a margin around the patterns as they are enlarged. Lay each skeleton illustration under its matching body picture, making sure that the skeleton lies within the body outline. Cut around the illustrations, leaving a one-inch margin around the top and sides, and a larger margin along the bottom. Insert a wide craft stick between the two pictures, making sure that the stick does not cover any part of either illustration. Apply a thin stream of glue around the edges of and between the two illustrations. Press them together and allow the project to dry. Encourage students to hold the puppets up to a light source such as a window or lamp so that the skeleton illustrations are visible through the animal pictures.

More Books About Bones

The Skeleton Inside You
Written by Philip Balestrino
Illustrated by True Kelley
Published by Thomas Y. Crowell

Body Books: Bones
Written by Anna Sandeman
Illustrated by Ian Thompson
Published by Copper Beech Books

Eyewitness Books: Skeleton
Written by Steve Parker
Published by Alfred A. Knopf

Skeletons! Skeletons! All About Bones
Written by Katy Hall
Illustrated by Paige Billin-Frye
Published by Scholastic Inc.

Patterns
Use with "Mr. Funny Bones Big Book" and "The Knee Bone's Connected To The Leg Bone..." on page 192 and "All About Bones" on page 193.

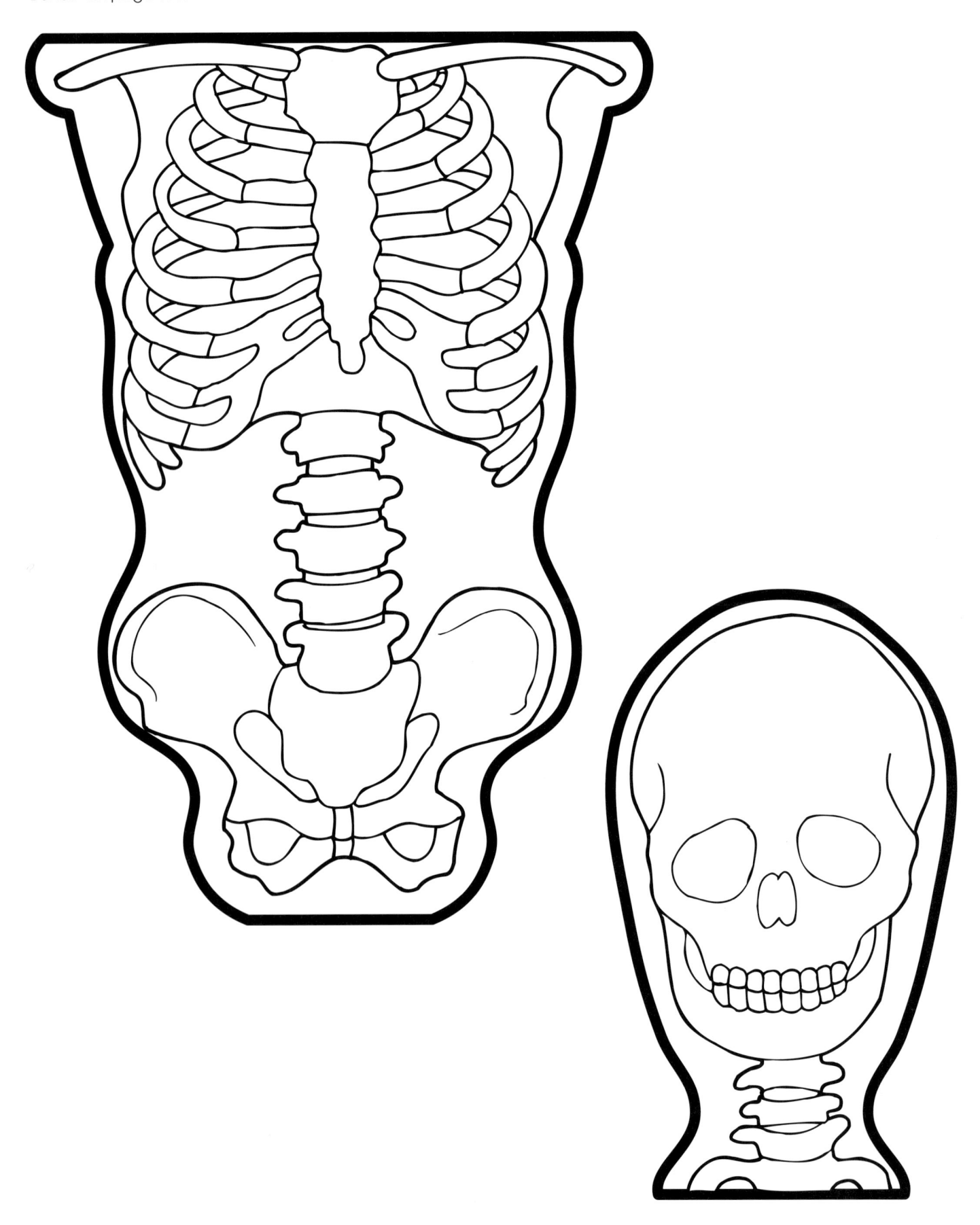

Patterns

Use with "The Knee Bone's Connected To The Leg Bone..." on page 192 and "All About Bones" on page 193.

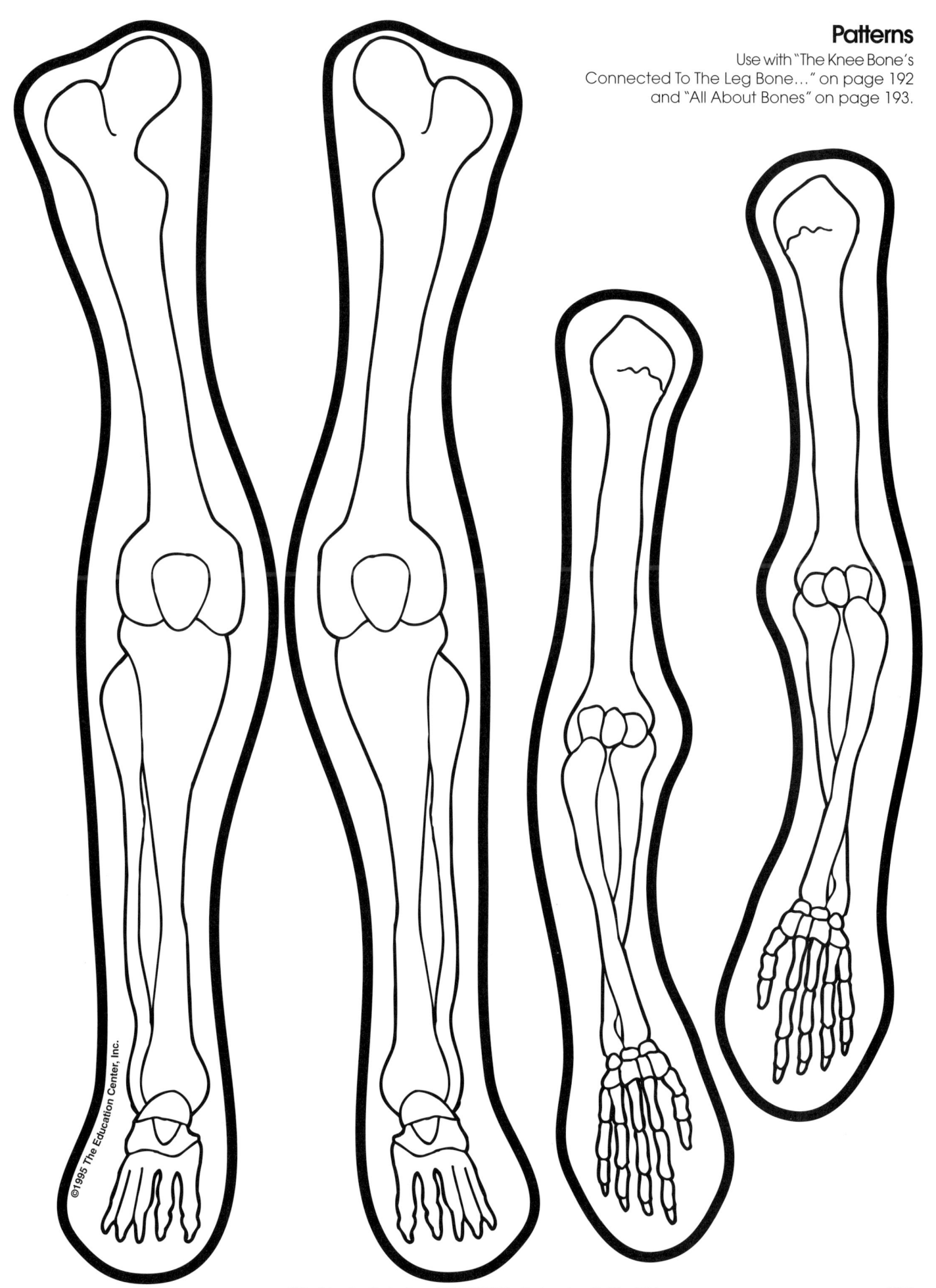

Animal Skeletons Booklet
Use with "Animals Have Skeletons, Too!" on page 192 and "An Inside Look" and "All About Bones" on page 193.

Animals With Skeletons

by _____

©The Education Center, Inc. • THE MAILBOX® • Kindergarten • Oct/Nov 1995

This is a dog.

1

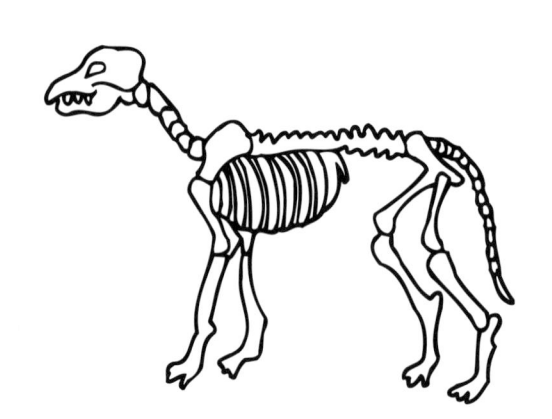

This is a dog skeleton.

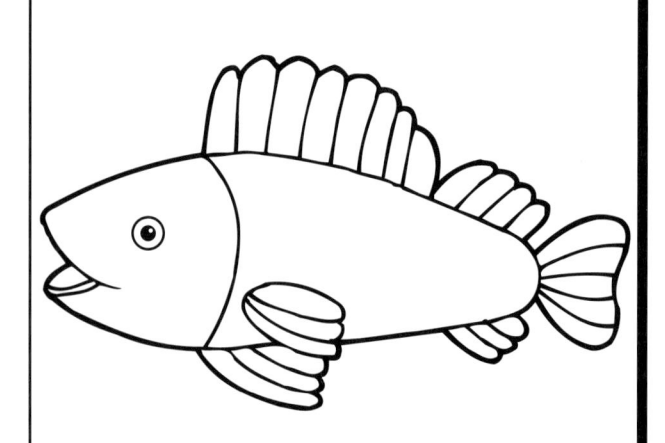

2

This is a fish.

3

Animal Skeletons Booklet

Use with "Animals Have Skeletons, Too!" on page 192 and "An Inside Look" and "All About Bones" on page 193.

This is a fish skeleton.

4

This is a frog.

5

This is a frog skeleton.

6

This is a duck.

7

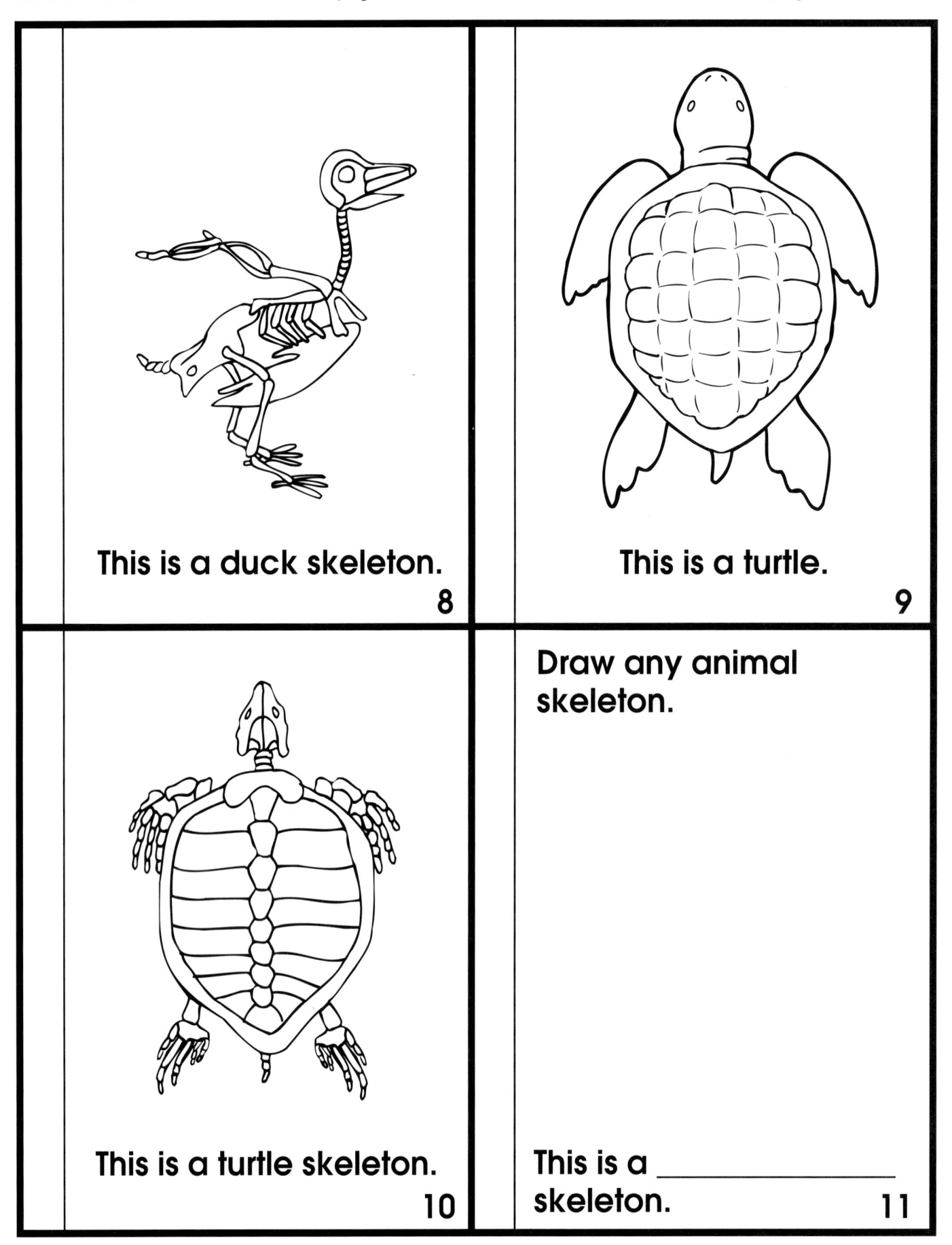

Animal Skeletons Booklet
Use with "Animals Have Skeletons, Too!" on page 192 and "An Inside Look" and "All About Bones" on page 193.

This is a duck skeleton.

8

This is a turtle.

9

This is a turtle skeleton.

10

Draw any animal skeleton.

This is a _____ skeleton.

11

Scarecrow Pattern
Use with "Scarecrow Books" on page 201 and "Counting Crows" on page 203.

If I Only Had A... Scarecrow!

Swing into the scarecrow season with this multidisciplinary unit including activities to reinforce skills in reading and language, social studies, math, science, large-motor movements, and more!

ideas by Lucia Kemp Henry

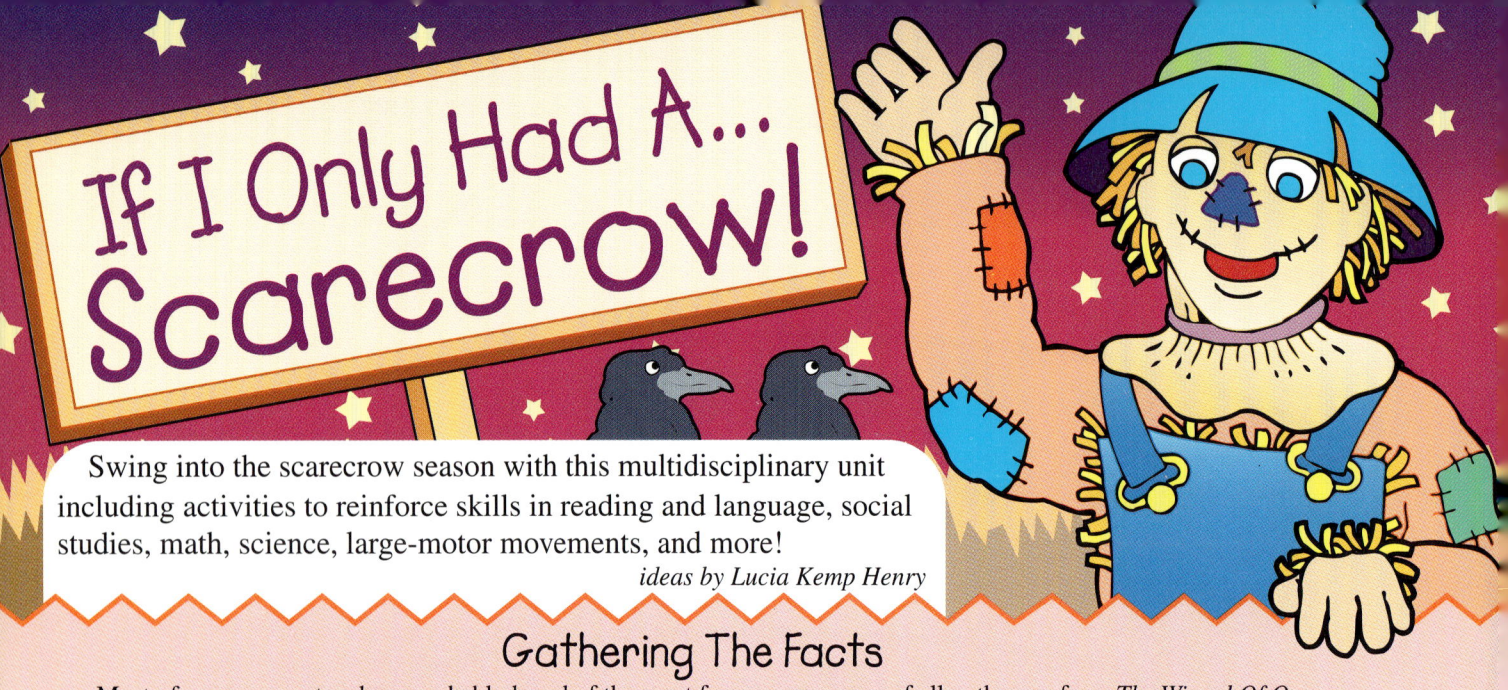

Gathering The Facts

Most of your youngsters have probably heard of the most famous scarecrow of all— the one from *The Wizard Of Oz*. But how many of your little ones actually understand the real-life purposes of scarecrows? Before posing that question to your students, get the facts for yourself by reading *Scarecrow!* by Valerie Littlewood (Dutton Children's Books). Since some of the text in this book may be too advanced for young children, prepare to paraphrase the information that is appropriate for your group.

Cut three large pumpkin shapes from orange paper. Title one pumpkin "What We Know"; the second, "What We Want To Know"; and the third, "What We Learned." Mount the pumpkins on a wall or board along with a scarecrow cutout. Then ask your children to share what they already know about scarecrows. Record the information on the first cutout. Find out what youngsters would like to know about scarecrows, and record that information on the second cutout. Then share the illustrations from Valerie Littlewood's *Scarecrow!* while you paraphrase the text. Afterwards ask children to share what they learned from reading the book. Record the new information on the remaining cutout. As you continue your scarecrow unit, add new discoveries to this list.

What We Know
- Scarecrows stand on a farm.
- Scarecrows can be very tall.

What We Want To Know
- How do scarecrows stand up if they're not alive?
- How do scarecrows scare the birds?

What We Learned
- Scarecrows can look like boys or girls.
- Scarecrows stand up on a stick.
- Scarecrows that are alive are really people.

Scarecrow Action Poem

Get your little ones moving—scarecrow style—with this simple action poem! Write the poem on a piece of chart paper. Encourage youngsters to use their growing reading skills to identify words or letter sounds in the poem. Then read the poem aloud. Move each body part—scarecrow style—as it is mentioned in the poem. In no time at all, youngsters will join you in reciting the simple rhyme and flopping around accordingly!

The Floppy Scarecrow

The floppy, floppy scarecrow
Guards his field all day.
He waves his floppy, floppy **hands**
To scare the crows away!

Repeat the poem, replacing the boldfaced body-part word with each of the following in turn: arms, elbows, head, legs, knees, feet, ankles, toes....**Can your youngsters think of any others?**

Soft-Sculptured Scarecrow

Enlist the help of your youngsters to create a scarecrow reading buddy for your classroom. Ask parents for donations to go towards making the scarecrow. Specify needed items such as old clothes, boots, gloves, an old pillowcase, and a hat. Have children stuff each of the body parts with newspaper, straw, or leaves; then use twine to close up any openings. Use large safety pins to secure the pieces together to form a scarecrow. Using fabric paint, add facial features to the face (pillowcase). When the scarecrow is finished, hold a classroom vote to name him. Then situate your original scarecrow in your reading center so youngsters can take turns reading with their new buddy.

Scarecrow Books

There's a whole harvest of language experiences awaiting each child who participates in making these class scarecrow books. In advance, program a classroom supply of white construction paper with "The scarecrow sees...." Then encourage each youngster to imagine that he is a scarecrow standing in a field. Have children brainstorm lists of items (by category) that they might see as they watch over their fields. For example, you might suggest categories such as *signs of fall, farm animals, vegetables,* or *Halloween things.* Write children's responses on the board or chart paper (in categories). Then give each child a sheet of the programmed paper. Have each child choose one of the items listed and illustrate it on his paper.

For each category mentioned, make a book cover by duplicating the scarecrow pattern (page 199) on construction paper. Color and cut out the scarecrow patterns; then glue each scarecrow to a different sheet of construction paper. Title these covers "The Scarecrow Sees [fill in the category]." Display the covers in a pocket chart. Then, when the children's illustrations are complete, have each child share his illustration with the group and then determine in which category his page belongs. Ask that child to place his picture under the appropriate book cover. When each child has shared and categorized his page, staple the covers and pages together. Make the finished books available for free-time reading throughout your scarecrow studies.

Scarecrow Colors Booklet

Color-word recognition will fall into place when youngsters hang out with these colorful little fellows. For each child, duplicate the booklet patterns (pages 204-207) on construction paper. Cut apart the pages. Give each child a set of booklet pages. After identifying the cover, have each child sequence her pages; then staple them together at the top. Then have each child color the cover as she likes and the remaining pages according to the color words. Read the booklets together; then encourage students to take their books home and read them to family members.

Barry Slate

201

Wings A-Flappin'

Little wings will be a-flappin' when youngsters practice counting with this scarecrow-themed subtraction song. Before singing, choose one child to be the scarecrow and ten children to be birds. Have the scarecrow strike a pose in front of the class; then begin singing the song. When you sing the fourth line of the song, encourage the birds to flap around the scarecrow. As you sing the second verse, have the scarecrow "scare" one of the birds away. Repeat the second verse (replacing the boldfaced number word with the appropriate number word) until all of the birds have been scared away.

(sung to the tune of "Have You Ever Seen A Lassie?")

Have you ever seen a scarecrow,
A scarecrow, a scarecrow?
Have you ever seen a scarecrow
With ten hungry birds?
Ten birds, ten birds,
Ten wing-flapping birds.
Have you ever seen a scarecrow
With ten hungry birds?

Have you ever seen a scarecrow,
A scarecrow, a scarecrow?
Have you ever seen a scarecrow
Scare one bird away?
One bird, one bird,
One wing-flapping bird.
Have you ever seen a scarecrow
With **nine** hungry birds?

by Lucia Kemp Henry

Suit Yourself

These child-made scarecrow costumes help reinforce shape-recognition skills and they're also perfect for fall-themed dress-up. For each child, cut out head and arm holes from a large brown paper bag. Also cut a variety of geometrically shaped patches from fabric scraps. Provide a supply of water-diluted white glue and paintbrushes.

To make a scarecrow shirt, have each child apply her choice of patches to her bag. To apply a patch, brush an area of the bag with thinned glue. Press the patch onto the glue; then brush more of the glue mixture over the patch. Repeat the process as desired. Have each child wear her scarecrow shirt with her own shirt, jeans, hat, and other scarecrow accessories. Use face paint to decorate each child's face to resemble a scarecrow.

Halloween Hoedown

A rhythmic reading of the magical *Barn Dance!* by Bill Martin Jr. and John Archambault (Henry Holt And Company) will inspire a Halloween hoedown in any classroom! Read the book aloud to your youngsters. (Don't be surprised if you're asked to read it more than once!) Then have each child wear his scarecrow costume (see "Suit Yourself") as he dances to some real hand-clappin', foot-stompin', hoedown harmonies!

More Scarecrow Books

Don't Be Scared, Scarecrow
Written & Illustrated by Pirkko Vainio
Published by North-South Books

Hello Mr. Scarecrow
Written & Illustrated by Rob Lewis
Published by Farrar Straus Giroux

The Scarebird
Written by Sid Fleischman
Illustrated by Peter Sis
Published by Greenwillow Books

Counting Crows

After completing this motivating learning center, each student will have an opportunity to gather in the harvest! For each number that you would like to study, photocopy the scarecrow (page 199) and that amount of crows (this page) on construction paper. Use markers to color each scarecrow and crow; then laminate and cut out all the pieces. Use a permanent marker to program each scarecrow's hat with a numeral or number word. Store the crows and a small bag of candy corn in a resealable plastic bag. Tape each scarecrow to a different empty quart-sized milk carton.

To use this center, a child first places the bag of candy corn on a table. Then he arranges the scarecrows around the corn. Next he scatters all of the crows around the scarecrows. Each scarecrow can protect the corn from the number of crows that is programmed on his hat—no more, no less! The child reads the number word or numeral on each scarecrow, then places that many crows near the appropriate scarecrow. When all the crows have been accounted for, the corn has been successfully protected and the child may take a piece of candy corn to celebrate!

Patterns
Use with "Counting Crows" on page 203.

crows

©The Education Center, Inc. • THE MAILBOX® • Kindergarten • Oct/Nov 1995

203

Booklet Pages — Use with "Scarecrow Colors Booklet" on page 201.

The hat is **brown.**

1

Scarecrow Colors

204 ©The Education Center, Inc. • *THE MAILBOX®* • *Kindergarten* • Oct/Nov 1995

Use with "Scarecrow Colors Booklet" on page 201.

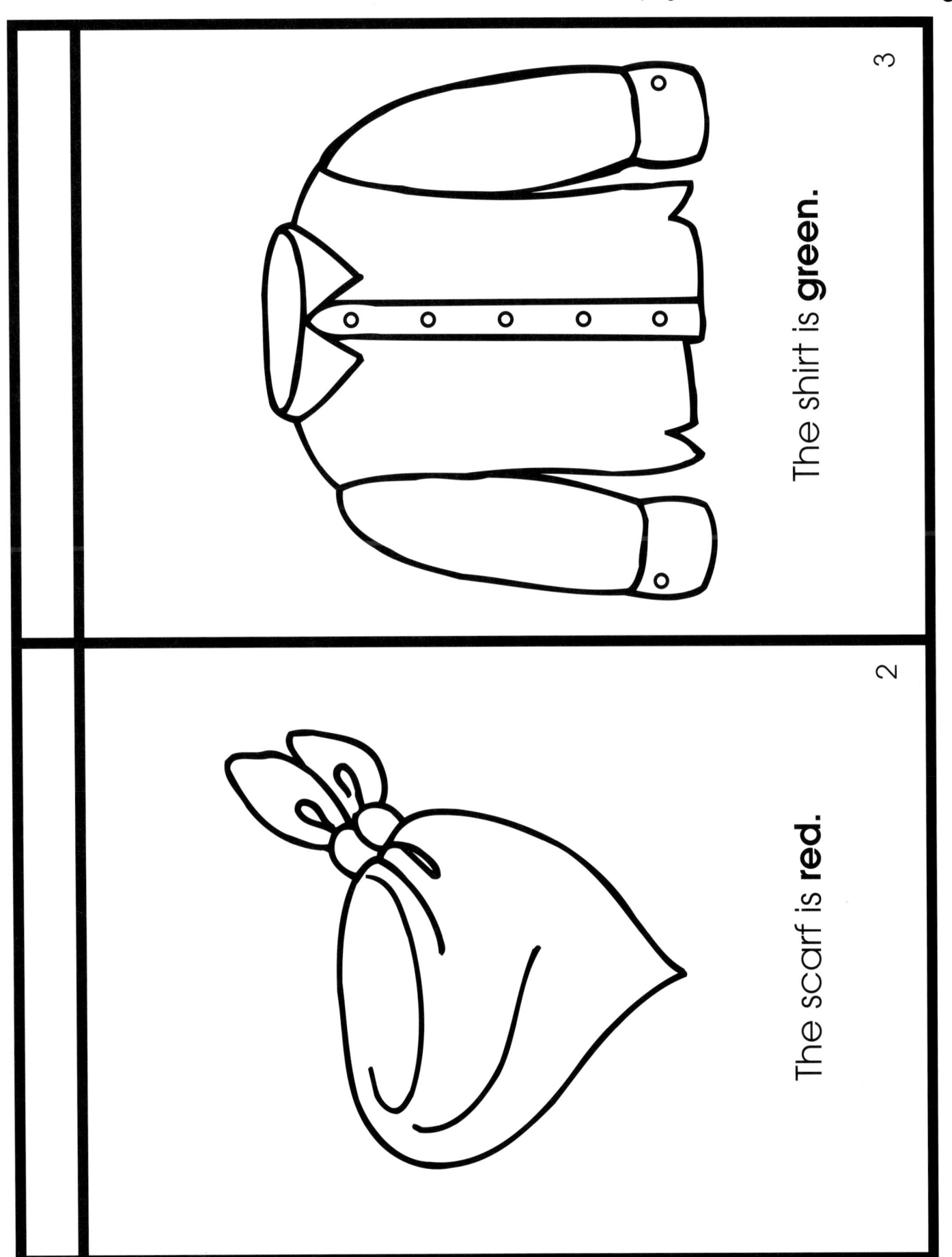

Booklet Pages

The shirt is **green**.

3

The scarf is **red**.

2

©The Education Center, Inc. • *THE MAILBOX®* • *Kindergarten* • Oct/Nov 1995

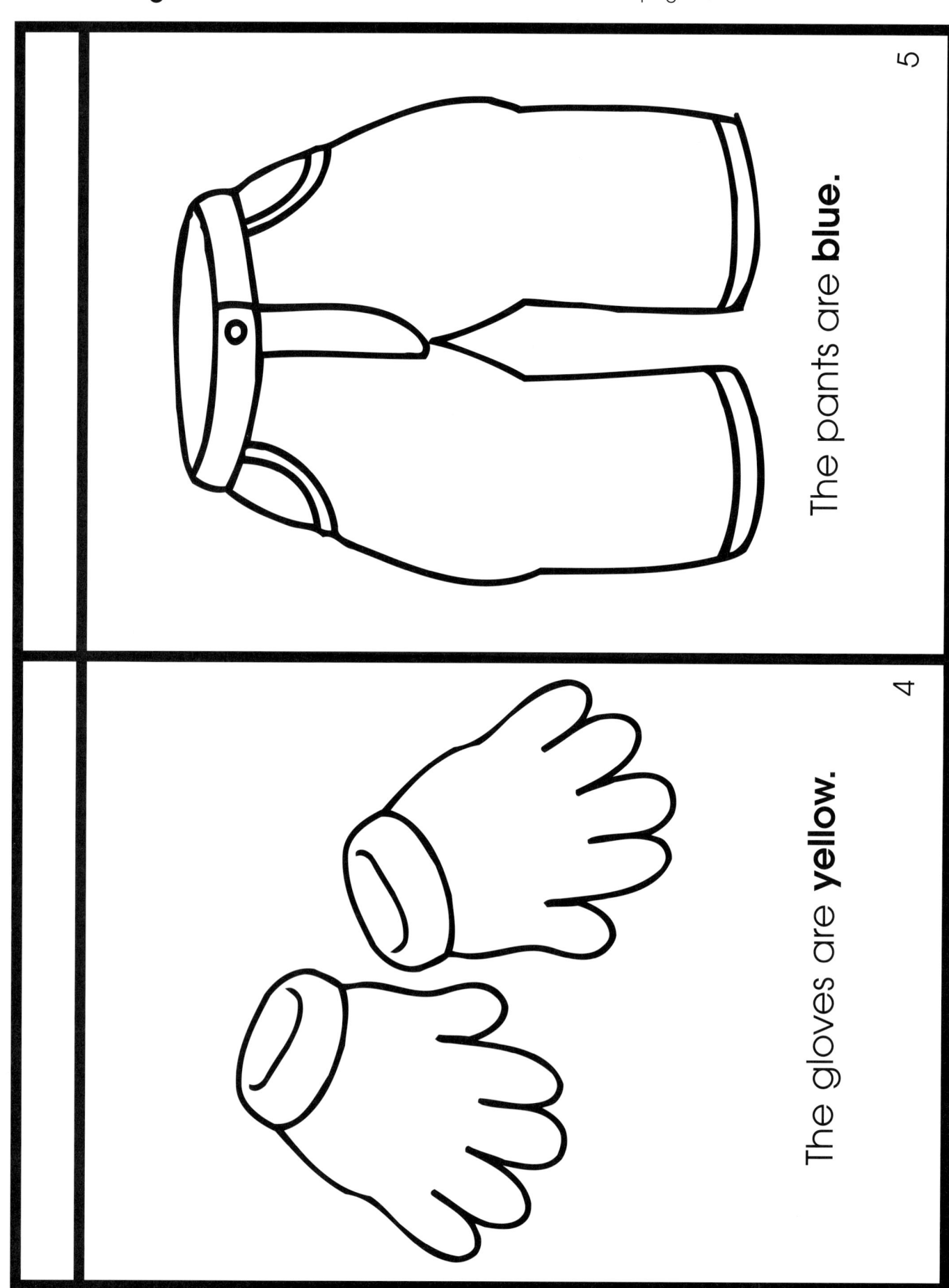

Booklet Pages Use with "Scarecrow Colors Booklet" on page 201.

The pants are **blue.**

5

The gloves are **yellow.**

4

Booklet Pages

206 ©The Education Center, Inc. • *THE MAILBOX®* • *Kindergarten* • Oct/Nov 1995

Use with "Scarecrow Colors Booklet" on page 201.

Booklet Pages

7

brown, red, green, yellow, blue, black, yellow, blue, black

6

The boots are **black.**

Paws, Claws, A Roar—And More!

Cash in on today's lion craze by presenting this unit on lions and other members of the cat family. The child-centered activities in this unit reinforce skills across the curriculum including scientific skills such as observation, comparison, and classification. So give a nice, long stretch; a low, rumbly roar—and prepare to meet the king and his cousins!

ideas by Lucia Kemp Henry

What A Family!

Your youngsters will be intrigued to learn that the majestic-looking lion and the sweet, cuddly kitten are members of the very same family—the cat family! Ask children to name other animals that they think might be members of the cat family. Write their responses on a sheet of chart paper. Then share Bobbie Kalman and Tammy Everts's *Big Cats* and *Little Cats* (both books published by Crabtree Publishing Company). As each member of the cat family is introduced in the books, check your list to be sure that each particular cat is on your list. If not, encourage youngsters to use the book as a reference and call out the letters in a particular cat's name as you add it to the list. Have you ever seen such a large family?

Define That Cat

After exploring the many members of the cat family (see "What A Family!"), encourage your youngsters to cooperatively write a definition for *cat*. Begin by having children brainstorm definition ideas as you write each idea on the board. Then, as a class, incorporate all of the ideas into a final definition. Write the new class-created definition on a large sheet of paper and attach it to the list of cat-family members from "What A Family!"

fur   eats meat
4 legs   whiskers
claws

A cat is a four-legged mammal that eats meat. A cat has claws and whiskers. Cats can be big or small and make noises like purring or roaring.

Here, Kitty, Kitty!

Captivating illustrations, repetitive text, common sight words—all this and more is found in *Have You Seen My Cat?* by Eric Carle (Scholastic Inc.). In this story, a young boy goes on a round-the-world quest in search of his lost cat. Throughout his search, he encounters many members of the cat family—but none of those cats is *his* cat. At long last, he finds his cat—and a very special surprise awaiting!

After sharing the story, have youngsters revisit the illustrations. Encourage them to use their observation skills and describe the different characteristics of each cat-family member such as body parts, size, and fur coloration. (If desired, have youngsters also look through books containing actual photos of cats such as those mentioned in "What A Family!") Then give each child a sheet of construction paper and ask him to use art supplies (such as paints, crayons, and tissue paper and water-diluted glue) to illustrate a picture of his favorite member of the cat family. Have him write/dictate the name of the cat he chose and why he likes that particular cat. Then bind all of the pages between construction-paper covers entitled "This Is MY Cat!" Have each child share his page during a group reading time.

Jacob
This is my favorite cat because he is the biggest. It's a tiger.

This is a kitten. I like her because she is so cute. Katie

The King Of Cats

Lions seem to be a hot topic with youngsters these days. So capitalize on your students' natural interest in the king of beasts, and take a look at lions by making this informational booklet. Duplicate the booklet pages (pages 211–213) for each child; then cut the booklet pages apart. Follow the directions for each page. After each child has made his booklet, read the books together. Then encourage children to take their booklets home to share with other friends and family members.

Booklet Cover: Read the title of the booklet together. Have each child write his name on the cover, then color the page.

Booklet Page 1: Read the text. After a round of roaring, tell youngsters that a lion's mane helps protect him during fights. The long, thick fur helps to soften the blows from his enemies. A lion's mane can be blond, brown, black, or a mixture of these colors. Have each child color the lion's body, then add a long, thick mane by gluing pieces of yellow, brown, and/or black yarn onto the picture.

Booklet Page 2: Read the text. Inform children that lionesses do most of the hunting for their families. Lions eat animals that run faster than they do (such as zebra and antelope) so the lions have to sneak up on their prey. Explain that lions live in grassy plains and areas of thorny scrub trees. Discuss the term *camouflage;* then ask children to think of ways that the lioness might camouflage herself. Guide them to determine that the lioness's color blends in with her surroundings. Then have each child color the lioness. Next give each child a 2 1/2" x 7 1/4" strip of white construction paper. Have him color it to resemble the lion's habitat, then use scissors to fringe one edge to resemble grass. Then direct each child to glue the grass to the bottom of the page.

Booklet Page 3: Read the text. Have each child color the cubs (being sure to leave spots on their coats). Discuss the word *thicket* and have each child color a thicket in the scenery. (A thicket is a dense growth of shrubbery or small trees.)

Booklet Page 4: Read the text. Discuss what kinds of small animals might be in Africa where most lions live (butterflies, lizards, tortoises). Have each child use art materials to make a small animal, then color the page and glue the student-made animal to the scene.

Booklet Page 5: Read the text and follow the directions. Discuss the page, and review new vocabulary words from the booklet such as *male, mane, female, lioness, camouflage, cubs, thicket,* and *pride.* Have each child sequence his pages, then staple them together along the left side.

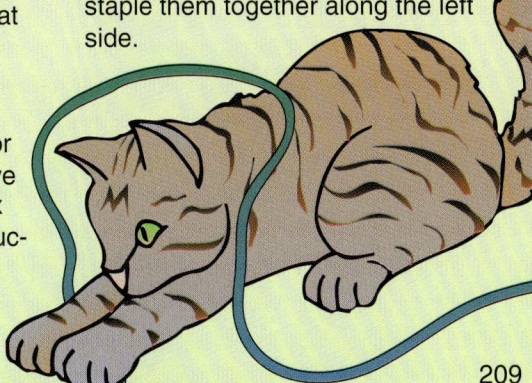

The Long And Short Of It

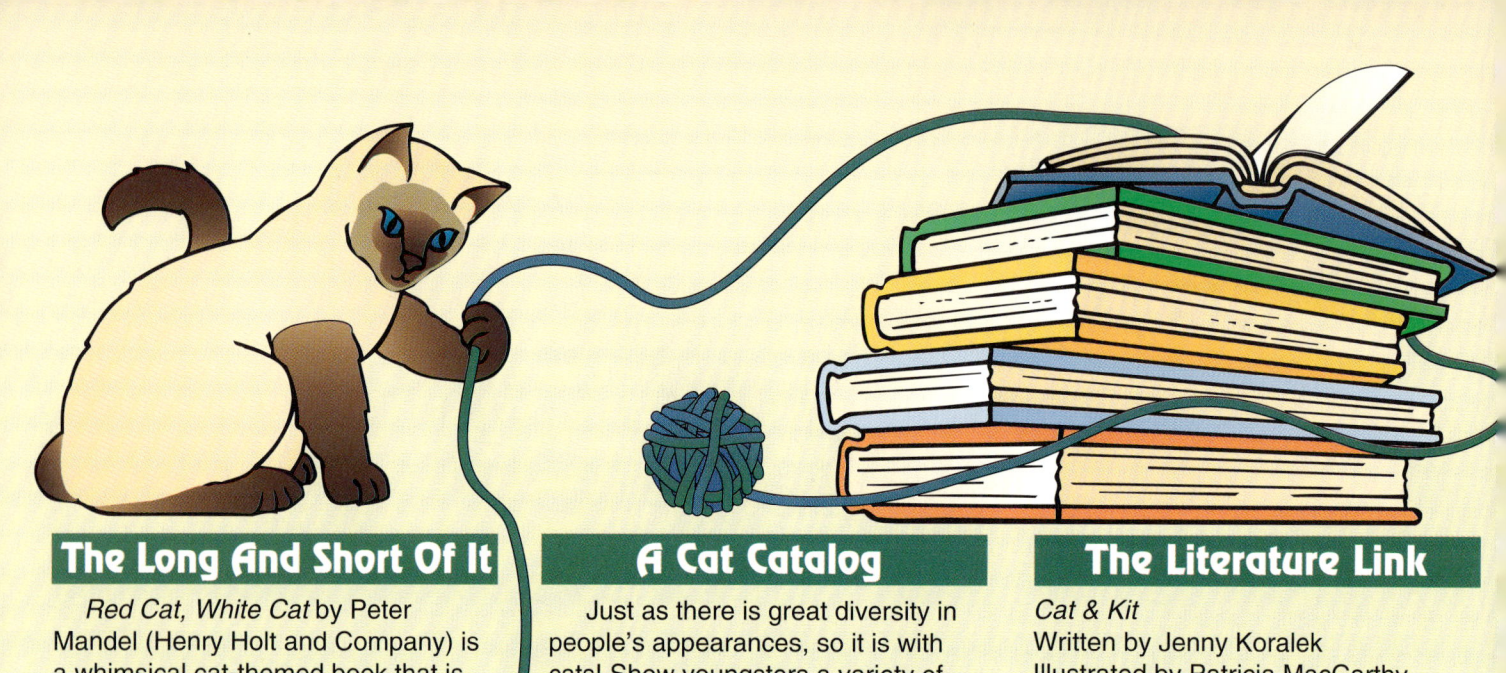

Red Cat, White Cat by Peter Mandel (Henry Holt and Company) is a whimsical cat-themed book that is loaded with learning opportunities. Share the book with your youngsters, encouraging them to look at the pictures as well as the text. (There are many common sight words in this text.) After you've read through the book one time, read it again, encouraging youngsters to read along with you as they are able. Then add a dash of music! Write the words from the book on a sheet of chart paper. As you point, have your youngsters *sing* the text to the tune of "Twinkle, Twinkle."

When children are familiar with the text (that is written on the chart paper), ask them to find pairs of opposite words. When a child has spotted an opposite pair, give him two pieces of highlighting tape or a highlighting marker and have him highlight the pair of words. When all of the opposite words have been highlighted, encourage youngsters to rewrite the song using new opposite words such as big/little, fat/skinny, sweet/mean. Write the new child-created lyrics on another sheet of chart paper and sing the new song!

A Cat Catalog

Just as there is great diversity in people's appearances, so it is with cats! Show youngsters a variety of domestic cat pictures/photographs from encyclopedias. Encourage them to notice things such as whether the cats they see are all one color, a combination of colors, different colors only in certain places, longhaired, shorthaired, etc. Then give each child a copy of a cat pattern. Provide a variety of art supplies such as paint, chalk, crayons, and pastels. Encourage each child to color his cat as he likes, then cut it out. Have him glue the cat to the top of a large sheet of construction paper. Then have each child write/dictate about his cat. Bind all of the pages between construction-paper covers entitled "Our Cat Catalog." Have each child share his page with the class.

The Literature Link

Cat & Kit
Written by Jenny Koralek
Illustrated by Patricia MacCarthy
(Hyperion Books For Children)

The Cats Of Tiffany Street
Written & Illustrated by Sarah Hayes
(Candlewick Press)

Kitten For A Day
Written & Illustrated by Ezra Jack Keats
(Aladdin Books)

The Lion And The Little Red Bird
Written & Illustrated by Elisa Kleven
(Dutton Children's Books)

Nanta's Lion
Written & Illustrated by Suse MacDonald
(Morrow Junior Books)

Poonam's Pets
Written by Andrew & Diana Davies
Illustrated by Paul Dowling
(Viking)

Lion Booklet Pages
Use with "The King Of Cats" on page 209.

A Look At Lions

by

An adult male lion has a **mane**.
He can roar! Can you?

1

Lion Booklet Pages
Use with "The King Of Cats" on page 209.

An adult female lion is called a **lioness**.
Her brownish-yellow fur helps her hide in the grass.
Where do you hide?

2

Baby lions are called **cubs**.
Cubs are born with their eyes closed.
Their fur has spots.
Cubs sleep in a thicket.
Where do you sleep?

3

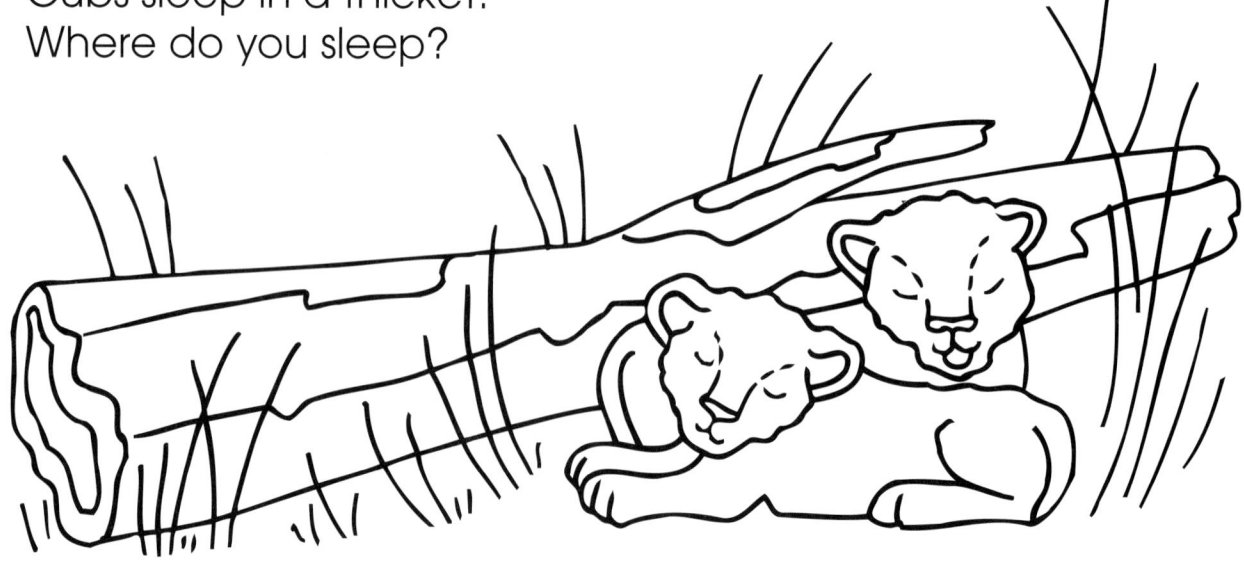

Lion Booklet Pages
Use with "The King Of Cats" on page 209.

When the cubs get older, they like to play.
They wrestle with each other and
  chase small animals.
How do you play?

4

A group of lions is called a **pride.**
Find the male lion. Color his mane.
Find the lioness. Draw a tail on her.
Draw some cubs. Color the page.

5

At The Bakery

'Tis the season for the sights, sounds, smells, and tastes of the bakery! Your youngsters will love the bakery-related activities in this unit as well as the bakery-themed language, literature, and art projects.

ideas by Lucia Kemp Henry

Bakery Fare

Roll into the bakery theme by involving your youngsters in a bakery-brainstorming session. Ask each child to think about what kinds of foods might be found in a bakeshop. Then ask children to name bakery items as you list their responses on a large cake cutout. Encourage children to generate lots of vocabulary by expanding on broad categories. For example, if one child suggests "bread," you could encourage children to expand the list to include different types of bread such as rye, wheat, white, pumpernickel, potato, cinnamon, etc. Oooh—just thinking about it can make you hungry!

cakes, rolls, pies, twisty bread, rye bread, cupcakes, cinnamon rolls, doughnuts

Bakery Poem

Copy this rhythmic poem onto chart paper; then share it with your students to give them just a taste of what's in store at the bakery.

Choose a treat, buy a treat
At the bakery shop.
There's so much I'd like to eat,
I may never stop!

White bread, wheat bread,
Sourdough, and rye.
Pumpernickel, honey oat
My, oh, my!

Apple pie, pumpkin pie,
Sweet potato, plum.
Blackberry, blueberry,
Yum! Yum! Yum!

Sugar cookies, butter cookies,
Oatmeal treats.
Chocolate chip and peanut butter
Nice and sweet!

Chocolate cake, lemon cake,
Angel food and spice.
Wedding cake, birthday cake
Oh so nice!

Choose a treat, buy a treat
At the bakery shop.
There's so much I'd like to eat,
I may never stop!

Showcase Display

Brush up on classification skills with this mighty tasty-looking learning center. To make the center, duplicate the baked-goods patterns (pages 217–218) onto white construction paper. Color, laminate, and cut out the patterns. Store all of the pictures in a resealable plastic bag. Then use narrow masking tape to divide a large tray or cookie sheet into three sections. Label the sections "breads," "pies," and "cakes" respectively. (If desired, glue a sample picture in each section.) To use the center, a child sorts each of the pictures into the appropriate category.

If you'd like to make this center self-checking, write each of the categories in a different color. Then color a corresponding dot on the back of each pattern piece. When a child has sorted all of the baked goods, he flips each piece over to see if the color dot matches the color of the category heading.

Baking Song

Simmer in the baking mood by singing this simple song with your little ones.

(sung to the tune of "Here We Go 'Round The Mulberry Bush")

What would you like to bake today,
Bake today, bake today?
What would you like to bake today
So early in the morning?

I'd like to bake some **bread** today,
Bread today, **bread** today.
I'd like to bake some **bread** today
So early in the morning.

Repeat the second stanza of the song, replacing the boldfaced word each time. Encourage children to think of examples such as *pie, cake, muffins,* and *rolls.* After singing the song, discuss why bakers might need to bake "so early in the morning."

A Holiday Bakery Book

Sofie's Role written by Amy Heath (Four Winds Press) is a beautifully illustrated story that links the bakery theme with the holiday season. Young Sofie's family owns a bakery. As the holiday approaches, every person in the busy bakery has an important job to do. As Sofie soaks in the enchantment of the holiday, she eventually becomes somewhat daunted as she wonders what important job *she* can do.

As you read the story aloud, have youngsters discuss the bakery jobs that are described. Encourage them to think about whether each job would be appropriate for someone about their age. Afterwards have each child decide which bakery job she would most like to do if she worked at a bakery. Have each child illustrate and write about herself doing the job of her choice. Then bind all of the pages between decorated construction-paper covers. Have each child share her page during a group reading time.

Off We Go!

After introducing the bakery theme, what could be more educational than the real thing? Take your children to tour a nearby bakery! Before the trip, review the brainstormed list from "Bakery Fare" (page 214). Ask children to be particularly aware of any food items they see that are not on the list. (Be sure to add the new entries to your list when you return.) Also encourage youngsters to take note of the different jobs that they see people doing. Later have children name and describe the jobs as you write them on a sheet of chart paper. For each job listed, ask children if they think that is a job that they would like to do. Then further explore the bakery scene with "A Holiday Bakery Book," "Classroom Kitchen," and "Bakery Buddies."

To thank your tour guide and the bakery staff, make and deliver this luscious-looking thank-you card. Cut a large cupcake shape from tagboard. Have children add "sprinkles" by making multicolored thumbprints with paint. Then have each child write his name under his print. Add a class-dictated thank-you message—and off you go!

Classroom Kitchen

This classroom kitchen concocts lots of learning opportunities through role playing and free exploration. Use your sand/water table for a measure-and-mix area. Stock the area with an assortment of manipulatives such as dried beans, rice, foam packing pieces, and buttons. Provide a variety of measuring spoons, cups, bowls, and aprons; then encourage children to mix and measure to their hearts' content!

Bakery Buddies

Budding bakers will rise to new heights at this center that carries the bakery theme into math, art, and social studies! Use your dramatic-play area to create a bakeshop. Stock the center with baking pans, empty baked-goods containers or bags, and baked goods that your youngsters make from art supplies. Set up a table and chairs, and a cash register with play money. Encourage youngsters to try out various roles as they set up the bakery displays, take customer orders, operate the cash register, or come into the bakery as customers. Good morning! May I help you?

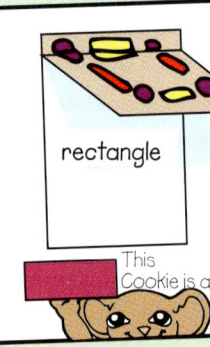

Barry Slate

My Shape-Cookie Book

Each child can express his own creative style as he decorates a differently shaped cookie for each page of this booklet. For each child, photocopy the booklet pages (pages 219-220) on white construction paper and the cookie shapes (page 221) on tan or light brown construction paper. Set up cookie-decorating stations using your choices from the ideas listed below. Then have each child decorate each of his cookie patterns as he likes and color the booklet pages. When the cookie shapes are decorated and dry, have each child cut out his cookies, then glue each shape to the corresponding booklet page (see the Note To The Teacher on page 221). After cutting apart the booklet pages, have each child sequence and staple his pages together. Encourage pairs of children to read each other's shape-cookie books. Then send the booklets home to be shared with family members.

Cookie-Decorating Techniques:
- Glue on: glitter, sequins, tissue-paper pieces, bits of colored cellophane, felt scraps, or nonpareils.
- Sponge-paint: white frosting, chocolate chunks, red berries, green leaves or trees.
- Color the designs of your choice.
- Squeeze on colored glue or glitter glue.
- Apply colorful stickers.

Extend this activity by decorating real slice-and-bake cookies. Mmmm!

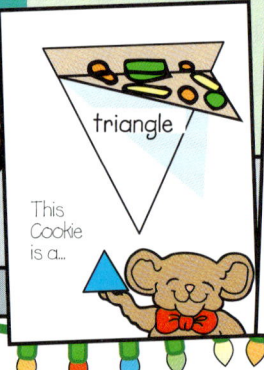

The Literature Link

The Baker's Dozen: A Colonial American Tale
Retold by Heather Forest
Illustrated by Susan Gaber
Published by Harcourt Brace Jovanovich

Bread, Bread, Bread
Written by Ann Morris
Photographed by Ken Heyman
Published by Lothrop, Lee & Shepard Books

The Cactus Flower Bakery
Written by Harry Allard
Illustrated by Ned Delaney
Published by HarperTrophy

Tony's Bread
Written & Illustrated by Tomie dePaola
Published by G. P. Putnam's Sons

A Visit To The Bakery
Written by Sandra Ziegler
Photographed by Pilot Productions, Inc.
Published by Childrens Press®

Baked-Goods Patterns
Use with "Showcase Display" on page 214.

217

Baked-Goods Patterns
Use with "Showcase Display" on page 214.

Cookie Booklet Pages
Use with "My Shape-Cookie Book" on page 216.

My Shape-Cookie Book

1
circle.
This cookie is a...

2
square.
This cookie is a...

3
rectangle.
This cookie is a...

Cookie Booklet Pages

Use with "My Shape-Cookie Book" on page 216.

4

triangle.

This cookie is a…

5

oval.

This cookie is an…

6

heart.

This cookie is a…

7

star.

This cookie is a…

Cookie Shapes

Use with "My Shape-Cookie Book" on page 216.

©The Education Center, Inc. • THE MAILBOX® • Kindergarten • Dec/Jan 1995–96

Note To The Teacher: Fold each cookie on the narrow line. Glue each cookie to its page along the folded portion only.

POSITIVELY PEANUTS!

What's in a peanut? Plenty! There's new vocabulary, opportunities for creativity, African-American history, math, reading, and science. Use these suggestions to get you started studying peanuts. But beware—it's hard to stop once you've started in on peanuts!

some ideas contributed by Sharon Hale—Gr. K, Wee School, Fairborn, OH

What's In A Name?

A peanut is a peanut, is a peanut—right? Well, not always! Use the following activity to introduce your children to the vocabulary surrounding peanuts. Begin by passing a few peanuts around the room. Trying **not** to use the word *peanut,* have each child examine the "object" and ask her what she calls it. Record any of the names mentioned on a large, peanut-shaped cutout. Then tell youngsters that because peanuts grow underground, they are sometimes called *groundnuts.* Have your youngsters ever heard of that? Also add that peanuts are sometimes called *goobers, goober peas, groundpeas,* and *pindas.* Write each of these names on the peanut cutout; then practice reading the new vocabulary throughout your peanut studies.

Nutty Names

After reviewing the vocabulary that was introduced in "What's In A Name?", encourage each child to make and name his own nutty peanut. To begin, have each child cut out a large peanut shape from a double thickness of grocery-bag paper. Using a variety of art supplies (such as crayons, buttons, fabric, and glue), have each child decorate his top peanut cutout. Encourage each child to think of a nutty name for his peanut and write that name on the cutout. Then help each child staple the lower two-thirds of both peanut shapes together. Direct each child to gently stuff the shape with crumpled, plastic grocery bags; then staple the peanuts closed. Display these nutty peanuts around your room in recognition of National Peanut Month (March)!

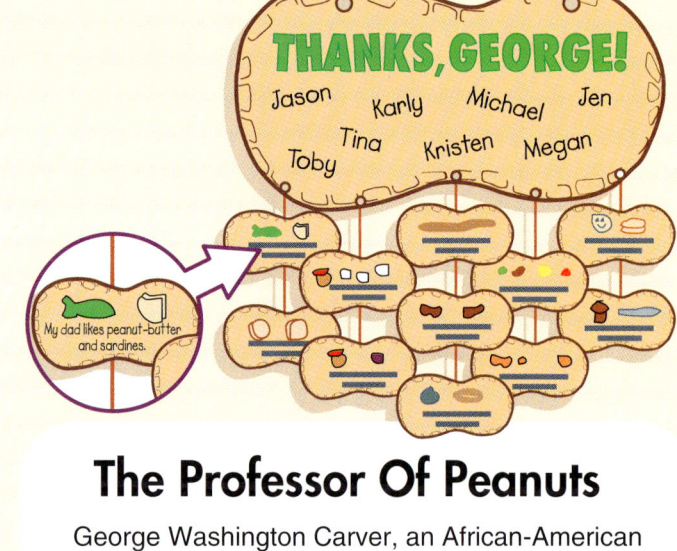

The Professor Of Peanuts

George Washington Carver, an African-American scientist, is indeed an important person in the history of peanuts—not to mention the history of the world! As a boy, George had a natural interest in and talent with plants. With those abilities and an incredible amount of hard work and study, George Washington Carver eventually became a professor and researcher at the Tuskegee Institute in Alabama. During his studies, Mr. Carver made over 300 products from peanuts!

Highlight George Washington Carver's contributions to our world by creating a mobile with your class. Cut out a large peanut shape from tagboard. Write "Thanks, George!" on the cutout; then punch two holes in the top of it. Ask each child to spend a day or two thinking of peanut uses. Then have him report his favorite peanut uses to the class. Have each child write about and illustrate his response on a smaller peanut cutout. For every three or four pictures, punch a hole in the bottom of the large tagboard peanut. Attach a length of string to each hole and tape several pictures to each string. As a child's picture is added, have him sign his name on the large peanut. Use yarn or string to suspend the entire mobile for all to be reminded of the importance of George Washington Carver.

And The Survey Says…

Creamy, chunky, or extra chunky? Everyone has input on this positively peanut report. Draw a four-column graph on a sheet of paper. Label the columns "creamy," "chunky," "extra chunky," and "not at all," respectively. Photocopy the graph for each child. Have each child take the graph home and survey his family members and friends to find out how each person likes peanut butter. In turn, have each child record his results on a large version of the graph. When each child has recorded his findings, discuss what the graph reveals. What's *your* pleasure?

creamy	chunky
Tara	Billy
Mom	Grandma
Dad	Takisha
Jake	Aaron
Levi	

Peanut Plants

George Washington Carver was fascinated with plants—particularly peanut plants. The same seeds just might be planted in your youngsters' minds with this peanut-planting activity. For each child, use a screwdriver or nail to poke several holes in the bottom of a clear plastic cup. Give each child a prepared cup, two raw peanuts, soil, and water. Have each child personalize his cup and fill it with soil. Then instruct him to plant his peanuts about two inches deep in the soil. Encourage each child to lightly water the soil, then place his cup in a gravel-filled tray. Place the tray in a warm place (at least 65°–70°) near a window. Ask each child to draw a picture of the planting process in his science journal. Then encourage him to predict how long it will take his peanut to sprout. As each child checks on his plant daily—watering it as necessary—have him record any visible changes in his journal. When sprouts appear, usually within seven days, compare the actual sprouting time with the child's prediction. Hey—my peanut plant just popped up!

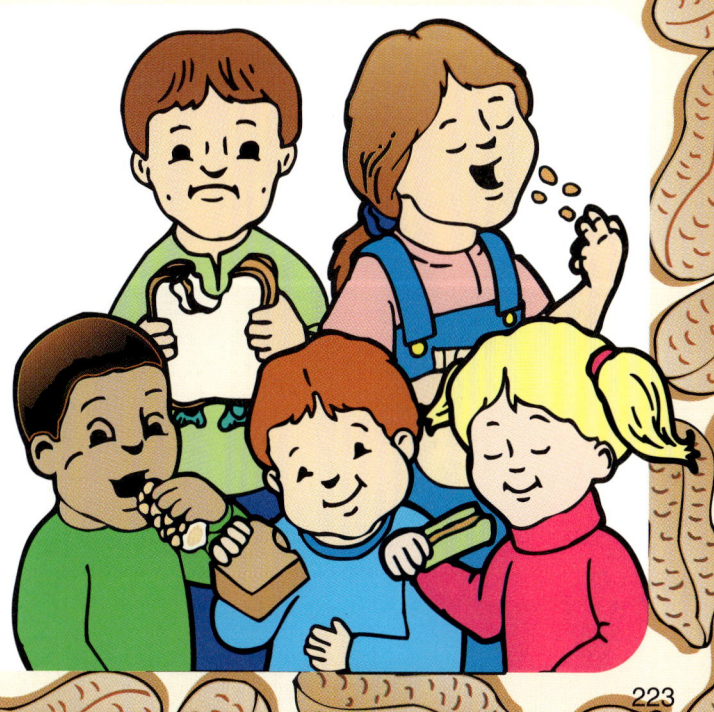

P Is For Peanut

If you're studying the letter *P* along with your peanut theme, this is the perfect time to practice letter recognition and formation. Place a large supply of unshelled peanuts, glue, pencils, and half-sheets of construction paper in a center. As each child visits the center, have her use a pencil to draw a large letter *P* on a sheet of construction paper. Next have her squeeze a generous line of glue along the *P* outline. Then encourage her to crack as many peanuts as she needs to cover the glue outline. When the peanut *P* is dry, display it in your classroom with your other peanut projects.

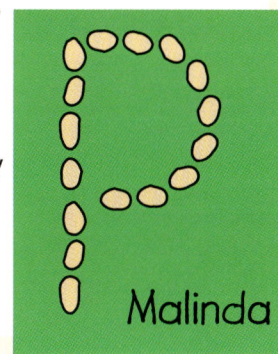

"Peanutty" Snacks

Encourage everyone to sample a portion of these positively "peanutty" snacks:

- roasted peanuts—salted and unsalted
- peanut butter and celery
- peanut butter and crackers
- peanut butter–and–jelly sandwiches
- crisp-rice cereal bars made with peanut butter
- chocolate–covered peanuts
- peanut–butter fudge
- peanut–log candy bars
- peanut butter-and-sardine sandwiches—if you dare!
- boiled peanuts

PIGS APLENTY!

The popularity of pigs is quite evident these days in current books, movies, and decorating items. So pepper your teaching with these perky-pig activities, and watch your youngsters go hog-wild for learning fun!

by Lucia Kemp Henry

A NEW PEEK AT PIGS

If your youngsters are like most people, they might not have a lot of accurate information regarding these curly tailed farm dwellers. So take advantage of the pig's present popularity and reintroduce these clever fellows. *All Pigs Are Beautiful* by Dick King-Smith (Candlewick Press) is a uniquely inviting work of nonfiction that introduces the reader to the characteristics and habits of pigs. After sharing this appealing book with your children, ask them to discuss what they learned from the book. *Now* what do you think of pigs?

A LITTLE PIG POEM

This little poem rolls together science, reading, and language to create a "pig-ture-perfect" learning opportunity. Copy the poem onto chart paper. After reading the poem aloud, have youngsters join you in reading it a second time. Using different colors of highlighting markers, have children take turns highlighting the skills of your choice. For example, if you're working on rhyming (see pages 241–245), have three different children each highlight a pair of rhyming words. You might also direct a child to draw a circle with a squiggly tail around the word *pigs* in a given stanza, draw a heart around the word *love*, or highlight sight words that he knows. Display the poem in your classroom and incorporate it in your "read-the-room" materials. Read the poem together periodically during your pig theme. Children will squeal with delight at their own reading skills!

Pigs have ears. Pigs have tails.
Pigs have four little feet.
Pigs love dirt.
Pigs love mud.
And pigs just love to eat!

Pigs can oink.
Pigs can grunt.
Pigs can squeal and snort.
Pigs can be fat.
Pigs can be thin.
And pigs can be long or short.

Pigs can be brown.
Pigs can be pink.
Pigs can be spotted black and white.
Pigs can be tan.
Pigs can be gray.
And pigs can be as black as night!

A PIG BIG BOOK

Your young artists will scramble at the chance to illustrate one of the pages of this class-made big book. In advance, write each line from the poem (on page 224) on a large sheet of construction paper. Add one additional page at the end that says, "Sleep tight!" Then assign each line of the text to a different artist. (If you have more children than pages of the book, assign pairs of students to work on some of the pages and/or other students to create a cover.) When each page is complete, bind the pages in order between construction-paper covers. Be sure to have each child/group share his page during a group reading time.

COUNTING LITTLE PIGGIES

Count up, count down, count all around! To prepare this activity, reproduce the flannelboard patterns (page 228) two times on construction paper. Color, laminate, and cut out each picture; then prepare it for flannelboard or magnet-board use. Use the pictures as manipulatives as you recite the rhyme below. If your students are ready for skip-counting, add a challenge by photocopying and preparing 20 pigs to correspond to the alternate verse. Count on!

One little, **two** little, **three** little piggies.
Four little, **five** little, **six** little piggies.
Seven little, **eight** little, **nine** little piggies.
Ten little piggies in a pen.

Repeat the verse counting backwards.

Alternate verse:

Two little, **four** little, **six** little piggies.
Eight little, **ten** little, **twelve** little piggies.
Fourteen little, **sixteen** little, **eighteen** little piggies.
Twenty little piggies in a pen.

Repeat the verse counting backwards.

A PIG PLAY

If you vary "A Pig Big Book" (above) just a bit, you can take the act on the road! When each child's page is complete, have him stand in line with his picture according to the order of the text. In turn, have each child read/recite his page aloud, show his picture, and provide any actions or sound effects that might enhance his performance. (If a particular line requires one of your little actors to have full use of his hands and feet, assign another child to hold the picture and read the line as the actor throws himself wholeheartedly into the pig part!) When the last child shows his picture and says "Sleep tight!" direct each child to curl up in a little ball and pretend to be a sleeping pig. As the applause explodes, have each little piggy rise to all fours and take a pig-style bow.

THIS LITTLE PIGGY

Here's a fun action poem with a porcine plot. Recite the poem below as you perform corresponding motions or sound effects. Encourage each child to follow along with you. Repeat the poem, going just a little faster each time you say it. Your perky little piglets will pucker right out!

This little piggy can wiggle its ears,
Wiggle its nose,
And wiggle its toes.
This little piggy can jump up and down,
Turn around,
And touch the ground.
This little piggy can grunt when it's sad,
Squeal when it's mad,
And oink when it's glad.
This little piggy can eat very fast,
Splish and splash,
Then sleep in the grass.

PLENTY OF PIGS

Youngsters will be pleased and proud to be able to read these pig booklets all by themselves. For each child, duplicate the booklet patterns (pages 229–231) on construction paper. Have each child cut out each page along the rectangular outline, then staple his set of pages together. Read through the text together. Then encourage each child to illustrate each line of text. (If desired, photocopy the pigs on page 228; then have youngsters glue individual pigs to the boxes to get their illustrations started.) When the booklets are complete, have youngsters sit in a circle. Read the booklets together, taking time for youngsters to show their pictures after each page has been read.

PIGGY LIT.

David McPhail has created a perfectly pleasing portrait of pigs in *Pigs Aplenty, Pigs Galore!* (Dutton Children's Books). The story is packed with a wealth of rambunctious pigs who perform unusual and unpiglike stunts. As you share the book, encourage youngsters to look for each of the pigs that the author describes. Afterwards ask children to imagine how the pigs might have gotten into the house in the first place. Then have each child share her idea with the group.

As a follow-up activity, encourage each child to make a contribution to this amusing bulletin board. In advance, mount construction-paper curtains to a bulletin-board background entitled *"Pigs Aplenty, Pigs Galore!"* Then provide a variety of art supplies and ask students to create whimsical pigs of their own. (Encourage children to revisit the illustrations in the book for inspiration.) Have each child choose a place to mount his pig on the board. When all the pigs have been placed, encourage each child to write/dictate about his pig on a strip of paper. Staple the creative writing near each pig; then have each child share about his own personal pig.

PIG'S POCKET OF P WORDS

Use this simple take-home activity to reinforce beginning sounds. For each child, duplicate the Pig's Pocket pattern on page 232. Have each child color and cut out her pattern, then glue it to a small manila envelope. Send a Pig's Pocket envelope home with each child and encourage her to draw or cut out pictures that begin with *P*. Have each child place her pictures in the pocket before bringing it back to school. When each child has returned her pocket, have children glue their pictures to a large construction-paper pig shape. P words seem to be popping out all over!

PIGGY BANKS

Math and money concepts abound in *Pigs Will Be Pigs* by Amy Axelrod (Simon & Schuster Books For Young Readers). After sharing the book with your children, explore a number of math skills with these specialized piggy banks. Using the pig pattern on page 229, make a pig tracer. For each number that you'd like to study, cut out one construction-paper pig shape. Add details if desired; then laminate the cutouts. Program each pig with the skill of your choice, such as numerals, number words, or monetary amounts. Then place all the pigs in a center with a supply of pennies or a combination of coins. To do this activity, a child first sequences the pigs, then places the appropriate number of pennies/coins on each pig.

Adapt this center by masking out the title and byline on the pig on page 229. Then reproduce the pattern several times for each child in your class. Program each page with a different numeral or number word. Place the reproducibles, a pig stamp, and a stamp pad in a center. As a child visits the center, he chooses a page or two, then stamps the corresponding number of pigs onto that page.

THE LITERATURE LINK

The Book Of Pigericks: Pig Limericks
Written & Illustrated by Arnold Lobel
(Harper & Row, Publishers)

Perfect The Pig
Written & Illustrated by Susan Jeschke
(Holt, Rinehart and Winston)

Pig Pig Gets A Job
Written & Illustrated by David McPhail
(Dutton Children's Books)

Pig Surprise
Written & Illustrated by Ute Krause
(Dial Books For Young Readers)

Pigs From 1 To 10
Written & Illustrated by Arthur Geisert
(Houghton Mifflin Company)

A Pile Of Pigs
Written by Judith Ross Enderle & Stephanie Gordon Tessler
Illustrated by Charles Jordan
(Boyds Mills Press)

Suddenly!
Written & Illustrated by Colin McNaughton
(Harcourt Brace Children's Books)

The Three Little Wolves And The Big Bad Pig
Written by Eugene Trivizas
Illustrated by Helen Oxenbury
(Scholastic Inc.)

We Keep A Pig In The Parlor
Written & Illustrated by Suzanne Bloom
(Clarkson N. Potter, Inc.)

Flannelboard Patterns
Use with "Counting Little Piggies" on page 225 and "Plenty Of Pigs" on page 226.

©1995 The Education Center, Inc.

Pig Booklet Cover

Use with "Plenty Of Pigs" on page 226 and "Piggy Banks" on page 227.

PLENTY OF PIGS

BY

©The Education Center, Inc. • THE MAILBOX® • Kindergarten • Feb/Mar 1996

Pig Booklet Page
Use with "Plenty Of Pigs" on page 226.

one pig	old pig
two pigs	new pigs

Pig Booklet Page
Use with "Plenty Of Pigs" on page 226.

muddy pig

farm pig

wet pig

pet pig

2

Patterns
Pig's Pocket Use with "Pig's Pocket Of *P* Words" on page 227.

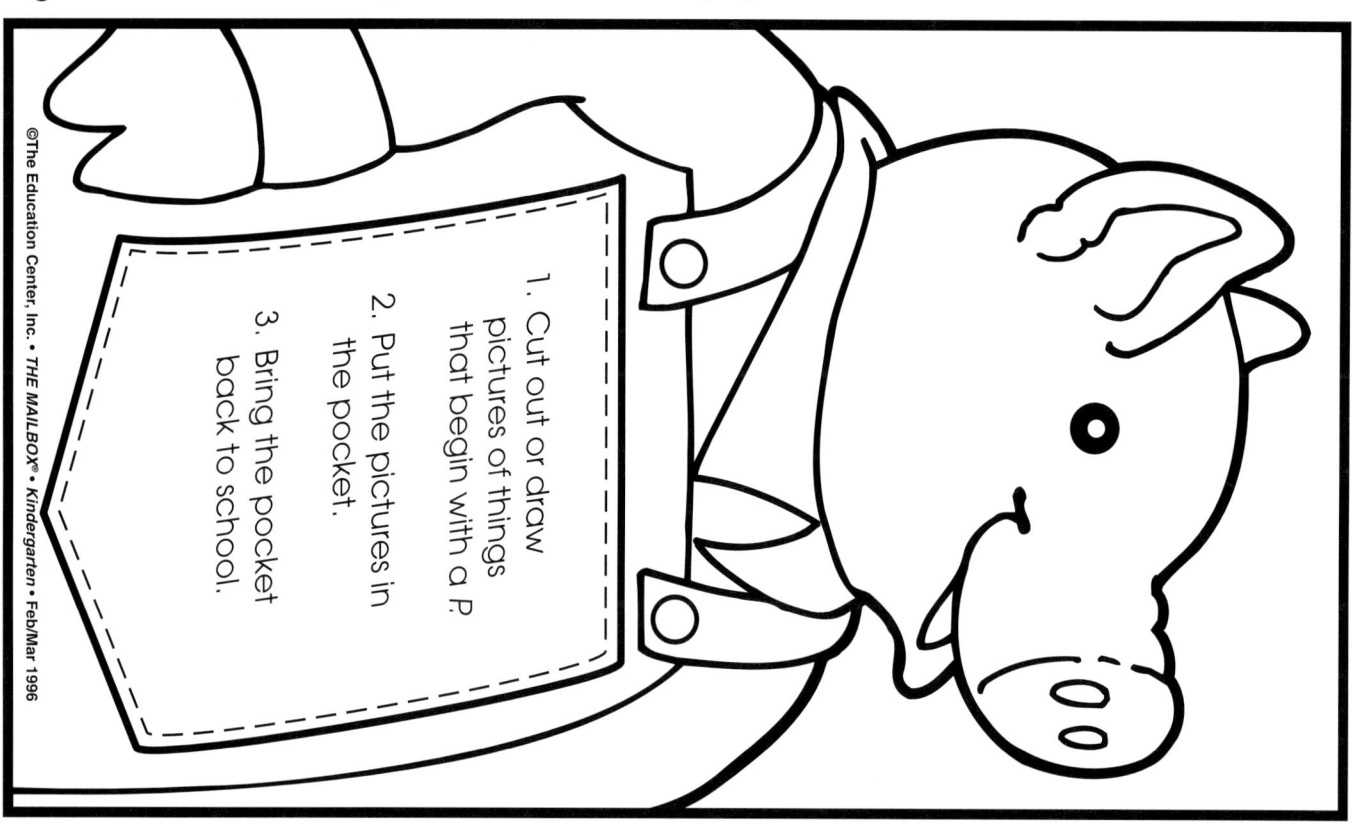

1. Cut out or draw pictures of things that begin with a *P*.
2. Put the pictures in the pocket.
3. Bring the pocket back to school.

©The Education Center, Inc. • THE MAILBOX® • Kindergarten • Feb/Mar 1996

Award For each child, duplicate the award and personalize it before sending it home.

CONGRATULATIONS, _____!

YOU'VE DONE FIRST—PRIZE WORK AS WE'VE LEARNED ABOUT PIGS!

1

©The Education Center, Inc. • THE MAILBOX® • Kindergarten • Feb/Mar 1996

On Top Of The World

The Arctic—a land that many think of as a vast, frozen wasteland—just might surprise you! Use this collection of activities to explore the tip-top of the world and some of the wonderful creatures who call it home.

ideas by Elizabeth Trautman

Where In The World!

Top and bottom, above and below, north and south—what do these opposite words have to do with the Arctic? Plenty! In advance, explain that a globe shows what our world looks like from a long, long way away. Then display a globe in your classroom for free exploration. Later tell your young geographers that you are going to study the area around the North Pole and, just for fun, you'll also locate the South Pole. Explain that the North and South Poles are located at the *top* and *bottom* of the globe. Have youngsters point to the top and bottom of your classroom globe. Can they guess which area is the *North Pole?* How about the *South Pole?* After determining the location of the respective poles, point out your state. Ask children whether each respective pole is *above* or *below* your state. This method of introduction not only orients students to the polar regions, but also is a practical reinforcement of the concept of opposites!

Globe Ball, Anyone?

Exercise those large-motor muscles and reinforce the location of the world's polar regions at the same time. In advance, blow up an inflatable globe. Encourage children to examine the area around the North Pole. Explain that the area of continuous cold around the North Pole—roughly shown by the Arctic Circle on a globe—is called the *Arctic.* Have children trace around the Arctic Circle with their fingers. Also explain that the area around the South Pole includes only one landmass that is called *Antarctica.*

To play Globe Ball, have youngsters stand in a circle. Toss the inflated globe to a child. When the child catches the globe, have the rest of the class whisper, "Freeze!" At that point, the catcher must "freeze" his hands on the globe. Ask him to see if any of his fingers are on either of the polar regions. If so, ask him to name the region(s). Then have that child toss the ball to another child. Continue playing in the same manner until interest wanes. If desired, add a little math interest to your game. Label a two-columned chart with appropriate vocabulary words (such as "North Pole" and/or "Arctic" for one column, and "South Pole" and/or "Antarctica" for the other column). Each time a child's fingers land on one of the poles, have another child make a tally mark in the respective column(s). At the end of the game, count the tally marks in each column and discuss the results. Think fast—you've got the *whole world* in your hands!

A Very Cold Pole

When youngsters get a feel for the Arctic winter, it's likely to make your seasonal hardships seem like a walk in the park! Introduce the Arctic climate by sharing Madeleine Dunphy's *Here Is The Arctic Winter* (Hyperion Books For Children). As you show the book's cover, draw attention to the words in the title as you read it. Then have youngsters read it again with you. As you share the book, ask children to read along with you each time that sentence is repeated in the text. Also encourage students to explore the illustrations in order to gather information about the Arctic winter. Record children's comments on a sheet of chart paper. Then share the facts below and ask the follow-up questions. You're bound to determine that the Arctic sure is a cold pole!

- Winter temperatures in the Arctic average around –30°F.
  What is today's temperature where you live? Is it warmer or colder than the average Arctic winter temperature?
  What kinds of outdoor activities do you do in the winter? How might outdoor activities be the same or different during an Arctic winter?

- July temperatures in the Arctic average around 45°F.
  What is the average July temperature where you live? How does that compare to the Arctic?
  What kinds of outdoor activities do you like to do in July? Could you do the same activities in the Arctic? Why or why not?

Arctic Art

After experiencing *Here Is The Arctic Winter* (see "A Very Cold Pole"), set up an art center in which youngsters can create their own Arctic winter scenes. Enlarge and photocopy the animal outlines on the last page of the book. Trace the animals onto plastic stenciling sheets (available at craft stores); then use a razor blade to cut them out. Put the animal cutouts and the stencils in a center along with construction paper, colored chalk, crayons, white paint, and old toothbrushes. Encourage each child to use the stencils, cutouts, and supplies to make the Arctic animals of his choice. Next have him glue his animal(s) to a sheet of construction paper, then use crayons and/or chalk to add scenery. (The chalk is especially effective for drawing the northern lights!) Add the finishing touch by having the child lightly dip a toothbrush in white paint. As he holds the brush over his picture, direct the child to rub his thumb along the bristles, causing "snow" to scatter lightly over his picture. When it's dry, lightly spray the entire picture with hairspray. Display the finished projects on a bulletin board entitled "Here Is The Arctic Winter."

Bear For A Day

There's hardly a child who can resist the intrigue of the ominous King of the Arctic—the polar bear. So come along and visit with this mighty mammal in *White Bear, Ice Bear* by Joanne Ryder (Morrow Junior Books). In this story, a boy changes into a large, furry polar bear...just for a day. After sharing this story, encourage your youngsters to distinguish fact from fantasy. Look through the illustrations again, asking youngsters to tell which events they think could really happen to a boy and which events could really happen to a polar bear. Then reread the story, having youngsters act out the part of the polar bear as you read aloud.

Compare To A Bear

After doing the activities in "Bear For A Day" (see page 234), youngsters will get a kick out of comparing their lifestyles with that of the polar bear. For each child, reproduce the booklet pages and picture choices (pages 237–240) on construction paper; then cut apart the pages. To complete the booklet pages, encourage youngsters to recall facts that they learned from *White Bear, Ice Bear*. Also assist children in using other references from the literature list for further information discovery. Follow the directions below to complete each booklet page. When each child has completed his booklet, have student pairs read their booklets to each other. Then encourage children to take their booklets home and share them with their families.

Booklet Page 1
Read the text together; then have students suggest possible answers as you write them on the board. (Encourage youngsters to give a variety of answers such as their town, state, county, or country.) Have each child fill in the blank on his booklet page, then draw a picture of his home.

Booklet Page 2
Read the text together. Show pictures of a polar bear's den (see *Animal Close-Ups: The Polar Bear* and/or *Arctic Animals* in the literature list) and discuss them. Then have each child draw a picture to complement the booklet text.

Booklet Page 3
In addition to the booklet page, give each child a copy of the picture choices (page 240). Read the text at the top of the page together. Have each child write/illustrate to complete the sentence starter. Then read the text on the bottom part of the page. Have each child examine the picture choices, then color and cut apart the appropriate pictures *(seal, lemming, leaves and berries)*. Then have him glue them in the spaces provided to complete the sentence starter.

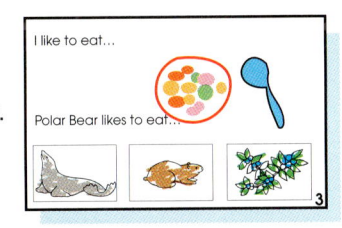

Booklet Page 4
Read the text at the top of the page together. Have each child illustrate his favorite type of weather. Then read the text at the bottom of the page together. Encourage each child to illustrate to complete the sentence starter.

Booklet Page 5
Read the text together. Discuss your youngsters' favorite outdoor activities; then have each child illustrate one of his favorite activities.

Booklet Page 6
Read the text together. Have children examine the remaining picture choices. Direct them to color and cut apart the pictures that best complete the sentence, then glue them in the space provided.

Booklet Cover
Read the partial title together; then have each child write his name to complete the title. Encourage each child to decorate the polar bear using cotton and glue. Then have each child draw a picture of himself standing next to the polar bear. If desired, have him add snow-covered ground by gluing crinkled pieces of white and blue tissue paper to the page. When the glue is dry, have each child sequence his pages and staple them together along the left edge.

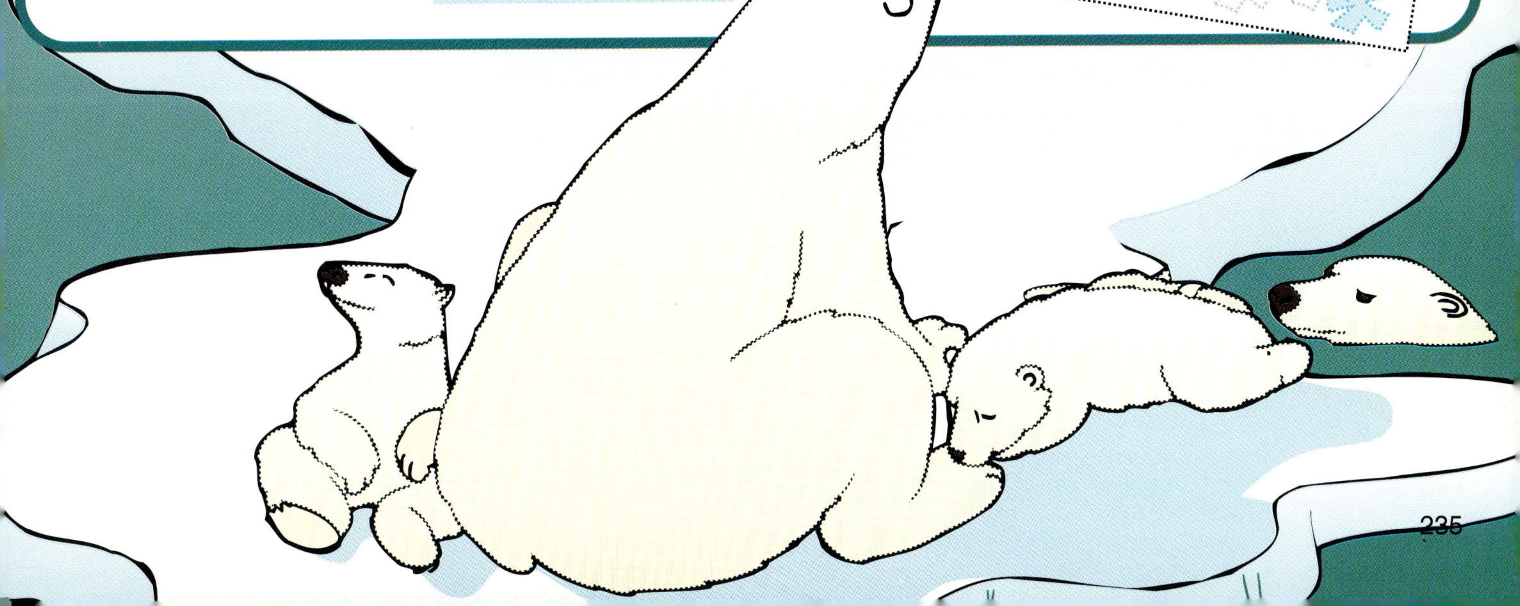

Wonderful Whales

Whether it's Willy from the movies or Baby Beluga from Raffi's book and song, it seems that children just can't resist a whale tale! According to Raffi's experience, "Children love this song ("Baby Beluga") because it is a bright and tuneful love song for a baby whale. Hearing it and singing it is enough for them; they don't need to be told that it's trying to teach them anything."

Share Raffi's *Baby Beluga* (Crown Publishers, Inc.) with your youngsters. Without even knowing it, your little ones will be introduced to many of the other creatures that call the Arctic home. After reading the book aloud, refer to the music at the back of the book and *sing* the book together! ("Baby Beluga" is on the cassettes and CDs entitled "Baby Beluga" and "Raffi On Broadway." Both are available from Music For Little People; 1-800-727-2233.)

Polar Parkas

Though the Arctic weather is rather cold, there are some animals that remain on the tundra or in the icy waters year-round. How do these animals stay warm? Have your youngsters name articles of clothing that children might wear to help them stay warm. Then explain that just as people have special cold-weather clothing, so do the Arctic animals! Encourage youngsters to think of what the animals' cold-weather clothing might be; then write their responses next to your first list. Then explain that in addition to thick coats of fur and skin, most of the Arctic animals also have a thick layer of fat that adds extra warmth.

Demonstrate how a layer of fat provides protection from the cold with the following activity. You will need two quart-size Ziploc® bags, a rubber band, a spoon, 1 1/2 cups of solid vegetable shortening, a large bucket of ice water, and paper towels. Spoon the shortening inside one bag. Then turn the second bag inside out and place it inside the bag with the shortening. Zip the two bags together so that the first bag is sealed to the second bag. Then evenly spread the shortening between the bag layers.

In turn, have each child insert one hand inside the zipped-together bags. To secure the bags on his hand, place the rubber band around the tops of the bags. Then have the child dip both of his hands into the bucket of ice water, decide which of his hands stays the warmest, then remove and dry his wet hand. After everyone has had a turn, discuss which hand stayed the warmest and why.

Literature Link

Animal Close-Ups: The Polar Bear
Written & Photographed by Valérie Tracqui
Published by Charlesbridge

Arctic Animals
Written & Photographed by Bobbie Kalman
Published by Crabtree Publishing Company

Arctic Spring
Written by Sue Vyner
Illustrated by Tim Vyner
Published by Viking

The Blue Whale
Written by Philip Steele
Illustrated by Ian Jackson
Published by Kingfisher

Frozen Land: Vanishing Cultures
Written & Photographed by Jan Reynolds
Published by Harcourt Brace & Company

Little Polar Bear (also available in Spanish)
Written & Illustrated by Hans de Beer
Published by North-South Books Inc.

Mama, Do You Love Me?
Written by Barbara M. Joosse
Illustrated by Barbara Lavallee
Published by Scholastic Inc.

The Seasons And Someone
Written by Virginia Kroll
Illustrated by Tatsuro Kiuchi
Published by Harcourt Brace & Company

To The Top Of The World: Adventures With Arctic Wolves
Written & Photographed by Jim Brandenburg
Published by Walker and Company

Use with "Compare To A Bear" on page 235.

Booklet Pages

I live in _____.
This is my home.

1

Polar bears live in the **Arctic.**
This is the home of a mother polar bear.

2

Booklet Pages Use with "Compare To A Bear" on page 235.

I like to eat...

Polar Bear likes to eat...

3

My favorite weather is...

Polar Bear's favorite weather is...

4

Use with "Compare To A Bear" on page 235.

Booklet Pages

When I play outside, I like to…

5

When polar bears play outside, they…

6

Booklet Cover And Picture Choices Use with "Compare To A Bear" on page 235.

Polar Bear And _____

©The Education Center, Inc. • THE MAILBOX® • Kindergarten • Feb/Mar 1996

240 ©The Education Center, Inc. • THE MAILBOX® • Kindergarten • Feb/Mar 1996

PRESENTING... VAL'S PALS IN RHYME TIME

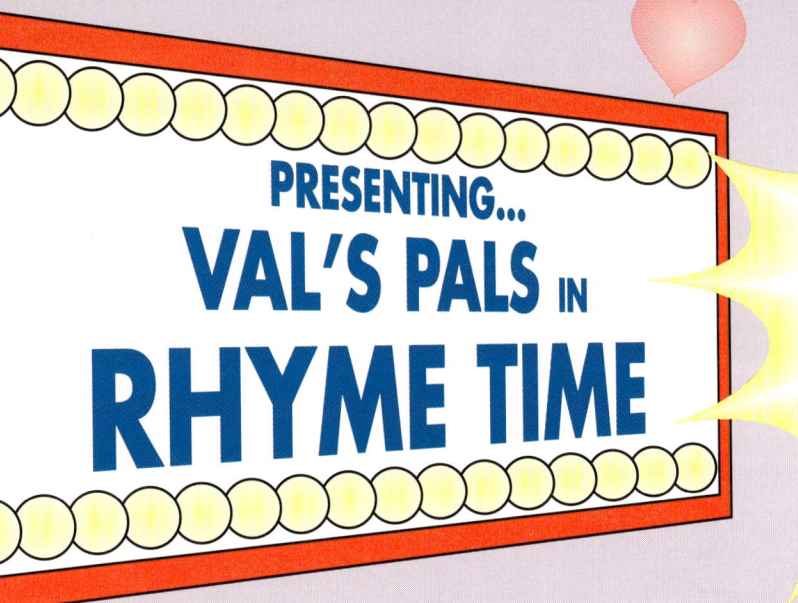

Ladies and gentlemen...it is with a great deal of appeal that we bring this fling to you. Val and her pals start from the heart, and strive to keep rhyming alive. So without any further ado, we give you— Val...and her pals!

Find Your Partner!

Your youngsters will dance their way into rhyming when they move to the groove in this fun activity. In advance, collect sets of rhyming pictures. To prepare the game, mount each picture on a tagboard card; then laminate the cards for durability. Compile card pairs or sets, matching the total number of cards to children in your class. To play, give each child one card. (With younger children, you might want to have each child name the picture on his card before you begin playing. If abilities permit, have each child simply look at his own card, then hold it in his hand.) Play music as children dance around the room. When you stop the music, have each child find his rhyming partner(s). Then, in turn, have each set of students say their rhymes aloud. If the class agrees that that set of students does indeed have a rhyme, continue around the room in the same manner. If someone disagrees, he may say, "I challenge!" Then study the words together and rearrange students if necessary. To continue play, say "Exchange"; then have each child exchange his card with someone who was not in his rhyming group. Then restart the music and begin round two!

Adapted from an idea by Stephanie Bolton—Gr. K
The Ellison School
Vineland, NJ

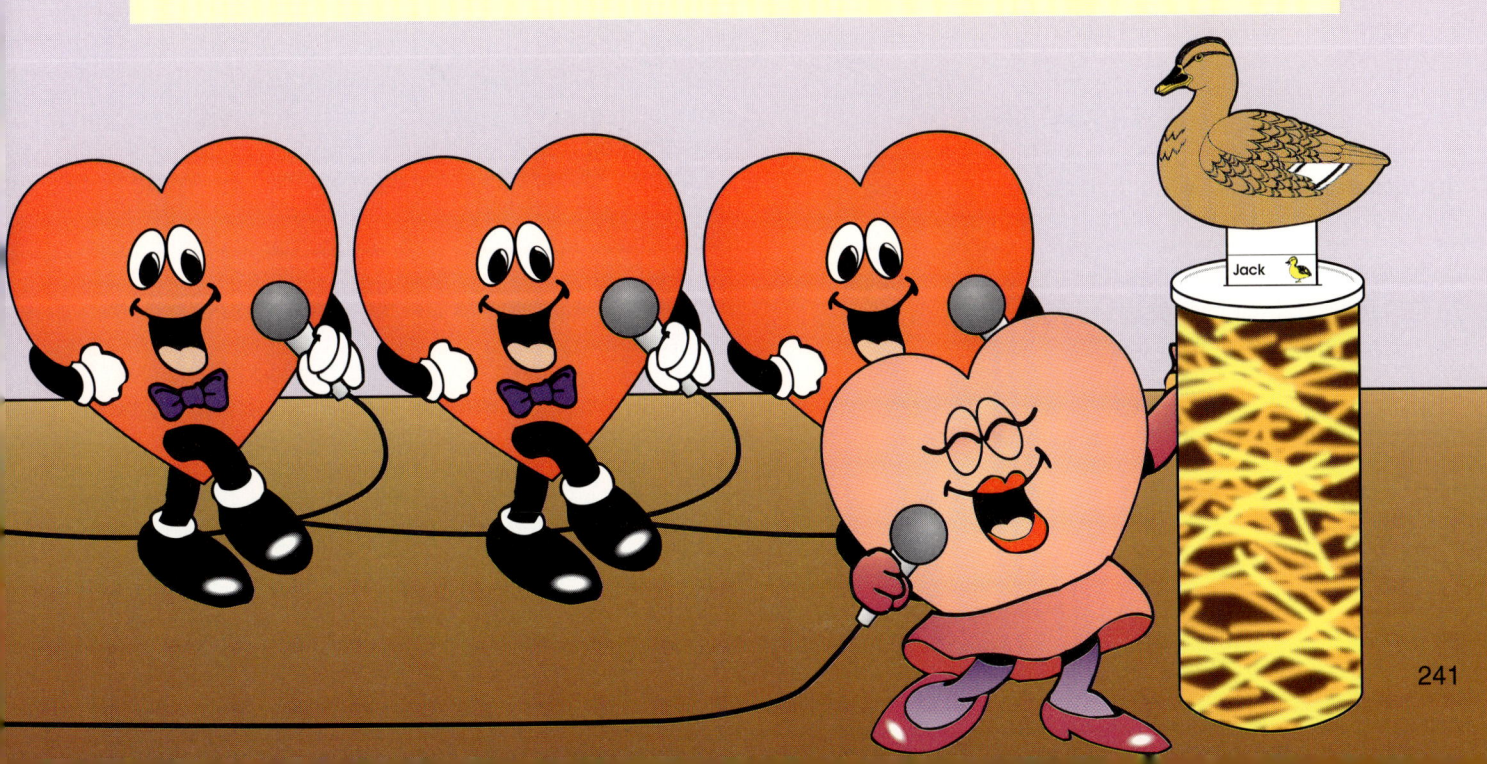

The Kindergarten Feud

Youngsters will ask to play this variation of "The Family Feud" time and time again! In advance, cut apart the riddles (on pages 246-247); then glue each riddle on a construction paper strip. Draw a scoreboard on the chalkboard. Then divide your class into two teams. Ask each team to decide on a rhyming name for their team. Write the team names on the scoreboard. Then, acting as the host, read one of the riddles aloud, addressing it to the first person on Team A. If the first person can answer it, he does so aloud. If his answer is correct, give that team a point. If his answer is incorrect, the first person on Team B can try to "steal" the point by answering the riddle. If Team B's answer is incorrect, the same riddle goes back to the second person on Team A, and so on until an appropriate word is said. Beginning with Team B, continue playing in this manner until all the riddles have been answered. (If you're playing this game in February, award each participating team member a candy heart when the game is over!)

Adapted from an idea by Gloria Barrow—Gr. K, Dundee Elementary, Dundee, FL

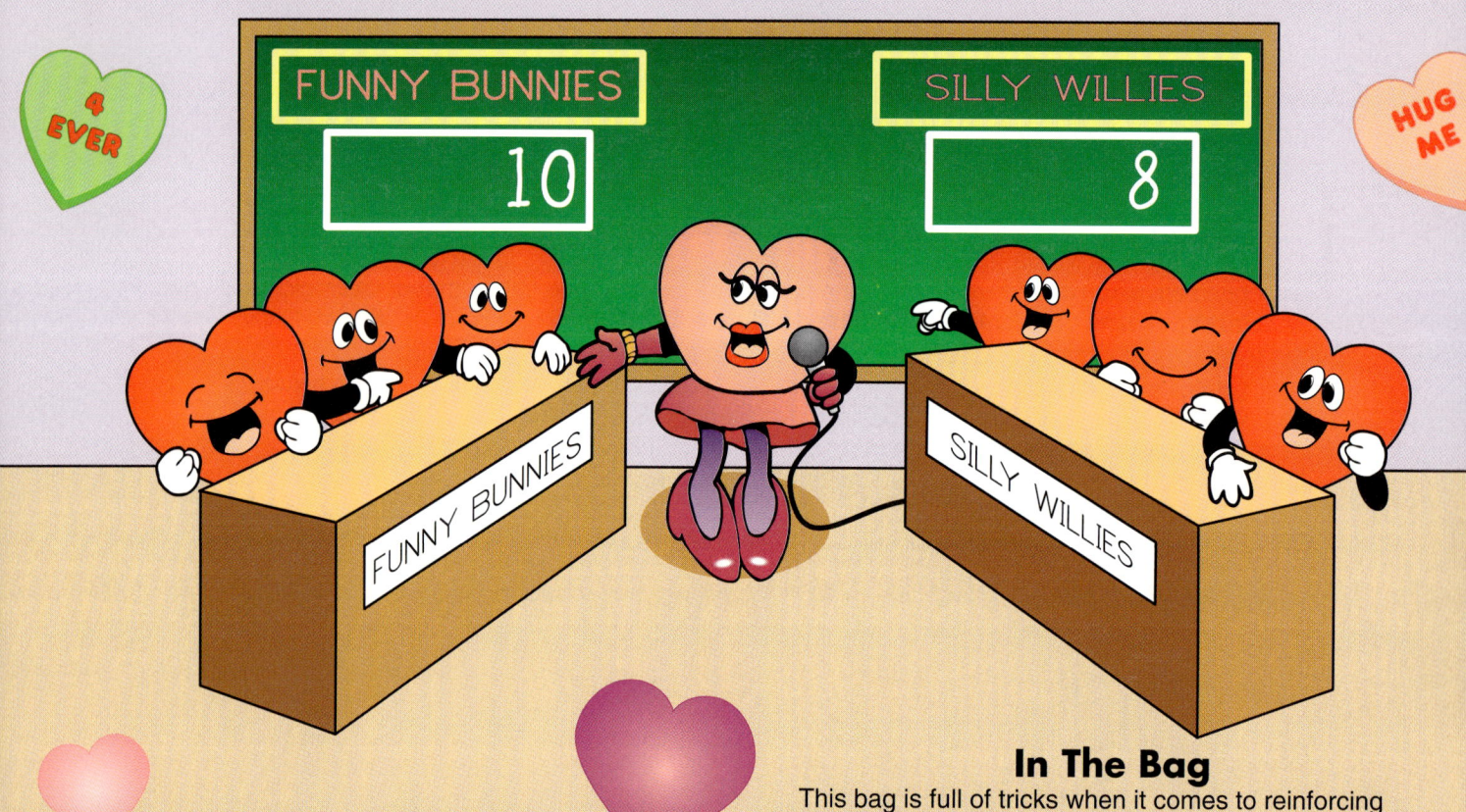

Time To Line Up!

Take advantage of your natural line-up times—and practice rhymes! Announce that each child may line up when she hears a word that rhymes with her name. Then, for each child, call out a word (or nonsense word) that rhymes with her name. In spite of the giggles, listening skills will be at their peak and children will begin to generate rhyming words of their own!

Tara Stefanich—Gr. K, Merritt Elementary, Mt. Iron, MN
LeeAnne Fuller—D-K, Montessori & More, Des Moines, IA

In The Bag

This bag is full of tricks when it comes to reinforcing rhyming. Place a variety of rhyming objects in a cloth bag. (You might also like to ask children to look for rhyming objects to bring in from home.) Have one child take an object from the bag and show it to the class. Then call on another child to try to find a rhyming object in the bag. When that child chooses an object, have him stand next to the first child. Encourage the class to say the name of each object together. If the objects rhyme, both children remain standing. Begin the process again by asking another child to choose an object from the bag; then continue in the same manner. Each time a new student is added to the line of standing students, have the whole class say the name of each object in the line. When all of the objects are out of the bag, have the children remain in place while you collect each of the objects. Then, just for fun, see if the class can say what each person was holding—from memory!

Sarah Teimouri—Gr. K, Guilford Primary School, Greensboro, NC
Audrey Smith—Gr. K, Church Street Elementary, Riverdale, GA

Rhyme Lines

Everyone moves and everyone learns with this rhyming activity. In advance, collect a rhyming object or picture for each child in your class. Choose one child to be captain for each family of rhymes. Give each captain an object or picture, and have her stand. Then distribute the remaining objects and pictures. At your signal, have each child line up behind the captain who is holding a rhyme for her object or picture. To check each line, have the whole class chant the objects in each line. Hey—you've made a *fine line!*

Sarah Teimouri—Gr. K
Guilford Primary School
Greensboro, NC

The Secret Password

This dismissal method reinforces rhyming skills—and crowd control just happens to be a fringe benefit! As children are preparing to exit your classroom, tell them that they must know the secret password in order to leave. Explain that you will announce a key word when everyone is in line. In order to leave the room, each child must tell you a word that rhymes with the key word before he passes through the door. (Announce new key words as appropriate.) Youngsters will soon learn that listening skills must be in fine form because, in addition to the key word changing in midstream, no child may use the exact same password as the child in front of him. See you later, alligator!

S. Bell—Grs. K and JK
Fairview Avenue Public School
Dunnville, Ontario, Canada

Go Rhyme

Two to four players will be fishing for rhymes with this adapted version of Go Fish. In advance, prepare sets of rhyming cards as described in "Find Your Partner!" on page 241. To play, shuffle the cards; then deal five cards to each player. Place the remaining cards facedown in a pile. Each player looks at his cards. If a player has any rhymes in his hand, he lays them down faceup. (Other players may play on an opponent's exposed rhymes at any time.) Player A addresses the player of his choice and says, "Do you have a rhyme for [whale]?" If that player has a rhyme for whale, he gives the card to Player A. Player A lays the rhyming cards faceup, and play continues in the same manner with Player B. If, on the other hand, the asked player does not have a rhyme for [whale], he says, "Go rhyme." Player A then draws a card from the pile. If he chooses a card for which he has a rhyme, he may lay that set down and play continues with the next player. If he does not have a rhyme for the drawn card, he says, "Pass," and play continues with the next player. Play until all the cards have been matched. (If players reach a stalemate, draw cards from the pile until all cards have a rhyming match.)

Lisa Cohen—Gr. K, Laurel Plains Elementary, New City, NY

Finish It Up

"Finishing up" rhymed poetry will reinforce rhyming, listening, and emergent reading skills. Besides all that—it's plain old fun! Read aloud a selection of rhyming poetry or a rhyming story (see the literature list on page 245). After discussing the selection, tell youngsters that you are going to read it again. This time, however, *they* are going to supply the rhyming words! Begin reading aloud. When you reach a rhyming word, pause expectantly, waiting for children to complete the sentence. (For example, you might say, "Hey diddle, diddle, the cat and the…..") Afterwards write each set of rhyming words on a sheet of chart paper, and discuss each pair's beginning and ending sounds. Lead children in drawing conclusions that are appropriate to their abilities (such as: rhyming words have the same ending sound and rhyming words are not always spelled alike).

Jeanene Engelhardt—Gr. K
Workman Avenue School
West Covina, CA

Show-And-Guess

When you're studying rhyming, adapt your show-and-tell time to show-and-guess time. Ask each child to find two rhyming items or pictures at home, put them in a bag, and bring them to school. In turn, have each child show one of his items to the class. After sharing his first item, have the class guess what the second item might be. Hmmm…could it be a bat? A mat? A hat? Oh, no—not a rat!

Robin Goddard—Gr. K
Mt. Vernon Elementary
St. Petersburg, FL

Down By The Bay

Raffi's *Down By The Bay* (Crown Books For Young Readers) is a wonderfully appealing and motivating literature selection to complement your rhyming theme. In this book, two friends use their imaginations and rhyme to create some of the silliest scenes you have ever laid eyes on! Share *Down By The Bay* with your children. After reading and discussing the book, teach the tune to your children and sing the song. Then ask each child to imagine what he might see at the bay. Give each child a large sheet of construction paper that has been programmed, "Have you ever seen a…?" Then have each child write about, draw, and color an imaginary rhyming scene to complete the page. Bind the pages together between decorated construction-paper covers. Then sing the song again, using students' pages to complete the song each time you sing it. This book is so much fun to read and sing, you might want to make it a traveling book so each family can share in the fun! As a variation, have children paint original *Down By The Bay* scenes; then display them on a bulletin board.

Wanda D. Jones—Gr. K, Smyrna West Kindergarten, Smyrna, TN
Kathryn Brophy—Gr. K, Kidwatch Plus®, Inc.; Chicago, IL

Flip Books

When your youngsters have become very familiar with rhyming, encourage each child to author a rhyming flip book. To make one book, fold a large sheet of construction paper in half horizontally (as shown). Then fold it in half (widthwise) two times. Open the paper to show eight sections; then refold it on the first fold only. Cut on the four folds **through one layer of paper only.** You now have four flip pages in your book. To program the top page of each section, gather pictures for which the student is likely to be able to think of rhyming words. Glue one picture to each section of the book. (Be sure that you don't glue two pictures that rhyme on the top pages.) Next have a child flip each top page up; then illustrate a different rhyming word on each bottom section. Encourage children to share their flip books by reading them to each other and their families.

Jennifer Barton—Gr. K, Elizabeth Green School, Newington, CT

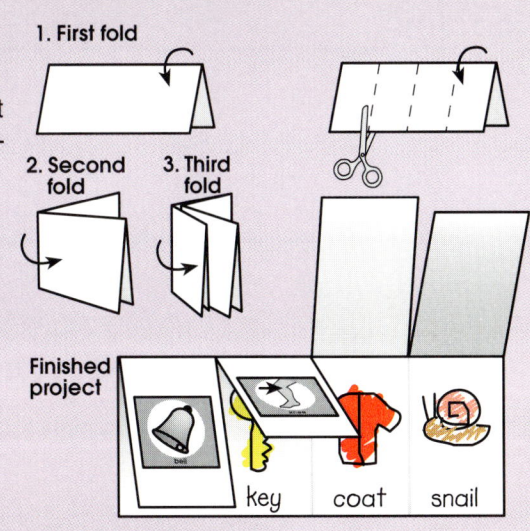

Rhyme-Time Challenge

Culminate your rhyming activities with a rhyme-time challenge. In advance, make a list of words for which you think your youngsters are likely to be able to think of more than one rhyming word (see the illustration). Then prepare an invitation and use it to officially challenge another class to play the game with your class—or just divide your own students into two teams. To play, announce the first word on the list. Encourage each team to think of corresponding rhyming words. Alternating from Team A to Team B, repeatedly ask each team to say a different rhyming word until one team is unable to think of another rhyme. Then give the last team to say a rhyming word a point. Continue play in the same manner as long as interest lasts. (By the way—did you know that *orange* and *pint* don't have rhymes? You might amuse your students by tossing out one of these words during the game.) Afterwards celebrate everyone's rhyming achievements by serving *chips* and *dips*!

Adapted from an idea by Betsy Pottey—Gr. K
Abington ECC
Abington, MA

Disappearing Act

Nothin' up your sleeve, but things *will* be disappearing! Draw a simple scene on a chalkboard or dry-erase board. In turn, have each child come to the board and hold the eraser. Then give him a simple rhyme (such as the one shown in the illustration) and have him erase the appropriate part of the picture. Continue in this manner until the entire scene has disappeared. Abracadabra!

Leslie O'Donnell—Gr. K, Sedalia Park School, Marietta, GA

The Literature Link

Sheep In A Jeep
Written by Nancy Shaw
Illustrated by Margot Apple
Published by Houghton Mifflin Company

*Sing A Song Of Popcorn:
Every Child's Book Of Poems*
Published by Scholastic Inc.

Ten Cats Have Hats
Written by Jean Marzollo
Illustrated by David McPhail
Published by Scholastic Inc.

Is Your Mama A Llama?
Written by Deborah Guarino
Illustrated by Steven Kellogg
Published by Scholastic Inc.

Poems For The Very Young
Selected by Michael Rosen
Illustrated by Bob Graham
Published by Kingfisher Books

Please Don't Squeeze Your Boa, Noah!
Written by Marilyn Singer
Illustrated by Clément Oubrerie
Published by Henry Holt and Company

Riddles Use with "The Kindergarten Feud" on page 242.

- You sleep in me. I rhyme with *sled*.
  What am I? *bed*

- You need me to play baseball. I rhyme with *hat*.
  What am I? *bat*

- You use me on a very hot day. I rhyme with *tan*.
  What am I? *fan*

- You can wear me on your finger. I rhyme with *sing*.
  What am I? *ring*

- You use me to write on the board. I rhyme with *walk*.
  What am I? *chalk*

- I keep you warm outside. I rhyme with *boat*.
  What am I? *coat*

- I sometimes sing a chirping song. I rhyme with *third*.
  What am I? *bird*

- I'm a drink that helps you grow. I rhyme with *silk*.
  What am I? *milk*

- I give you shade on sunny days. I rhyme with *bee*.
  What am I? *tree*

- Some people live in me. I rhyme with *mouse*.
  What am I? *house*

Use with "The Kindergarten Feud" on page 242.   **Riddles**

- I keep your hands toasty warm. I rhyme with *kittens*. What am I? *mittens*

- You need me to catch a fish. I rhyme with *book*. What am I? *hook*

- I'm just right at a birthday party. I rhyme with *rake*. What am I? *cake*

- I tell you when it's time to go. I rhyme with *sock*. What am I? *clock*

- I twinkle high up in the sky. I rhyme with *car*. What am I? *star*

- I'm funny and I make you laugh. I rhyme with *down*. What am I? *clown*

- You use me to wash your hands. I rhyme with *rope*. What am I? *soap*

- I'm furry and I can purr. I rhyme with *rat*. What am I? *cat*

- I hold you up when you're sitting. I rhyme with *hair*. What am I? *chair*

- Some people write with me. I rhyme with *hen*. What am I? *pen*

Animal Parents And Their Kids!

All parents start out as babies—in one form or another. Ducks were once ducklings, cats were once kittens, and large gorillas were once little, tiny babies! Use the ideas in this unit to explore animal parents and their offspring.

by Lucia Kemp Henry

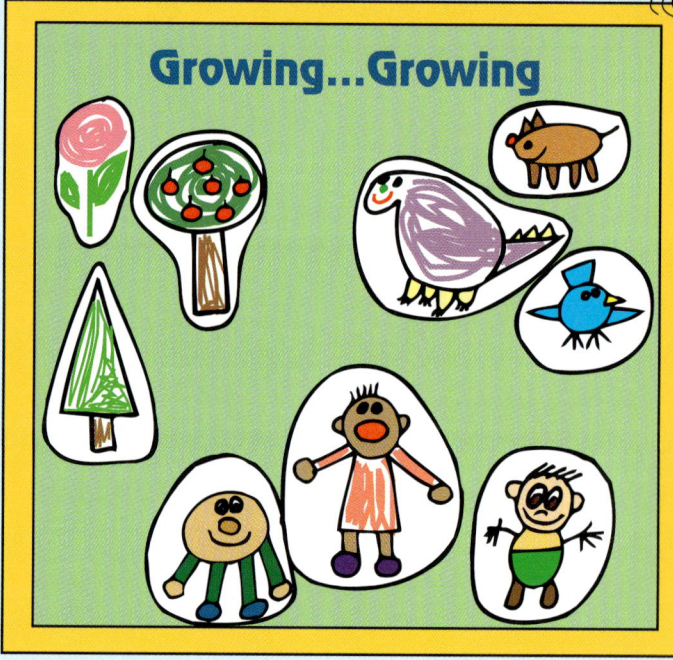

Growing...Growing

Stimulate your youngsters' thoughts on growth by asking them what it means to grow. Then encourage them to brainstorm a list of things that grow. Next have each child select one item from the list. Have him illustrate his selection, then cut it out. Encourage children to think of different ways in which they could sort their cutouts (such as by plants, animals, and people). Then mount the pictures on a bulletin board entitled "Growing...Growing." When the display is finished, encourage children to look at the board and discuss the similarities and differences in growing things. (For example, how is the growth of an apple different from that of a puppy?)

Read All About It

Fascinating photography and a text to match make each of the nonfiction selections below a treasury of information for your kindergarten classroom. Share your choice of these books with your youngsters, allowing plenty of time for independent study of the photographs. (Although the text is a little lengthy in some of the books, the pictures are worth a thousand words!)

Amiable Little Beasts
By Roger A. Caras & Steve Graham
Published by Macmillan Publishing Co., Inc.

Baby Animals
By Bernice Rappoport
Published by World Book, Inc.

The Baby Zoo
By Bruce McMillan
Published by Scholastic Inc.

My First Book Of Nature: How Living Things Grow
By Dwight Kuhn
Published by Scholastic Inc.

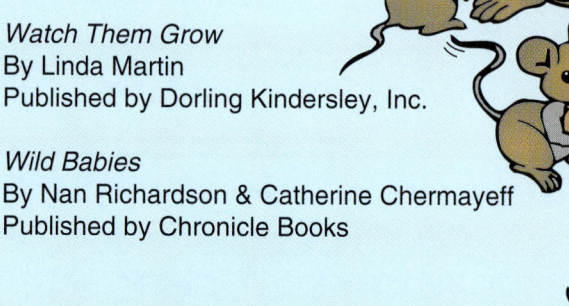

Raising A Family
By Paul Bennett
Published by Thomson Learning

Watch Them Grow
By Linda Martin
Published by Dorling Kindersley, Inc.

Wild Babies
By Nan Richardson & Catherine Chermayeff
Published by Chronicle Books

Who Are You?

As you explore together the books listed in "Read All About It," youngsters may start to notice that some animal babies are referred to by specific names. Make a chart to record this new information. Ask children to name all of the animals that they have been reading about. Write their responses on chart paper. Then assign a different animal to each child/small group. Ask each child to look through the literature to find a picture of her assigned animal. As abilities permit, have each child copy the corresponding baby-animal name on the chart, or dictate the letters in the baby animal's name that you point out. Then display the chart in your classroom to incorporate in your read-the-room activities.

Animal Parents And Their Babies

Young animal lovers will delight in illustrating and then reading these child-made booklets. For each child, duplicate the booklet patterns (pages 252–255) on white construction paper. Have each child color the mother animals. Then have youngsters use the art techniques described at the right to illustrate each of the baby animals, or encourage them to design their own illustrations. If appropriate, have each child write the name of the baby animal on each booklet page.

To complete booklet page 7, encourage each child to draw a parent or caregiver on the left side of the page, then glue a photocopy of his school picture on the right side of the page. To assemble the booklet, cut out each half-sheet section along the bold outlines. (You should have eight sections.) Glue booklet page 7 to a piece of cardboard cut to size. (Do not cut page 7 in half.) Then cut the cover and the rest of the booklet pages along the dotted lines. Stack the mother-animal pages in order on the left side of page 7; then staple along the left edge. Stack the baby-animal pictures in order on the right side of page 7; then staple along the right edge.

Booklet Cover: Use your fingertip to spread a thin layer of glue over the cub. Then shake coffee grounds (in a salt shaker) onto the glue. Let it dry; then shake off the excess grounds.

Booklet Page 1: Draw a lamb on the page. Use your fingertip to spread a thin layer of glue over the lamb. Glue stretched-out pieces of cotton on the lamb. Let it dry.

Booklet Page 2: Study a variety of kitten pictures. Color a kitten just for you!

Booklet Page 3: Cut out a duckling shape from a piece of felt. Glue the felt to the page. Then use markers to add details.

Booklet Page 4: Draw and color a piglet. For the tail, glue on a curled piece of curling ribbon.

Booklet Page 5: Glue a piece of fabric to the page to resemble a blanket. Then look through old magazines for pictures of puppies. Cut out one of the puppies; then glue it to the page.

Booklet Page 6: Use paint to make thumbprints on the page. When the paint is dry, use fine-tipped markers to add chick details.

Reinforce baby-animal names with the poem below. If desired, enlarge and trace the art onto a large sheet of poster board. Then add the text. Display the poster in your baby animals display.

Baby Names

A baby goose is a **gosling**.
A baby bear is a furry, little **cub**.
A baby dog is a **puppy**
That needs a lot of love!

A baby duck is a **duckling**.
A baby cow is a wobbly **calf**.
A baby cat is a **kitten**
That sometimes makes me laugh!

A baby horse is a **foal**.
A baby pig is a little **piglet**.
A baby kangaroo's a **joey**.
In his mama's pouch—a perfect fit!

A baby deer is a **fawn**.
A baby seal is a shiny, black **pup**.
A baby goat is a **kid**…
And *we're* the kids you'd like to cuddle up!

The Simple Bare Necessities

This activity takes you back to the basics of animal care. As a group, brainstorm a list of wild and domestic animals. Have each child choose one of the animals listed to research. Encourage children to look through your collection of baby-animal books to find out the needs of her particular animal. Children might also choose to draw on their own experiences, or interview people who know about their chosen animals. Then have each child illustrate one or more of the facts that she has learned. Bind all of the pages between construction-paper covers. Have each child share her page during a group reading time.

The Bare Necessiti[es]
by Ms. Mallard's Class

A fawn needs a hiding place.

The Show Must Go On

With some creative costuming and a few rehearsals, your little ones will be ready to take their act on the road—or at least a classroom stage! Using the "Baby Names" poem on page 250, assign each line of text that names an animal to a different student. Assist these students in creating simple costumes/puppets for their parts. (See the illustration for ideas.) Also assign the last lines of the first three stanzas to different students. Encourage these students to memorize and act out their lines. Assign the last line to the remaining children. Have these children create a mural of kids by encouraging them to draw pictures of themselves on a long sheet of bulletin-board paper.

To perform the play, arrange the children in rows according to the poem. For example, position the gosling, the cub, the puppy, and the child with the last line of the first stanza in the first row. Arrange the next "stanza of students" similarly behind the first row of students, and so on until the last line of the entire poem. Have the creators of the mural stand in the last row holding the mural. (You will end up with five rows.) In sequence, have each child recite and dramatize his line. As the last line of each stanza is said, direct that row of children to sit down. After the last line of the entire poem has been said, have all of the children stand and take a bow!

A baby goose is a **gosling**.

A baby bear is a furry, little **cub**.

A baby dog is a **puppy**

That needs a lot of love!

Experience The Movement

Since it might not be convenient to have a zooful of baby animals in your classroom, role-playing just might be the next best thing! Have each child find a spot in the classroom where he can freely move about. Then call out the name of a baby animal, such as a colt. Encourage each child to pretend to be that animal during the first days, weeks, and months of its life. When the animals seem to have grown up, call out another animal and encourage the children to play the parts once again. If possible, videotape these animal antics. Then, when you view it, turn the sound down and ask youngsters to identify each animal as it is dramatized.

The Literature Link

Kitten For A Day
By Ezra Jack Keats
Published by Four Winds Press

Mother Night
By Denys Cazet
Published by Orchard Books

Time For Bed
By Mem Fox
Published by Harcourt Brace & Company

Booklet Cover And Pages

Use with "Animal Parents And Their Babies" on page 249.

Animal Parents

by

And Their Babies

This is a sheep.

Her baby is a _____.

1   1

Booklet Pages 2 And 3
Use with "Animal Parents And Their Babies" on page 249.

This is a cat.

Her baby is a _____.

2 | 2

This is a duck.

Her baby is a _____.

3 | 3

©The Education Center, Inc. • *THE MAILBOX*® • *Kindergarten* • April/May 1996   253

Booklet Pages 4 And 5
Use with "Animal Parents And Their Babies" on page 249.

This is a pig.

Her baby is a _____.

4 | 4

This is a dog.

Her baby is a _____.

5 | 5

254 ©The Education Center, Inc. • THE MAILBOX® Kindergarten • April/May 1996

Booklet Pages 6 And 7

Use with "Animal Parents And Their Babies" on page 249.

This is a hen.

Her babies are _____.

6 | 6

This is my _____ ...and this is me!

7

The Strawberry Patch

Mosey on down to this strawberry patch that is loaded with basketfuls of learning opportunities including language arts, math, science, art, fine-motor skills and more!

ideas by Lucia Kemp Henry

A Strawberry Tale

To introduce your strawberry unit with irresistible appeal, read aloud Don and Audrey Wood's *The Little Mouse, The Red Ripe Strawberry, And The Big Hungry Bear.* This sweetly suspenseful tale is available in paperback and hardcover, and on videotape and audiotape from Child's Play: 1-800-639-6404. A big book and teaching guide are also available from Scholastic Inc.: 1-800-325-6149. After sharing the story with your youngsters, choose from among the rest of the ideas in this unit that are just ripe for the picking!

The Real Thing

There's just no substitute for the real thing—so let's get it! In advance, ask several parents to each donate a basket of strawberries. After washing hands and strawberries, have small groups of children examine several strawberries. As they look at the berries, encourage children to talk about what they observe. Write their comments on a strawberry-shaped cutout. Then give each child a blank index card, crayons, and markers. Encourage each child to draw a detailed picture of a strawberry based on his observations. Have each child sign his illustration; then laminate the pictures to use in "Strawberry Treats" on page 257. (Save the real strawberries for activities to come in this unit!)

- It's bumpy.
- It's red.
- It has a green part.
- It's speckley.
- They might have seeds.

Is It Ripe?

After sharing *The Little Mouse, The Red Ripe Strawberry, And The Big Hungry Bear,* do this activity with your youngsters to dip into science concepts and vocabulary building. Begin the activity by writing the book's title on a sheet of chart paper. (If you haven't read the book, simply write "The Red Ripe Strawberry.") Using highlighting tape or markers, have student volunteers highlight words that they recognize in the title. Then draw your youngsters' attention to the word *Ripe*. Ask children what they think the word means. Also ask what they think might make an unripe strawberry ripen. Then divide your students into small groups and have each group work with a basket of washed strawberries (bananas and pears also work well if strawberries are not available). Ask the groups to sort their strawberries according to ripeness. Record the number of strawberries in each category on a class graph. Then provide plastic knives for cutting and encourage each child to taste a slice of a ripe and an unripe (or less ripe) strawberry. Which do they like best? Make a human graph by having each child stand in a line to indicate his preference. Which line is longer? Discuss what the human graph reveals. (Save the remaining strawberries for activities on page 257.)

To be ripe, or not to be...

Half-And-Half

The Little Mouse, The Red Ripe Strawberry, And The Big Hungry Bear provides a delicious introduction to fractions. First ask children how the little mouse saved the strawberry in the story. Then revisit the illustrations on which the text reads "Cut it in two," and "Share half with me." Encourage children to look at the pictures and suggest ideas to define the word *half*. Guide children to conclude that to halve something, it must be separated into two equal parts, and that two halves make a whole. Then, after washing hands, give each child a couple of strawberries and a plastic knife. Have her practice cutting the strawberries in half; then discuss the results. Is it easy to cut a strawberry *exactly* in half? If you put one half and one half together, what do you have? When all of the strawberries are cut, have each child put her strawberries in a bowl. Save the sliced strawberries for "Strawberry Shortcake" (below).

Pam Warren—Gr. K
DeSoto Trail Elementary
Tallahassee, FL

Strawberry Shortcake

Your youngsters will love making—and eating—these luscious-looking strawberry shortcakes. To prepare, slice the halved strawberries (from "Half-And-Half") into smaller pieces. Put them in a large bowl; then sprinkle the strawberries with sugar and gently stir the mixture. For each child in your class, cut a slice of angel food cake. Arrange the cake slices and strawberries in your cooking center along with paper plates, a bowl of whipped topping, serving spoons, and a fork for each child. Duplicate the recipe–page 265, then place it at children's eye level. As each child visits the cooking center, encourage her to make her very own serving of strawberry shortcake by following the pictures and the simple directions on the recipe. Mmmm—berries at their best!

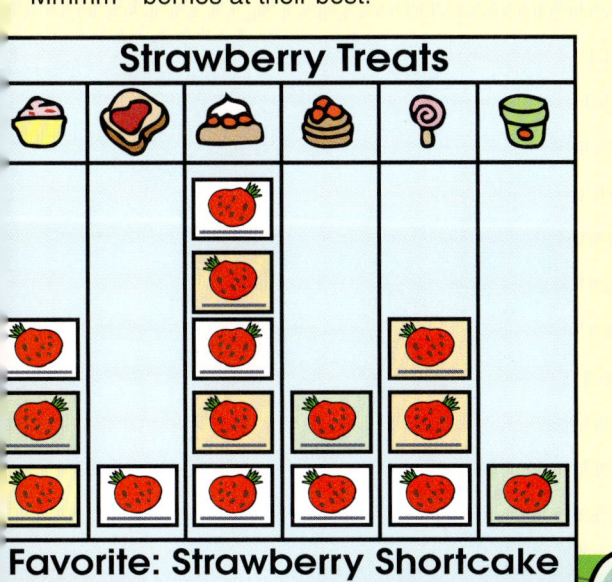

Strawberry Treats

After sampling their own strawberry shortcakes, youngsters will be in the mood to do this strawberry graphing activity. Ask each child to think of foods that are made with strawberries. Write the responses on a strawberry cutout. (Challenge your youngsters to add to the list as you continue your strawberry theme!) Then make a graph with one column for each food mentioned. Have each child indicate his favorite strawberry food by taping his strawberry card (see "The Real Thing" on page 256) in the appropriate place on the graph. Use the graph to discuss concepts such as favorite, least favorite, more, less, and equal.

Strawberry Counting Booklet

Youngsters will pick up a basketful of math skills—and more—when they make this strawberry counting booklet with a surprise ending. For each child, duplicate the booklet cover (page 261), the text strips (page 262), and the last booklet page (page 263) on construction paper. Have each child color his cover and cut it out along the bold outline. Then provide each child with five 8 1/2" x 7 1/2" white construction-paper pages. After reading each text strip together, instruct each child to cut the strips apart and glue each strip to the bottom of a different page. Then, in five separate work stations, have each child follow the directions to complete each page. As they work, draw students' attention to the mouse on each page. Ask children what they think the mouse is feeling. Do they think the mouse will get what he is wishing for?

When each child has completed pages 1–5, show him the last booklet page. Have him examine the illustration as you read the text aloud. Then have each child color the last page to reflect what he thinks happened. Be sure to read your booklets together during a group reading time.

Booklet Page One
Write the numeral 1 at the top of the page. Cut one large strawberry from red gift wrap; then glue it to the page. Also cut a green leaf crown from green gift wrap; then glue it to the top of the strawberry.

Booklet Page Two
Write the numeral 2 at the top of the page. Using the stencil pattern (page 264), cut strawberry stencils from tagboard or plastic stenciling sheets. Using two large stenciling brushes, and red and green paint, stencil two strawberries on the page. (Remember to use a different brush for each color of paint!)

Booklet Page Three
Write the numeral 3 at the top of the page. Cut three strawberry shapes from red fabric; then glue them to the page. Glue small, artificial leaves to the top of each berry.

Booklet Page Four
Write the numeral 4 at the top of the page. Cut a strawberry shape from a sponge. Using red paint, sponge-print four strawberries on the page. Use the corners of sponge scraps that have been dipped in green paint to sponge-print green leaves on the top of each berry.

Booklet Page Five
Write the numeral 5 at the top of the page. Cut out five strawberry shapes from red-toned magazine pictures; then glue them to the page. Cut small pieces of green curling ribbon; then glue them to the tops of the berries to resemble leaves.

Rhythm And Rhyme

Ripen up a vineload of skills with this Strawberry Counting Chant. It can serve as an introduction to subtraction, a reinforcement of number words and counting, and a chance to let those emerging reading skills really shine! In advance, duplicate the strawberry pattern (page 264) ten times on construction paper. Color, cut out, and laminate each strawberry. Then write the poem on chart paper. Read the poem aloud several times, encouraging children to join in as they are able. Then give one strawberry cutout to each of ten children. Have those children pretend to be strawberries on a plate by standing in a side-by-side line. As you recite the poem together, have the appropriate child squat down and hide his strawberry until all of the strawberries are gone. (For a variation, use this poem as a fingerplay. Have each child hold up all ten of his fingers. As you recite the poem together, each child manipulates his fingers to correspond with the words.)

Strawberry Counting Chant

One berry, two berries,
Three berries, four.
Five berries, six berries,
Seven berries—more!
Eight berries, nine berries,
Ten berries—wait!
Where are the berries that
were on my plate?

Stuffed Strawberries

Have each child make several of these colorful crafts that can be used as produce in your dramatic play area, as manipulatives for counting activities, as classroom decorations, or as springtime gifts. To make one strawberry, follow the directions below.

1. Form a golf-ball-sized ball of crumpled newspaper. Compress one end of the ball to form a somewhat pointed strawberry shape. Wrap a few pieces of clear tape around the pointed end to retain its shape.

2. Wrap the strawberry shape with a 7" x 7" red tissue-paper square. Use clear tape to secure the tissue paper at the top of the strawberry. Cut away any excess paper.

3. Paint the entire berry with water-diluted white glue. Let it dry.

4. Tape or glue a fabric or construction-paper leaf crown to the top of the berry.

5. Use a fine-point marker to add seeds to the berry.

Step 1
Step 2
Step 3
Step 4
Step 5

Strawberry-Basket Workshop

At this independent workshop, children's fine-motor skills combine with creativity and patterning to produce an original work of art. Stock a center with a supply of small berry baskets and a wide variety of ribbon, yarn, pipe cleaners, and construction-paper and fabric strips. As each child visits the workshop, she chooses a combination of materials to weave in and out of the holes in the basket. The finished baskets can be used to store each child's stuffed strawberries (from above).

Share-A-Berry Game

Pickin' these berries will promote cooperation and communication, as well as reinforce the skills of your choice. For every two children in your class, photocopy one large strawberry (page 264) on construction paper. (If you have an uneven number of children, photocopy one extra strawberry and you can play too!) Color, laminate, and cut out each strawberry. Then use a permanent marker or construction-paper cutouts to program the top half of each strawberry with a skill (see sample skills in the illustration). Then program the bottom half of each strawberry with the corresponding skill. Puzzle-cut each strawberry; then place all of the pieces in a basket. To play, designate an area of the room (such as the carpet) to be the strawberry patch. Then have each child select a strawberry piece. At your signal, encourage each child to find her match. When two children think they have a match, they may put their pieces together to check. If they have a perfect match, they take their berry to the strawberry patch. As additional children enter the patch, encourage the children to sort or arrange themselves according to skill. When all the berries are in the patch and sorted, discuss how they arranged themselves. If desired have each child exchange his berry piece for a nonmatching piece, and begin round two!

The Grey Lady And The Strawberry Snatcher
Written by Molly Bang
Published by Four Winds Press

This wordless Caldecott Honor Book blends fantasy and humor to tell a rich tale of wonder and suspense. Place the book in your reading center and encourage children to look through the book individually or in student pairs. Then share the book with your whole group. After discussing the story, encourage students to create text for each page (or spread) of the book. Write students' dictation on sticky notes and attach each note to the bottom of the appropriate page. Then share the book again, having student volunteers read the child-dictated text.

Strawberries Coming Out Of Your Ears?

Youngsters will expand their language skills as well as get a kick out of exploring some familiar American idioms with *Molly And The Strawberry Day* by Pam Conrad (published by HarperCollins). Begin by asking your youngsters if they have ever heard a phrase such as "I'm up to my ears in housework!" Find out what they think that saying means. Then explain that you are going to share a strawberry book that has a saying like that (an idiom) in it. Ask them to *be on the lookout* for the saying. Then read the story aloud. Each time the father refers to having strawberries coming out of their ears, ask your youngsters what they think the father means. Then finish reading the story to see Molly's fanciful conclusion to her strawberry day. (Note: Remind students that it is really ONLY a saying and they should never put objects in their ears.) Afterward, propose some of the idioms below and ask youngsters what they think each phrase means. Then discuss the actual meanings.

- a fork in the road
- raining cats and dogs
- getting your ducks in a row
- mark my words
- keep your cool
- fishing for a compliment
- throw in the towel

Barry Slate

Booklet cover
Use with "Strawberry Counting Booklet" on page 258.

My Strawberry Counting Book

by

©The Education Center, Inc. • THE MAILBOX® • Kindergarten • April/May 1996

Booklet text strips
Use with "Strawberry Counting Booklet" on page 258.

One red strawberry,
Juicy and sweet.

Two red strawberries,
So *tempting* to eat!

Three red strawberries,
Hanging on a vine.

Four red strawberries,
Can't *one* of them be mine?

Five red strawberries,
Looking *so* delicious...

Booklet—last page
Use with "Strawberry Counting Booklet" on page 258.

No more strawberries—

I just got my wishes!

Patterns

Use with "Strawberry Counting Booklet" and "Rhythm And Rhyme" on page 258, and "Share-A-Berry Game" on page 260.

stencil pattern

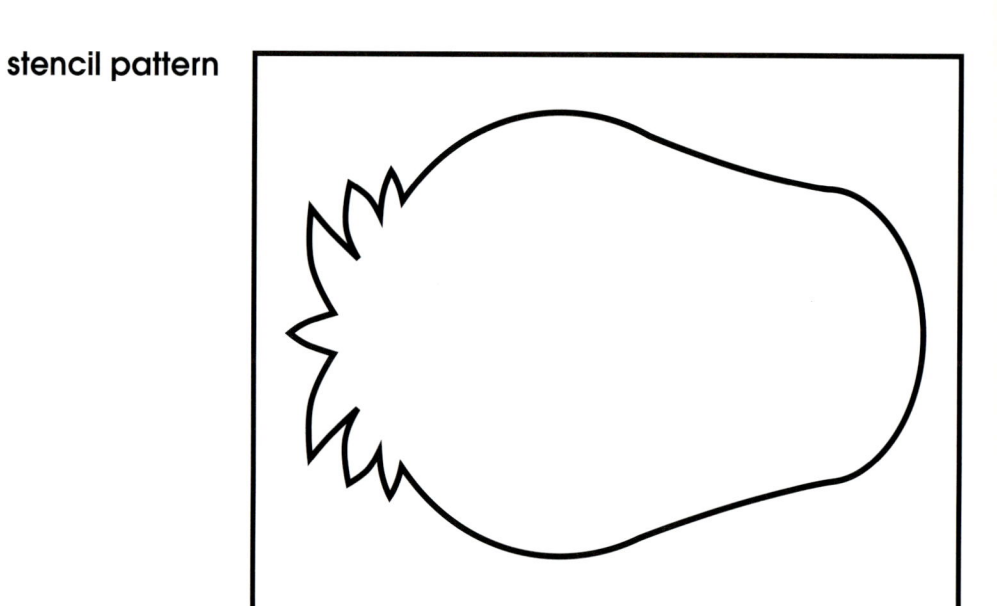

strawberry

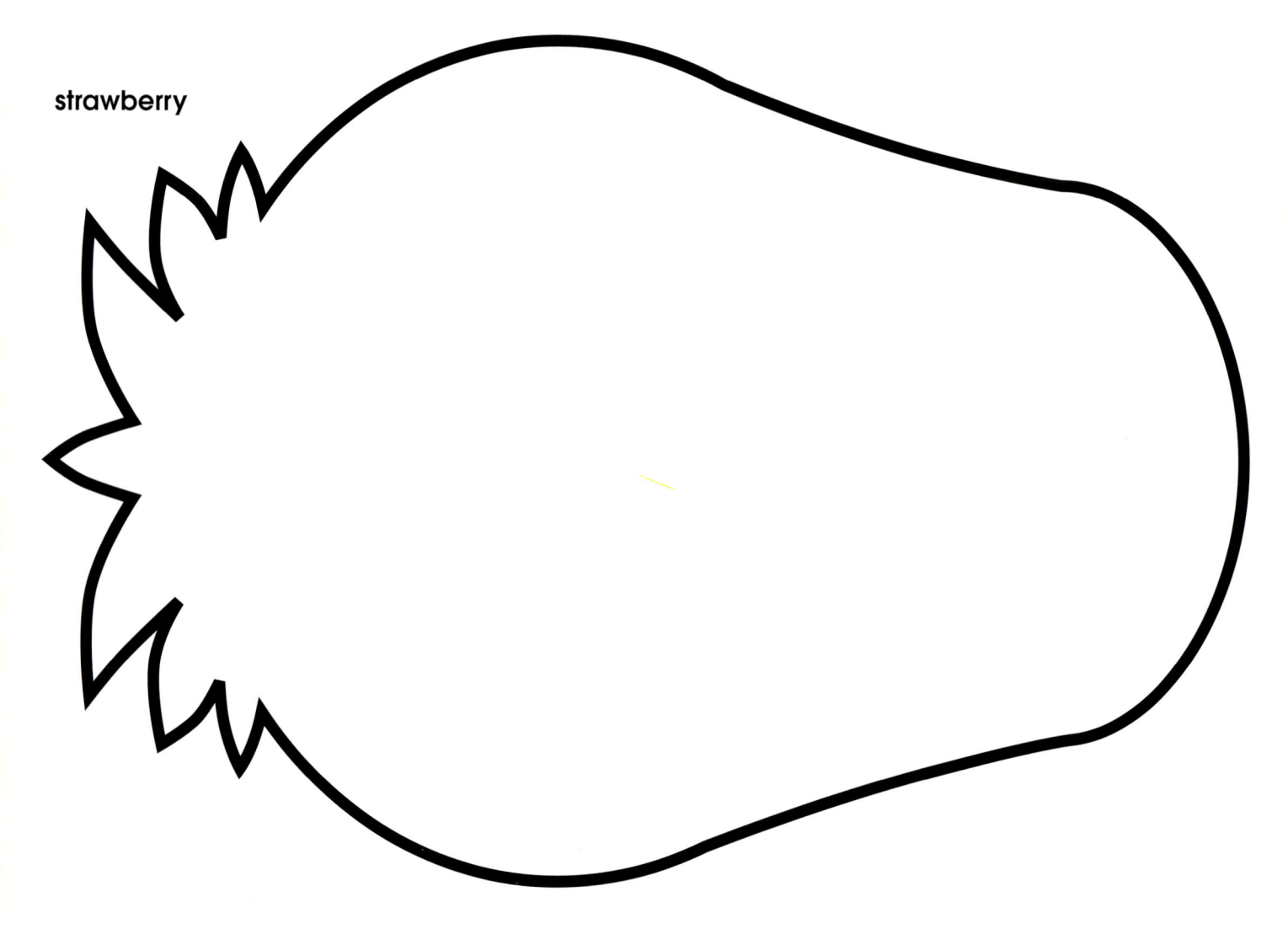

©The Education Center, Inc. • THE MAILBOX® • Kindergarten • April/May 1996

Strawberry Shortcake

1. Put the cake on a plate.
2. Add strawberries.
3. Add topping.

Barry Slate

Note To The Teacher: Use with "Strawberry Shortcake" on page 257.

©The Education Center, Inc. • THE MAILBOX® • Kindergarten • April/May 1996

We're Talkin' Turtles!

Your youngsters will topple for turtles—and learn a whole lot more—with the activities in this multidisciplinary unit.

by Lucia Kemp Henry

Turtle Tips For Teachers

- *Sea turtles* rank among the largest of all turtles. A leatherback may measure up to eight feet long! Sea turtles have powerful front flippers for swimming. Only female sea turtles ever leave the water, and that is only to lay their eggs on the sandy beach.

- *Box turtles* are usually very gentle creatures that live on land. For protection, a box turtle can pull all four legs and its head inside its shell. Box turtles eat mainly fruits, flowers, and leaves, but will also eat worms, insects, and other small animals.

- *Snapping turtles* live in freshwater lakes, marshes, ponds, and rivers. They are quite aggressive and will bite with their powerful jaws. The shell of a snapping turtle has ridges and its tail is spiny. Snappers eat fish and plants and other animals that they catch in the water, such as frogs and salamanders.

- *Soft shelled turtles* have a round, flat, leathery shell and a tubelike snout that serves as an underwater breathing tube. They may bite when they are disturbed and can strike out with lightning speed. Soft shelled turtles almost never leave the water.

- *Painted turtles* can be found in or near the quiet waters of freshwater lakes, ponds, and streams. Markings of bright red and yellow give painted turtles their name. Being quite timid, a painted turtle will dive into the water at the slightest sound.

- *Tortoises* are turtles that live on land. They have legs and elephantlike feet rather than flippers or webbed feet. There are about 40 types of tortoises. The Galápagos tortoise is among the largest of the land turtles, measuring up to four feet long and weighing up to 600 pounds!

Turtles In The Wild

Introduce your students to a variety of wild turtles with a wonderful Reading Rainbow selection titled *Turtle And Tortoise* by Vincent Serventy. (If this title is not available, see the literature list on page 269 for additional recommendations.) Up close photographs clearly show the turtles in their natural environments and are accompanied by informative text. After reading and discussing the book, the stage is set to use the poem on page 267 to present a little scientific information for those kids who are curious about turtles.

Turtle Types

A little rhythm and rhyme always seem to aid in absorbing information. So try using this science-related poem to present some interesting turtle facts. In advance, write the poem on chart paper. Photocopy the turtle patterns on pages 272-273. Color each turtle picture; then cut loosely around its outline. Mount each cutout on a piece of tagboard. Laminate the turtle pictures for durability; then prepare them for flannelboard or magnetboard use. As you mention each specific turtle in the poem, display its picture on the board. As they are able, encourage youngsters to join you in reading/reciting the poem. When children are familiar with the poem, distribute the turtle pictures and have youngsters place them on the board at the appropriate time.

Turtle Types

Some turtles swim in the ocean.
Some turtles walk on the land.
Some turtles are quite enormous
And some fit in the palm of your hand!

Sea turtles live in the ocean
And swim and glide all day.
They only come out to lay eggs on the beach,
Then return to the sea right away.

A **box turtle** is usually gentle
And lives upon the land.
Some people keep them at home for pets.
You can even hold them in your hand!

A **snapping turtle** moves quickly.
He strikes out with the speed of a snake.
You might find this spiny-tailed creature
In a pond, a stream, or a lake.

A **soft shelled turtle** likes water—
You may see him swimming about.
He lives in freshwater places.
He has webbed feet and a long, pointy snout.

A **painted turtle** is pretty,
But also quite quiet and shy.
He lies in the sun by a pond or a stream,
But may hide if you pass too close by!

A **tortoise** lives on the land.
It has four legs and can walk about.
But if it's in danger or frightened,
You won't see its head popping out!

Turtle Habitats

This classification activity doubles as a turtle display for your science area. Photocopy a supply of the turtle patterns (from pages 272-273). Also fold a length of white mural paper in three vertical sections. Label one of the sections "Freshwater," one "Land," and one "Sea." Place the mural at a workstation and encourage children to paint each of the sections according to its label. Next have each child choose a turtle pattern, cut it out, and color it. If desired, refer children to the poem and the colored turtle pictures for guidance. Then encourage each child to glue his turtle in the appropriate habitat on the mural. Turtles, turtles everywhere...but of the snapping ones—beware!

Get Back In That Shell!

In some cases, children are urged to come out of their shells. Well, *The Foolish Tortoise* (written by Richard Buckley, illustrated by Eric Carle, published by Scholastic Inc.) is a story about a little fellow who tried doing just that! After reading and discussing the story with your children, ask them why they think the author called the tortoise *foolish*. Find out if your youngsters agree with the author.

Extend the story by asking children what purpose the shell of a real turtle or tortoise might serve. Then encourage youngsters to examine the photographs in some of the nonfiction titles listed in the literature list on page 269. Encourage discussion regarding which turtles' shells look like they might offer the most protection. Then look again at the colored turtle pictures prepared in "Turtle Types" on page 267. After categorizing them into land and nonland turtles, ask youngsters if they see any difference in the shells of the land and the nonland turtles. *(Land turtles have higher, domelike shells while sea turtles have lower, more streamlined shells.)*

The leatherback is bigger than Jen and Meg put together!

Evan can hold the little one in his hand and his fingers still stick out.

Little...Big...Giant!

Since adult turtles come in a wide array of sizes—from the tiny three-inch mud turtle to the giant eight-foot leatherback—measurement and size-related activities crawl right on into your turtle studies! To give your youngsters a lifelike idea of turtle sizes, try the following activity. First reduce one of the turtle patterns (from pages 272-273) until it is approximately three inches in length. Duplicate it on construction paper; then color and cut it out. Next use an opaque projector to project the leatherback turtle pattern onto a long sheet of mural paper. (If an opaque projector is not available, trace the pattern onto a sheet of acetate and use an overhead projector.) Position the projector so that the leatherback image reaches about eight feet in length. Trace the pattern; then paint it and cut it out. Laminate both of the patterns; then display them on the floor. Encourage youngsters to interact with the patterns, then guide students to draw conclusions. Record children's responses on a sheet of chart paper.

Travelin' Along

Most land turtles travel very slowly...but just *how* slowly? The following activity will put it in perspective. If you've been walking regularly with your class, plan to walk a half mile together and time your walk. Right as you leave, set a timer in your classroom for 2 1/2 hours. Tell your children that the timer will represent a land turtle's speed if it were to walk the same distance that you are about to walk. Upon returning from your walk, check the timer. Of course, it will still be ticking. Then continue with your daily activities, being sure to be in the room when the timer will go off. When it does go off, youngsters will likely have forgotten that they were even waiting for that imaginary turtle to cross the finish line!

"Down In The Meadow"

Change just a few of the words in this classic little song and it will be just right for singing about turtles and movement—and you can even add a little subtraction on the side! To make manipulatives or puppets to use with the song, use the patterns on pages 272-273. Or have youngsters use art supplies to make their own little turtles.

Down in the meadow in a little bitty pool
Swam ten little turtles and a mama turtle, too.
"**Swim**," said the mama turtle. "**Swim** like I do."
So they **swam** and they **swam** all over the pool.

Repeat the song several times, changing the action word each time. Use words like *splash, dive,* and *float.* Vary the activity by reducing the number of turtles by one each time you sing a verse, counting down from ten to one.

Turtle Books

The turtle-book patterns on pages 270-271 can be used in a variety of ways. Scan the options below and choose the ones that best suit your little ones' needs. To make one book, reproduce the back page (page 270) on tagboard and several copies of the book page (page 271) on construction paper. Color the back page; then align the book pages on top of the turtle shell and staple along the left edge.

Turtle Tips: Youngsters will be proud to record and share their newfound knowledge in their very own turtle-shaped books. As each child makes new turtle discoveries during your studies, suggest that he write about and illustrate each new fact on a page of his book. Encourage children to share their books during a group time.

T Is For Turtle: When your children make this book, all ears will be attuned to the sound of *T*—sometimes when you least expect it! Encourage your students to be on the lookout for pictures or words that begin with the *T* sound. Have each child glue her pictures or illustrate *T* words in her turtle book. If necessary, add more pages to the turtle books and see who has the biggest turtle around!

Turtle Math: Reproduce a supply of the turtle patterns (pages 272-273) on construction paper. Enlist the help of your students to color the patterns; then laminate and cut them out. Program each page of each child's book with an appropriate math problem. (Or tell a simple story and have the student write the appropriate information in his book. For example, you might say, "Three painted turtles were sitting on a log. One turtle dove into the pond. How many turtles are left?") Encourage each child to use the turtle cutouts as manipulatives to figure out the problems, then record the information in his book.

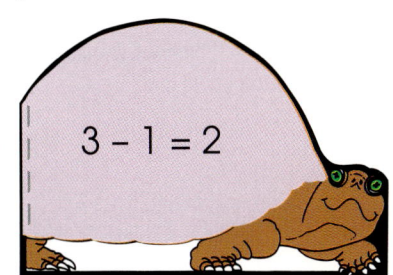

More Turtle Tales

Nonfiction

The Galápagos Tortoise
by Susan Schafer
(Dillon Press)

Look Out For Turtles!
by Melvin Berger
(HarperCollins Publishers)

Sea Turtles
by Frank Staub
(Lerner Publications Company)

Sea Turtles
by Gail Gibbons
(Holiday House, Inc.)

What's Under That Shell?
by D. M. Souza
(Carolrhoda Books, Inc.)

Tracks In The Sand
by Loreen Leedy
(Delacorte Press)

Fiction

The Smallest Turtle
by Lynley Dodd
(Gareth Stevens, Inc.)

Tomorrow, Up And Away!
by Pat Lowery Collins
(Houghton Mifflin Company)

I Wish I Could Fly
by Ron Maris
(Greenwillow Books)

How Turtle's Back Was Cracked: A Traditional Cherokee Tale
retold by Gayle Ross
(Dial Books For Young Readers)

Follow The Moon
by Sarah Weeks
(HarperCollins Publishers)

Box Turtle At Long Pond
by William T. George
(Greenwillow Books)

©1996 The Education Center, Inc.

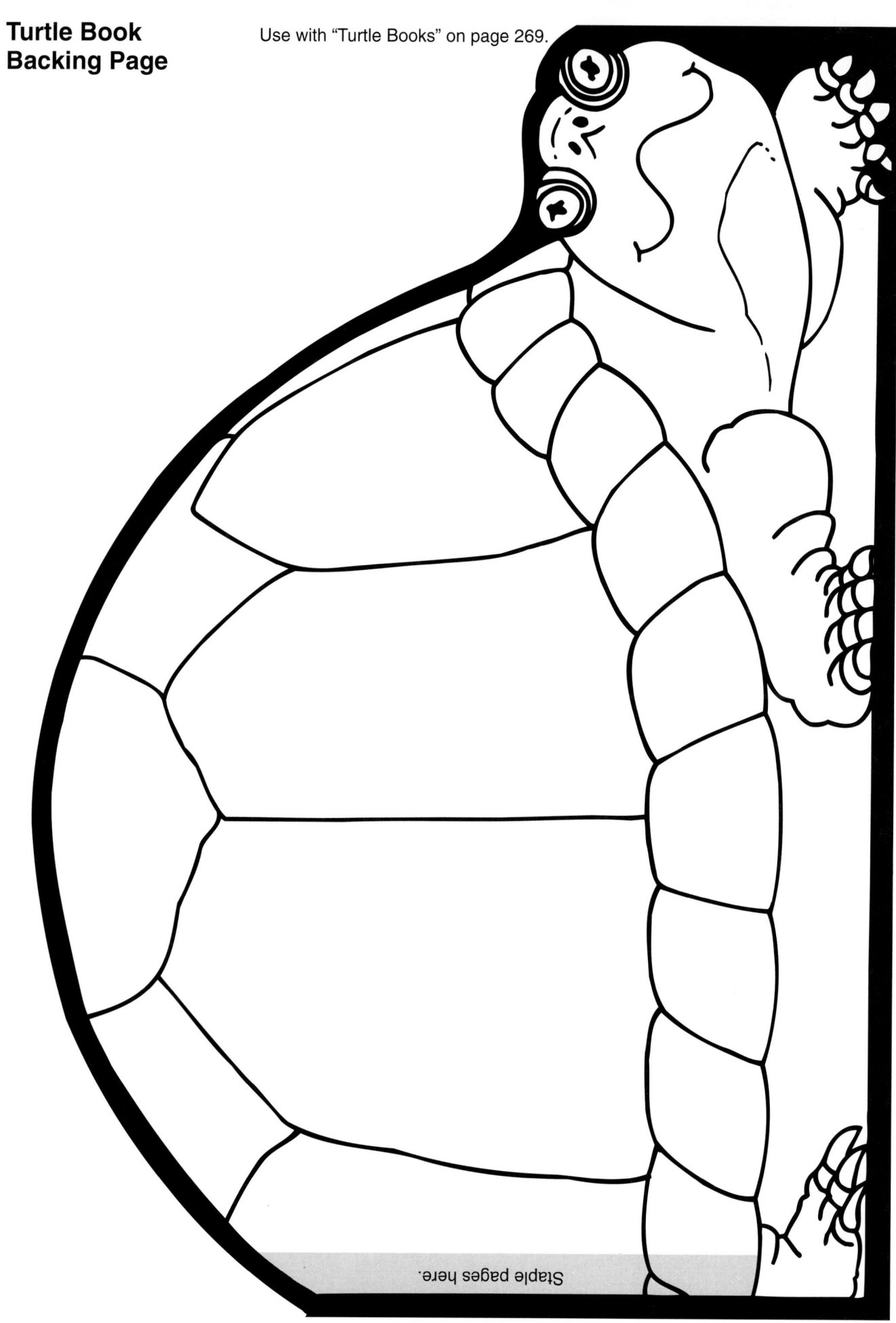

Turtle Book Backing Page

Use with "Turtle Books" on page 269.

Staple pages here.

270 ©The Education Center, Inc. • THE MAILBOX® • Kindergarten • June/July 1996

Turtle Book Page
Use with "Turtle Books" on page 269.

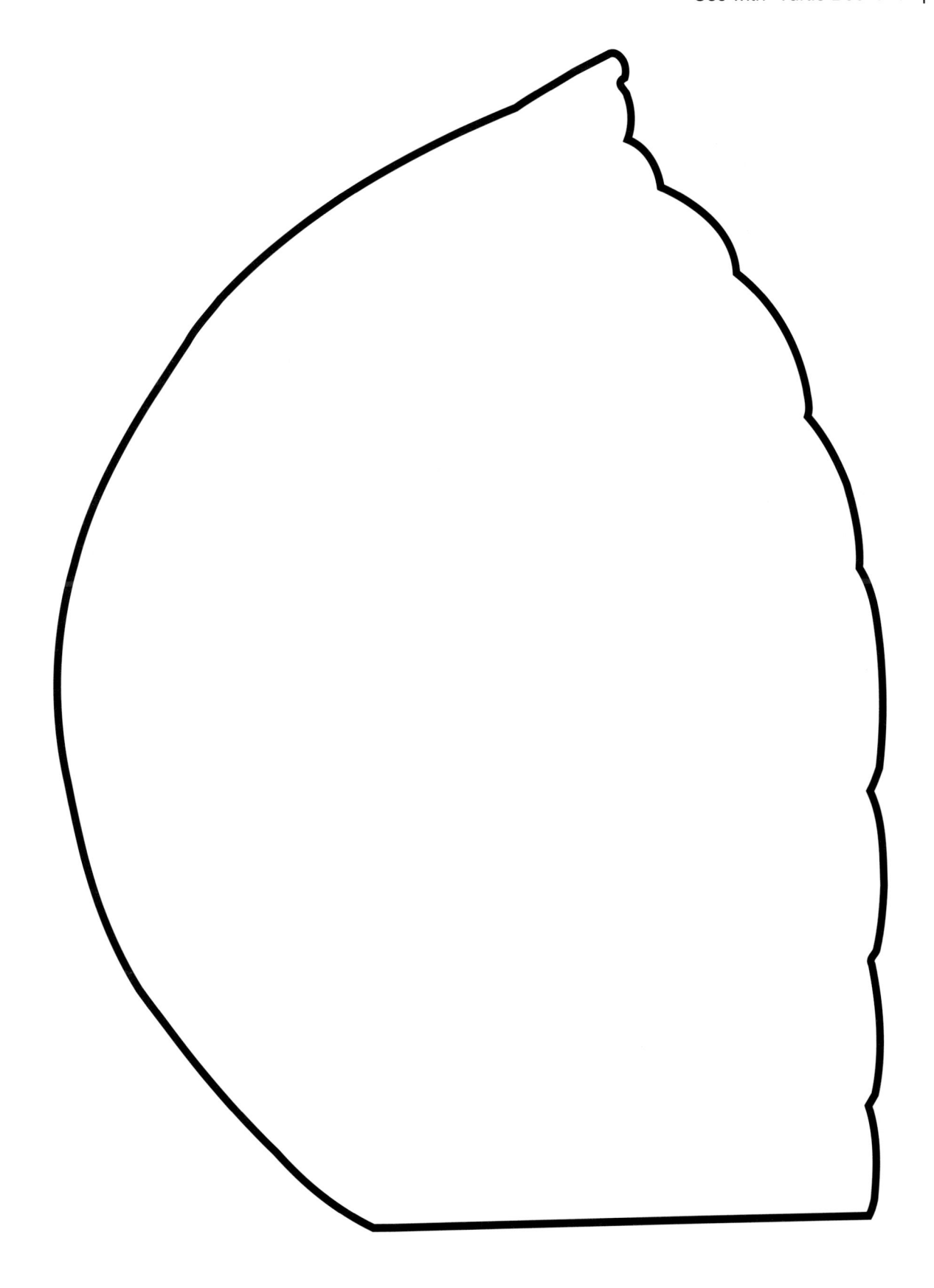

Turtle Patterns

tortoise

soft shelled turtle

box turtle

Note To The Teacher: See the directions in "Turtle Types" on page 267. Use these with "Turtle Habitats" on page 267, "Get Back In That Shell" on page 268, "Little…Big…Giant" on page 268, " 'Down In The Meadow' " on page 269, and "Turtle Books" on page 269.

Turtle Patterns

leatherback

green turtle

painted turtle

snapping turtle

Note To The Teacher: See the directions in "Turtle Types" on page 267. Use these with "Turtle Habitats" on page 267, "Get Back In That Shell" on page 268, "Little…Big…Giant" on page 268, " 'Down In The Meadow' " on page 269, and "Turtle Books" on page 269.

©The Education Center, Inc. • THE MAILBOX® • Kindergarten • June/July 1996

The Wild, Blue Yonder!

What lurks beyond our human vision of this wild, blue yonder that we call *space*? Whatever it is, it has fascinated children and grown-ups alike throughout the ages. Use the ideas in this unit to take a child-sized peek into the stars, the moon, the sun, and the planets.

Pictures In The Sky

Begin your study of the wild, blue yonder with one of the most familiar types of heavenly bodies—the stars. Inspire a discussion about stars by asking your youngsters to share their stargazing experiences. When the discussion subsides, explain that a very long time ago, people spent a lot of time looking at the stars—and many people still do! After a while, those people long ago began to think that certain groups of stars looked like pictures or outlines of things—such as an animal, a person, or an object. These star groups were called *constellations*. Write the word "constellation" on the board and practice saying it together. Guide your group to summarize that a *constellation* is "a picture in the sky."

Maybe I should call it the pepperoni pizza constellation.

The one on the far left is my Uncle Irving!

Create A Constellation

Solid science information and your youngsters' imaginations are the ingredients that make these projects just heavenly! Begin by displaying several pictures of constellations. (Suitable illustrations can be found in *Stargazers* by Gail Gibbons [Scholastic Inc.], *The Stars* by Patrick Moore [Aladdin Books Limited], and *The Kingfisher Young World Encyclopedia*.) Emphasize how much imagination must have gone into the naming of each constellation.

Then encourage your little ones to launch their own imaginations. Give each child a sheet of black construction paper and self-adhesive foil stars. Invite each child to arrange his stars on his paper. Encourage each child to study his arrangement of stars, then use white chalk to connect the stars as he desires. Have each child write or dictate the name of his constellation on the paper. Encourage each child to share his picture with the group; then save these kid-created constellations to use in "Star Stories."

Jennifer Barton—Gr. K, Elizabeth Green School, Newington, CT

Stargazing— Classroom Style!

Once your youngsters realize the origin of the constellations, the night sky will take on new meaning for them. However, since it isn't likely that you'll be able to do much *real* stargazing as a class, why not make up a sky for your own stargazing pleasure? To prepare, spread a long sheet of black mural paper on a flat surface in your art center. Stock the center with a supply of colored chalk and minimarshmallows. Encourage each child to visit the center and use the chalk to draw a constellation, then sign and label it. Then have him glue minimarshmallows on his picture to resemble stars. When the glue is dry, display the mural so that children will be able to do some peaceful stargazing during rest time.

Mrs. M. Duffy—Gr. K
Memorial School
Paramus, NJ

Star Stories

When your little ones have created their own constellations (see "Create A Constellation"), creative writing is a natural spin-off. Tell your children that the people who named the constellations long ago also made up stories about them. Have each child examine her constellation picture. Then encourage her to write or dictate a story about her constellation. She might decide to explain how her constellation ended up in the sky or perhaps what purpose it serves now that it's up there. Glue each child's story to another sheet of construction paper. Bind all of the stories together so that each child's writing is across from her illustration. Encourage children to read this book with partners during free time. When parents visit, children will twinkle with delight to be able to share their pages with their parents.

Are You Kidding Me?

You may be met by looks of disbelief when you tell your youngsters that the sun is actually a star. How can that be when the stars we see are tiny, twinkling specks in the sky? Give your students just a little perspective on the relative sizes of these celestial bodies. Cut out a 2 3/4-inch construction-paper circle and label it "Earth." Also cut out a 3/4-inch circle and label it "moon." Then take your students outside to a flat area. Draw (or use string to indicate) a circle with a 25-foot diameter. Label this circle "sun." Position the paper circles near the big circle. Tell your youngsters that if the smallest paper circle represents the size of the moon and the other paper circle represents the size of the Earth, the large circle would be the size of the sun. And in reality they are all much, much bigger! Can you imagine that?

Planet Play

Thousands of years ago, stargazers noticed bright spots of light moving very slowly among the stars. These sky watchers of old named the spots of light *planets,* which came from their word that meant "wanderer." There are nine planets in our solar system. To illustrate the planets and depict an impressive new vocabulary word—*orbit,* cut out construction-paper circles. (If you'd like your paper circles to represent relative size, see the list below.) Then glue each circle to a different sheet of construction paper. Label the planets respectively; then laminate each sheet. Punch two holes in the top of each sheet and tie on a length of yarn to make a necklace. Give each necklace to a child and have those children line up— side by side—in a spacious area. (Planets' order from the sun is indicated by the order in which they are listed below.) Select one child to be the sun and stand next to Mercury.

To do this activity, sing the first verse of the song below. As you begin the second verse, all of the "planets" hold hands. With the sun remaining in one place, all of the planets orbit around the sun. Change actors and repeat the song until each child has had a turn playing a part.

(sung to the tune of "The Mulberry Bush")
I am a planet in the sky,
In the sky, in the sky.
I am a planet in the sky.
I orbit around the sun.

Here we go orbiting round the sun,
Round the sun, round the sun.
Here we go orbiting round the sun.
Orbiting round the sun.

Adapted from an idea by Rachel Meseke Castro
Madison, WI

Relative Size Of Planets

Mercury	about the size of a green pea
Venus	about the size of a nickel
Earth	about the size of a quarter
Mars	about the size of a dime
Jupiter	about the size of a ten-inch circle
Saturn	about the size of an eight-inch circle
Uranus	about the size of a softball
Neptune	about the size of a large orange
Pluto	about the size of a dried lentil

Gravity And Moon Jumps

Introduce the word *gravity* to your youngsters. Find out if they would like to offer any possible definitions for the word. Then explain that *gravity* is "the invisible force on Earth that pulls things down." To illustrate, have each child toss a Nerf® ball, a pom-pom, a penny, or a similar item in the air. What happened? What pulled the objects back down? Why didn't they keep going up? Next have everyone stand up. Is there anyone among you who is floating up into the sky? What is keeping you firmly planted on the ground? It's that old gravity!

After talking about gravity, your youngsters will be intrigued to know that the gravity on the moon is very weak. So weak, in fact, that if your students were on the moon, they wouldn't even be able to stand on the ground without a special space suit. Amaze your little ones by telling them that if their houses were on the moon, they'd be able to jump onto their own roofs! Encourage dramatic play based on this fact and a shared reading of *Regards To The Man In The Moon* by Ezra Jack Keats.

The Phases Of The Moon

Begin this discussion by asking youngsters what shape they think the moon is. Ask a volunteer to draw that particular shape on the board. Then find out if your students have ever seen the moon appear to be another shape. Ask volunteers to draw those shapes on the board. Find out if your youngsters have any explanation for the changing shape of the moon. Then explain that the moon is always round. The reason that the moon appears to be different shapes to us is because, on Earth, we can only see the part of the moon that is lit up by the sun. The different shapes of the moon that we see are called the moon's *phases*. Label a sheet of chart paper "The Phases Of The Moon." Then ask youngsters to draw all the different phases of the moon that they have ever seen. Keep this chart and refer to it as you do the activity in "Once In A Blue Moon."

Celestial Art

Wrap up your space studies with a display fit for the heavens. In advance, trace the patterns on page 279 onto plastic stenciling sheets. Using a razor blade, cut out the patterns and save both the stencils and the patterns. Put the stencils and the cutouts in an art area with stencil brushes, paints, and a supply of art paper. Encourage children to use the supplies to make the designs of their choice. Mount each dried piece of artwork on a colorful sheet of construction paper. Then display these heavenly designs on a board titled "Celestial Art"!

Once In A Blue Moon

Scientific observation and recording are all part of this blue-moon activity. Photocopy a page of the calendar grid on page 278. Then program the calendar with the dates of the month during which you will be studying the moon. (Save the original, unprogrammed copy for future use!) Duplicate the programmed calendar for each child. Then instruct your youngsters to take the calendar home. Each night, have them look at the moon and draw its shape in the appropriate box on the calendar. (You might choose to draw the previous evening's moon shape on the board each morning for those children who were not able to see the moon for themselves.)

When the month is over, have each child bring his calendar back to school. Discuss what is revealed by the drawings. Then explain that we usually see one full moon in a month. On rare occasions, we might see two full moons in one month. That second full moon is called a *blue moon*. It isn't really blue, but that's what it's called. Sometimes people say, "Once in a blue moon," when they mean, "Once in a very long while." Did you get a blue moon this month?

BARRY SLATE

Blast Off! Poems About Space
Selected by Lee Bennett Hopkins
Illustrated by Melissa Sweet
Published by HarperCollins Publishers

What Is The Sun?
Written by Reeve Lindbergh
Illustrated by Stephen Lambert
Published by Candlewick Press

Blast Off! A Space Counting Book
Written by Norma Cole
Illustrated by Marshall Peck III
Published by Charlesbridge Publishing

Twinkle, Twinkle, Little Star
As Told And Illustrated by Iza Trapani
Published by Whispering Coyote Press, Inc.

Under The Sun
Written & Illustrated by Ellen Kandoian
Published by Dodd, Mead & Co.
Check your school or local library.

277

Calendar Pattern Use with "Once In A Blue Moon" on page 277.

Patterns
Use with "Celestial Art" on page 277.

©The Education Center, Inc. • *THE MAILBOX® • Kindergarten* • June/July 1996

Kindergarten Café

Kindergarten Café

To prepare each cooking activity, duplicate a classroom supply plus one extra of the chosen recipe cards (pages 283-284). Cut the cards apart; then color one set of cards. Display the colored cards in sequence in the cooking center. Arrange the ingredients and utensils near the recipe cards. As a small group of children visits the cooking center, ask each child in the group to color a set of recipe cards to match the sample set. As each student completes his cards, have him sequence them; then ask him to explain the steps on each card. According to each child's abilities, have him circle letters, numerals, or sight words. Staple the cards together, creating a recipe booklet for the child to take home. Get ready, get set...cook!

August

Happy Face Muffin

Ingredients for one:
one-half of an English muffin
peanut butter or cream cheese
2 raisins
1 round carrot slice
1 red pepper slice
alfalfa sprouts

Utensils:
plastic knife or craft stick

Teacher Preparation:
Slice a red pepper into thin strips. Cut a carrot into round slices.

Include Happy Face Muffins in a self-awareness or back-to-school unit.

* Step-by-step directions on page 283.

September

Johnny Appleseed Sandwich

Ingredients for one:
2 apple slices
peanut butter

Utensils:
plastic knife or craft stick

Teacher Preparation:
Cut apples horizontally into round, quarter-inch-thick slices. Sprinkle with lemon juice to prevent browning.

On September 26th, celebrate the birthday of John Chapman, better known as Johnny Appleseed. Read aloud *Johnny Appleseed* written and illustrated by Steven Kellogg (published by Morrow Junior Books); then snack on these nutritious treats.

* Step-by-step directions on page 284.

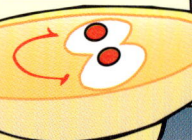

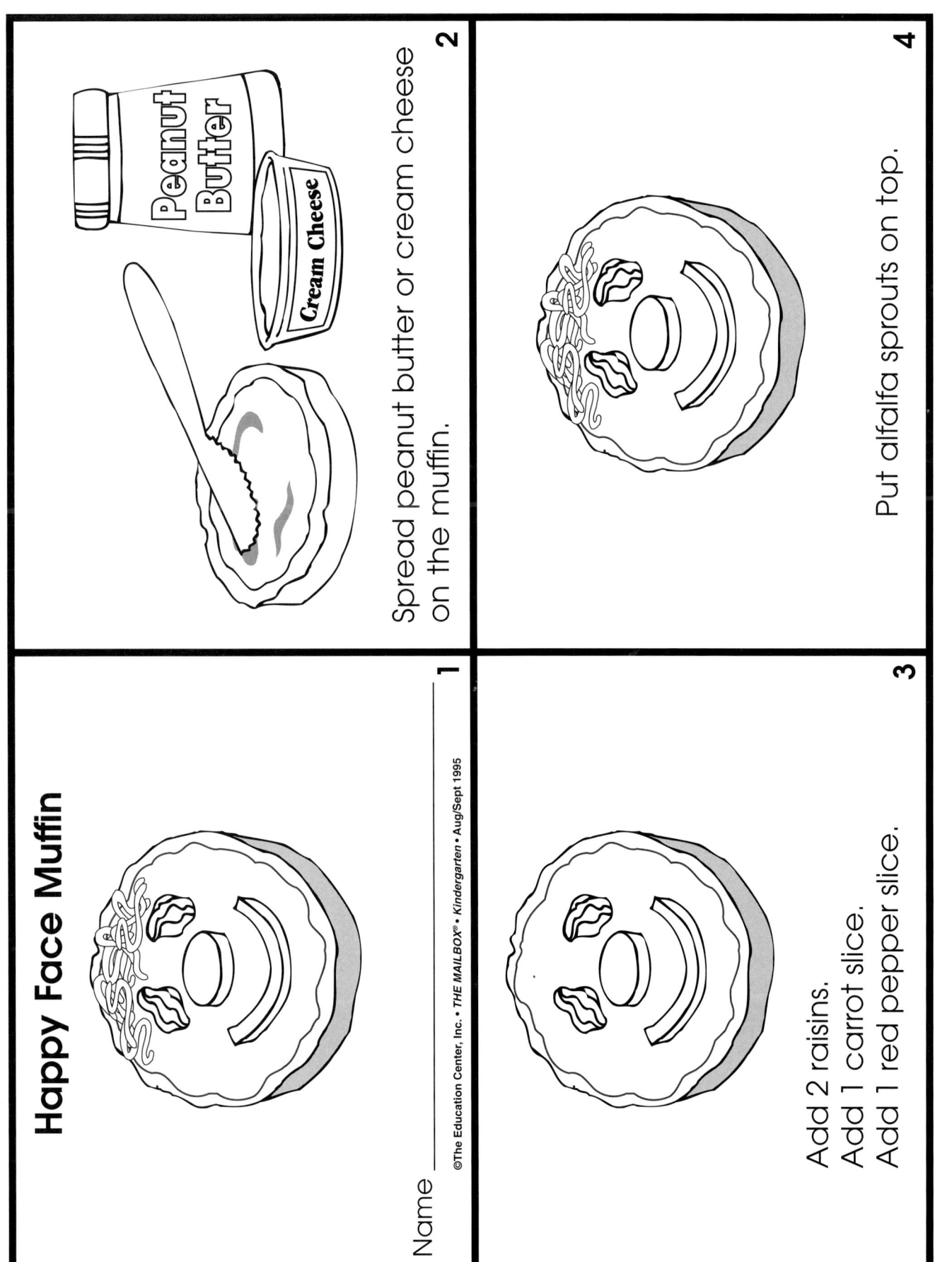

Pattern
August—Happy Face Muffin

Happy Face Muffin

Name _____

2. Spread peanut butter or cream cheese on the muffin.

3. Add 2 raisins.
Add 1 carrot slice.
Add 1 red pepper slice.

4. Put alfalfa sprouts on top.

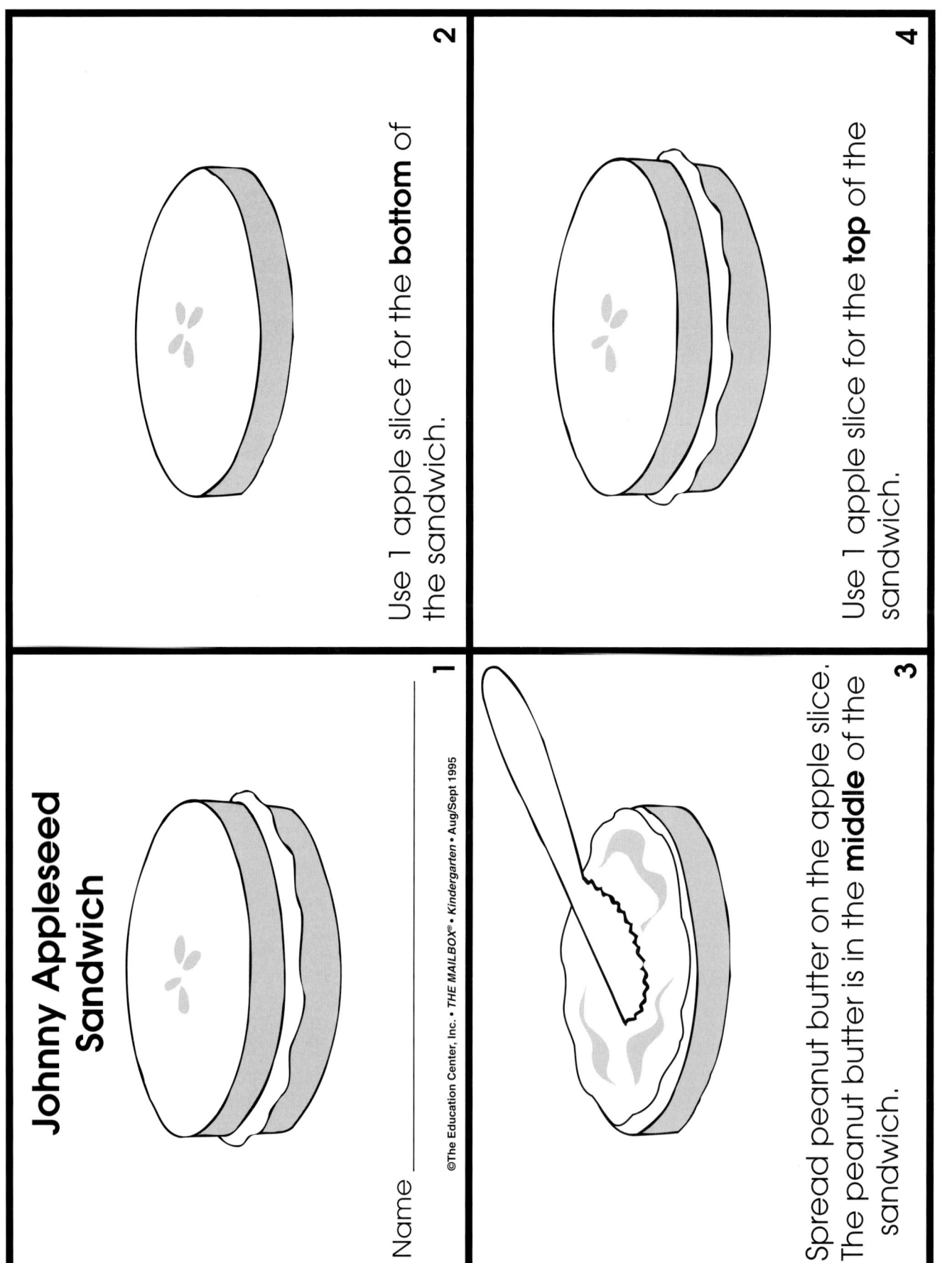

Pattern
September—Johnny Appleseed Sandwich

Johnny Appleseed Sandwich

Name _____

2. Use 1 apple slice for the **bottom** of the sandwich.

3. Spread peanut butter on the apple slice. The peanut butter is in the **middle** of the sandwich.

4. Use 1 apple slice for the **top** of the sandwich.

©The Education Center, Inc. • *THE MAILBOX®* • *Kindergarten* • Aug/Sept 1995

284

Thank-You Note

We're really cooking now!
Thank you for your help!

name
date

Award

Look who's cooking!

name
has discovered the recipe for success!
teacher

Request List

Dear _____,

Here's what's cooking in the Kindergarten Café:

_____

Please send the following ingredients:

_____
_____
_____
_____

Thank you for shopping for our cooking activity!

©The Education Center, Inc. • *THE MAILBOX®* • *Kindergarten* • Aug/Sept 1995

Invitation

Kindergarten Café

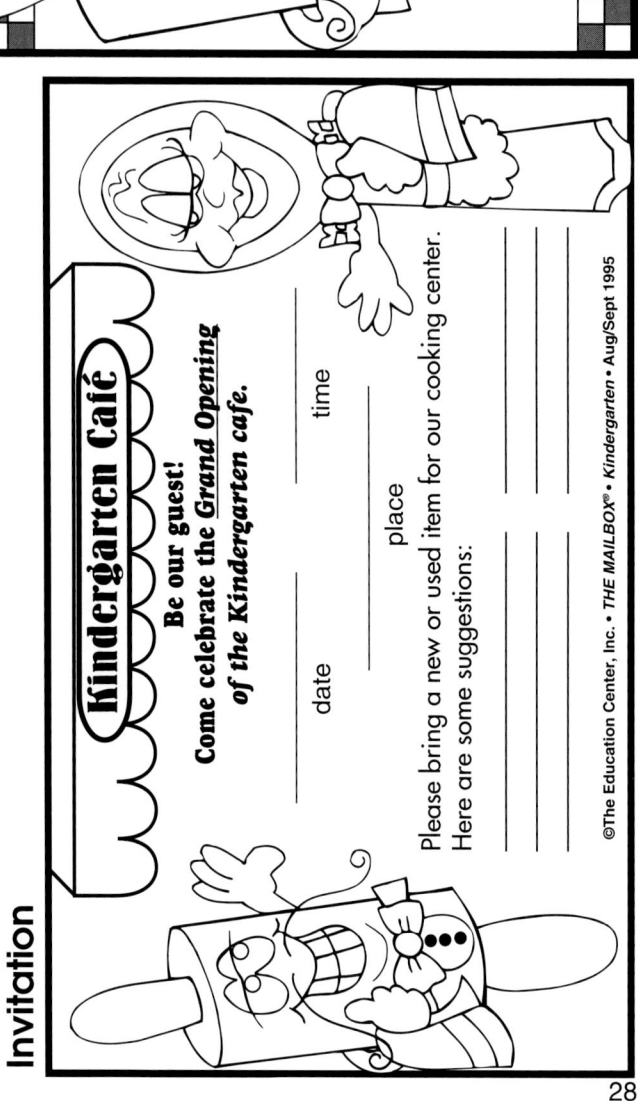

Be our guest!
Come celebrate the *Grand Opening* of the Kindergarten cafe.

date
time
place

Please bring a new or used item for our cooking center.
Here are some suggestions:

©The Education Center, Inc. • *THE MAILBOX®* • *Kindergarten* • Aug/Sept 1995

285

Kindergarten Café

To prepare each cooking activity, duplicate a classroom supply plus one extra of the chosen recipe card (pages 287-288). Cut the cards apart. Color one set of cards; then laminate them. Sequence the colored cards; then display them in the cooking center. Arrange the ingredients and utensils near the recipe cards. As a small group of children visits the cooking center, ask each child in the group to color a set of recipe cards to match the sample set. As each student completes his cards, have him sequence them; then ask him to explain the steps on each card. Based on each child's abilities, have him read the words and numerals that he knows. Staple the cards together, creating a recipe booklet for the child to take home. Then get ready, get set...cook! (These recipes are also great to use when a parent offers to do an activity with your class!)

October
Awesome Owl Snack

Ingredients For One:
creamy peanut butter
1 rice cake
2 banana slices
2 raisins
6 Froot Loops®
1 cheese triangle

Utensils And Supplies:
plastic knives or craft sticks

Teacher Preparation:
Slice the bananas. Sprinkle them with lemon juice to avoid browning. Cut small triangles from cheese slices.

November
Harvest Pumpkin Pie

Ingredients For One:
1/4 cup of vanilla pudding
1 teaspoon of canned pumpkin
dash of pumpkin pie spice
1 single-serving-size graham-cracker crust
1 candy pumpkin

Utensils And Supplies:
1/4 cup measuring cup
teaspoon
spoons
small bowls

Teacher Preparation:
Prepare vanilla pudding according to the package directions.

Pam Crane

Pattern
October—Awesome Owl Snack

Awesome Owl Snack

Name _____

©The Education Center, Inc. • THE MAILBOX® • Kindergarten • Oct/Nov 1995

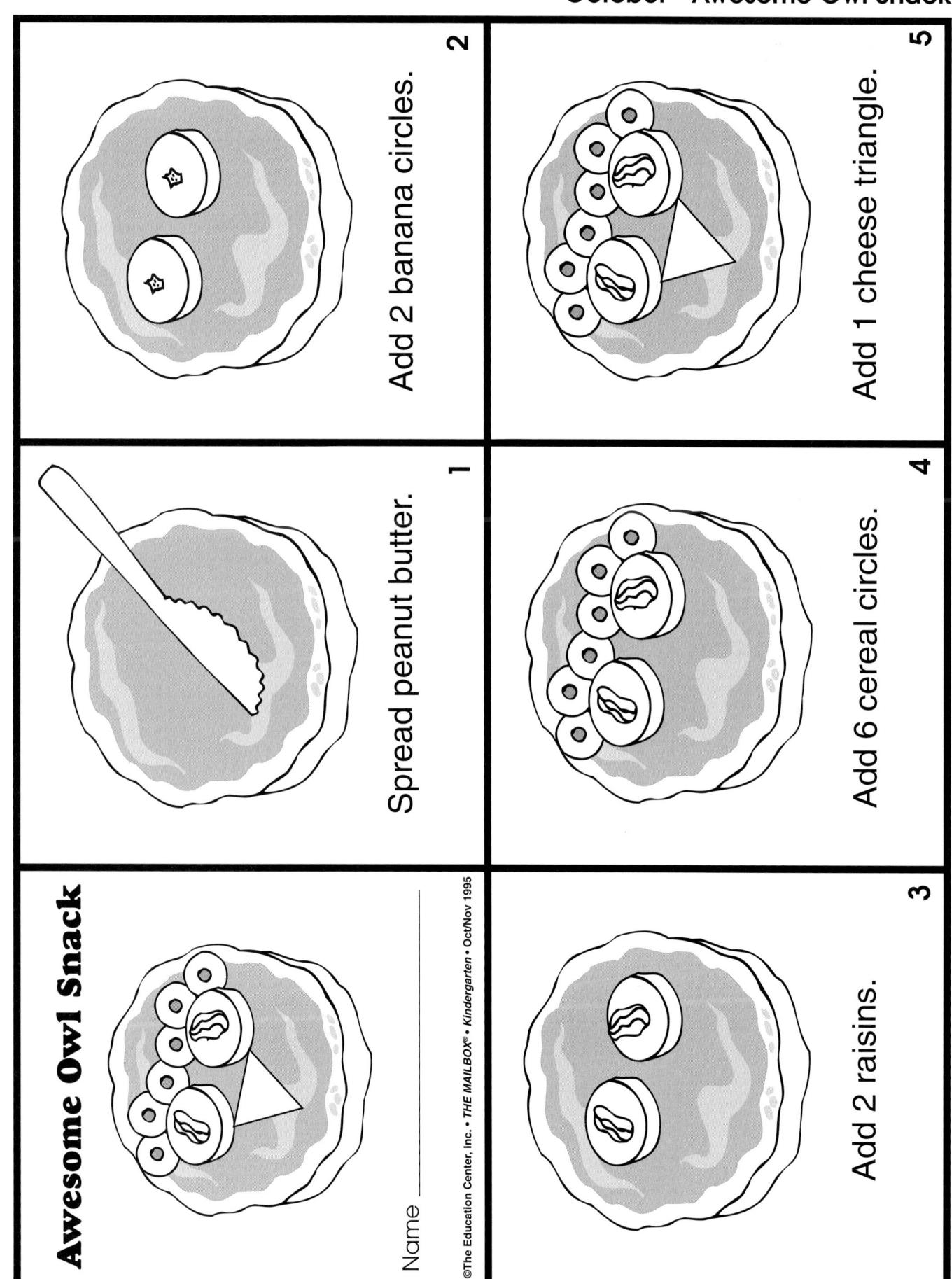

1. Spread peanut butter.
2. Add 2 banana circles.
3. Add 2 raisins.
4. Add 6 cereal circles.
5. Add 1 cheese triangle.

287

Pattern
November—Harvest Pumpkin Pie

Harvest Pumpkin Pie

Name _____

1. Measure:
   1/4 c. pudding
   1 tsp. pumpkin spice
   dash

2. Stir.

3. Spoon into the crust.

4. Chill.

5. Decorate and eat!

©The Education Center, Inc. • THE MAILBOX® • Kindergarten • Oct/Nov 1995

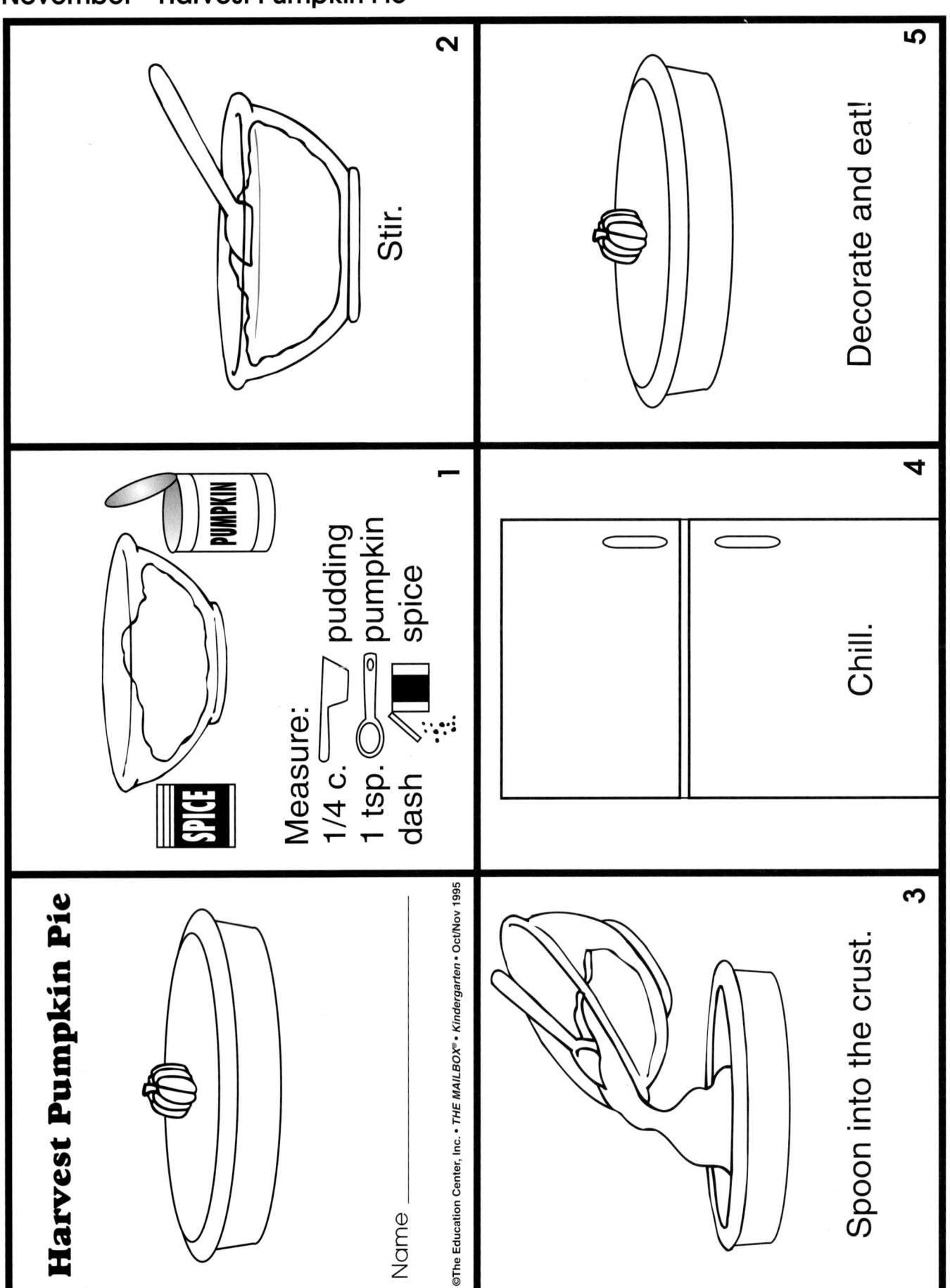

Kindergarten Café

To prepare each cooking activity, duplicate a classroom supply plus one extra of the chosen recipe cards (pages 290-291). Cut the cards apart. Color one set of cards; then laminate them. Sequence the colored cards; then display them in your cooking center. Arrange the ingredients and utensils near the recipe cards. As a small group of children visits the cooking center, ask each child in the group to color a set of recipe cards to match the sample set. As each student completes his cards, have him sequence them; then ask him to explain the steps on each card. Based on each child's abilities, have him read or circle letters, numerals, or sight words. Staple the cards together, creating a recipe booklet for each child to take home. Then get ready, get set...cook!

December
Reindeer Refreshments

Ingredients For One:
1/2 cup of granola
5 chocolate chips
10 peanuts (shelled)
15 M&M's®
20 raisins

Utensils And Supplies:
1/2 cup measuring cup
small bowls
brown paper lunch bags

Note To The Teacher:
When each child has one serving of reindeer refreshments in his bag, have him decorate the bag if desired. Fold the top corners of the bag toward the middle, then down to form a triangle-shaped reindeer face. Glue a paper nose and eyes to the face. Trace both hands onto brown paper; then cut out the hand shapes. Glue the cutouts to the top back of the bag for antlers. Attach the "How To Feed The Reindeer" note to the front of the bag.

January
Hot Cocoa Mix

Ingredients For One:
3 spoons of Nestlé® Quik®
2 spoons of nondairy creamer
1 spoon of dry milk
1 spoon of powdered sugar
3 large marshmallows (optional)
decorating gel (optional)

Utensils And Supplies:
plastic spoons
resealable plastic bags
plastic stirring sticks (optional)

Note To The Teacher:
When a child has made a serving of the hot cocoa mix, attach the "Dear Parent" note to the plastic bag. (If desired, have each child make a snowman stirring stick to use with his cup of hot cocoa. Push a plastic stirring stick through two or three marshmallows; then use decorating gel to add snowman features.)

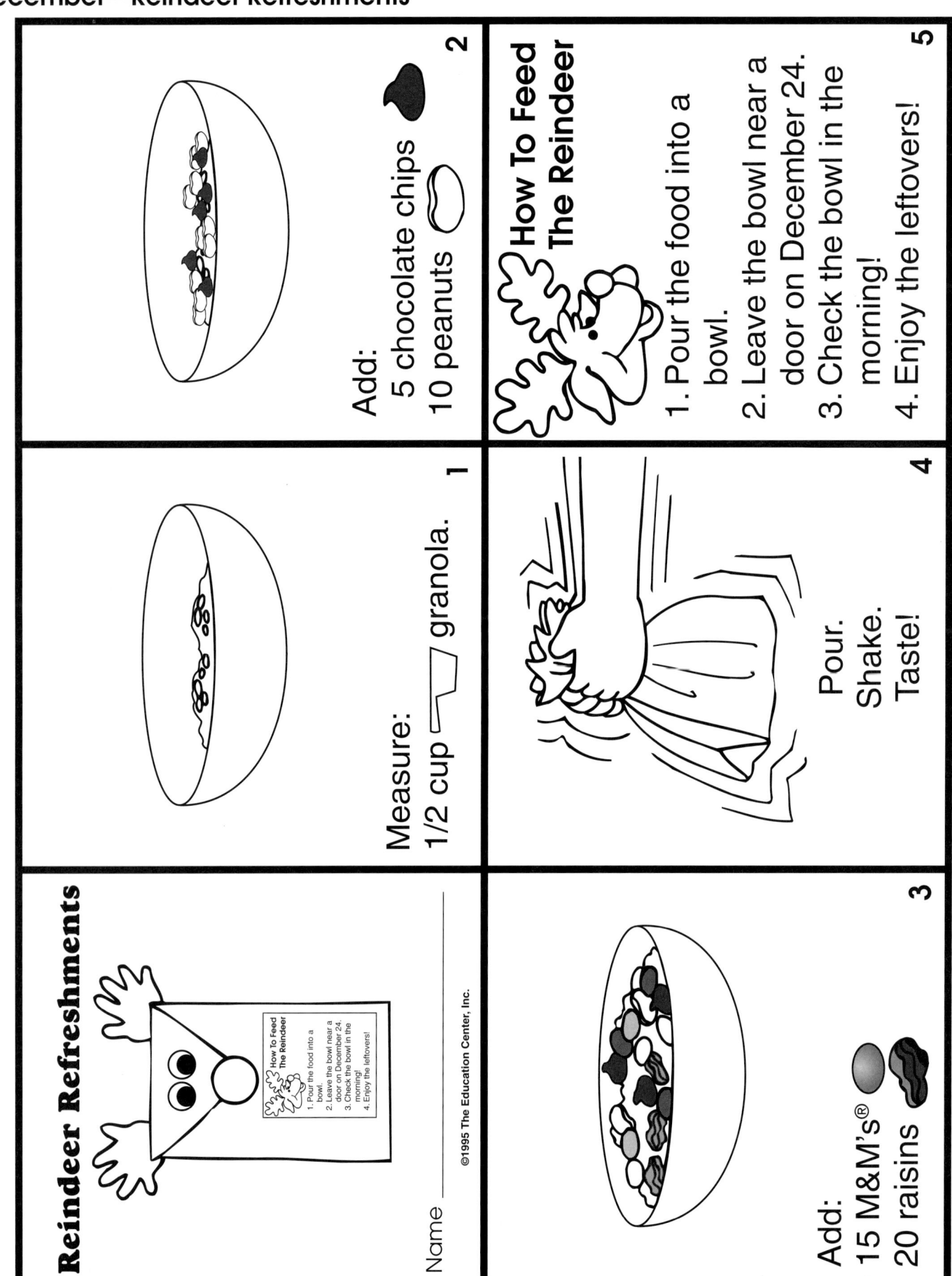

Recipe Cards
December—Reindeer Refreshments

Reindeer Refreshments

Name _____

©1995 The Education Center, Inc.

1

Measure:
1/2 cup granola.

2

Add:
5 chocolate chips
10 peanuts

3

Add:
15 M&M's®
20 raisins

4

Pour.
Shake.
Taste!

5

How To Feed The Reindeer

1. Pour the food into a bowl.
2. Leave the bowl near a door on December 24.
3. Check the bowl in the morning!
4. Enjoy the leftovers!

©The Education Center, Inc. • THE MAILBOX® • Kindergarten • Dec/Jan 1995–96

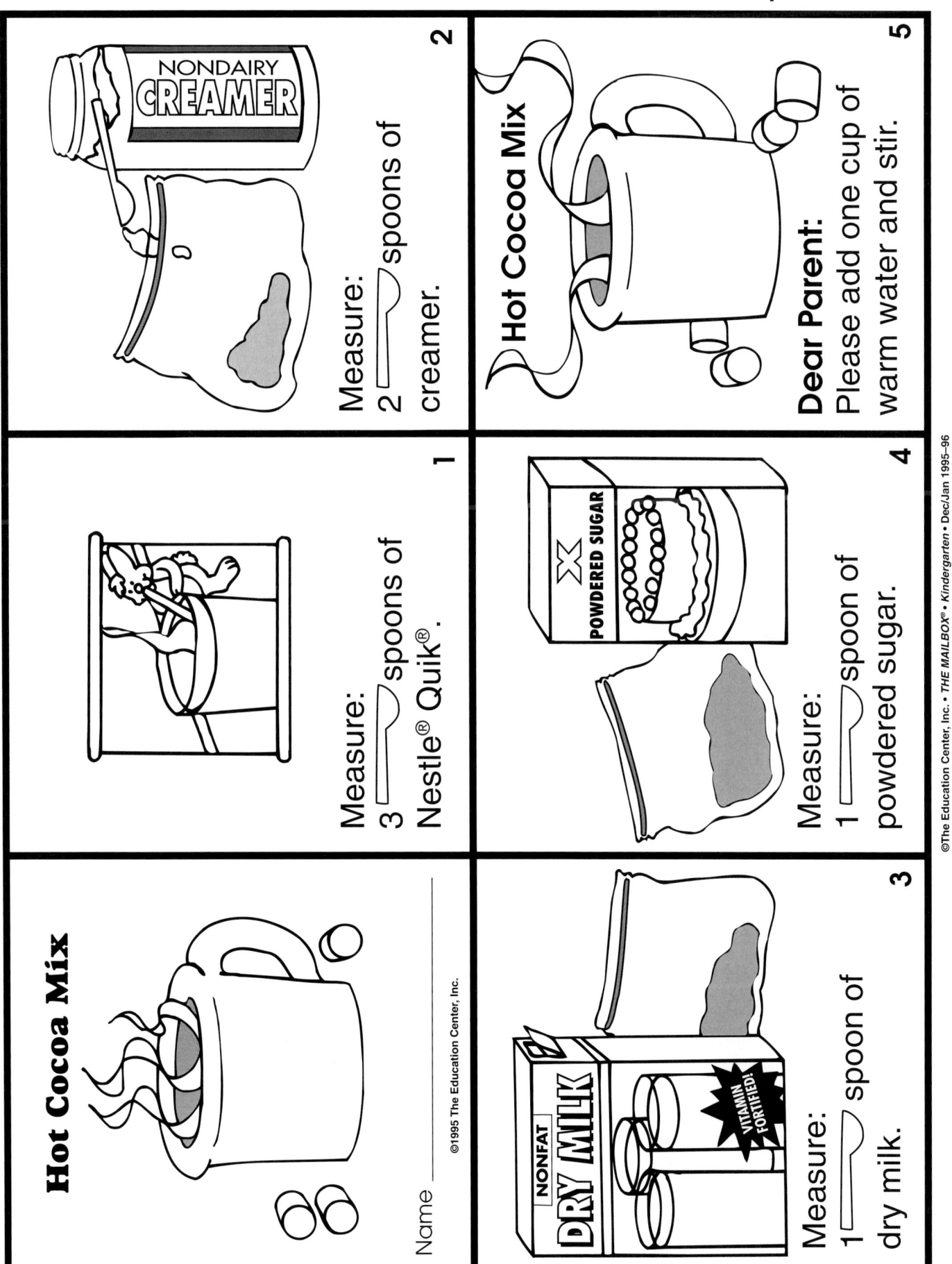

Recipe Cards
January—Hot Cocoa Mix

2

Measure:
2 🥄 spoons of creamer.

5

Hot Cocoa Mix

Dear Parent: Please add one cup of warm water and stir.

1

Measure:
3 🥄 spoons of Nestlé® Quik®.

4

Measure:
1 🥄 spoon of powdered sugar.

Hot Cocoa Mix

Name _____

©1995 The Education Center, Inc.

3

Measure:
1 🥄 spoon of dry milk.

©The Education Center, Inc. • THE MAILBOX® • Kindergarten • Dec/Jan 1995–96

Kindergarten Café

To prepare each cooking activity, duplicate a classroom supply plus one extra of the chosen recipe cards (pages 293-294). Cut the cards apart. Color one set of cards; then laminate them. Sequence the colored cards; then display them in your cooking center. Arrange the ingredients and utensils near the recipe cards. As a small group of children visits the cooking center, ask each child in the group to color a set of recipe cards to match the sample set. As each student completes his cards, have him sequence them; then ask him to explain the steps on each card. Based on each child's abilities, have him read or circle letters, numerals, or sight words. Staple the cards together, creating a recipe booklet for each child to take home. Then get ready, get set...cook!

February
Groundhog Day Cupcakes

Ingredients For One:
1 cupcake
chocolate frosting
2 vanilla wafers
3 M&M's®
2 miniature marshmallows

Utensils And Supplies:
spreading knife

Teacher Preparation:
Bake a cupcake for each child.

Susan Snyder—Preschool–Gr. 1 • North Main Street Christian School • Butler, PA

March
Shakin' Shamrocks

Ingredients For One:
square of lime-flavored Jell-O® Jigglers™
can of whipped cream
gold cake-decorating sprinkles

Utensils And Supplies:
shamrock-shaped cookie cutter

Teacher Preparation:
Prepare a pan of lime-flavored gelatin by following the package directions for Jell-O® Jigglers™. Cut the gelatin into individual squares that are slightly larger than your shamrock-shaped cookie cutter.

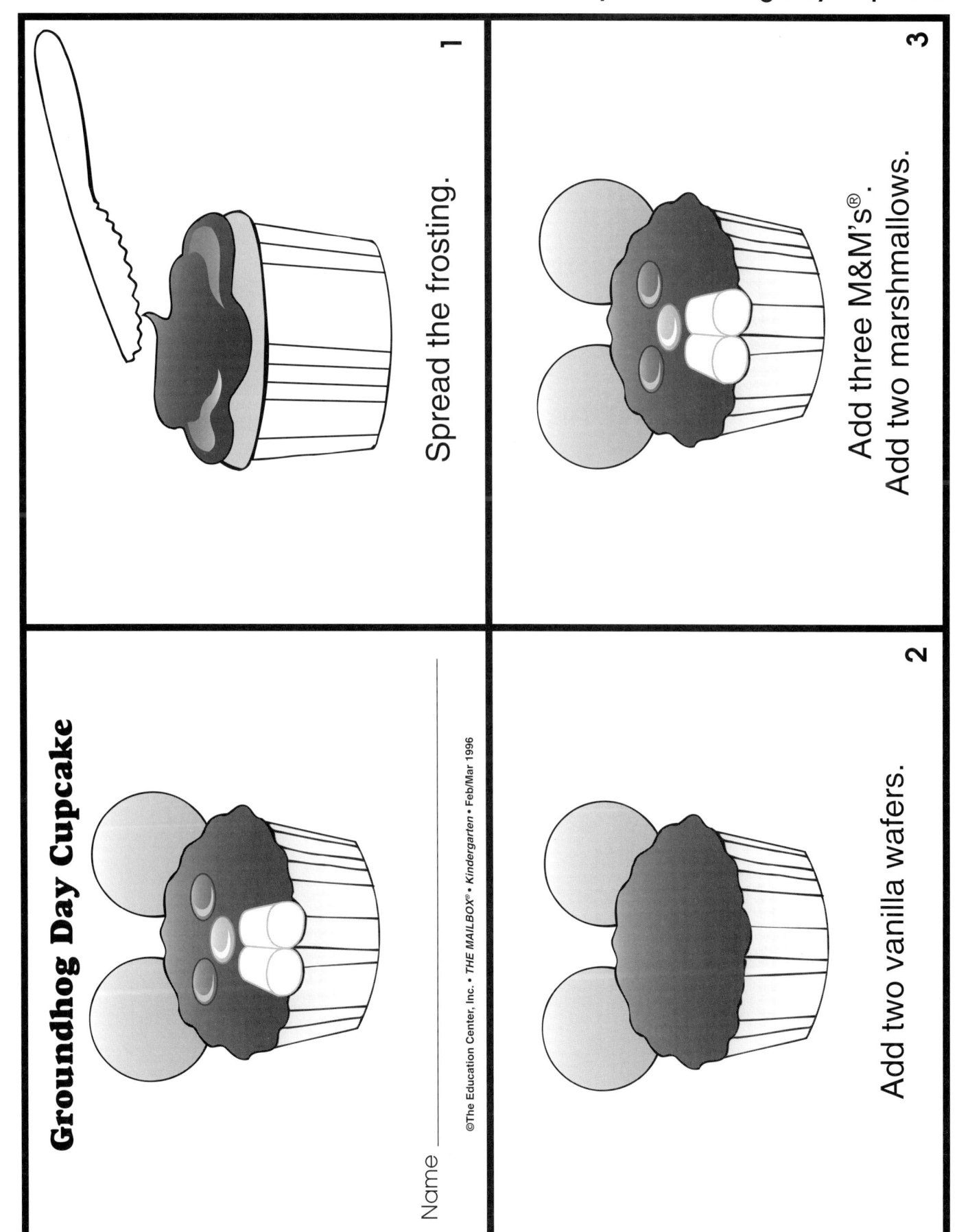

Pattern
February—Groundhog Day Cupcake

1

Spread the frosting.

3

Add three M&M's®.
Add two marshmallows.

Groundhog Day Cupcake

Name _____

©The Education Center, Inc. • *THE MAILBOX*® • *Kindergarten* • Feb/Mar 1996

2

Add two vanilla wafers.

293

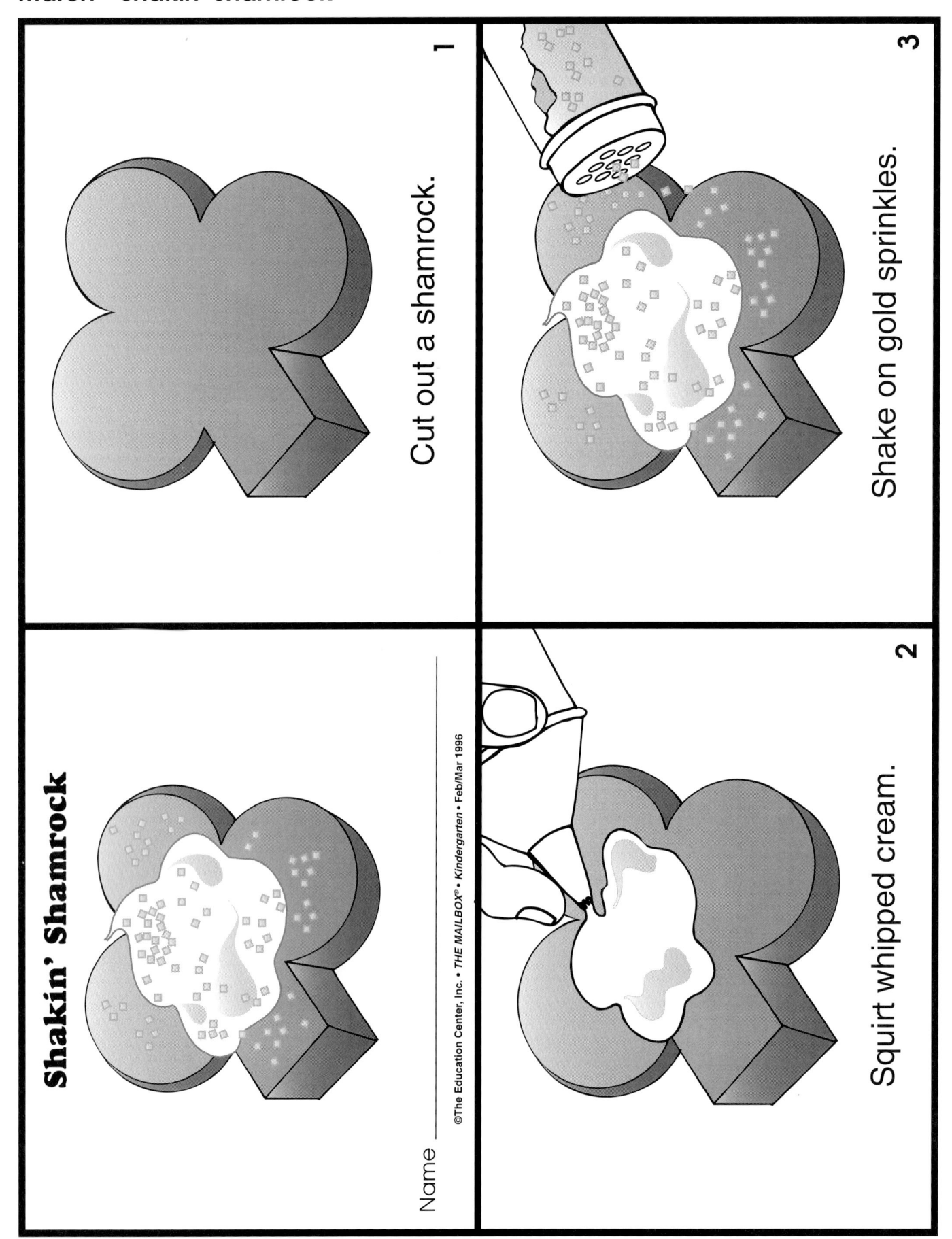

Pattern
March—Shakin' Shamrock

1. Cut out a shamrock.

2. Squirt whipped cream.

3. Shake on gold sprinkles.

Shakin' Shamrock

Name _____

©The Education Center, Inc. • THE MAILBOX® • Kindergarten • Feb/Mar 1996

294

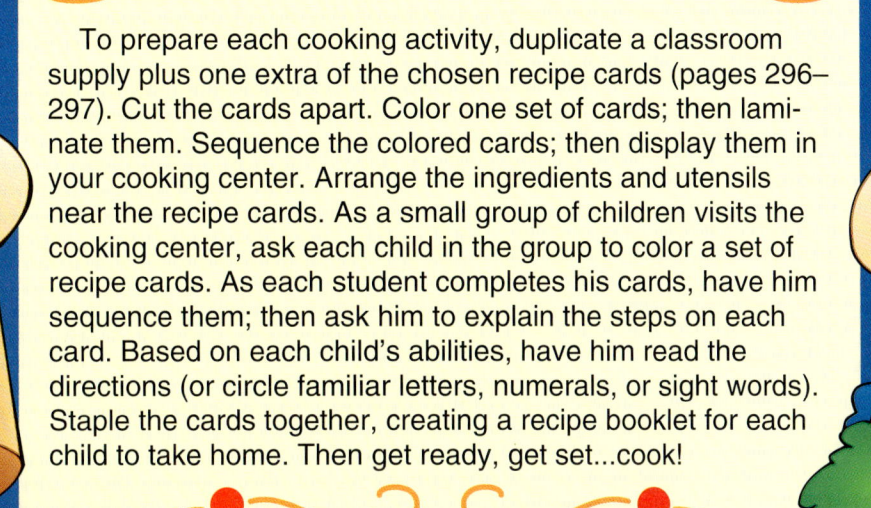

Kindergarten Café

To prepare each cooking activity, duplicate a classroom supply plus one extra of the chosen recipe cards (pages 296–297). Cut the cards apart. Color one set of cards; then laminate them. Sequence the colored cards; then display them in your cooking center. Arrange the ingredients and utensils near the recipe cards. As a small group of children visits the cooking center, ask each child in the group to color a set of recipe cards. As each student completes his cards, have him sequence them; then ask him to explain the steps on each card. Based on each child's abilities, have him read the directions (or circle familiar letters, numerals, or sight words). Staple the cards together, creating a recipe booklet for each child to take home. Then get ready, get set...cook!

April
Peter Rabbit's Lunch

Ingredients For One:
lettuce leaves
8 carrot slices
4 cucumber slices
10 croutons
1 cherry tomato

Utensils And Supplies:
bowls of salad dressing
serving spoons
bowls
forks

Teacher Preparation:
Prepare the ingredients in the list above.

May
Deviled Eggs

Ingredients For One:
1 hard-boiled egg for each child
Thousand Island dressing

Utensils And Supplies:
small paper plates
plastic knives
spoons
bowls

Teacher Preparation:
Hard-boil one egg for each child. Pour Thousand Island dressing in a bowl.

Colleen Huston, Rock Branch Elementary, Nitro, WV

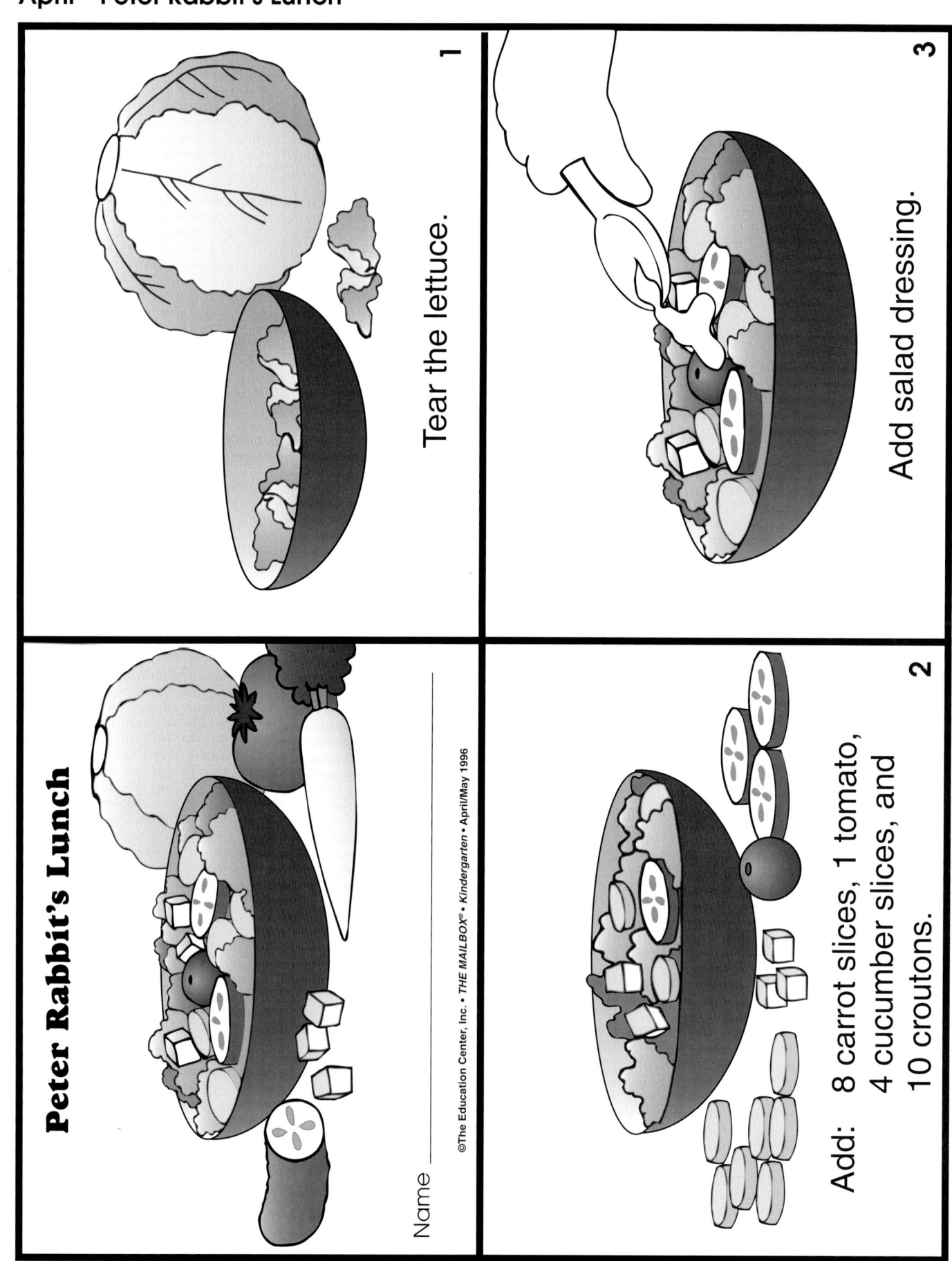

Recipe Cards
April—Peter Rabbit's Lunch

Peter Rabbit's Lunch

1. Tear the lettuce.

2. Add: 8 carrot slices, 1 tomato, 4 cucumber slices, and 10 croutons.

3. Add salad dressing.

Name _____

©The Education Center, Inc. • *THE MAILBOX®* • *Kindergarten* • April/May 1996

Recipe Cards
May—Deviled Eggs

1

Peel the egg.
Cut the egg in half.

2

Scoop out the yolk.
Add 1 spoon of Thousand Island dressing.
Stir.

3

Spoon the mixture into the egg halves.

Deviled Eggs

Name _____

©The Education Center, Inc. • *THE MAILBOX®* • *Kindergarten* • April/May 1996

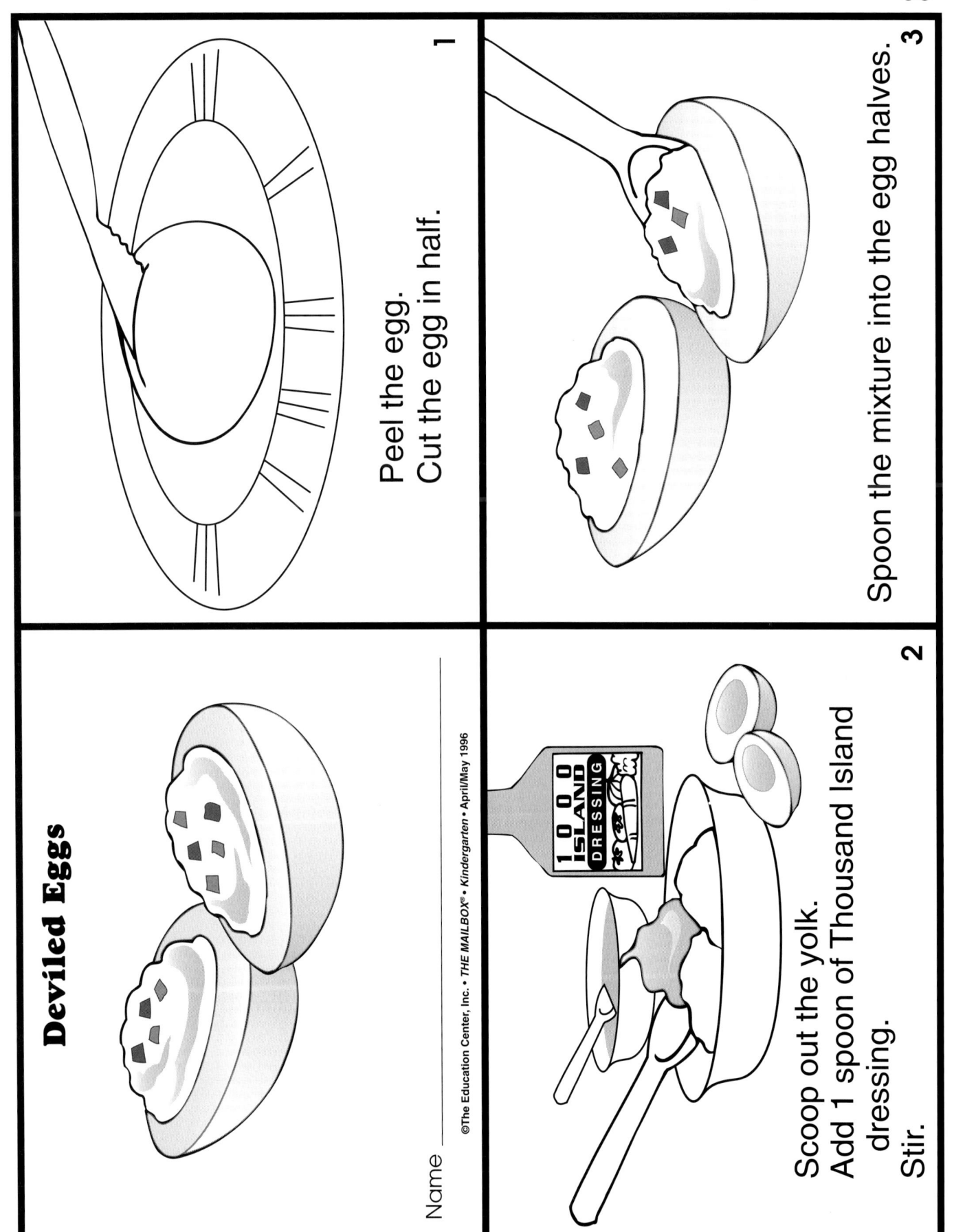

Kindergarten Café

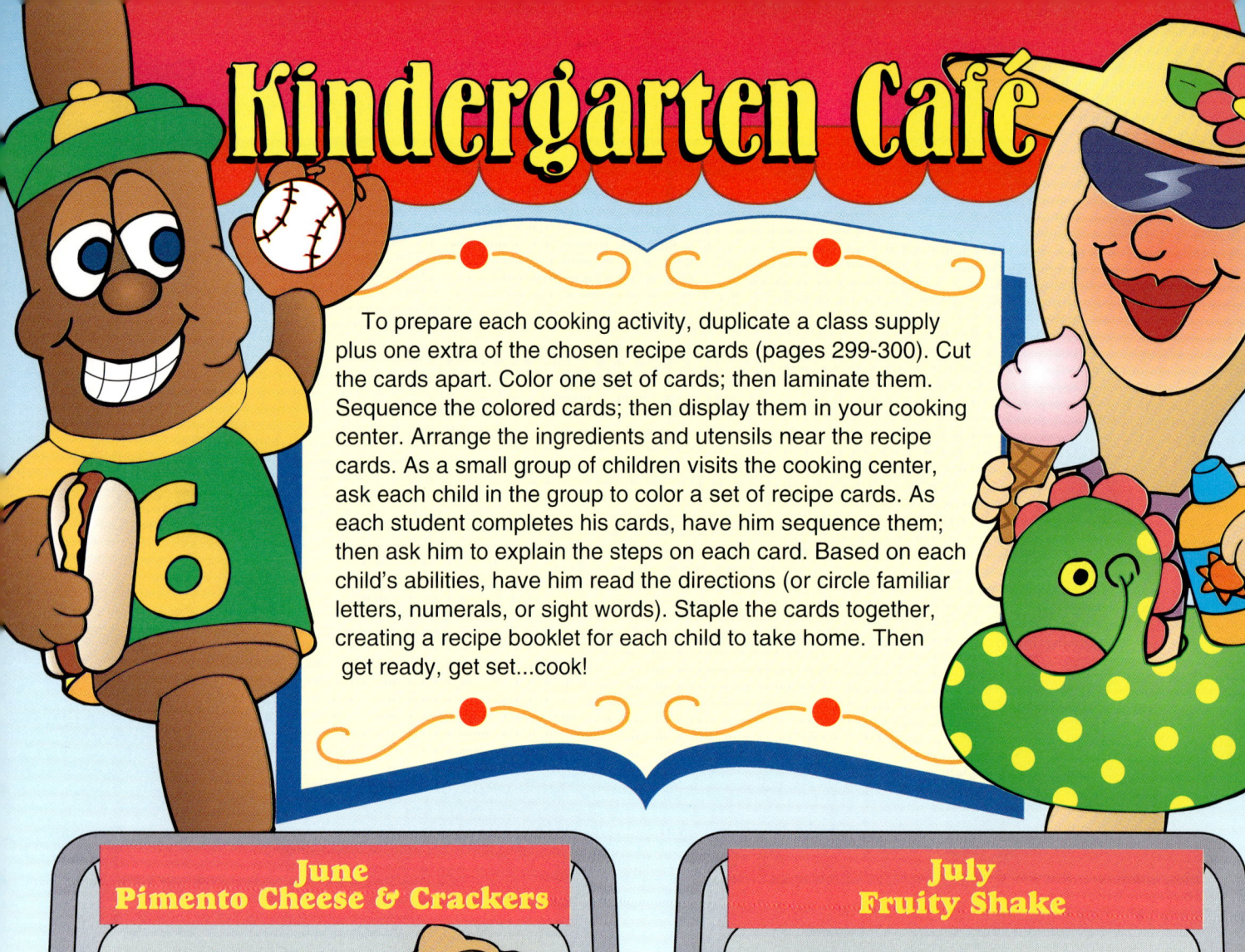

To prepare each cooking activity, duplicate a class supply plus one extra of the chosen recipe cards (pages 299-300). Cut the cards apart. Color one set of cards; then laminate them. Sequence the colored cards; then display them in your cooking center. Arrange the ingredients and utensils near the recipe cards. As a small group of children visits the cooking center, ask each child in the group to color a set of recipe cards. As each student completes his cards, have him sequence them; then ask him to explain the steps on each card. Based on each child's abilities, have him read the directions (or circle familiar letters, numerals, or sight words). Staple the cards together, creating a recipe booklet for each child to take home. Then get ready, get set...cook!

June
Pimento Cheese & Crackers

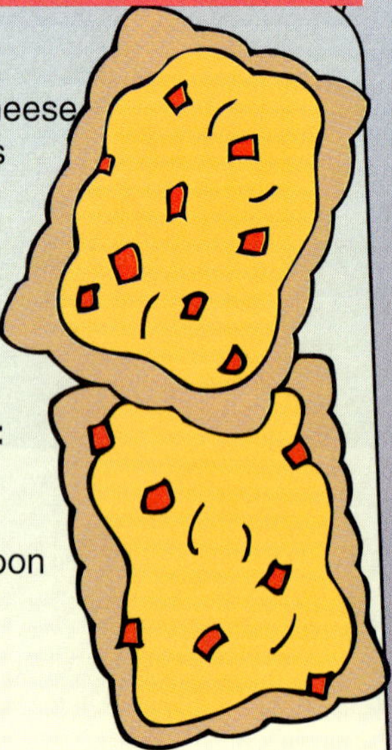

Ingredients For One:
1/4 c. grated cheddar cheese
2 tsp. chopped pimentos
2 tsp. mayonnaise
pinch of minced onion
pinch of pepper
crackers

Utensils And Supplies:
serving bowls
1/4-cup measuring cup
teaspoon measuring spoon
small bowls for mixing
spoons
paper plates

Teacher Preparation:
Put each of the ingredients listed above in serving bowls for easy student access. Describe and demonstrate the meaning of the word *pinch* when it is used in recipes.

July
Fruity Shake

Ingredients For One:
1 c. cold milk
2 Tbs. flavored gelatin (any flavor except lemon)

Utensils And Supplies:
measuring cup
shaker (container with an airtight lid)
tablespoon measuring spoon
drinking glasses
straws

Teacher Preparation:
Open the boxes of different flavors of gelatin. Help pour the milk, depending on your students' abilities.

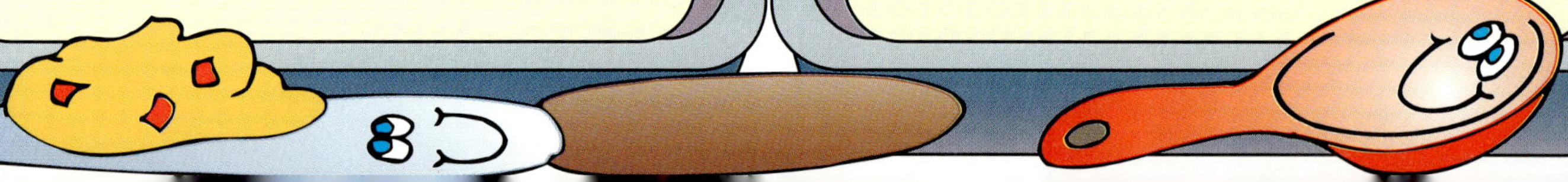

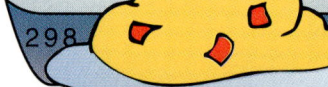

Recipe Cards
June—Pimento Cheese & Crackers

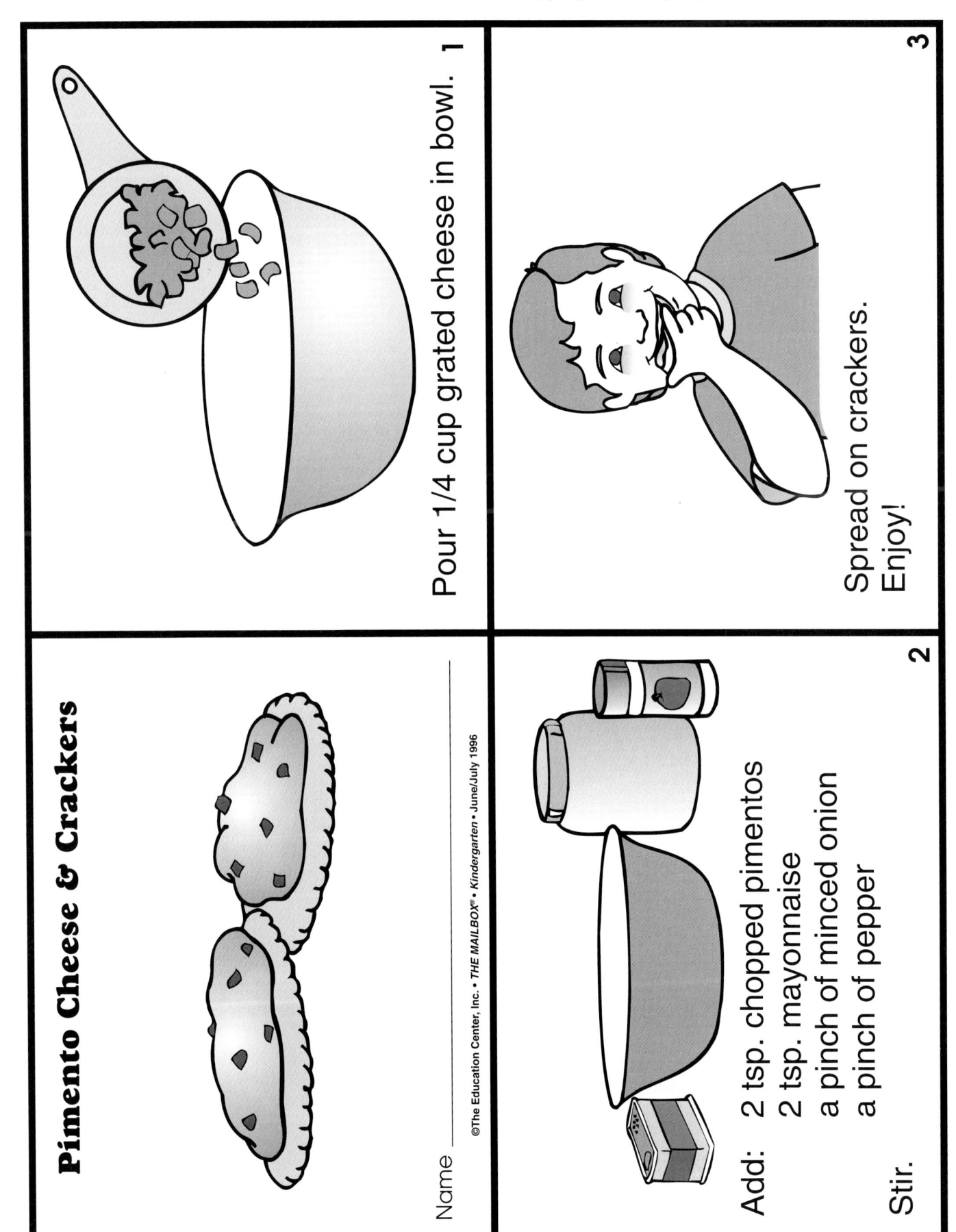

Pimento Cheese & Crackers

1. Pour 1/4 cup grated cheese in bowl.

2. Add: 2 tsp. chopped pimentos
   2 tsp. mayonnaise
   a pinch of minced onion
   a pinch of pepper

   Stir.

3. Spread on crackers. Enjoy!

Name _____

©The Education Center, Inc. • THE MAILBOX® • Kindergarten • June/July 1996

299

Recipe Cards
July—Fruity Shake

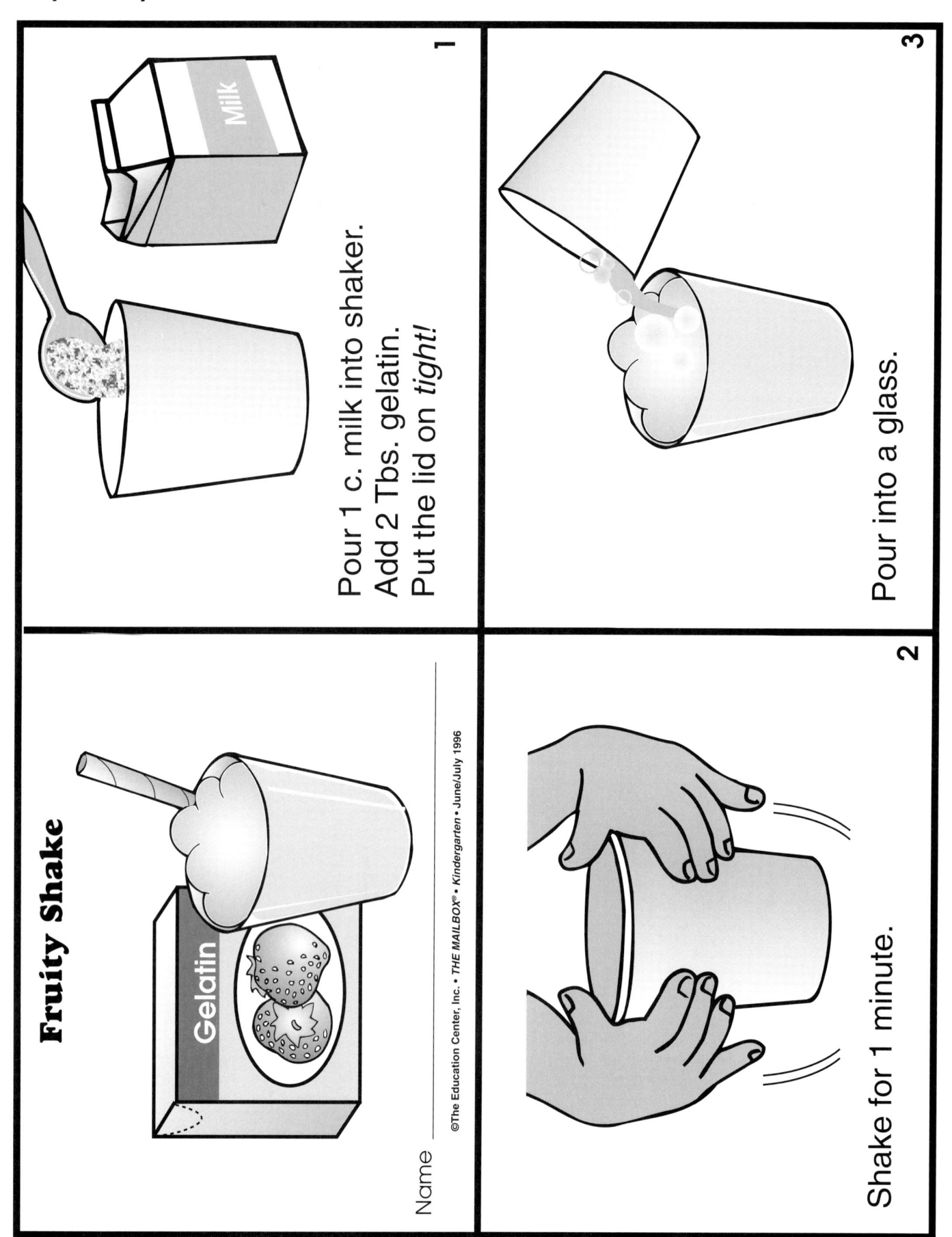

Fruity Shake

1. Pour 1 c. milk into shaker. Add 2 Tbs. gelatin. Put the lid on *tight!*

2. Shake for 1 minute.

3. Pour into a glass.

Name _____

©The Education Center, Inc. • THE MAILBOX® • Kindergarten • June/July 1996

Management Tips

GETTING YOUR DUCKS IN A ROW

The ABCs Of Kindergarten

Inform parents about the basics of kindergarten with this unique welcome-to-school booklet. Organize an alphabetical list of information that you would like parents to know, such as school policies and classroom procedures. Type the information; then duplicate copies to present to each parent during orientation sessions or parent conferences. Parents are sure to appreciate this valuable resource that they can refer to throughout the year.

Kathleen Miller—Gr. K
Our Lady of Mt. Carmel School
Tenafly, NJ

Class Address Book

Keep students' phone numbers and addresses at your fingertips with this suggestion. At the beginning of the year, record each child's home information in an inexpensive address book. Keep the book conveniently located near your phone at home. In this book, you'll also be able to record the date and topic of phone conversations as they take place. At the end of the year, enclose the book and a class picture in an envelope for your records.

Patt Hall—Gr. K
Babson Park Elementary
Lake Wales, FL

Sticker Tags

Here a name! There a name! Where's *my* name? Use eye-catching stickers to help little ones find their own names on cubbies, tables, and coat hooks. For each child, collect multiple copies of a specific sticker design. As you prepare name labels for each child, attach the same sticker design to each of that child's name labels. This use of picture cuing will enable youngsters to find their own places and identify their names in no time at all.

Esther Gorelick—Gr. K
Yeshiva Zichron Moshe
South Fallsburg, NY

Here Are The Highlights

If you prepare lesson plans in advance, use a highlighting marker to accent materials that need to be purchased or created. A glance at your plans will remind you what you need to do. What an outstanding tip!

Krista Leemhuis
The Kid's Place
Ottawa, IL

Helping Hands

This personalized helpers' chart will display a spectrum of colorful helpers. To make a chart, cut approximately eight-inch-wide strips of tagboard. About two inches above the bottom of the long edge of each tagboard strip, write students' names in colors according to the order of the rainbow: red, orange, yellow, green, blue, and violet. Have each child make a handprint above her name, matching the color of paint for the handprint to the color used to write her name (or using the paint color of her choice). Once they're dry, hang the strips in a row across the top of a chalkboard.

Draw a picture for each job assignment (such as a milk carton for the milk helper). Laminate these pictures; then attach a clothespin upside down to the top back of each picture. Hang each picture under a different child's name. By moving the pictures to the right each day, you'll have the opportunity to reinforce left-to-right movement for reading readiness. Once a picture has been moved completely down the line of names, be sure to move it back to the beginning to start again. At the end of the year, cut the handprints apart and send them home as thank-yous to your happy helpers.

Peggy Bierma—Gr. K
Calvin Christian School
Edina, MN

Versatile Containers

Here's a versatile use for the empty condiment containers available from your school cafeteria. Decorate the cleaned containers with permanent markers; then fill them with math manipulatives or art supplies. For a simple science experiment, pour water into an empty container. Observe the water level daily as the water slowly evaporates. Keep an empty jar handy for impromptu estimation activities. The possibilities are endless!

Lori Moosa
St. Edmund Elementary
Eunice, LA

Word Cards

This idea is a ringer! Mount a cup hook under each letter of your alphabet line. As you study each letter, write words that begin with that letter on cards. When it is time to move on to the next letter, punch a hole in the corner of each of the word cards and place them on a metal ring. Hang the ring of cards on the hook under the appropriate letter. Young writers will be able to use and replace the word cards with ease.

Judy Bingle—Gr. K
Hitchens Elementary
Addyston, OH

GETTING YOUR DUCKS IN A ROW

We're Growing...Growing...
With this cute little guy around, good behavior will be growing by leaps and bounds! Begin by cutting out a designated number of construction-paper circles (20, for example). Decorate one circle to resemble the face of a caterpillar and mount that circle on a wall. Add construction-paper feet to the remaining circles. Tell your class that each time they demonstrate positive behavior, you will mount a circle behind the caterpillar face. When the caterpillar reaches a length of 20 circles, everyone will celebrate. (To heighten the anticipation for younger children, you might like to put a piece of tape on the wall to indicate what will be the finished length of the caterpillar.)

Virginia Chaverri, Costa Rica, Central America

The Cleanup Train
When your classroom needs a little extra straightening up, announce that it's time for The Cleanup Train. Ask each child to line up behind you and hold on to the waist of the person in front of her. Begin quietly chugging around the room. As you see an area that needs attention, call out (for example), "First stop, block center." Then the first child behind you steps off the train and begins to clean up the block center. Meanwhile the train continues quietly chugging along, calling out stops such as "Second stop, art area" and "Third stop, trash can." Each time a stop is announced, the child directly behind you steps off the train to tend to that stop. When a child's work is done in a particular area, she rejoins the train at the end of the line. When your room is in order, you say, "Last stop!" and the whole class joins you in a round of "Toot! Toot!"

Chava Shapiro, Beth Rochel School, Monsey, NY

It's In The Bag
If your classroom isn't equipped with built-in cubbies, this idea *clearly* solves that problem. For each child, label a large, resealable, heavy-duty freezer bag. Punch two holes (through both thicknesses of the bag) approximately one inch below the sealing strip. Then thread a strong cord through the holes in just one side of the bag. Tie the cord so that it fits over the back of a child's chair. As a child completes his work or you hand out take-home papers, have each child store his papers in his personalized bag. With just a glance at each day's end, you can clearly see who has left his work behind. (If a bag receives excessive wear and tear during the semester, simply rethread the cord through the holes on the opposite side of the bag.)

Jeannine Bergeman—Gr. K
League Street Elementary School
Norwalk, OH

Last-Minute Labels
Have you ever needed to quickly label oddly shaped crafts, projects, or even your students themselves? With this tip, you'll be prepared to label anything—in an instant! In advance, use a computer-label program to make a supply of name labels for each child in your class. (Many label programs have attractive graphics that can be added to the labels.) Then, when you need a label on the spur of the moment, just peel and stick!

Farrelyn Lee, Bloomfield, NM

Movable Nametags
These convenient nametags help promote organization as well as add a decorative flair to your classroom. For each child, collect an empty, plastic yogurt container with a lid. To make a movable nametag, cover the container with decorative adhesive covering. Personalize a construction-paper flower or seasonal cutout; then laminate it if desired. Tape the cutout to a pencil "stem"; then poke the pencil through the center of the lid on the container. Use these name tags to indicate seating or groupings, or to label freestanding artwork.

Kristy Curless—Gr. K
Walnut Creek Day School
Columbia, MO

Where's That Pointer When I Need It?
If you're constantly searching for your big-book pointer, try this easy location tip. Cut off a section of Velcro® tape. Stick one side of the tape on the pointer, and the other side on your big-book holder. Each time you are through using your pointer, attach it to the big-book holder. The next time you need it—there it is!

Patt Hall—Gr. K, Babson Park Elementary, Lake Wales, FL

The Messenger
Help strengthen the home-school connection with these handy carriers. For each child, label the left side of a two-pocket folder "Return To School." Label the right side "Completed." Put finished student work and notes/memos in the right side. Place any papers that need to be returned to school in the left side. Encourage responsibility by having each child bring his folder to and from school every day. As children arrive, have them place their folders in a designated basket. You can quickly look through the folders to retrieve any returned papers or other home communications.

Debbie Perry—Gr. K
St. Brigid School
Midland, MI

GETTING YOUR DUCKS IN A ROW

Get Clipped
Clip off some of your paper-searching time by using this handy organizational tip. Label a large spring-type clip with a subject name. Then use the clip to hold together your sorted papers for that topic. When you need to get your hands on a particular paper, simply flip through the papers held by the appropriately labeled clip. There it is—right where you clipped it!

Saundra Bridgers
Wee Care Preschool
Fuquay, NC

Wipe And Wash
When a sink is not conveniently located, the mess created by art projects can be quickly wiped away with this cleanup hint. Keep a container of baby wipes available in the art center. Encourage your children to use the wipes to clean their hands before going to the sink to wash. Also use the wipes to clean the art tables and other surfaces. Cleanup is as simple as wipe and wash.

Gretchen R. Ganfield
McHale Child Care–Preschool
Plymouth, MN

All Wound Up
Do you ever wind up with a roomful of excitable youngsters after certain activities? If so, try using a music box to help your little ones unwind in preparation for the next activity. Wind the music box. While the music is playing, have the children relax by lying down or resting their heads on the tables. When the music stops, students will be calmer and prepared for the next transition.

Pablo Millares—Gr. K
Van E. Blanton Elementary
Miami, FL

Easel Ease
With the use of S-hooks, you can simplify switching sheets of paper on an easel so students can succeed at doing this themselves. First hang two large S-hooks (available from hardware stores) over the top of the easel. Next use a hole puncher to make holes in the top left- and right-hand corners of several sheets of art paper. Then slip the papers onto the hooks, and the easel is set up for your young artists. As each child completes her work, she can lift her paper off the hooks, leaving a fresh sheet for the next student. Those S-hooks are simply super!

Suzanne Bell
Fairview Avenue Public School
Dunnville, Ontario, Canada

Big-Book Boxes
Convert a deep big-book box into a convenient storage container for your big books when they are not in use. First open the center of the box to remove the books; then tape the box together again at the center. Next seal the bottom of the box with tape. Trim off the top flap. Apply Con-Tact® covering to the box to improve its appearance and life span. Then slide your big books into the top of the box for quick and easy storage.

Terry Schreiber—Gr. K
Holy Family School
Norwood, NJ

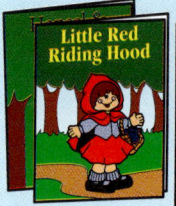

Colorful Centers
With this color-coded system of learning center assignments, your little ones will know at a glance where to go for center time. From construction paper cut a large crayon of a different color for each center in your classroom. For each child cut a set of smaller crayons to correspond to the colors of each center. (The small crayons may be cut from construction paper or bulletin-board border.) Punch a hole in the top left-hand corner of each crayon cutout. Use a key tag to hold each set of cutouts together. Label each tag with a child's initials. Then label a Peg-Board with each student's name. With the color of his assigned center in front, hang the child's set of crayons on his peg. When center time arrives, each child can check his peg for the color of his assigned center. Before the next center time, flip a new color to the front of each child's set to give him the opportunity to visit a different center. What a colorful idea!

Trudy White—Gr. K
Mayflower Elementary
Mayflower, AR

Job Gallery
Your youngsters can remember their daily job assignments with the help of this picture job chart. Take photographs of items that represent each of the jobs assigned to your students. For example, you may photograph a broom to represent the job of sweeping, an aquarium for pet care, or a trash can for emptying the trash. Attach the pictures to a low bulletin board so the children can easily see them. Place the name of the student responsible for each job under the picture for that job. Throughout the day, the children can check the job chart to remind themselves of their jobs. It's a picture-perfect way to promote independence and responsibility.

Jan McManus—Gr. K, Our Mother of Sorrows, Cincinnati, OH

Our Readers Write

Our Readers Write

"Class-y" Stationery

Your correspondence will make quite an impression when it's written on this one-of-a-kind stationery. To make the stationery, cut out a photograph of each child. Glue the photos onto the top of a piece of paper. Label the paper with your name, students' names, or a catchy phrase; then duplicate the paper (in color if possible). Send important messages home with a touch of class when using this unique stationery.

Barbara Meyers—Gr. K, Fort Worth Country Day, Fort Worth, TX

Macaroni Math Manipulatives

Try using fun-shaped pasta as inexpensive math manipulatives. Dye the pasta by mixing it with rubbing alcohol and food coloring. Encourage youngsters to use the different colors and shapes of pasta for sorting and patterning activities.

Susan Lind—Preschool and Gr. K
Lincoln Elementary School
Clarksville, TN

Laundry Bottle Possibilities

Don't throw away laundry-detergent bottles! Try these new uses for those old household bottles. Cut a bottle into three sections as shown. Turn the top portion of the bottle into a hat by decorating it with markers and stickers. To create sturdy nametags, cut the middle section into rectangles and program each with a name. Then tape a large safety pin to the back of each cutout. The bottom of the bottle has a variety of uses, such as a no-spill paint tray or an easy-to-fill bird feeder. With a little imagination, the possibilities are endless.

Becky Gibson
Camp Hill, AL

Animal-Cracker Art

Here comes the circus! Include this easy craft during a circus unit or just for fun. Give each child several animal crackers to glue onto a piece of white art paper. Ask him to imagine a circus scene around his crackers. Then provide him with crayons or markers, and encourage him to draw his imagined scene on the paper. For the big finish, give everyone the remaining animal crackers to snack on.

Deanna Evans—Gr. K
Richland, MO

Magic Alphabet Balls

This back-to-school door decoration will magically turn into a learning tool throughout the year. On your door, display a large clown cutout. Above the clown attach a set of circle cutouts, each programmed with a different student's name. Through the year, as you focus on each letter of the alphabet, remove the balls from the door and attach them to a chalkboard or bulletin board in the shape of the letter being studied. Students will believe the balls magically appeared!

Danvis Calhoun—Gr. K
Collins Elementary
Collins, MS

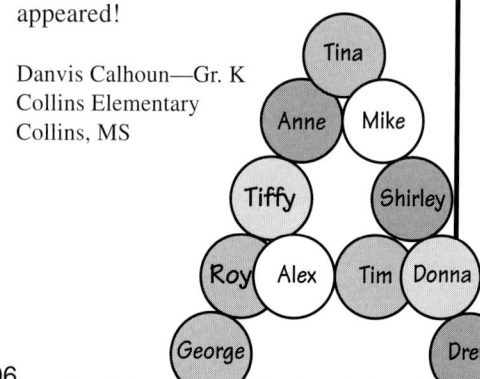

Tree Branch Display

Go out on a limb with student artwork by using this unique decorating idea. Using eye hooks and clear fishing line, suspend a tree branch from the ceiling. Next hang paper clips from the branches with fishing line. Display students' art projects (such as leaves, ghosts, or snowflakes) from the branches by hooking them onto the paper clips. Change the hanging projects each season for an intriguing display throughout the year.

Helynn Bode—Gr. K
Charter Oak–Ute School
Ute, IA

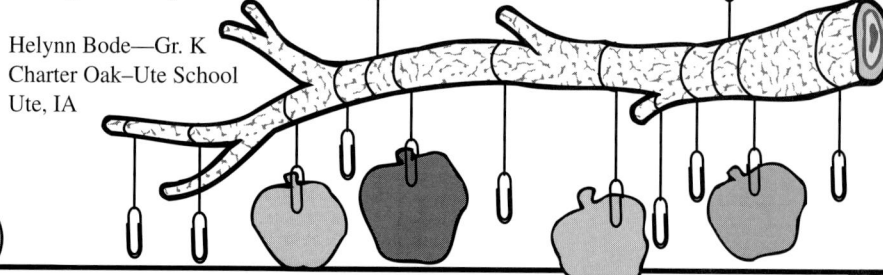

"Kinder-Graphics"

If you would like a record of classroom-created graphs, try this idea. After each graphing activity, take a photo of the graph or draw a representation of the graph results on graph paper. Include the photo or drawing in a notebook labeled "Kinder-Graphics." Place the notebook in a center for children to look at during free time. During conferences or Open House, share the notebook with parents. At the end of the year, you'll have an organized record of your classroom graphs.

Judy Kelley—Gr. K, Lilja School
Natick, MA

Helpful Hands Quilt

You won't be able to keep little hands off this class project. In fact, you'll want them all to leave their marks! To begin provide each child with a large square cut from solid-colored fabric. Using a fabric pen, have her write her name on the square. Then have her dip her palms in paint and press her hands onto the square. When the paint dries, use double-sided tape to attach a photograph of the child to the center of the square. Sew the completed squares together with a border to create a quilt that will be treasured for years to come.

Kim Wilson—Gr. K
Morris Central School, Morris, NY

All Tied Up

Are you all tied up tying youngsters' shoelaces? Try using this tip to teach them to tie their shoelaces themselves. Fold a white shoelace in half. Using permanent markers, color one-half of the shoelace red, and the other half blue. After removing the original shoelace from a child's shoe, lace the colored shoelace in its place. Refer to the colors on each half of the lace as you explain and demonstrate the steps for tying a shoelace. Youngsters will learn to tie quickly with the help of these colorful shoelaces.

Betty Lynn Scholtz—Gr. K
St. Ann's Catholic School
Charlotte, NC

Rewriting Mother Goose

Supplement your traditional nursery-rhyme activities with this novel idea. After learning a nursery rhyme, have youngsters think of creative ways to change the rhyme. For example, students might add a new ending or change the characters. Ask students to illustrate the new rhyme; then display the rhyme and student illustrations for others to enjoy.

Annette Hamill—Gr. K
Collins Elementary, Collins, MS

Mystery Sentence

Teach an abundance of reading skills with this fun activity. Each morning, select a child to whisper a sentence to you. Write the child's sentence on a chart or dry-erase board. Ask students to look for familiar words and use their knowledge of letter sounds to decipher the sentence. This quick, simple activity will help take the mystery out of learning to read.

S. Reneé Martin—Gr. K
Westwood Hills Elementary, Waynesboro, VA

Cooperation Tastes Good!

Use a favorite story, *The Little Red Hen*, to introduce the concept of cooperation to your new batch of kindergartners. Read or retell the classic story of the busy hen and her lazy barnyard companions. Explain that, as in the barnyard, everyone in the classroom will need to share the work in order to share the rewards. Put this lesson about cooperation into action by baking bread as a class; then give all of the helpers a piece of bread to enjoy. Be sure to send a letter home explaining how the story of the little red hen was used to teach cooperation in the classroom. Mmm! Cooperation tastes good!

Betty W. Caskey—Gr. K, Magnolia, AR

Reusing Helium Balloons

Have you ever wondered what to do with deflated Mylar® balloons? Here are some ideas for reuse. Use flattened balloons as an accent on bulletin boards. For a 3-D effect, cut a hole in the back of each balloon, stuff the balloon with plastic grocery bags, and seal the hole with clear tape. Open the door to fun with this final idea. Secure an eye hook to the top right corner of a door. Secure a second eye hook in the ceiling above and to the right of the door. Attach a lengthy piece of string to the top of a stuffed balloon. Thread the string through the eye hook in the ceiling; then tie the string to the eye hook on the door. Each time the door opens and closes, the balloon will go up and down.

Shell Gossett, Sebring, FL

Letter Of The Week

If you study a different letter each week, try this nifty display idea. Title a bulletin board "Letter Of The Week." Ask each student to bring in an item that begins with the letter you are currently studying. Display the items along with a large cutout of the letter on the board. Place items that can not be mounted in a plastic bag; then attach the bag to the board. Label each item displayed on the board. Now that's hands-on letter learning!

Elaine Hercenberg—Gr. K
Bet Yeladim School
Columbia, MD

"Cat-O'-Lantern"

For a different twist on your pumpkin carving, try making a cat-o'-lantern. Cut off the top of a pumpkin; then remove the seeds. (Be sure to save the seeds for baking and snacking on later!) Cut out a nose and a mouth shape from the pumpkin; then cut out two triangle eyes from the pumpkin. Place the top on the pumpkin. To create the cat's ears, secure the cut-out triangles on the pumpkin with toothpicks. Using a black marker, color six toothpicks. Insert the colored toothpicks into the pumpkin to resemble whiskers. As a conclusion, make a class book sequencing the steps for making a cat-o'-lantern.

Stacy Fleischer—Grs. K–1 Special Education
Educational Center Primary School
West Seneca, NY

Clip It With Clothespins

Need an easier way to hang charts around the room? Looking for a quick solution for storage of small items that seem to get lost easily? Grab a hot glue gun and a supply of spring-type clothespins, and you're ready to go! Using the hot glue gun, mount the clothespins inside cabinets, on doors, and across walls. The solution is simple—clip it with clothespins!

Robin McDonald—Gr. K
Westside Elementary
Clewiston, FL

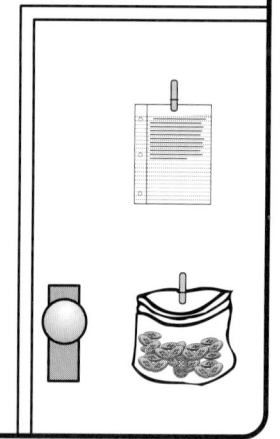

Laminated Leaves

Rake up a supply of colorful fall leaves to use in your classroom. Press the leaves flat and allow them to dry slightly. Then heat-laminate the leaves. Place the laminated fall foliage in a math center for sorting and classifying practice.

Pat Bollinger—Gr. K
Leopold R-3
Leopold, MO

Fruit Salad Fun

Here's a healthful alternative to the cupcakes and candy traditionally served at holiday parties. Request that each child bring a piece of her favorite fruit on the day of a class party. Use the fruit for a variety of sorting and graphing activities. Wash the fruit and cut it into equal portions. Provide each child with a plate, a plastic knife and fork, a cup, and a portion of each different kind of fruit. Have each child cut her assorted fruit pieces into smaller pieces on the plate. Then have her put her cut fruit in the cup and mix it. Try using red and green fruit for a Christmas party or only red fruit at a Valentine's Day party.

Patt Hall—Gr. K
Babson Park Elementary
Lake Wales, FL

Ring! Ring!

Hello? Here's an idea you won't want to put on hold. Help each youngster learn his phone number with this easy-to-make phone. Cut out an oaktag telephone base and receiver. Punch a hole on one side of both pieces; then join them with a length of yarn. Cut slits in the top of the phone base so that the receiver can rest on the base. Glue a duplicated copy of a phone dial to the phone base. Write a different child's name and his phone number on each phone. Encourage youngsters to use these phones to practice "dialing" their phone numbers.

Kathleen Miller—Gr. K
Our Lady of Mt. Carmel
Tenafly, NJ

The Great Divide

Separate classroom learning centers with an attractive, yet inexpensive, divider. Obtain a dressmaker's cutting board from a fabric store. Have youngsters give the divider a creative touch by decorating it with markers or paint. To use the divider as a display area, attach student work to the board with Sticky-Tac.

Jodi Lee McNamara—Gr. K
Jolly Tots, Inc.
Columbus, OH

Days Of The Week

To help students learn to read and sequence the days of the week, add an interactive element to your class calendar display. Under the calendar, insert seven pushpins into the bulletin board. Cut seven seasonal shapes from construction paper and label each shape with a different day of the week. Punch a hole in the top of each shape. To do this activity, have a child hang the shapes on the pushpins in the correct sequence.

Wilma Droegemueller—Preschool–Gr. K
Zion Lutheran School
Mt. Pulaski, IL

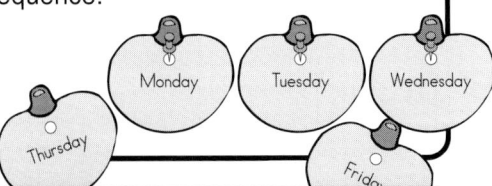

From Cradle To Kinder

This take-home project will send families on a trip down memory lane. Provide each child with a length of white bulletin-board paper to take home. Attach to the paper a letter to the child's parent. Request that the parent and child together create a timeline of the child's life. Display the projects in a school hall or on a bulletin board for teachers, students, and parents to admire.

Kiely Miller—Gr. K
St. Thomas More
Kansas City, MO

Book Bags

Use resealable plastic bags to create books. Simply place a supply of bags between laminated pieces of construction paper and bind them with a bookbinder. Here's a tip for keeping the bags in place while punching the holes for binding. Cut a piece of cardboard the width of the resealable bag. Using the binder, punch holes in the cardboard. Slip the cardboard inside the bag; then punch holes in the bag with the binder. The cardboard will hold the bag in place as the holes are punched. An alternative suggestion for perfect placement of the holes is to reinforce the bag with clear tape before punching the holes.

Jackie Wright—Grs. K–2
Summerhill Children's House
Enid, OK

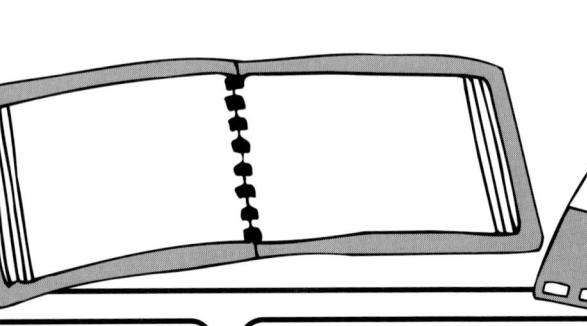

Apple-Butter Finger Paint

Pudding is an inexpensive substitute for finger paint. However, children with milk allergies need a substitute for pudding. Try using apple butter!

Dianne Donahoo Youngdahl—
Early Childhood Family
  Education Coordinator
ISD #880
Howard Lake, MN

Long-Playing Games

These gameboards are sure to be a hit! Here's how to make a gameboard from an old LP record. Cut out a paper circle that is the same size as the label in the center of the record. Glue or color a picture on the paper circle; then glue the circle to the center of the record. Next glue a trail of colored dots around the record toward the center. Provide dice or program a set of cards with numerals or directions. Store the games in record racks.

Tilda Sumerel
Spruce Pine, AL

Super Spinner

To make a spinner that is sturdy and simple to assemble, you will need a large safety pin, a washer, a brad, and a square piece of tagboard. On the tagboard, draw a circle. Visually divide the circle into equal sections; then program them as desired. Place the washer over the center of the circle; then place the small end of the safety pin over the washer. Insert the brad through the hole of the safety pin and the washer; then press it through the tagboard. Open the ends of the brad and press until they are flat. Give it a spin!

Stayce Rich—Gr. K
West Side Kindergarten
Magnolia, AR

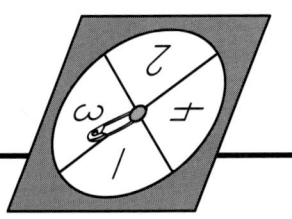

A Holiday Quilt

Deck the halls with a holiday quilt! To make the quilt, ask each child to write his name on a white, construction-paper rectangle and decorate it with craft items. Glue each child's rectangle to a larger rectangle of red or green paper. Glue all of the red and green rectangles to a white bulletin-board paper background in a patterned design. Complete the quilt by adding bows at intervals and a red border around the edge of the white background. This display is sure to send warm holiday wishes to all who admire it.

Elinor Gesink—Gr. K
Sheldon Christian School
Sheldon, IA

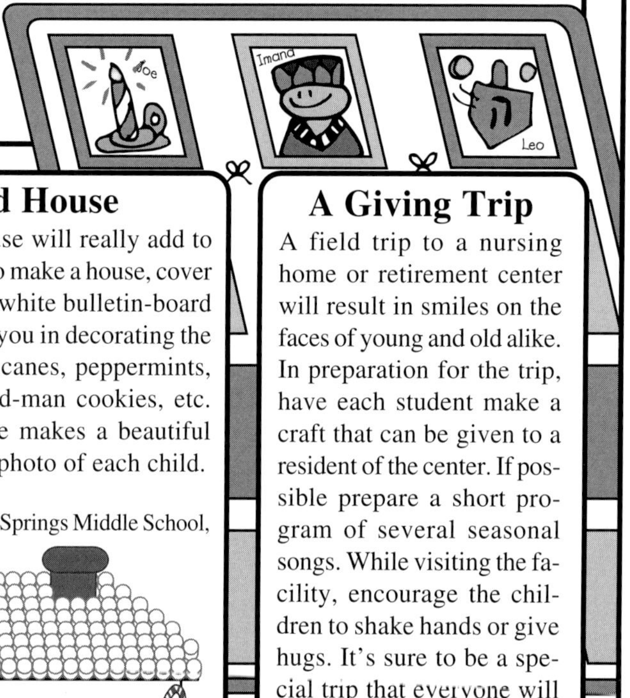

Deer Greetings

Parents are sure to love this special holiday-photo greeting. To make the antler hat that each child will wear in the photo, have each child trace both hands onto brown construction paper. Cut on the resulting outlines, leaving a strip of paper below the hand shapes as shown. Fit each child's antler hat on his head; then staple the ends of the hat together. Mix equal parts of red tempera paint and dish soap; then paint the tip of each child's nose with the mixture. Gather your class around yourself and have an adult volunteer take the picture. To prepare the card, program the bottom of a sheet of paper with the phrase, "We love you 'deer-ly'!" On the opposite side of the paper, have each child write his name. Duplicate a class supply of both sides onto red paper. Attach the photo and fold the paper in half; then send a card home with each child.

Toni Gardiner—Gr. K
Lincoln Park Elementary School
Muskegon, MI

Gingerbread House

This giant gingerbread house will really add to your holiday decorations! To make a house, cover a large appliance box with white bulletin-board paper. Have students assist you in decorating the house by gluing on candy canes, peppermints, marshmallows, gingerbread-man cookies, etc. When complete, this house makes a beautiful background for a seasonal photo of each child.

Mary Kitchens—Gr. K, Crystal Springs Middle School, Crystal Springs, MS

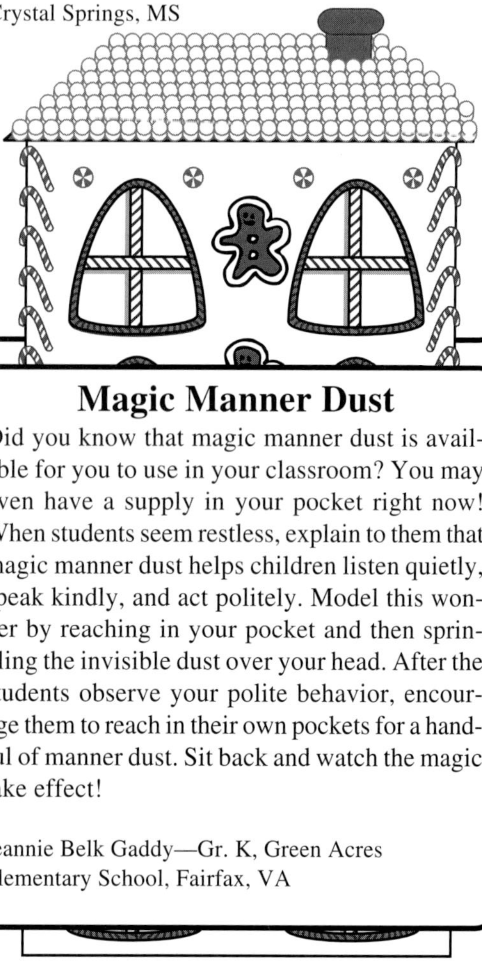

A Giving Trip

A field trip to a nursing home or retirement center will result in smiles on the faces of young and old alike. In preparation for the trip, have each student make a craft that can be given to a resident of the center. If possible prepare a short program of several seasonal songs. While visiting the facility, encourage the children to shake hands or give hugs. It's sure to be a special trip that everyone will remember.

Wilma Droegemueller—Gr. K and Preschool, Zion Lutheran School, Mt. Pulaski, IL

Magic Manner Dust

Did you know that magic manner dust is available for you to use in your classroom? You may even have a supply in your pocket right now! When students seem restless, explain to them that magic manner dust helps children listen quietly, speak kindly, and act politely. Model this wonder by reaching in your pocket and then sprinkling the invisible dust over your head. After the students observe your polite behavior, encourage them to reach in their own pockets for a handful of manner dust. Sit back and watch the magic take effect!

Jeannie Belk Gaddy—Gr. K, Green Acres Elementary School, Fairfax, VA

The Language Of Holidays

Invite parents to a holiday party with activities that are not only fun, but provide opportunities for language development as well. In advance organize learning centers with a holiday theme. For example, you might want to prepare a center in which parents and children can listen to a story and make an ornament, or a center in which parents and children follow directions to decorate cookies. To each different learning center, tape a different-colored light shape from construction paper. As each child and his parent/adult volunteer arrive, provide them with a length of string with a white, construction-paper light shape for each center in the room. As each child and parent complete each center, provide them with a stick-on dot (the same color as the light shape at that center) for them to attach to one of their white light shapes. After each parent and child complete every center, conclude the party with cookies, punch, and a round of holiday songs. A good time will be had by all!

Cathie Pesa, Paul C. Bunn School, Youngstown, OH

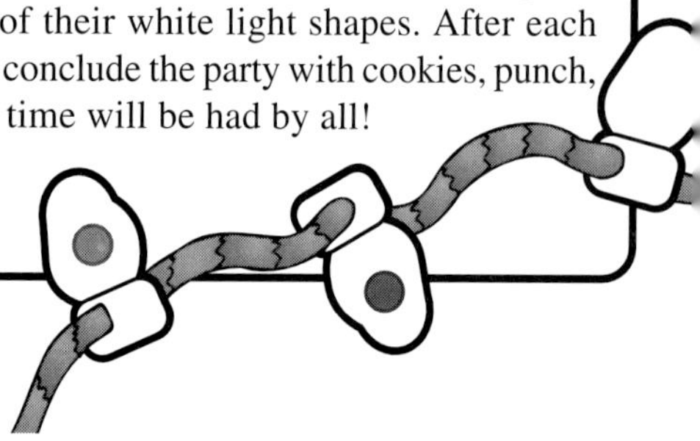

Grocery-Bag Art

Promote the joy of reading in your community with grocery-bag art. After reading a book aloud in class, give students the opportunity to illustrate the story on grocery bags obtained from a local grocery store. Attach a note (similar to the one shown) to each illustrated bag; then return the bags to the participating grocery store. Students will be thrilled to receive mail from the customers who admire their illustrations on the bags. Consider sending a letter home to parents explaining the program and encouraging their patronage of the cooperating business.

Betsy Short—Gr. K
Locust Grove Elementary
Locust Grove, GA

Growler's Grocery is cooperating with Mrs. Short's Kindergarten class to promote interest in reading. A student in the class listened to the story and illustrated it on this bag. Please take a moment to write a note to the student and mail it to: Stockbridge Elementary School, 4617 Henry Blvd, Stockbridge, GA, 30281

Berlioz The Bear
by Jan Brett
by Ben M.

Christmas-Tree Crayons

These nifty crayons make inexpensive gifts that children are sure to enjoy receiving. Peel and sort a supply of old or broken crayons. Melt the crayons; then pour the wax into candy molds that are shaped like Christmas trees. When the wax has cooled, pop the shapes out of the molds and package them. What a great gift idea!

Patty Schmitt—Gr. K
St. Patrick's School
Portland, MI

Pinecone Presents

With a creative touch, a pinecone and a plastic lid make the perfect gift for a parent. Hot-glue a pinecone to a lid. Spray-paint the lid and the pinecone green or silver. While the paint is wet, sprinkle the pinecone with glitter. Oh Christmas Tree!

Stacy Fleischer
Williamsville, NY

Paper Chains

Your class can practice an abundance of skills when making paper chains. To practice creating patterns, provide students with two or three different colors of construction-paper strips to glue together to form a chain. Use the chains to practice counting or for measurement activities. For a lesson on cooperation, provide each child with ten construction-paper strips. Ask each child to glue his chain to another child's chain. When the chains are complete, mount them on a bulletin board for a unique border.

Erin Nigro—Gr. K
Hale School
Everett, MA

Magnetic Skills

If you have a magnetic chalkboard, this idea is for you! Cut out a supply of corresponding shapes, such as snowmen and hats or dogs and bones. Label the shapes with the skills you would like for students to practice, such as uppercase and lowercase matching or number skills. Attach magnetic tape to the back of each shape; then randomly place the shapes on the board. As each student visits the board, she can match or sequence the shapes. With this magnetic idea, the skills are sure to stick.

Jeannine Bergeman—Gr. K
League Street Elementary School
Norwalk, OH

The Question Box

Develop your youngsters' thinking skills with this fun activity. Place an object familiar to students in a box. Allow time for each child to ask a question about the mystery object. Then encourage each child to use the information to guess the identity of the object. If necessary allow students to feel the object to assist them with their guesses. The Question Box is a great way for youngsters to learn to ask questions and draw conclusions from information.

Suzanne C. Bryant—Gr. K
Jacksboro Elementary School
Jacksboro, TN

Numbered Cupboards

What's behind door number one? It's a great numeration idea! If you have a row of cupboards in your classroom, label each cupboard door with a different numeral. When directing a student to get supplies from a cupboard, you can say, "It's in cupboard number three," for example. Referring to the cupboards by number not only saves time, but can also be used as an assessment tool.

Linda Crosby—Gr. K
Hill Crest Community School
Fort Vermilion
Alberta, Canada

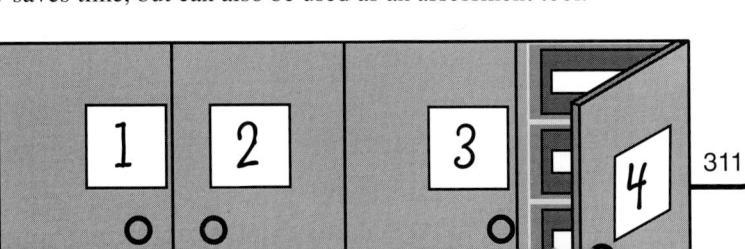

A Valentine Tree

This Valentine's Day display is simply lovely! Paint a tree branch white. When it's dry, set the branch in a small coffee can; then fill the can with cement. Decorate the secured tree branch with valentines and students' February art projects. If desired, decorate the tree each month with art projects related to the current holiday.

Debbie Musser—Gr. K
Washington Lee Elementary
Bristol, VA

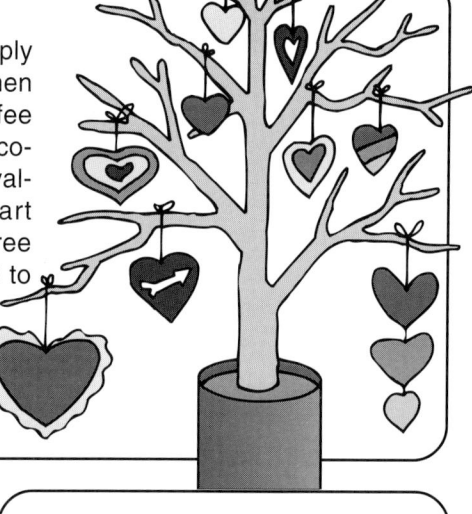

The Compliment Quilt

In addition to being a permanent self-esteem booster for your student-of-the-week, this compliment quilt makes a charming display in your writing center. Staple colorful bulletin-board paper to a small board; then title it with the phrase "[Child's name]'s Compliment Quilt." Stock the center with markers and a paper square for each student in the class. Encourage each child in the class to write (or dictate) a complimentary statement about the featured child on a square; then have him draw a picture to illustrate his statement. Glue the squares onto the bulletin board in rows so that the finished product resembles a quilt. At the end of the featured child's special week, give him the compliment quilt to take home and treasure.

Lee Butler—Gr. K
Morrow Elementary School
North Lauderdale, FL

The Letter's In The Mail!

If your youngsters are learning their home information or your theme is community helpers or transportation, this project is addressed to you! To make a mail truck, fold a sheet of white construction paper in half so that the folded side is at the bottom. At the top, cut a section from both thicknesses so that the folded paper resembles a mail truck. Glue a red strip, a blue strip, and black circles to the front of the truck. Label the truck with the phrase "U.S. MAIL." Glue the sides of the truck together. When every child has made his own truck, have him write his name and address on a blank envelope. Direct each child to attach a sticker or a stamp to his envelope. Then have each child slide his envelope in the truck.

Linda Hroncich
North Bergen, NJ

Mail Call

Here's a first-class way for students to share news and develop their writing skills. If youngsters have special news that they would like to share with the class, encourage them to write the news on a piece of paper at home and place the paper in an envelope labeled with your name. The next day have them deliver the envelope to your class mailbox. Each day collect the mail from the box and read it aloud. Be sure to respond to each child's news by writing him a letter in return. Place the letter in an envelope labeled with the child's name; then deposit the letter in the mailbox. Each day have a mail call by delivering outgoing mail and reading aloud new mail.

Duane Blake—Gr. K
RTR Elementary
Ruthton, MN

Stevie's Compliment Quilt

He is nice.	He is good in math.	Stevie is fair.
He is a good boy.	He has manners.	Stevie is a good reader.
He knows jokes.	He is a very smart boy.	Everyone likes him.

Wear A Pattern

Purchase a supply of inexpensive plastic bracelets. Encourage children to wear their choice of bracelets so that the bracelets display a pattern. For example, a student might wear a set of alternating pink and green bracelets. Be sure to ask your fashionable students to explain the bracelet patterns that they are wearing.

Marcia Boone and Robin Gattis—Gr. K
Seagoville Elementary School, Seagoville, TX

Jumbo Writing

Encourage students to write in a big way by adding easel writing pads to your writing center. (To collect the pads, consider asking local hotels or convention centers to donate the blank writing pads that presenters leave behind.) If you have shelves with pegboard backs, place pegboard hooks in the holes; then hang the pads on the hooks. The easel writing pads will be easy to store and just the right height for youngsters to write on.

Beth Lemke, Coon Rapids, MN

Seasonal Art Hangers

Hung up on where to display students' artwork? Make these seasonal hangers and hang it up! For each child, cut a large seasonal shape (such as a heart or shamrock) from appropriately colored poster board. Using the scraps, cut smaller versions of the same shape. Use craft glue to glue the smaller shape to a wooden clothespin; then glue the clothespin to the larger shape. Mount the seasonal hanger to the wall with pushpins or tape. Or punch two holes near the top of each hanger. Connect the hangers with clear fishing thread and suspend them from the ceiling. Clip the artwork to the shapes for a display that is always in season.

Alana Holley—Gr. K
Windmill Point Elementary
Port St. Lucie, FL

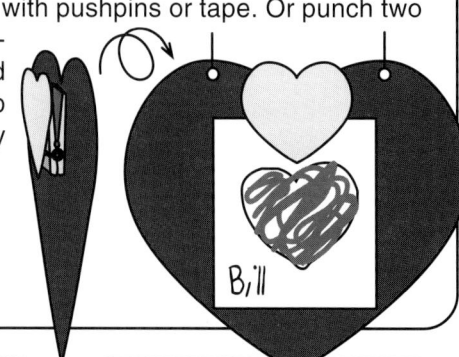

Cereal-Box Books

Recycle empty cereal boxes by using the front and back panels as journal or booklet covers. Simply cut the front and back panels from a cereal box. If desired cover the panels with Con-Tact® covering. Then place a supply of paper between the panels and bind together with plastic binders. If you cover the panels, encourage each student to decorate his journal or booklet with markers.

Deanie Pizzillo
Garfield Elementary
Spokane, WA

If I Live 100 Years...

On the 100th day of school, ask students what they believe they will look like, feel like, or be able to do if they live to be 100 years old. Then provide each child with art paper and have him complete the phrase "If I live 100 years...." Have each child illustrate his statement; then bind the pages between covers. Be sure to send this class book home for parents and grandparents to enjoy!

Mary Johnson—Gr. K
Grandville Christian School
Grandville, MI

Stove-Top Covers

If you have stove-top covers that have been slightly burned, don't toss them out! Paint the covers and use them as magnet boards. What an attractive idea!

Kristy Hedinger
Creative Corner's Preschool
Corning, IA

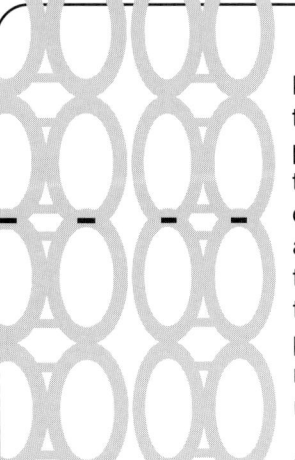

Decorate With Plastic!

Help the environment by collecting the plastic rings used to hold six-packs of soda cans. By stapling them together end to end, you can create a curtain! Use the curtain as a divider between classroom centers by hanging it from the ceiling tiles. Clip artwork to the curtain with paper clips for a new decorative dimension in your classroom. Decorating with plastic—how original!

Sue Thompson—Gr. K
Woodridge Elementary School
Stone Mountain, GA

Class Pictionary

A class pictionary will help your students address their valentines all by themselves! Take a picture of each child in the class. Mount the developed pictures on a chart; then label the chart with the children's names. Place the pictionary in a center set up for addressing valentines. To encourage youngsters to use the pictionary after Valentine's Day, display the chart in a mail or writing center.

Helaine Rooney—Gr. K
Georgian Forest Elementary
Silver Spring, MD

Index

abc's. *See* alphabet; emergent reading skills; learning centers.
acceptance of others, 67
Action Alphabet, 104
adding, 56, 80
address book, class for, 302
Ahlberg, Janet and Allan, 145
adjectives, 99
African-Americans.
   Carver, George Washington, 222
African-American History Month, 222
Ahlberg, Janet and Allan, 145
Aliki, 66
All Pigs Are Beautiful, 224
Allsburg, Van, Chris, 187
alphabet, 47, 48, 51, 56, 78, 99, 302. *See also* emergent reading skills; manual alphabet; learning centers.
   Action Alphabet, 104
   A Swim Through The Sea, 99
   Eight Hands Round: A Patchwork Alphabet, 78
   The Handmade Alphabet, 105
alphabetical order, 48, 56
Amazing Anthony Ant, 186
amounts,
   coins, 51, 309
   estimate/estimating, 55
   measure/ measuring 52, 55, 160, 215, 311
   monetary, 227, 309
   pour/ pouring 52, 55
   volume, 52
   weighing, 55
   weight and shape, 89
angel, 30
animals,
   Artic, 236
   babies, 248-255
   counting, 106
   farm, 112, 113, 119, 120
   growth, of, 248
   mobile, 74
   nocturnal, 74
   ocean, 72
   pond, in, 117
   puppets, 193
   skeletons of, 192, 196–198
   sounds of, 112, 119
   trees, sleeping in, 74
   zoo-animals, cages for, 24
Animal Parents And Their Kids!, 248–255
Animals At Night, 106
Antarctica, 233
ants, 184–190
Ant Cities, 184
apples, 24
apron, 41. *See also* Arts and Crafts; Father's Day
Arnosky, Jim, 98
Arthur's Valentine, 105
Artic, 233–236
arts and crafts, 23–41. *See also* gifts
   animal-cracker pictures, 306
   animal puppets, 193
   apples, 24
   angel, 30
   apple, wind-sock, 24
   apples, stained-glass, 24
   apron, 41
   Artic winter scenes, 234
   autumn, 55, 26, 27, 28
   balloons, hot-air, 36
   basket, spring, 38
   batik (fabric prints), 167
   bears, coffee, 41
   bee, 15, 17, 33
   birds, 39
   birthday, cakes, decorative tagboard, 25
   blankets, Native American, 80
   bumblebees, crayon shavings, 36
   bunny, 38
   cards, greeting, 34, 73, 310
   card, cupcake-shaped, thank you, 215
   chicks, cotton ball 93
   connected figures, folded and cut from paper, 65
   constellations of minimarshmallows, 275
   Christmas, 30, 31, 32
   Christmas tree, 30
   critter cages, 24
   coat, patchwork, for class mascot, 81
   cookies, paper decorated, 216
   crayon, Christmas-Tree, 311
   decorating body shape, 6
   dreidel, 162
   Easter, 38
   eggs, 38, 94, 94

fall leaves, 26, 27
Father's Day, 41
finger puppet, 116
fish, alphabet, 99
fish, multi-colored, 66
flag, German, 154
flowers, 23, 39, 122
friendship necklaces, 66
frames, 25, 33, 123, 182
fruit, clay sculpted from, 163
fruit painting, scented, 139
gingerbread, 32
goodnight scene, 74
grocery bag art, 311
happy birthday, 25
hand-shaped cutout, 187
hat for the moon, 73
horseshoe, lucky 35
hot air balloons, 36, 165
Indian cloth, 167
Indian corn, 27
jack-o-lanterns, 26, 27, 308
jellyfish, 36
jewelry, 72
leaf nests for ants, 186
lift-the-flap, animals in trees, 106
lobster, 36
magnets, refrigerator 25, 41
mkeke (placemat), 163
mailbox, 105
Menorah, 162
ornament, Christmas, 30
peacock, 166
peanut-shaped mobile, 222
penguins, 114
people, 183
pigs, little three, houses for, 104
Pig's Pocket envelope, 227
pillowcase, 123
pin, eyeglass, 54
pinwheels, 87
popcorn cutouts, 132
posters, 92
prints, 31
pumpkins, 8
owls, 103
quilt, 78, 80, 81,82, 307
rag coat, 81
rainbow, eggshell 35
rainbow, wand, 35
rhymes, illustrated, 109
robin, 36
salt, designs, 39
Santa, 31
scarecrow costumes, 202
sea-life, 36
self-portrait, 68, 123, 174, 257
snow, 32
spring, 36,39
strawberry index card, 256
strawberry, stuffed, 259
stocking, 30
suitcase, 120
summer sunflowers, 23
Thanksgiving, 56
trees, 23, 32
trees, pinecone, 32
T-shirts, 26
turkeys, 28
Valentine kisses, Styrofoam ®, 105
Valentine's cards, 34
vase, 39
whale with waterspout, 110
wind sock, 24
winter, 32
winter snow scene, 32
wrapping paper, 31
wreaths, 31
art techniques,
batik (fabric prints), 167
bubble solution, background, 100
clay sculpting, 163
crayon melt, 36
crayon shavings, 36
crayon resist, 94
drawing, 65, 71, 87, 92, 98, 110, 113, 123, 133, 139, 149, 188, 251, 256, 277
eggshells, crushed, 35
fabric paint/pens, 26, 30, 41, 81, 307
fabric printing, 167
finger painting, 15, 94
finger/thumb prints, 28, 74, 100, 159, 184, 215
fabric scraps, 6, 16, 120, 202
Friendly Plastic ® jewelry, 72
handprints, 9, 12, 31, 41, 302, 307
mobiles, 73, 74, 110, 222
murals, 10, 72, 86, 251, 267, 275

paint, 8, 16, 17, 23, 78, 110, 115, 117, 244
print, 27
rubbing, 71, 141
scented soap drawing, 149
silhouette, 12
sponge painting, 16, 31, 38, 166, 184
tracing, 25, 30, 32, 54, 66, 97, 115, 187
Asch, Frank, 73
astronauts. *See also* moon; space
art project, 71
I Want To Be An Astronaut, 71
pattern of, 76
Auch, Mary Jane, 94
Author Units, 107-123
   Carlstrom, Nancy White, 120–121
   Fleming, Denise, 116–119
   Henkes, Kevin, 122–123
   Pfister, Marcus, 114-115
   Raffi, 108–111
   Tafuri, Nancy 112-113
autumn. *See* fall
awards, 65, 175, 232
Axelrod, Amy, 227
Baby Beluga, 110, 236
Bacon, Ron, 87
Bailey Goes Camping, 122
bakery, 214-221
balloons, 307
Bang, Molly, 260
barnyard, 119
Barnyard Banter, 119
Barton, Ron, 87
basket, spring, 38
bat, (mammal)309
bears. *See also* arts and crafts
   bulletin board, 11
   coffee-bears, 41
   Better Not Get Wet, Jesse Bear, 121
   It's About Time, Jesse Bear: And Other Rhymes, 121
   Jesse Bear, What Will You Wear?, 121
   polar, 235
bee, 15, 17, 36, 56
behavior, encouraging good student, 310
Bein' With You This Way, 67
Bently & Egg, 93
Better Not Get Wet, Jesse Bear, 121
bibliographies. *See also* literature; song books
   animal babies, 248, 251
   ants, 188
   bakery, 216
   blankets and quilts, 8
   bones, 193
   Carlstrom, Nancy White, 121
   cats, 210
   eggs, 95
   England, 157
   family, 183
   fish, 101
   Fleming, Denise, 119
   France, 165
   friendship, 69
   Hanukkah, 162
   Henkes, Kevin, 123
   Kwanzaa, 163
   moon and night, 75
   Norway, 160
   Pfister, Marcus, 114
   pigs, 227
   rhyme, 245
   scarecrows, 202
   school and such, 175
   science, 139, 141 (senses)
   smell, sense of, 149
   sound, 143
   space, 277
   Tafuri, Nancy, 113
   touch, sense of, 141
   turtles, 269
   whales, 236
   wind, 89
Big Cats, 208
Big Hungry Bear, The, 256
birds, 13, 36, 37, 103, 114, 116, 161, 202
birthdays, 25, 132
blankets, books about,
   Geraldine's Blanket, 80
   Owen, 80
   Ten Little Rabbits, 80
blankets, favorite, 80, 123
body parts, learning 111
Blow Away Soon, 88
Blowing In The Wind: A Collection Of Books About The Wind, 84-89
bones. *See* skeleton
Bones & Skeleton Book, 193
Books. *See* authors; bibliographies; literature; song books
Boy And The Cloth Of Dreams, The, 81

Boy And The Quilt, The, 80
book, making a, 65, 66, 67, 71, 74, 76, 79, 80, 86, 91, 92, 98, 99,103, 104, 113, 116, 118, 121, 126, 134, 157, 158, 201, 208, 209, 210, 215,216, 225, 226, 235, 244, 245, 249, 250, 258, 269, 275, 313
Brett, Jan, 104, 159
Brown, Marc, 105
Brown, Margaret Wise, 71
Buckley, Richard, 268
bulletin boards, 5–20. *See also* patterns; reproducibles
    accomplishments, student, 17
    aquarium, 17
    baby animals, "Growing...Growing," 248
    bees, 15, 17
    Christmas, 10
    Columbus Day, 8
    Down By The Bay, original scenes, 244
    end of the year, 16
    families, 79 (suggested activity for *The Patchwork Quilt*)
    family portraits, 182
    family traditions, 183
    "Favorite Things, A Few Of, Our," 123
    fish, 66
    friendship, 6, 7, 65, 67
    gardens, 15
    ghosts, 9
    gingerbread house, appliance box, 310
    Halloween, 8, 9
    Hanukkah, 10
    jellyfish, 40
    Letter Of The Week, 308
    listening skills, 309
    Martin Luther King Day, 12
    moon and stars, 71 (suggested activity for *Goodnight Moon*)
    mountains and valleys, 88 (suggested activity for *The Gates Of The Wind*)
    nutrition, 15
    octopus, 7
    owls, 103
    patriotism, 16
    pets, 17
    Pigs Aplenty, Pigs Galore!, 226
    Pilgrims, 157
    pond life in, 117
    quilts, 82
    self-esteem, 6, 13, 14, 17
    snow, 11
    spring, 13, 14
    Thanksgiving, 9
    unity, promoting, 6
    Valentine's Day, 12
    vowels, 15
    welcome, 7
    wind, 89
    winter, 11
bunny, cake shaped as, 72
Burton, Robert, 91
butterflies 119
Button Box, The, 103
calendars, 277–278
cameras. *See* photographs
camping, 122
cards,
    greeting, 34, 73, 310
    invitation, 287
    thank you, 215, 287
    Valentines, 313
Carle, Eric, 66, 71, 87, 208
Carlston, Nancy 183
Carlstrom, Nancy White, 85
carpet squares, 309
Carrot Seed, The, 106
categorizing, 42, 214, 268
cats, 208-213,
    defining, 208
    identification, of, 209
cats, books about,
    Big Cats, 208
    Have You Seen My Cat?, 208
    Little Cats, 208
    Red Cat, White Cat, 210
celebrations, multi-cultural. S*ee* cultural celebrations
centerpiece, hot air balloon, 40
centers. *See* learning centers
Chanukah. *See* Hanukkah
chanting, 185, 258
character,
    courage, finding within, 81
charts, means of hanging, 308
Chermayeff, Catherine and Nan Richardson, 98
Chickens Aren't The Only Ones, 91
Children's Literature, 63–102
Christmas,10, 30, 31, 32, 49, 50, 127, 214, 310, 311. *See also* learning centers; holidays; bulletin boards; winter
Chrysanthemum, 68, 122
circle time,
    mathematical twist for, 126

musical patterns, 128
physical actions in patterns, 129
reading, 226
role playing, activity for, 104
sense of sight, 145
Circle-Time Fun, 129
classification, 99, 103, 267
classroom management,
    big books storage, 304
    charts, hanging, 308
    cleanup, 304
    easel, 304
    establishing quiet, 304, 310
    job chart, 304
    labels, 303
    nametags, 303
    pointer location, 303
    positive behavior, 303
    purchasing items, 302
    reducing paper-searching time, 304
    room divder, 304
    straightening, 303
    storage space, 303
clocks, 103, 143, 155, 167
Clocks And More Clocks, 103
cloth, Indian, 167
clothing, 121, 236
coats, books about patchwork,
    Coat Of Many Colors, 81
    Rag Coat, The, 81
Coat Of Many Colors, 81
Cohen, Miriam, 65
coins, 00, 309
collecting, reinforcing skill of, 130
Cole, Joanna, 98
color recognition, 45, 46, 50, 52
color-word recognition, 45, 50, 52, 201
Columbus Day, 8
communication,
    oral, 67, 275
    story telling, 74
comparing, 72, 98, 104
cooking. *See* recipes
cooperation, 6, 78, 81, 307, 311
Conrad, Pam, 260
consonants, initial, 56
constellations, 274
counting, 42, 45, 46, 51, 54, 56, 68, 80, 97, 99, 106, 109, 113, 122, 126, 129, 166, 185, 225, 258, 259, 309, 311
    M&M's R Brand Chocolate Candies Counting Book, The, 126
Count Your Way Through India, 166
crayons,
    Christmas-Tree shaped, 311
    cookie-cutter, 309
    melt, 36
creativity, 47, 73, 116, 117, 163, 259
Crinkleroot's 25 Fish Every Child Should Know, 98
Cuckoo-Clock Cuckoo, 155
cultural celebrations,
    Chinese Harvest Moon Festival, 72
    Hanukkah, 10
    Kwanzaa, 163
    Nigerian creation myth, 72
Cumbaa, Stephen, 193
Daly, Nikki, 72
decoration, classroom, 259, 310
describing word. *See* adjective
dinosaurs, 11
displays. *See also* bulletin boards; reproducibles
    alphabet, 105
    anthill, 184
    Artic winter scenes, 234
    baby animals chart, 249
    back-to-school, 174
    bat or ghost, 309
    Celestial Art, 277
    Christmas, 30
    classroom charts, 308
    classroom unity, 183
    duck pond, 112
    drawing of the effects of the wind, 87
    fall leaves, 26
    first day of school, 174
    fish scenes, 100
    flowers, 122
    fruit and vegetables, 118, 163
    Holiday Quilt, 310
    Kwanzaa, 163
    miniature paper quilts, 82
    peanuts, grocery bags made from, 222
    pigs, poem about, 224
    Quilt, Compliment, 312
    rainbow fish, (two)m 115
    rhymes, illustrations of, 109
    seasonal hangers for, 313
    self-portraits of students, 174

scarecrow for reading center, 200
sense of touch/tactile poster, 141
sharks, 98
sight, 144, 145
story quilts, 78
techniques, 306
tree branch, 306
turtles, 267
Valentine's Day, 312
vibrations of sound, 142
whales, 110
dismissal, 242, 243
displaying, reinforcing skill of, 130
diversity, 67
    friendship in, 74
    physical differences, 67
dividing, 68, 257
Doorbell Rang, The, 68
door decoration,
    alphabet balls, 306
    first-day, 172
Dorros, Arthur, 184
Down By The Bay, 109, 244
Do You Want To Be My Friend?, 66
drama. *See* also role playing
    "Baby Names," 251
    Play, A, 225
Drawing
ducks, 111, 112
Dunphy, Madeleine, 234
Each Peach Pear Plum, 145
eggs, 53
Early Morning In The Barn, 112
ears, 309
Easter,
    bulletin boards, 14
    bunny, 19
    bunny, sponge painted, 38
    center, 53
    Easter Egg Farm, The, 94
    eggs, 91
    eggs, coloring center, 93
    fancy eggs, 38
    Peter Rabbit's Lunch, 295
Easter Egg Farm, The, 94
Egg: A First Discovery Book, The, 91
Egg: A Photographic Story Of Hatching, 91
Eggbert, The Slightly Cracked Egg, 93
Eggs All Around, literature unit, 90-95
eggs, books about, 90-95
    Bently & Egg, 93
    Chickens Aren't, 91
    Easter Egg Farm, The, 94
    Eggbert: The Slightly Cracked Egg , 93
    Egg: A First Discovery Book, The, 91
    Egg: A Photographic Story Of Hatching, 91
    Extraordinary Egg, An, 92
    Green Eggs And Ham, 93
    Hatch, Egg, Hatch!, 93
    Nessa's Story, 92
    Nest Full Of Eggs, A, 91
    Surprise Family, The, 92
    Yes, 92
eggs. *See also* arts and crafts; Easter; literature; science
    fancy eggs, 38
Ehlert, Lois, 72, 99
E-I-E-I-O, 128
Eight Hands Round: A Patchwork Alphabet, 78
Elementary School Kindergartners, 67
emergent reading skills, 15, 48, 51, 54, 56, 98, 99,104, 111, 119, 27, 129, 200, 208, 226, 234, 235, 256, 258, 302, 307. *See also* phonics
Enchantment Of The World: Germany, 154
Enchantment Of The World: India, 167
end of the year,
    bulletin board, 16
England, Jolly Olde, 156–157
Ernst, Lisa Campbell, 78
environments, 110, 116, 266
estimating, 49, 55, 309
Ets, Marie Hall, 87
Extraordinary Egg, An, 92
fact from fiction, separating, 92, 98, 234
facts, recognizing, 98
fairy tales, 104, 105, 155
fall. *See also* bulletin boards; holidays
    foliage, 23, 26
    Indian corn, 27
    jack-o-lanterns, 26, 27, 307, 308
    leaves, 307, 308
    leaf prints, 27
    pumpkin patch, 8
    scarecrows, 200-202
    trees, 23, 133
    turkeys, 28, 29
family,
    life in Norway, 158

315

memories, 79
show-and-tell, 183
Surprise Family, The, 92
ties, 79, 92
traditions, 162, 183
Family In Norway, A, 158
farm, 112, 113, 119, 120. *See also* animals
  barn, 112
  Barnyard Banter, 119
  ducks, 118, 112
  Early Morning In The Barn, 112
  E-I-E-I-O, 128
  Have You Seen My Duckling?, 112
  Rise And Shine!, 120
  Spots, Feathers, And Curly Tails, 113
farm, classroom, 112
Father's Day,
  apron, 41
  magnet, refrigerator 41
Fathers, Mothers, Sisters, Brothers: A Collection Of Family Poems, 182
field trip,
  bakery, 215
  nursing home or retirement center, 310
fine-motor skills,
  hooking candy canes, 49
  lacing, 45
  practice, 46, 54
  strawberry basket workshop, 259
  tweezers, 54
  wrapping, decorating blocks and boxes, 49
first day of school, 6, 123, 306, 172
  acclimation, 173
  bus-shaped totes, 173
  door decoration, for, 172
  nametags for students, 172
  rules, establishing, for students, 174
  school-bus booklet, 173
  singing: *Wheels On The Bus,* 172; "We're So Glad You're In Our Classroom," 175
  travel to school, discussing, 175
  welcome aboard, 174
  welcome-to-school booklet, 302
  welcome-to-school pack, 172
  youngster's feelings about, 65
fish, 42, 66, 97, 115. *See also* jellyfish; lobster; sharks
  bulletin board, 7
fish, books about, 96–101
  Crinkleroot's 25 Fish Every Child Should Know, 98
  Fish Eyes, 99
  Fishy Facts, 98
  Fish Skin, The, 99
  Hungry, Hungry Sharks, 98
  Million Fish...More Or Less, A, 100
  Sawfin Stickleback: A Very Fishy Story, The, 100
  Sea Dragons And Rainbow Runners: Exploring Fish With Children, 98
  Swim Through The Sea, A, 99
  Swimmy, 100
  What's It Like To Be A Fish?, 97
Fish Eyes, 99
Fish Skin, The, 99
Fishy Facts, 98
Five Little Ducks, 111
flags,
  French, 164
  German, 154
flannelboard, 80, 88, 106, 209, 225, 267
Fleming, Denise, 116–119
Flournoy, Valerie, 79
flowers, 16, 23, 122
food, 118
  cheeses of France, 164
Foolish Tortoise, The, 268
fractions, 257
frames, 25, 33, 123
France, Vive La, 164-165
France,
  flag of, 164
  geography of, 164
Friend, Catherine, 100
Friends, 65
friends,
  animals, 65
  imaginary, 68, 123
  things they do together, 66
  traits, of a, 65
friendship, 7, 65–69. *See also* social skills
  fostering friendships, 65
  friendship necklaces, 66
  "Reach Out And Be A Friend," bulletin board, 7
friendship, books about,
  Bein' With You This Way, 67
  Chrysanthemum, 68
  Doorbell Rang, The, 68
  Do You Want To Be My Friend?, 66
  Friends, 65

Jamaica's Find, 67
Jessica, 68
My Friends, 65
Rag Coat, The, 81
Rainbow Fish, The, 66
We Are All Alike...We Are All Different, 67
We Are Best Friends, 66
Will I Have A Friend?, 65
frog, 117
fruit, 118, 308. *See also* arts and crafts; vegetables; nutrition; recipes
  apples, stained glass, 24
  apple wind-sock, 24
  Each Peach Pear Plum, 145
  Fruit Kabobs, 127
  Fruit Salad Fun, 308
  Lunch, 118
  patterning, 127
  What's Your Favorite Apple?, 130
Fruit Kabobs, 127
Fuchshuber, Annegert, 155
games,
  ant-trail, 185
  cake walk, 88
  Cleanup Train, The, 303
  Disappearing Act (rhyme), 245
  "Down In The Meadow," 269
  dreidel, 162
  ducks, 111
  Find Your Partner! (rhyme), 241
  "Finishing up," rhyming, 244
  Go Rhyme, 243
  Globe Ball, 233
  guessing, 106, 113
  In The Bag (rhyme), 242
  I Spy, 145
  "I've Got Ants In My Pants" dance, 187
  Kindergarten Feud, The, (rhyme) 242
  London Bridge, 156
  lost and found, 67
  Make Way For Rhyming, 241
  matching, 193
  naming that sound, 147
  obstacle course, 93
  Pin The Tail On The Donkey, variation of, 100
  pinning character to board, 112
  planets orbiting the sun, 276
  race, seed, 87
  rhyming, 109
  Rhyme Lines, 243
  Rhyme-Time Challenge, 245
  Secret Password, 243
  seed search, 109
  show-and-guess, 244
  spider, 111
  Time To Line Up!, 242
  touch and tell, 148
  X-ray play, 191
Ganeri, Anita and Jonardon Ganeri, 167
garden, bulletin board, 15
Gates Of The Wind, The, 88
Geisel, Theodor. *See* Seuss, Dr.
Geraldine's Blanket, 80
Germany, Journey To, 154–155
Germany, similarities and differences between and United States, 154
Gerson, Mary-Joan, 72
Getting Kids Into Books, 103–106
ghost, 9, 309
Gibbons, Gail, 105, 274
gifts. *See also* arts and crafts; Father's Day; National Grandparent's Day
  apron, Father's Day 41
  crayons, Christmas-Tree, 311
  eyeglass pin, 34
  frame, National Grandparents Day, 25
  gift sack, 79 (*The Keeping Quilt*)
  magnet, Father's Day
  pinecone, for parents, 311
  Valentine kisses, Styrofoam®, 105
  vase, 39
Gilberto And The Wind, 87
gingerbread house, giant, 310
globe, 164, 233
  inflatable, exercise with, 233
Glow-In-The-Dark Book Of Animal Skeletons, 192
Goffin, Josse, 92
Gomi, Taro, 65
Goodnight, Goodnight, 9
Goodnight Moon, 71
Good Night, Owl!, 9
gourds, 47
graphing, 68, 97, 109, 182, 223, 307
graphing, learning unit, 130–136
  Happy Birthday!, 132
  Is It Ripe?, 256
  Look What's Poppin', 132

My Favorite Center, 133
Once Upon A Time, 133
Peanut Graph, 130
Ready, Set, Roll, 134
roll of die, 134
seeds, number found, 109
Skittles®, 131
Sneakin' Around, 130
Soup's On, 131
Sources Of Light, 134, 136
Strawberry Treats, 257
Traveling Book Of Graphs, A 134
Trees For All Seasons, 133
What's For Lunch, 132
What's Your Favorite Apple?, 130
Yes Or No?, 131
graphing, notebook record of, 307
gravity, 276
Green Eggs And Ham, 93
Grey Lady And The Strawberry Snatcher, The, 260
Grossman, Virginia, 80
Groundhog Day, 293
grouping 68. *See also* graphing; sets
Guback, Georgia, 79
Halloween, 8, 9, 26, 27, 307, 308, 309. *See also* arts and crafts; holidays
Handmade Alphabet, The, 105
Hanukkah, 10, 162
Hanukkah Lights, Hanukkah Nights, 162
Happy Birthday, 132
Happy Birthday, Moon, 73
Hargrove, Jim, 154
Halloween, 8, 9, 26, 27, 307, 308, 309
Haskins, Jim, 166
Hatch, Egg, Hatch!, 93
hats, 73. *See also* headbands
hats, birthday, 132
Have You Seen My Cat?, 208
Have You Seen My Duckling?, 112
Havill, Juanita, 67
headbands, 91, 127. *See also* hats
hearing, sense of, 142-143, 144, 147
hearts, (Valentine's), 12, 34, 241–245
Heath, Amy, 215
Heine, Helme, 65
Heller, Ruth, 91
Henkes, Kevin, 68, 80
Henry, Lucia Kemp, 191
Here Is The Artic Winter, 234
hibernation, 11
Hoberman, Mary Ann, 182
holidays
  Christmas, 10, 30, 31, 32, 49, 50, 127, 161, 214, 310, 311
  Columbus Day, 8
  Easter, 14, 19, 38, 53, 91, 94, 295
  Father's Day, 41
  Groundhog Day, 293
  Halloween, 8, 9, 26,27, 307, 308,309
  Hanukkah, 10, 162
  Independence Day, 16
  Kwanzaa, 163
  Martin Luther King, Jr. Day, 12
  Mother's Day, 39
  St. Patrick's Day, 13, 35, 296
  Thanksgiving, 9, 28, 157
  Valentine's Day, 12, 34, 241–245, 312, 313
Hopkinson, Deborah, 78
home information, learning, 308, 312
hot-air balloons, 36, 165
How Does The Wind Walk?, 85
How Night Came From The Sea: A Story From Brazil, 72
How The Wind Plays, 85
Hungry, Hungry Sharks, 98
Hutchins, Pat, 9, 68, 86, 103
idioms, 260
imagination, 68, 71, 109, 113, 116, 157, 201, 226, 244, 258, 274
interpreting information, reinforcing skill of, 130
It's About Time, Jesse Bear: And Other Rhymes, 121
Independence Day, 16
India, 166–167
India, 166
India, similarities and differences between and United States, 166
Indian corn, 27
Inside-Outside Book Of London, The, 158
Inside-Outside Book Of Paris, The, 165
In The Small, Small Pond, 117
In The Tall, Tall Grass, 116
invitations,
  to Sensory Fair, 150
It's About Time, Jesse Bear: And Other Rhymes, 121
Iva Dunnit And The Big Wind, 85
I Want To Be An Astronaut, 71
I Went Walking, 103
jack-o-lanterns, 26, 27, 308
Jamaica's Find, 67
James, Betsy, 88

jellyfish, 40
Jenkins, Priscilla Belt, 91
Jesse Bear, What Will You Wear?, 121
Jessica, 68, 123
Jeuness, Gallimard and Rascale de Bourgoing, 91
Johnston, Tony, 79
Jonas, Ann, 81
journal science, making a, 139
Joyce, William, 93
Jug Lids, 129
Kahney, Regina, 192
Kalman, Bobbie, and Tammy Everts, 208
Keats, Ezra Jack, 276
Keeping Quilt, The, 79
Keller, Holly, 80
Kimmelman, Leslie, 162
King Bidgood's In The Bathtub, 157
Kingfisher Young World Encyclopedia, The, 274
King-Smith, Dick, 224
Koralek, Jenny, 81
Krakauer, Hoong Yee Lee, 72
Krauss, Ruth, 106
Kurtz, Shirley, 80
Kwanzaa, 163
labeling, 97, 98, 103, 105, 121, 131
lacing, shoes, 45, 307
languages,
    English, 156
    French, 165
    German, 154
    Hindi, 166
large-motor muscles, 233
Lasky, Kathryn, 88
laundry bottles, plastic, recycling for classroom, 306
learning centers, 43–62
    addition, 56
    alphabet, 99
    alphabetical order, 48, 56
    ants, 188
    bakery theme for math, art, and social studies, 216
    bees, 15
    bulletin boards: participatory, 6, 7, 8, 9, 11, 12, 13, 14, 15, 16, 17, 71
    carpet, making for, 309
    classification, 103, 214
    color-coded assignment system, 304
    color recognition, 45, 46, 50, 52
    color-word recognition, 50, 52
    counting, 42, 45, 46, 51, 54, 56, 97, 202
    dinosaur, 128
    discovery, fish, 42; gourds, 47; nature, 46
    Easter, 53
    egg coloring, 93
    egg hatching, learning about, 91
    farm animals, 128
    fine-motor skills, 45, 46, 49, 54
    fish matching, 98
    fish watching, 42
    holidays, 310
    Kwanzaa art, 163
    lacing, 45
    letter recognition, 47, 51, 56, 105
    letter sounds, 56
    mail, 66, 105
    masks for role playing, 72
    matching, 45, 51, 53, 54, 55, 56
    math/money, 227
    message, 51
    name recognition, 48
    nature, 46
    numbers, 42, 48, 53
        numerical order, 51, 53
        numeral recognition, 45, 47, 48, 51
    numeration, 56, 311
    paint, 82
    patterning, 49, 52, 53
    phonics, 56
    play, 121
    prints, 47
    reading, 54, 200, 241
    scent, 139
    science, 42, 46, 54, 122
    science display, interactive, 97
    seashell, 54
    senses, 55
    sensory, 55
    sharks, 98
    skeleton, 193
    sorting, 42, 48, 50
    spelling, 48, 56
    sound, 143
    touch, 141
    visual discrimination, 51, 55
    water table, 52
    word recognition, 45
    writing, 50, 51, 55, 313
    leprechaun, 13, 18

letter formation, 223
letter matching, 47, 56, 311
letter recognition, 47, 51, 56, 223, 308
letter, upper case and lower case matching, 311
letter sounds, 56, 307
letter writing, 50, 55, 66, 105, 108, 311. *See also* learning centers; mail; writing
light, sources of, 134, 136
Like Me And You, 108
Lionni, Leo, 92, 100
lining up, pattern forming when, 129
Lipson, Michael, 85
listening skills, 120, 309
listing, 73, 74, 78
literature. *See also* song books
    Action Alphabet by Marty Neumeier, 104
    All Pigs Are Beautiful by Dick King-Smith, 224
    Amazing Anthony Ant by Lorna and Graham Philpot, 186
    Animals At Night by Sharon Peters, 106
    Arthur's Valentine by Marc Brown, 105
    Baby Beluga by Raffi, 110
    Bailey Goes Camping by Kevin Henkes, 122
    Barnyard Banter by Denise Fleming, 119
    Bein' With You This Way by W. Nikola-Lisa, 67
    Bently & Egg by William Joyce, 93
    Better Not Get Wet, Jesse Bear by Nancy White Carlstrom, 121
    Big Cats by Bobbie Kalman and Tammy Everts, 208
    Big Hungry Bear, THe, by Don and Audrey Wood, 256
    Blow Away Soon by Betsy James, 88
    Bones & Skeleton Book, The, by Stephen Cumbaa, 193
    Boy And The Cloth Of Dreams, The by Jenny Koralek, 81
    Boy And The Quilt, The, by Shirley Kurtz, 80
    Button Box , The by Margarette S. Reid, 103
    Carrot Seed , The by Ruth Krauss, 106
    Chickens Aren't The Only Ones by Ruth Heller, 91
    Chrysanthemum by Kevin Henkes, 68, 122
    Clocks And More Clocks by Pat Hutchins, 103
    Coat Of Many Colors by Dolly Parton, 81
    comparing and contrasting, 80, 81
    Count Your Way Through India by Jim Haskins, 166
    Cuckoo-Clock Cuckoo by Annegert Fuchshuber, 155
    Doorbell Rang , The by Pat Hutchins, 68
    Do You Want To Be My Friend? by Eric Carle, 66
    Down By The Bay by Raffi, 109, 244
    Each Peach Pear Plum by Janet and Allan Ahlberg, 145
    Early Morning In The Barn by Nancy Tafuri, 112
    Easter Egg Farm , The by Mary Jane Auch, 93
    Egg: A First Discovery Book, The created by Gallimard Jeuness and Pascale de Bourgoing, 91
    Egg: A Photographic Story Of Hatching by Robert Burton, 91
    Eggbert: The Slightly Cracked Egg by Tom Ross, 93
    Eight Hands Round: A Patchwork Alphabet by Ann Whitford Paul, 78
    Enchantment Of The World: Germany by Jim Hargrove, 154
    Enchantment Of The World: India by Sylvia McNair, 167
    Extraordinary Egg , An by Leo Lionni, 92
    Family In Norway, A, by Jetty St. John, 158
    Fathers, Mothers, Sisters, Brothers: A Collection Of Family Poems by Mary Ann Hoberman, 182
    Fish Eyes by Lois Ehlert, 99
    Fish Skin, The by Jamie Oliviero, 99
    Fishy Facts by Catherine Chermayeff and Nan Richardson, 98
    Five Little Ducks by Raffi, 111
    Foolish Tortoise, The, by Richard Buckley, 268
    Friends by Helme Heine, 65
    Gates Of The Wind , The by Kathryn Lasky, 88
    Geraldine's Blanket by Holly Keller, 80
    Gilberto And The Wind by Marie Hall Ets, 87
    Glow-In-The-Dark Book Of Animal Skeletons by Regina Kahney, 192
    Goodnight, Goodnight by Eve Rice, 9
    Goodnight Moon by Margaret Wise Brown, 71
    Good-Night, Owl! by Pat Hutchins, 9
    Green Eggs And Ham by Dr. Seuss, 93
    Grey Lady And The Strawberry Snatcher, The, by Molly Bang, 260
    Handmade Alphabet , The by Laura Rankin, 105
    Hanukkah Lights, Hanukkah Nights by Leslie Kimmelman, 162
    Happy Birthday, Moon by Frank Asch, 73
    Hatch, Egg, Hatch! by Shen Roddie, 93
    Have You Seen My Cat? by Eric Carle, 208
    Have You Seen My Duckling? by Nancy Tafuri, 112
    Here Is The Artic Winter by Madeleine Dunphy, 234
    How Does The Wind Walk? by Nancy White Carlstrom, 85
    How Night Came From The Sea: A Story From Brazil by Mary-Joan Gerson, 72
    How The Wind Plays by Michael Lipson, 85
    Hungry, Hungry Sharks by Joanna Cole, 98
    India by Anita Ganeri and Jonardon Ganeri, 167
    Inside-Outside Book of London, The , by Roxie Munroe, 156
    Inside-Outside Book Of Paris, The, by Roxie Munroe, 165
    In The Small, Small Pond by Denise Fleming, 117

In The Tall, Tall Grass by Denise Fleming, 116
Iva Dunnit And The Big Wind by Carol Purdy, 85
It's About Time, Jesse Bear: And Other Rhymes by Nancy White Carlstrom, 121
I Want To Be An Astronaut by Byron Barton, 71
I Went Walking by Sue Williams, 103
Jamaica's Find by Juanita Havill, 67
Jesse Bear, What Will You Wear? by Nancy White Carlstrom, 121
Jessica by Kevin Henkes, 68
Keeping Quilt, The by Patricia Polacco, 79
King Bidgood's In The Bathtub by Audrey and Don Wood, 157
Kingfisher Young World Encyclopedia, The, 274
Like Me And You by Raffi, 108
Little Cats by Bobbie Kalman and Tammy Everts, 208
Little Mouse, The, by Don and Audrey Wood, 260
Louanne Pig In The Perfect Family by Nancy Carlson, 183
Luka's Quilt by Georgia Guback, 79
Lunch by Denise Fleming, 118
M&M's ® Brand Chocolate Candies Counting Book, The by Barbara Barbieri McGrath, 126
Make Way For Ducklings by Robert McCloskey, 241
Million Fish...More Or Less , A by Patricia C. McKissack, 100
Mirandy And Brother Wind by Patricia C. McKissack, 88
Mitten. The by Jan Brett, 104
Molly And The Strawberry Day by Pam Conrad, 260
Moon Came Too , The by Nancy White Carlstrom, 120
Moonglow Roll-O-Rama , The by Dav Pilkey, 74
Moon Rope: Un Lazo A La Luna by Lois Ehlert, 72
"My Bones" by Lucia Kemp Henry, 191
My Friends by Taro Gomi, 65
Nessa's Story by Nancy Luenn, 92
Nest Full Of Eggs , A by Priscilla Belt Jenkins, 91
Night In The Country by Cynthia Rylant, 74
One Light, One Sun by Raffi, 110
Owen by Kevin Henkes, 80
Papa, Please Get The Moon For Me by Eric Carle, 71
Patchwork Quilt, The by Valerie Flournoy, 79
Penguin Pete by Marcus Pfister, 114
Penguin Pete, Ahoy! by Marcus Pfister, 114
Penguin Pete And Little Tim by Marcus Pfister, 114
Penguin Pete And Pat by Marcus Pfister, 114
Penguin Pete's New Friends by Marcus Pfister, 114
Pigs Aplenty, Pigs Galore! by David McPhail, 226
Pigs Will Be Pigs by Amy Axelrod, 227
Post Office Book, The by Gail Gibbons, 105
Quilt, The by Ann Jonas, 81
Quilt Story, The by Tony Johnston, 79
Rabbit Mooncakes by Hoong Yee Lee Krakauer, 72
Rabbit's Morning by Nancy Tafuri, 113
Rag Coat, The by Lauren Mills, 81
Rainbow Fish, The, by Marcus Pfister, 66
Red Cat, White Cat by Peter Mandel, 210
Red Ripe Strawberry, The, by Don and Audrey Wood, 256
Regards To The Man In The Moon, by Ezra Jack Keats, 276
Rise And Shine! by Nancy White Carlstrom, 120
Sam Johnson And The Blue Ribbon Quilt by Lisa Campbell Ernst, 78
Sawfin Stickleback: A Very Fishy Story , The by Catherine Friend, 100
Scarecrow! by Valerie Littlewood, 200
Sea Dragons And Rainbow Runners: Exploring Fish With Children by Suzanne Samson, 98
Sofie's Role by Amy Heath, 215
Somewhere In The World Right Now by Stacey Schuett, 167
Spider On The Floor by Raffi, 111
Spots, Feathers, And Curly Tails by Nancy Tafuri, 113
Surprise Family , The by Lynn Reiser, 92
Sweet Clara And The Freedom Quilt by Deborah Hopkinson, 78
Swimmy by Leo Lionni, 100
Swim Through The Sea , A by Kristin Joy Pratt, 99
Tar Beach by Faith Ringgold, 78
Ten Little Rabbits by Virginia Grossman, 80
Tiny Seed , The by Eric Carle, 87
Trouble With Trolls, The, by Jan Brett, 159
Turtle and Tortoise by Vincent Serventy 267
Two Bad Ants by Chris Van Allsburg, 187
We Are All Alike...We Are All Different by the Cheltenham Elementary School Kindergartners, 67
We Are Best Friends by Aliki, 66
Weekend With Wendell, A by Kevin Henkes, 123
What's It Like To Be A Fish? by Wendy Pfeffer, 97
Wheels On The Bus by Raffi, 172
White Bear, Ice Bear by Joanne Ryder, 234
Who's Counting? by Nancy Tafuri, 106
Who Gets The Sun Out Of Bed? by Nancy White Carlstrom, 120
Who's Counting? by Nancy Tafuri, 106
Who Gets The Sun Out Of Bed? by Nancy White Carlstrom, 120
Why The Sun And The Moon Live In The Sky by Nikki Daly, 72
Will I have A Friend? by Miriam Cohen, 65
Wind by Ron Bacon, 87

Wind Blew, The by Pat Hutchins, 86
Wind Garden, The by Angela McAllister, 87
Wind Says Good Night by Katy Rydell, 88
Yes by Josse Goffin, 92
literature, childrens', 63–102
Little Cats, 208
Little Mouse, The, 256
Littlewood, Valerie, 200
lobster, 40
London, sights of, 156
Look What's Poppin', 132
Luenn, Nancy, 92
Louanne Pig In The Perfect Family, 183
Luka's Quilt, 79
Lunch, 118
lunch choices, graph of, 132
M&M's ®Brand Chocolate Candies Counting Book, The, 126
McAllister, Angela, 87
McCloskey, Robert, 241
McGrath, Barbara Barbieri, 126
McKissack, Patricia C., 88, 100
McNair, Sylvia, 167
McPhail, David, 226
magnetic chalkboard, 225, 267, 311, 313
magnifying glass, 46, 145
mail, 105, 108. See also learning centers; letters; writing class center, 66, 105
    Like Me And You by Raffi, 108
Make Way For Ducklings, 241
Mandel, Peter, 210
manipulatives, 47, 48, 51, 78, 97, 186, 215, 225, 269, 306
manual alphabet, 105 (The Handmade Alphabet)
Martin Luther King, Jr. Day, 12
masks, 72
matching, 45, 51, 53, 54, 55, 56, 78, 98, 119, 138, 139, 143, 148, 185,186, 192, 193, 227, 241, 260, 311
math, 126, 125–136, 269.See also adding; counting; dividing; fractions; graphing; grouping; learning centers; patterning; sets; subtracting
math masquerade, 126
Math Units, 125–136
measurement, 52, 55, 160, 215, 311
    volume, 52
Menorah, 162
Million Fish...More Or Less, A, 100
Mills, Lauren, 81
minimural, In The Tall, Tall Grass, 116
Mirandy And Brother Wind, 88
Mitten, The, 104
mobiles, 73, 74 110
Molly And The Strawberry Day, 260
money, 51, 227, 309
    coins 51, 309
moon, 120.See also astronauts; space
    birthday party for, 73
    blue, 277
    climate on, 71
    mobile, man-in-the-moon, 73
    phases, of, 73, 277
moon, books about, 70–76,
    Goodnight, Goodnight, 74
    Goodnight Moon, 71
    Good-Night, Owl!, 74
    Happy Birthday, Moon, 73
    How Night Came From The Sea: A Story From Brazil, 72
    I Want To Be An Astronaut, 71
    Moon Came Too, The, 20
    Moonglow Roll-O-Rama, The, 74
    Moon rope: Un Lazo A La Luna, 72
    Night In The Country, 74
    Papa, Please Get The Moon For Me, 71
    Rabbit Mooncakes, 72
    Why The Sun And The Moon Live In The Sky, 72
Moon Came Too, The, 120
Moon, Once Upon A Blue, literature unit, 70–76
Moonglow Roll-O-Rama, The, 74
Moon Rope: Un Lazo A La Luna, 72
Moore, Patrick, 274
more and less, concept of, 186
most, least, same, 130 (Peanut Graph)
Mother's Day, 39
Moving Patterns, 128
movement, 35, 80, 85, 87, 104, 105,120, 128, 129, 192, 200 241, 226, 241, 251, 269
moving, 66
multi-cultural,
    Hanukkah, 10
multicultural ideas,
    Brazilian, myth explaining night, 72
    Chinese Harvest Moon Festival, 72
    England, 156–157
    France, 164–165
    Germany, 154–155
    Hanukkah, 10, 162
    India, 166–167
    Kwanzaa, 163
    Native American blankets, 80

Nigerian Creation Myth, 72
Norway, 158–161
Peruvian, folk tale, 72
Munroe, Roxie, 156, 165
murals, 10, 72, 86, 251, 267, 275. See also minimural
music,
    German, 155
    patterns in, 128
Musical Patterns, 128
"My Bones," 191
My Favorite Center, 133
My Friends, 65
names, liking own, uniqueness of, 68, 122
name recognition, 48, 302
nametags, 174, 175
nature, 46, 116
    Baby Beluga, 110
    cycle of, 99
    fish watching, center, 42
    Five Little Ducks, 111
    Good-Night, Owl!, 74
    Have You Seen My Duckling?, 112
    harmony in, 99
    items from, 46, 122
    One Light, One Sun, 110
    The Moon Came Too, 120
    The Moonglow Roll-O-Rama, 74
    Rabbit's Morning, 113
    Spider On The Floor, 111
    In The Small, Small Pond, 117
    In The Tall, Tall Grass, 116
    Night In The Country, 74
    Who Gets The Sun Out Of Bed?, 120
near and far, 103
Nessa's Story, 92
Nest Full Of Eggs, A, 91
Neumeier, Marty, 104
night,
    Goodnight, Goodnight, 74
Nikola-Lisa, W., 67
Night In The Country, 74
Nikola-Lisa, W., 67
northern lights, 160
Norway, 158—161
    Christmas, in, 161
    family life, in, 158
    natural environment/sagas, 158
number matching, 53, 311
number words, 258
numbers, ordinal, 113
numeral recognition, 45, 47, 48, 51, 53, 56, 113, 203, 311
numerical order, 51, 53, 97
nut, 48
nutrition,15. See also fruit; vegetables
    Lunch, 118
    lunch choices, 132
observation skills, 98, 256
Oliviero, Jamie, 99
Once Upon A TIme, 133
One Light, One Sun, 110
One Light, One Sun, mobile, 110
opposites, 210, 233
ordering. See sequencing
organizing, reinforcing skill of, 130
ornament, Christmas, 30
Our Readers Write, 305–313
Owen, 80, 123
Papa, Please Get The Moon For Me, 71
paper chains, learning skills from, 311
Parton, Dolly, 81
patience, 106
Patchwork Quilt, The, 79
patterns. See also bulletin boards; reproducibles
    Animal Skeletons Booklet, 196-198
    ant manipulatives, 190
    anthill workmat, 189
    ant, 189
    apple, 57
    astronaut, 76
    Awesome Owl Snack, 287
    baked goods, 217–218
    bee, 20, 61
    bird, 37
    booklet covers, 178, 221, 229, 261
    booklet cover and pages, 252–255
    booklet cover and picture choices, 240
    booklet, last page of, 263
    booklet pages, 179–181, 204–207, 211–213, 219–220, 230–231, 237–239
    calendar, 278
    car, 176
    celestial bodies, 279
    clock, 168
    class token, 176
    crows, 203
    Deviled Eggs recipe card, 297
    dog, 45

fishbowl, 102
Fruity Shake recipe card, 300
gingerbread person, 33
grid, 60
Groundhog Day Cupcake recipe card, 293
Happy Face Muffin recipe card, 283
Harvest Pumpkin Pie recipe card, 288
honey jar, 61
Hot Cocoa Mix recipe card, 291
Johnny Appleseed Sandwich recipe card, 284
label, 50
ladybug, 62
leprechaun, 18
nametag, 176
Peter Rabbit's Lunch recipe card, 296
pigs, 228
pig's pocket, 232
Pimento Cheese & Crackers recipe card, 299
quilt, 60, 80
rabbit, 19
Reindeer Refreshments recipe card, 290
riddles, 246–247
scarecrow, 199
Shakin' Shamrock recipe card, 294
school bus, 177
ship, 169
skeleton, 194-195
strawberry, 264
turkey, 29
Turtle Book Backing Page, 270
Turtle Book Page, 271
Turtle Patterns, 272–273
tree, 135
walking to school,
patterning, 49, 52, 53, 97, 127-129, 259, 311,312
Pattern Talk, 127
Pattern Wear, 127
Paul, Ann Whitford, 78
peacock, 166
Peanut Graph, 130
penguins, 114
Penguin Pete, 114
Penguin Pete, Ahoy!, 114
Penguin Pete And Little Tim, 114
Penguin Pete And Pat, 114
Penguin Pete's New Friends,114
personal information, learning own,
    address, 312
    phone number, 308
Peters, Sharon, 106
Pfeffer, Wendy, 97
Pfister, Marcus, 66, 114–115
Philpot, Lorna and Graham, 186
phonics,
    beginning sound of words, recognizing, 104, 227, 241, 269
    center, 56
    initial consonant sounds, 56
    letter sounds,56, 307
    sound words, 112, 119
    vowel sounds,bulletin board, 15
photographs
    bulletin boards, 6, 9, 13, 14, 88
    counting skills, taught with, 113, 126
    Father's Day magnet, 41
    first-day-of-school tour, 173
    frame, 25
    holiday, 310
    pictionary, 313
    spring, 14
    students with favorite blanket or quilt, 79
    Valentine's Day card, 34
Photo Opportunities, 126
picnic, 185
pigs, 224–232
Pigs Aplenty!, 224–232
Pigs Aplenty, Pigs Galore!, 226
Pigs Will Be Pigs, 227
Pilgrims, 157. See also Thanksgiving
Pilkey, Dav, 74
pinecone, 32, 46, 311
plants, See also seeds,
    seed, 87, 106, 109
    peanut, growing a, 223
plant growth, 106
plant life, pond, in, 117
poem, 29, 73, 80, 162, 182, 191, 200, 214, 224, 225, 226, 250, 258, 267
Polacco, Patricia, 79
poles, North and South, 233–234
pollution, 110 (Baby Beluga)
pond, 117
popcorn, 46, 132
position words, 80, 119
post office, 105, 108
Post Office Book, The, 105
pouring, 52, 55
Pratt, Kristin Joy, 99

318

predicting, 122, 130, 131, 132, 133
pumpkin, 8, 47, 200
puppets, 111, 115, 269, 309
Purdy, Carol, 85
puzzle, 119, 192, 260
quilts, 49, 307
quilts, books about, 77–82. See also blankets; coats
    Boy And The Cloth Of Dreams, The, 81
    Boy And The Quilt, The, 80
    Eight Hands Round: A Patchwork Alphabet, 78
    Keeping Quilt, The, 79
    Luka's Quilt, 79
    Patchwork Quilt, The, 79
    Quilt, The, 81
    Quilt Story, The, 79
    Sam Johnson And The Blue Ribbon Quilt, 78
    Sweet Clara And The Freedom Quilt, 78
    Tar Beach, 78
quilt pattern, 60
Quilt, The, 81
Quilt Story, The, 79
rabbits, 80
Rabbit Mooncakes, 72
Rabbit's Morning, 113
Raffi, 108—111, 172, 236, 244
Rag Coat, The, 81
rainbow, 35
Rainbow Fish, The 66, 115
Rankin, Laura, 105
rap, 67. See also rhythm
reading. See emergent reading skills
reading, promoting community, 311
reading, participatory, 112, 224, 234
reading, rhythmic, 202
Ready, Set, Roll, 134
recall, 104, 119
recipes, edible
    ants on a log, 188
    Awesome Owl Snack, 286
    Deviled Eggs, 295
    edible ants, 188
    edible "bird nests," 91
    egg, 91
    flat bread, 159
    fruit kabobs, 127
    Groundhog Day Cupcakes, 292
    Fruit Salad Fun, 308
    Fruity Shake, 298
    happy face muffin, 282
    Harvest Pumpkin Pie, 286
    Hot Cocoa Mis 289
    Johnny Appleseed Sandwich, 282
    Masal Chay (tea), 167
    peanutty snack ideas, 223
    Peter Rabbit's Lunch, 295
    Pimento Cheese & Crackers, 298
    Reindeer Refreshments, 161, 289
    sauerkraut, 155
    scones, 157
    Shakin' Shamrocks, 292
    strawberry shortcake, 257
recipes, non-edible
    baking dough, 28
    julenek, (bird food), 161
recycling, for use in classroom,
    cereal boxes, 313
    condiment containers, 302
    crayons, 309
    foam packing pieces, 117
    laundry bottles, 306
    milk cartons, 117
    Mylar® balloons, 307
    packing bubbles, 117
    paper grocery bags, 9, 148, 222, 311
    plastic can holders, 313
    plastic grocery bags, 110, 117, 222
    stove-top covers, 313
Red Cat, White Cat, 210
Red Ripe Strawberry, The, 256
Regards To The Man In The Moon, 276
Reid, Margarette S., 103
reindeer, 161, 310
Reiser, Lynn, 92
reproducibles. See also patterns
    booklet text strips, 262
    center label, 59
    cut-apart riddles, 246-247
    grid, 136
    invitation to parents to Sensory Fair,150
    invitation and thank you note to parents, 285
    pig booklet cover/manipulative, 229
    request form, 83
    sources of light graph, 136
    strawberry shortcake, 265
    taste chart,151
rhyme, 87, 109, 111, 116, 119, 121, 191, 224, 241-247, 258,
    267, 307

rhyming flip book, 245
rhyming, reinforcing skill of, 242
rhythm, 267
Rice, Eve, 9
Ring-A-Ling, 126
Ringgold, Faith, 78
Rise And Shine!, 120
robin, 36. See also spring
Roddie, Shen, 93
role playing, 72, 86, 104, 117, 118, 120, 215, 216, 225, 234, 251
Ross, Tom, 93
royalty,
    English, 157
    Norwegian, 159
Rydell, Katy, 88
Ryder, Joanne, 234
Rylant, Cynthia, 74
St. Patrick's Day, 13, 35, 296
St. Valentine's Day. See holidays; Valentines
Sam Johnson And The Blue Ribbon Quilt, 78
Samson, Suzanne, 98
Santa, 31
Sawfin Stickleback: A Very Fishy Story, The, 100
Scarecrow!, 200
Schuett, Stacey, 167
science,
    ants, 184
    bones, 191–198
    centers, 42, 46, 54
    constellations, 274–275
    dinosaurs, 128
    eggs, that animals lay, 92
    effects of moving air, 85, 87
    fat, insulating properties of, 236
    fish, habits and habitats, 97
    fish watching, center, 42
    gravity, 276
    light, 134, 136
    moon, 70-76, 120, 277
    peanuts, 222-223
    pollution, effect on whales, 110
    seasons, 23, 85, 117, 133
    senses, 138-151
    space, 274–279
    storms, 85
    sun, 120, 275–276
    wind, 84-89
Science Units, 137–151
    A "Please Touch" Display, 141
    Center For Touching, 141
    Dancing Rice, 142
    Double The Scents, 139
    Good Vibrations, 142
    Guess Who?, 145
    Hearing, 147
    Is It Hot Or Cold?, 140
    Look Around!
    No Bones About It!, 191
    No Peeking!, 145
    One Eye Or Two?, 144
    Positively Peanuts!, 222-223
    Scented Pictures, 139
    Science Journals, 139
    "Sense-sational Experiences With Hearing, 142
    "Sense-sational" Experiences With Taste And Smell, 138
    "Sense-sational" Experiences With The Sense Of Touch, 140
    "Sense-sational" Sensory Fair, The, 146
    Shake, Shake, Shake!, 143
    Sight, 146
    smell, 149
    space, 274–279
    Taste, 147
    Taste It, 139
    Taste Table, 139
    Texture Rubbings, 141
    Ticktock, 143
    touch, 148
    Touch And Tell!, 140
    We're Talkin' Turtles!, 266–273
    What's That Sound?, 143
    Wide-Eyed Activity, A, 144
    Wild, Blue Yonder!, The, 274–279
*Sea Dragons And Rainbow Runners: Exploring Fish With
    Children,* 98
seashells, 7, 46, 54
seasons, 23, 85, 117, 133. See fall; spring; summer; winter;
seasons, favorite, graph of, 133
seeds, 87, 106, 109
self-esteem, 6, 14, 67, 81, 174, 312
senses, 55, 138–151
Sensory Fair, 146-151
sequencing, 86, 91, 99, 104, 105, 113, 118, 129, 201, 216, 257
series books
    Penguins, 114
    Pfister, Marcus, 114; 114-115
Serventy, Vincent, 266
Seuss, Dr., 93

sets, 42, 47, 48, 50, 51, 53, 56, 103, 186
sharing, 66
sharks, 98. See also fish
sight, books about,
    Each Peach Pear Plum by Janet and Allan Ahlberg, 145
sight, sense of,144–145, 146
sight words, 208, 210
similarities and differences, 93, 154, 158, 166, 182, 248
singing, 85, 100, 104, 106 108, 109, 110, 111, 115, 119,
    172, 186, 202, 210, 215, 236, 244, 276. See also song books
size, order of, 209, 268, 275, 276
skeletons, 191–198
smell, sense of, 138, 149, 166, 185
Sneakin' Around, 130
social skills. See also friends; friendship; self-esteem
    acceptance of others, 67, 93
    appropriate and inappropriate behavior for sleepovers, 123
    caring, 115
    compromise, learning to, 79
    conflict resolution, 309
    cooperation, 260, 307
    courage, finding within, 81
    division of labor, 184
    friends, traits of, 65
    kindness, 81
    patience, 106
    problem solving, 68, 79, 80, 159
    qualities of a good family member or firend, 92
    respect, 81
    sharing, 68, 115
    stereotypes, learning to recognize, 78
    working and playing together, 174
social studies,
    England, 156–157
    France, 164–165
    Germany, 154–155
    India, 166–167
    Kwanzaa, 163
    Independence Day, 16
    Norway, 158–161
Sofie's Role, 215
Somewhere In The World Right Now, 167
song books
    Baby Beluga by Raffi, 110
    Down By The Bay by Raffi, 109
    Five Little Ducks by Raffi, 111
    Like Me And You by Raffi, 108
    One Light, One Sun by Raffi, 110
    Spider On The Floor by Raffi, 111
sorting, 42, 48, 50, 80, 89, 97, 103, 118, 131, 214, 248, 256
sound, 142–143
Soup's On, 131
Sources Of Light, 134, 136
space, 274-279. See also astronauts, moon, sun, stars
    astronauts, 71, 76
    moon, 71, 72, 73, 74,
spelling, 48, 56
Spider On The Floor, 111
Spots, Feathers, And Curly Tails, 113
Spotlight On Center, 43-62
spring, 13, 14, 23, 36, 39, 133. See also holidays
snow, 11, 32, 160
squirrel, 48
stars, 274
Stars, The, 274
Stargazers, 274
Stegosaurus Patterning, 128
stereotypes, 78
*Stitch In TIme: A Cozy Collection Of Books About Blankets
    And Quilts,* 77–83; See blankets; coats; quilts,
    stockings, Christmas, 30
subtraction, 10, 80, 202, 269,
summer, 23, 54, 133
sun, 120, 275-276
sun, books about,
    Why The Sun And The Moon Live In The Sky, 72
sun/unity, mobile, 110
sunflowers, 23
Surprise Family, The, 92
Sweet Clara And The Freedom Quilt, 78
Swimmy, 100
 Swim Through The Sea, A, 99
taste, 138
T-shirts, 26
Tafuri, Nancy, 106, 112–113
Tar Beach, 78
taste, sense of, 138, 147
taste and smell, senses of, 138–139
Ten Little Rabbits, 80
Thanksgiving, 9, 27, 28, 157
thematic units,
    animal babies, 248–255
    ants, 184–190
    Artic, 233–240
    bakery, 214–221
    bones, 191–198
    cats, 208–213

family, 182–183
peanuts, 222–223
penguins, 114
pigs, 224–232
scarecrows, 199–207
space, 274–279
strawberries, 256–265
turtles, 266–273
Val's Pals in Rhyme TIme, 241–247
Welcome To School, 172–181
thinking skills, 311
time, 103, 167, 268
Tiny Seed, The, 87
touch, sense of, 140–141, 148
Traveling Book Of Graphs, A, 134
trees, 23, 27, 46
tree branch, display, 306, 312
trees, pinecone, 32
trees, Christmas, 30
tree, Valentine's Day, 312
Trees For All Seasons, 133, 135
trolls, 159
Trouble With Trolls, The, 159
turkeys, 28
turtles, 266–273
Turtle And Tortoise, 266
Two Bad Ants, 187
tying shoes. S*ee lacing*
Valentine's Day, display, 12
Valentines, card, 34
Valentine's Day, 12, 34, 241–245, 312,313
vegetables,
    bulletin board, 15
    *Lunch, 1*18
verbal discription, 67, 226
vibrations, sound, 142
videotape, 251
visual discrimination, 51, 54, 55
vocabulary, 118, 119, 156, 209, 214, 222, 233, 256, 274, 276
vowels,
    bulletin board, 15
wear, thing students, 121
We Are All Alike..We Are All Different, 67
We Are Best Friends, 66
*Weekend With Wendell, A ,1*23
weighing, 55
weight and shape, 89
We're Talkin' Turtles!, 266—273
whales, 110, 236
What Comes Next, 129
What's For Lunch?, 132
What's It Like To Be A Fish?, 97
What's Your Favorite Apple?, 130
W*heels On The Bus,* 172
White Bear, Ice Bear, 234
Why The Sun And The Moon Live In The Sky, 72
W*ho's Counting?,* 106, 113
W*ho Gets The Sun Out Of Bed?,* 120
W*ill I Have A Friend?,* 65
Williams, Sue, 103
W*ind,* 87

W*ind Blew, The,* 86
wind, books about, 84–89
    B*low Away Soon,* 88
    Gates Of The Wind, The, 88
    Gilberto And The Wind, 87
    How Does The Wind Walk, 85
    How The Wind Plays, 85
    Iva Dunnit And The Big Wind, 85
    Mirandy And Brother Wind, 88
    Tiny Seed, The, 87
    W*ind,* 87
    Wind Blew, The, 86
    Wind Garden, The, 87
    W*ind Says Good Night,* 88
W*ind Garden, The* 87
W*ind Says Good Night,* 88
winter, 11, 23, 32, 114, 133, 160, 234. S*ee also* holidays
Wood, Audrey and Don, 157, 256
word recognition, 45, 224, 256, 302
workmats, 186
wrapping paper, 31
wreaths, Christmas, 31
writing, 12, 50, 51, 55, 65, 66, 71, 78, 105, 111, 116, 118, 120, 157, 182, 208, 215, 226, 260, 302, 312
Y*es,* 92
Yes Or No?, 131
zero, concept of, 175
zoo, animals, 24